A New Leaf
2

Also by Jim Gold

Books

Songs and Stories for Open Ears

Handfuls of Air: A Book of Modern Folk Tales

Mad Shoes: The Adventures of Sylvan Woods: From Bronx Violinist to Bulgarian Folk Dancer

Crusader Tours and Other Stories

Recordings

World of Guitar

American Folk Ballads

A New Leaf 2

Adventures in the Creative Life

Jim Gold

Full Court Press
Englewood Cliffs, New Jersey

First Edition

Copyright © 2001 by Jim Gold

All rights reserved. No part of this book may be reproduced or transmitted in any form or by any means electronic or mechanical, including by photocopying, by recording, or by any information storage and retrieval system, without the express permission of the author, except where permitted by law.

Published in the United States of America
by Full Court Press, 601 Palisade Avenue,
Englewood Cliffs, NJ 07632
fullcourtpress.com

ISBN 978-1-946989-51-2
Library of Congress Control Number: 2020904310

Editing and book design by Barry Sheinkopf

To Ma

"Wait for my index finger, Mommy."
"Why?"
"It's slow."
"It's slow because it's curious. Index is your explorer finger pointing the way, visiting strange, mysterious places, touching the unknown. It has to move ahead slowly, hesitantly, cautiously. . . but very bravely. Ah, what a brave finger you have. What a brave and lovely son!"

Table Of Contents

January–March 1995

Writing, *1*
Languages, *5*
Life, *7*
Money And Its Brethren, *22*
Performance, *23*
Business, *24*

April–June 1995

Writing, *45*
Languages, *61*
Life, *62*
Money And Its Brethren, *89*
Performance, *90*
Business, *96*
Inventions, *124*
God, *125*

July–September 1995

Writing, *127*
Languages, *140*
Life, *141*
Money And Its Brethren, *151*
Business, *152*

October–December 1995

Writing, *169*
Life, *173*
Money And Its Brethren, *184*

Performance, *188*
Business, *196*
Inventions, *208*

January–December 1996

Writing, *215*
Languages, *230*
Money And Its Brethren, *273*
Business, *286*
Inventions, *325*

January–March 1995

Henry Miller

When we went to California several years ago, we visited the Henry Miller Library at Big Sur. I put my name on the library mailing list and, a few weeks later, got a letter asking for a contribution. I made one and soon a copy of *Ping Pong: Journal of the Henry Miller Library* arrived in the mail. Reading "The Last Days of Henry Miller" by Barbara Kraft, I remembered the wonderful influence Henry Miller had on me. A true soul mate.

Reading him reminded me about the importance of writing, art, and the artist as rebel. Kraft: "He has no patience with government support of the artist. He was convinced poverty brought forth the greatest work. 'When I wrote the Tropics books I was a desperate man... I owe everything to poverty. I wouldn't have become what I am without it.'"

A Strange Nonverbal Place

I turned on the computer, concentrated on breathing, then did three rounds of Salute to the Sun. I did three more. Not bad. Three more. Again three more. That made twelve.

Does concentrating on breathing help you transcend the body? Yes. I focused on my breath as I did twenty-one sit-ups. Good. Does doing yoga with the computer turned on mean anything? Is it a wise idea to combine yoga, breathing, and writing? Can it be done? Should it?

When I finished yoga I started to write.

I've noticed that, if I exhale with raspy, breathy voice, I feel no pain in my knees when I get into the lotus position. If I focus my mind somewhere else, on my inner thigh, breath, or more distant body part, I bypass any pain in my knee. But when I focus directly on relaxing my knee, it hurts. Strange. Am I touching a power beyond thought? I believe so.

I don't have words for this place.

Publishing My Work

Publishing is a strength-building exercise. Should I self-publish my journal? I have three other books sitting in my basement. I know they are good, yet I've been hesitant to promote or sell them; it's the old "How-dare-I-own-my-own-creativity!" question.

So strange. I know my tours, folk dance classes, weekends, concerts, and my books are good. Yet I hesitate to promote and sell them. I manage only because I *have* to sell them in order to survive financially. But suppose I had enough money? Would I still sell them?

I am lucky to I have little money. It forces me to push beyond myself. If I had enough, would I stop all promotions and retreat into a cocoon?

Two New Businesses

I needed a break, a vacation. I took two weeks. Last night the old pre-writing feeling returned, that melancholy which I often describe as depression. A few days before I had read William Styron's book about his depression. How lucky he is, I thought. I wish I could get depressed. That's a true sign. With depression coming on, you know writing is right around the corner.

Now it's Sunday morning. I'm busy at my computer. It certainly make writing easier. I can put down words almost as fast as I can think. Talking to someone is often limited. Your thoughts are subtly influenced by their reaction. Writing has no immediate listeners. You can go directly into your soul.

While writing, I gave birth to two fertile ideas.

A New Guitar Business

After my New Year's Weekend guitar concert I took two weeks off. Evidently, I had conquered my fears. But paradoxically, it was fear of performance that drove me to practice and improve. Now I had conquered my fears. Why bother practicing? Failure and problem solving are incredible motivators. Once you succeed, you need to find new reasons to continue your activity. Old ones don't work anymore. That was my state of mind after the New Year's Weekend. I needed to find a new reason to play guitar.

So I took off a month while the cauldron heated up. The stew cooked for weeks without a bit of effort from me. The cook of the unconscious collected all the pots and frying pans, worked day and night, and soon created a new purpose.

My folk dance class had been cancelled due to inclement weather. I sat home with "nothing to do." I picked up the guitar; I started playing. Then I listened to a guitar tape I'd made of myself practicing about a month ago. It sounded soothing and relaxing. I thought about Mark Trapnell's desire to own *Trgnala Rumjana* from Bulgaria, and how I'd easily made him a tape of it. He was so happy and appreciative when I gave it to him. During class on the following week he came over to tell me he'd played it while driving to work. He liked it. I thought, if he liked such an inferior quality tape he might also like one of my classical guitar playing. I didn't have to make a perfect tape, just a "good enough" tape. He could listen to it as he drove to work. My soothing classical guitar playing is relaxing—just like *Trgnala Rumjana*.

So I started recording my practice sessions. When I played them back I saw many improvements I could make. I made them, then recorded again. I did this for several days until an idea occurred to me: *Why not make classic guitar tapes?* First I considered giving them away for nothing. Then I thought, *Why not sell them?* As this idea developed, it soon moved to making folk dance tapes. Suddenly, a new business was born.

Of course, I would need better recording equipment. I'd have to study a new industry, learn about electronics, recording styles and techniques, tape and CD productions, tape jackets, etc.

The next day I went to Sam Ash on Route 4 to investigate tape recorders. The salesman told me about Trutone, Inc. in Hackensack, which produces tapes from start to finish. I visited them and had a half-hour talk with Dennis Ostrom, the sales manager, about how to produce tapes and their costs. Two days later, I returned to Sam Ash and spent six hundred dollars for a new Yamaha four-track tape recorder, two microphones, jacks and tapes. I still need to get speakers, speaker connectors, head phones, and a microphone stand. More money. But I don't mind. It's part of my education. A new business is being born.

Not bad for a two-week writing break.

And that was only the first idea.

Tours

I'm trying to create next year's tour program. This year's is completed. I'm all set up for 1995. Budapest and Prague in March, Greece in May, Bulgaria in August—itineraries are in order. Only the selling remains. A big "only." Nevertheless, I'm ready to move on.

I planned the March, 1996 Budapest and Prague tour. I've added Romania—a new country and itinerary—for August. What about May? Should I do Turkey? Moravia and Slovakia? Both? If I do Turkey, should I return to Western and Central Turkey and include Cappadocia, or should I run a real adventure tour that, even though few will go on it, I want to experience before I die: Eastern Turkey?

A few days ago I decided: In May I'll organize a tour to Eastern Turkey. My rationalization: I'm running a tour to Greece this year, and even though I've got fifteen people on it, I'm still not making any money. I won't make money unless I reach twenty, and that possibility is very unlikely. I priced it too low. Usually I price it so that the first three people will pay for me. After that, it's pure profit. With Greece I priced it with me free, but with no profit until I reach twenty people. I'll never do that again. Still, it is a learning experience in this new county. But here's the point: if I can have fifteen people on my Greek tour and make no money, why not have three or four people on a tour to Eastern Turkey and make no money? The constant on both tours is making no money. But I still get a "free" adventure, a learning experience, an exploration of a new country. Thus I have rationalized running a tour of Eastern Turkey. I'll write Selim, describe my itinerary, ask him to be our guide and see if he has any suggestions.

What about Moravia and Slovakia? Wouldn't May be a good time to go there? But I can't do two tours in May. This question was answered when I got some brochures from Jasan Bonus. He's running a summer program to Slovakia, from June 30 to July 10, which included the Detva Folk Festival and the Vichodna Folk Festival. I'd like to visit these festivals. If I go in July I'll have enough time to recover from my Eastern Turkey tour in May. Then I'll lead my tour of Romania in August.

That's a lot of tours for 1996. Three of them are new. It may be too much. My wife thinks so. I think so, too. Yet when I decided to organize all these tours, I had an inner peace I hadn't had in weeks. It was a lot of work but it felt right. Bernice threw me off when she said it was too much travel, and she'd miss me. But Eastern Turkey in May and Romania in August will be okay. Even though both countries are new, there lots of rest time in between. Adding Slovakia is putting pressure on me. It is the third new tour. Yet early July is the best time for Slovakia.

What should I do?

This morning an idea struck me: why not plan to personally lead the tours to Budapest and Prague in March, Eastern Turkey in May, and Romania in August, and plan *not* to lead the one to Slovakia in July? I could advertise the Slovakia tour and see how the response is. If I get a lot of people—what a wonderful problem that would be—then I'll lead it myself. If I don't, I'll let Jasan lead it. He planned the itinerary; he knows the tour. I sell his tour. If I get enough people, I can lead it. I could do the same thing with Eastern

Turkey. I'll piggy-back the Eastern Turkey itinerary on top of the Pacha Tours itinerary. If I only get three or four people, I'll join their tour. If I get more, I'll lead my own. This is a new tour idea, selling other people's tours and, if I get enough people, leading the tour myself. Thus, I am both a travel agent and a tour leader. This way I don't have the pressure of filling up my tours. Since I am being backed by other tour companies itineraries, I won't have to cancel my tour if I don't get enough people. Good idea. In fact, I could run four tours in 1996 and possibly not go on any of them.

I have distanced myself from my tours by facing the one element I have little control over: registration.

LANGUAGES

Hungarian

Last night I sat in the First Congregational Church of Old Greenwich, reading my Hungarian grammar book. "I'm tired of making minimal effort to learn Hungarian," I said. "I stay the same. I never get worse, never get better." So I decided to *commit myself* to Hungarian study. What is a Hungarian commitment? It is temporal, emotional, and spiritual. It means I will sweat, cry, and struggle with all my Hungarian heart with all its Hungarian valves, ventricles, and auricles, with all my magyar soul in a day and night fight to master this Finno-Ugric jawsnapper.

I'll learn to *think* in Hungarian. English will become my *second* language. Not only will my thoughts be in Hungarian, but I will also translate Hebrew into Hungarian, even read the Torah in Hungarian. And of course, I'll start a hand-written journal in Hungarian.

The "Concept" of Hungarian

I have cracked the Hungarian code. I made my commitment; I thought, spoke, wrote, and lived exclusively within the Hungarian language for six weeks. Suddenly, I find Hungarian "easy."

I started by studying the adverbs and positions of the prepositions. Since Hungarian is an agglutinative language, adverbs and prepositions come at the end of a noun. This concept is so foreign to an English speaker that for years I could not "understand" the Hungarian way of thought. Everything in Hungarian seemed backwards and incomprehensible both intellectually and emotionally. But today I feel somewhat comfortable with it.

It feels strange, especially after so many years of living in a Hungarian linguistic fog.

Speaking in Tongues

Is there another purpose to my study of languages? Can it have something to do with *speaking in tongues?*

Through "tongues" I can transcended local language by speaking the universal language. It's true no one will understand me, at least not rationally. But "tongues" is not meant to be rational or even communicate to other human beings. Speaking in tongues goes directly to God. It is a personal talk with the Lord, a private consultation with no human ears listening ever ready to pounce on words and imprison them within walls of interpretation. Speaking in tongues is the ultimate language. Maybe that's what I'm aiming for by studying foreign languages. I may do better if I forget about communicating with other human beings and simply speak to God directly. I can't count on human beings understanding; they might or they might not. However, simply because others don't understand does not mean such speaking has no use. As long as God understands, that's enough. A conversation with God, whether private or public, will bring satisfaction, joy, and inner peace. That's pretty good for a conversation. It's the ultimate therapy. I can't say I often get such peace and satisfaction when I speak to human beings. Therefore, I'll put conversation with them on the back burner for awhile. Who can be sure if they can understand, anyway? But God does. And He is always there. I started studying Hungarian and other languages because I wanted to run better tours. But on this tour, I am happy to let our guide, Andrew, do the talking. I don't feel like speaking Hungarian unless I am forced. Maybe this signify an upward step in my confidence. I'm grasping many shades of strength. Strangely, losing my desire to learn Hungarian may be one of them.

Czech

I started studying Czech this morning. It seems rather dull compared to

Russian. No bite. Plus it uses the boring (for me) Latin alphabet, which lacks the beauty of the Cyrillic. But this could be just the beginning. My boredom may be based on ignorance. I'm sure the Czech language has some beauty. After all, Dvorak spoke it.

LIFE

Organization

I hate a mess. Therefore, I am taking a new look at organizing.

Organizing has beauty to it, the beauty of creating oneness and wholeness. It doesn't matter what I organize—tours, weekends, dance classes, words on paper, or notes on guitar. I see organization as fixing the mess of the world, a personal *tikkun* fitting broken parts into a larger unity.

Organizing expresses the urge towards oneness and the One.

Back Again

My back hurts. It's related to the increased registration for my Bulgarian tour. Too good! I'm too excited! Will the heavy hammer of success fall on my head, destroy me, alienate me from friends and family? I grew up with this attitude.

Why am I afraid of success? How could it hurt me?

I might be transported by enthusiasm, lose perspective, get sloppy, forget the transient nature of ups and downs. The hubris of success could blind me and create its opposite. Wouldn't it be better to modulate my enthusiasm and remain even?

There is the warning in my fear of success. It can destroy as easily as failure. But it can also uplift as easily as failure can sink. It depends on your attitude. Seeing failure and success as part of service to a higher self would help.

Leg Cramps and Self-Destruction

It's been a whirlwind week. I've been working on my tours since last Friday. I made my Bulgarian flier, send out a mailing, organized lists for my

Greek and Hungarian tours, banked the money, went over my accounting and finances, made more lists, and on and on, I waded through an endless pile of detail work. There is so much *detail* work in the tour business.

How can I remain creative? Doesn't dissatisfaction, pain, and suffering drive one to create? If I stop suffering, will I stop creating? Perhaps this is why I fear success.

But there is little chance I'll stop suffering. Simply witness how I look at my success: I *suffer* from it. Luckily, I can suffer whether I succeed or fail. My ability has not diminished, only changed. Thank God for it! It keeps me creative. Even success cannot destroy it.

Speaking of pain and suffering, I never had a worse leg cramp than two nights ago. I woke up screaming, jumped out of bed, and tried a counter-stretch, which only made it worse. This was a new muscle cramping. I'm "used to" cramps in my gastrocnemius and know the counter-stretch. But this muscle was different. I don't even know its function; perhaps an abductor. I doubt it was a hamstring. I'm not sure. I'll have to ask the doctor when I have my physical tomorrow. In any case, when it cramped and I screamed, other muscles started cramping too. I've never felt such pain! I screamed, sweated, and panted through. Could this be a heart attack? If it is, I hope I die right now. Anything is better than this.

The cramps wouldn't go away. Finally, exhausted by my screams, I fell back into bed. Slowly I gave up. As I did, the cramp subsided, and I fell asleep. This morning those muscles still hurt; they'll probably keep hurting for several days.

Why did my muscles cramp in the first place? Perhaps I hadn't stretched enough the night before my dance class. Then I considered a psychological explanation. Perhaps I had cramped as a reaction to the joy of my success. Could I have brought on such pain, not only in order to "punish myself for my success," but to keep me "in my place" and protect me from the ostracism, alienation, and loss of love that I believe I will take place when I am successful? A childish pattern. I learned it long ago from my mother. Was I creating my own cramps to both punish and protect myself from something even worse? What could be worse?

A leg cramp is nothing compared to being cast into the chasm of the rejected, forgotten, and damned. Why am I damned if I am successful? I don't know. Along with success goes a slap in the face from a higher deity. Ma said I was good. She gave me unconditional love. She loved me for what

I am. But she definitely did not love me for what I *did*. Instead of admiring my successes and encouraging me, she warned me not to overdo it, not to "get sick." I learned to see that success and sickness go together. Could I have created my cramps to make myself sick and fulfill my mother's wish?

What a radical idea! Could it be true? If my lower back cramps have a psychological origin, why not my legs? Leg cramps came after a successful Tuesday night folk dance class where we had fifty people, the best attendance in years. Coupled with great dancing, it was an incredible evening. Since my legs are the physical foundation of my folk dancing, perhaps by "destroying" them I could destroy my folk dance success. Is *that* why my legs cramped? I'm onto something.

Success Is Suffering on a Higher Level

Is there a fun aspect to martyrdom?

I hate suffering. But I don't want to give it up. Suffering is a source of creativity. I relieve my pain by creating.

The peace, stillness, and beauty of the place called "Success" has been a lifetime goal of mine. Now that I'm close, I'm getting scared. Suppose I was wrong? Suppose I don't want success after all? Isn't that strange? Struggle all your life to achieve something, and when you finally do, realize you don't want it?

It is strange. But I am strange, too.

Although I want inner peace, I don't want the death of creation I had pictured that takes place during "Success."

But now I see success as a location where you can suffer "on a higher level." I can be successful, keep suffering, and stay creative.

I've always thought success meant an end to suffering. I thought creativity would free me from suffering. It does—but only for the moment. When I create something, I float happy, transformed by the light of my creation; I skip down the street, smiling, dancing, singing, untouched by cares, no longer buffeted by wild tumultuous winds, free from all desires. . .including the desire to create.

But soon, I sink back again to my old suffering state; I start to worry, cringe, twist, itch, grimace, and twitch. Soon I want relief, so I become creative again.

My tours are a good example. They're exciting but also very difficult. The details annoy me, but I relish the organization: a beautiful two-edged sword.

I love *both* edges, even though the cuts make me suffer.

"O" in Organization

I am a good organizer because I love that letter "O". It symbolizes organization itself, the roundness of completion, the attainment of inner organization and harmony. When I am frazzled by errant thoughts, I remember the meaning of "O" and its organizing message of unity and inner peace.

Mission

Everyone on earth has a mission.
Nations and religions also have a mission.
If they forget their mission, they die.
I too have a mission. But I don't know what it is. The elation of success has distracted me. I'm losing my peace of mind though I am making lots of money in the process.

Reordering Priorities

It's time to reorder priorities. Last month I was amazed by my success. Could such things happen to me? Hard to believe. Yet they happened. Plus I wrote beautifully. I add writing to my successes.

I've spent years denying my talents. Admitting them had been too much of a threat. But now, acceptance of my talents, skills, and successes is the lesson of the month. It is an expression of faith. After all, isn't denial of talent a denial of God? He gave it to me. Denying His gift is a form of hubris.

I'm ready to move on. I'm returning to my miracle schedule.

Creation

The goal of creation is to move beyond creation.
Completion comes when one touches the everlasting. This transcendent space has nothing to do with creation, since it has existed and will exist forever.

Paradoxically, during the process of creation, I free myself from the need to create by placing myself in the unchanging center of the universe.

But it is so difficult to keep priorities in line, so easy to be thrown off track. During the past month, I have been derailed. Tours have haunted my brain. First, the creation of the August 1995 Bulgarian itinerary and the excitement of filling my Budapest/Prague and Greek tours (although this week has brought four Greek tour cancellations). Second, the planning of new tours for 1996: a May tour to Bohemia and Moravia, with an extension to Slovakia and Cracow, and an August tour to Romania, which will include Transylvania. Both tours go to places rarely visited by Americans. I'll probably be running the only Romanian tour in America. Will people register for such unique destinations? You never know.

But just because you can't predict the future doesn't mean you can't set up priorities. There are two kinds: thinking and doing. Regarding thinking: oneness, unity, transcendence, should be my constant thought. From such a high point everything else should come. Notice I am using the hated and dreaded "should" word, shunned and scorned by contemporary psychologists, a word devaluing the ego, pointing to straight-and-narrow paths and higher priorities. Generations have rebelled against "should." "Drop it!" they cry. "Don't tell *me* what I should do. Just give me what I want!"

I have lived much of life according to these so-called selfish principles. But I also have a strong "should" ingrained in me. Try as I may, there is no escaping its harsh commandments. Years of therapy, counter-thought, and rebellion have still not freed me from "should." Now I am reassessing it. I realize that within it may lie my own salvation. Ironically, it is the "should" word that has saved me from insanity, kept me on balance, brought me back from the edge, and forced me to keep my priorities straight.

What does "should" say to *me*?

What "should" *I* do? Think about the Ultimate. Work incessantly without regard for the fruits of your labor. These are healthy "shoulds." When I remember them and follow their dictates, they free me from my chains.

I forgot about them during the past three weeks. The tour business ground me down. Details, details, details. I stopped writing in the morning, playing guitar, running and yoga. By giving up these centers I sank into a sea of forgetfulness; I could not remembering who I was. Even the money flowing in from my tour registrations didn't make me feel any better. The more that came in, the more attached I became. As my money and attachment grew, I became a prisoner of my own success. How can I call myself successful if I am a prisoner? Success means being free. I am only a success if I am free. Freedom, the only success worth striving for, comes through detachment. As more registrations came in, as the monies multiplied both in actuality and in my mind, instead of feeling satisfied, I wanted more, more, more. Greed quickly replaced my old fears of failure. Now, a prisoner of my tours, I was chained to the hope for more checks in the mail and more phone calls from customers.

I descended slowly. Most people would see this descent as success. For awhile, I did, too. But as I became more attached to my success, my dreams, once visions of freedom, started to dissolve. That's what happened during the past month.

Disguised Realms

What if my mother found out how religious thinking and spiritual I am? Or my father? They'd think I was nuts. Stupid, too. How can I find such solace, wonder, peace, and wisdom in religion if it is the opiate of the people? "Religion?" they'd say. "It's for the ignorant. God? A fiction, an excuse used by the stupid to 'explain' their ignorance. Spirituality? Forget it. What is it but a collection of hocus-pocus, of silly superstitions. Spirituality is for the mentally lame; it is not for someone like you with a college education."

Then they'd state the party line: "Religion, spirituality, and God have always been used by capitalist moguls to suppress the proletariat. Religion protects the rich who control the means of production and the world."

This is how my mother "explained" religion. My father, although not exactly agreeing, did not disagree either.

Yet my parents did have a spiritual side. My father loved philosophy, writing, words, soft humor, human foibles, balance, and an even temperament; my mother loved art, science, and music. Indeed, my parents worshipped learning; they revered artists and intellectuals. They believed in dialectical materialism and rationalism. But they also loved passion—as long as it was their own kind of passion.

Where did this leave me? I was free to discover a gateway to religion through the worship of Beethoven, Mozart, and Mendelssohn. The arts were acceptable. So were scientists like Einstein, or intellectuals like Marx, Lenin, and Engels, who changed the world through their ideas.

I grew up within the orthodox secular religion of communism. My mother promoted orthodoxy, my father skepticism. Thus, our household did have spirituality, God, and religion, only not under those names. Those names were anathema, banned, relegated to the realm of the stupid.

Jumping Mind

My attempt to master the Indo-European, Finno-Ugric, Turkic, and Semitic languages is coming to an end. It's an impossible task. I'm constantly being pulled in one direction or another. No sooner do I study Hungarian than Hebrew calls, no sooner study Greek than Bulgarian calls, no sooner Czech than Turkish. The result is I study many languages and know none of them. Is this a satisfying way to go? Do I want to go another? What good is studying Hungarian if my next trip is to Greece, or Hebrew if I'm going to Bulgaria? I have three or four trips a year. How can I keep all these languages going?

Wise friends say you can't do everything at once. It only leads to frustration, impotence, and unhappiness. Better to concentrate on one language. Then you can really learn it. Intellectually, I agree. Yet agreement doesn't *stop* me from jumping from one activity to another, from business to art to folk dancing to tourism to weekends to guitar to concerts to running to yoga to history, and to philosophy. I suffer from a jumping mind. No wonder I am always searching for inner peace. Jumping may be good for dancing and pole vaulting, but not for peace of mind.

To some degree everyone suffers from a jumping mind. My degree just seems higher than most. Certainly it *feels* higher. In any case, others don't matter in this situation. The idea of "others" is simply another creation of the same mind, which flies from one person to the next as easily as from one country to the next. All this jumping can drive me crazy. Sometimes the only thing that saves me from the lunatic asylum is fatigue. I get so tired of jumping that I fall down in exhaustion and go to sleep. Of course, when I wake up next morning, or even in a few hours or minutes, I start jumping again.

So the problem is not so much in the subjects of my jumps but in the *nature* of jumping mind. How can I quiet it, keep a perspective on its jumping? Can I watch it jump and simultaneously realize another part of me exists that can remain still? I'll never be able to stop my mind for long. As long as I have a mind, it will jump. Sometimes I am its master; most times I am its slave.

I'd like to be stronger and more self-controlled, but I am not. God put such a mechanism in my brain to both torture me and open the gates of wisdom. The slippery frog is hard to hold. Every time you grab it, it jumps out of your hand. My mind is exactly the same. Every time I try to grab it, it jumps away. Other people are amazed I can do so many things. I myself walk the line between amazement and overwhelmed. I live life at the edge of out-of-control. Gears are slipping. Wheels are about to come off. They rarely do, but the possibility is always there. So I step on the gas, keep my engine racing so my car will stay on a road.

What will happen if my mind stops? Bliss. What a paradox. I *look* for bliss, for connection with the universal sparks. Yet even though I "know" how to achieve this ecstasy and have done so countless times, I keep my mind jumping in countless directions so I don't achieve it.

I know the goal of any meditation is to still the mind. Knowing all this is fine. How to do it and keep doing it is the question.

The Universal Lost-and-Found Department

A melancholy is descending upon me, a sadness. Does it have something to do with the coming of spring?

I experience it as a falling apart. I can't concentrate on any one thing. Tourism is driving me mad. I only find peace now in doing physical things like yoga, running, or teaching folk dancing. Paradoxically, when I write I'm focused, because I'm writing about my lack of focus.

I am doing too much. Doing too much is my problem. But it may also be the solution to my problem. Perhaps confusion and lack of focus are my road *to* concentration and focus. That statement feels right, though it heightens my confusion and I don't understand it.

Opposites were injected into my body at birth. Are tours an outer reflection of the inner search for a path? Old questions. I doubt I'll ever find an answer. Yet I know the answer. I knew it years ago. I even knew it yesterday. But today is a new day. I begin each new day forgetting what I learned yesterday.

Why did I forget the path this morning? Are today's truths different from yesterday's? Perhaps they're the same but the paths to them are different. Why not? Look at the world's religions. All seek out the same truth, yet all take different paths. If this is the cultural nature of religions, why shouldn't it be true of individuals as well? Truth is One. Paths are infinite. Perhaps it is normal to begin each morning completely lost. Living in the lost-and-found department may be the most creative approach to life.

Not that I have much choice in the matter. I'd prefer to know exactly where I am going. It's much easier, smarter, and more peaceful.

If this were so, the confusions, discomforts, and worries of the search would end. I could sit on my porch, beer in hand, looking out over the beautiful landscape of truth, filled with visions of Oneness. Puffs of cloud would float by framed by blue skies and lighted by a brilliant sun: an Arizona morning forever. How lovely it would be. I'd sit in my rocking chair, watch the sun rise and set, the moon rise and set, the light change to dark and back to light; I'd smile beatifically in full possession of the universe. That would be nice. Instead, most of my mornings begin with the vague discomfort of being lost. My daily project is to find myself again.

The Trinity-and-One Method

I want to do everything but have time to do almost nothing.

In order to do something, I must set priorities. They are: writing, yoga and running, and guitar. Notice there are not one, but three priorities, the holy trinity, the magic of *chai*—eighteen, a multiple of three.

I have recently incorporated these mystical, religious, and spiritual aspects of numbers and counting into my calisthenics and yoga practices, and this has given them a renewed spiritual base. By using multiples of the number 3 backed by the number 1, I am aiming to move my concentration from the material to the spiritual. It is working. The number 3 has put a new meaning into my yoga practices. I am concentrating on two levels: I visualize 3 and 1 at the same time.

When can I find time to practice my Trinity? Mornings are best. I begin with an hour of writing followed by an hour of yoga or running; then breakfast, followed by an hour of guitar playing. I can vary the order. Either way, I have three hours of Trinity work each morning before my "earth-work," world-of-business begins.

Where will I find these three hours? I used to rise at five or six a.m. to get an extra hour each morning. I need to return to that discipline.

How can I apply its magic, mystery, and spirit to the world of business? Concentrating, focusing on the number 3 while I visualize the number 1 behind it helps me keep my priorities straight and my mind in balance. It is also a constant reminder of the ever-present higher forces in the universe. When I remember these forces and my relationship to them—who I am—I feel at peace.

What is my trinity in business? Notice I use small letters for this trinity to distinguish it from the larger, more ethereal, artistic one. My business trinity is folk dance teaching, weekends, and tours.

What about miscellaneous interests like language, history, stocks, philosophy, reading, studying? There is a trinity involved here, too: language, philosophy, and history.

These are trinities within trinities, wheels within wheels. Standing behind each is the One. The Trinity-and-One method. What an excellent way to organize my life.

Mr. Bereshit Organizes the Basement

I love beginnings. I'm a *bereshit* person. I love starting new books, new paths, new adventures. That's why I'm reorganizing the basement. It's a metaphor and symbol for a fresh start, a new beginning.

I'm trying to find a piece of God in my basement: loveliness, beauty, truth, and light among the mess of files, boxes of folk dance tapes, loose photos lying in cartons and envelopes, scattered books and records, boutique items, blouses, pants, T-shirts, and maps. Is it possible for me to find that kind of uplift, hope, and even transcendence, there?

If not, can I at least find it in the metabasement world of business? Must I always "retreat" to art forms, solitary meditations, writing, and guitar to find inner peace and spiritual contentment? The Hasidim and Martin Buber say the Lord Himself, Hashem, is in the little things like washing dishes, sending your kids off to school, talking to a next door neighbor, or picking up trash. Can I find it in a little thing like tourism? Tourism? In the same category as art? I often get lost when I enter the material world of work, business, and people. Can't it be possible to find the same beauty and light in the "outside world" that I find when I am alone in my room? Can I find it in *organization?*

My favorite word in the bible is *bereshit*. "In the beginning God created heaven and earth." Then He also *organized* heaven and earth. Which came first? Are creation and organization inseparable?

I want to put some transcendence into my basement organization. I want to put it into my business life as well. I need a different tour attitude. There must be a reason my tours haunt me. I can't get them out of my mind.

Why?

Perhaps I need to find transcendence in the ordinary telephone calls I make, the confirmation letters I send out, the countless details of tour organization, in stamping and addressing letters, sending out ads, calling a customer, finding the right rooms, the buses, guides, travel agents, on and on. Is this what I'm looking for, a saintly life amid the refuse, to see heaven in a lump of sugar?

How to Wake up Early

I'm waking up at 5:00 a.m. Recently however, I have been turning over and sleeping until about 7:00. That is because I have nothing to get up for. The only way to wake up early is to have something you love to do waiting for you. Thus, first thing in the morning: Do something you love!

Where Is the Sun?

I walked off a cliff. A sudden sinking. Falling, falling, into darkness, a pit filled with snakes hissing at my frail, fragile form; clouds of bilious, black, unearthly fluid hovered above my head, dropping pellets of acrid, foul-smelling rainwater on me; a cold damp chill invaded my body; goose pimples covered every whitewashed inch of flesh. Crows of hopelessness flew into the pit, followed by hundreds of bats carrying loaded bombs of despair, misery, and depression. Where was the sun? Why this sudden fall? Things were going so well only a few minutes ago!

It has nothing to do with money, relations, friends, goals, or power.

Well, maybe power. I woke up this morning aching in every bone. Too much yoga and running yesterday? Or arthritis, which sometimes visits me when I get up in the morning so that I can hardly move. I hobble to the bathroom like an ancient turtle lumbering up the shore in the Galapagos; I sprinkle water on my face, brush my teeth, limp down the stairs, hobble outside to get the newspaper, bend over stiffly to pick it up, and limp back to the kitchen table, where coffee awaits me. I perform this ritual almost every morning. It takes about an hour. Then I write or play guitar. By nine or ten o'clock, my body is aching to move. I run, do yoga—performing squats, sit-ups, push-ups, head stands, foot stands, twists, running, and all kinds of amazing stretches I couldn't have dreamt of doing only a few hours ago.

Revisiting High School

I spoke to Paul Bachner yesterday afternoon, an old high school buddy I haven't seen in years. His mother just died. He now lives with his wife Susan in Lexington, Kentucky. Talking to him on the phone brought back so many high school memories, mostly of playing Mozart violin and piano sonatas on Saturday nights in his apartment. His Hungarian mother baked us cookies and fed us. How I loved those evenings, my music, the whole High School of Music and Art experience. What nostalgia!

I hate nostalgia and the melancholy it brings. I remember when leaving my house opposite the park and walking all the way from Riverdale to Dyckman Street, carrying my violin, was no big deal. I had lots of musical heroes to look up to who could point the way clearly into a light-suffused future, a musical firmament filled with stars, sun, and a universe of beautiful sound. My Milky Way sparkled with symphonies of Beethoven and Mozart, conducted by Toscanini, Guido Cantelli, Dmitri Metropoulos, and all the others. I played the violin in their image. It was heavenly.

If all that was so heavenly, why does remembering it make me so melancholy? Shouldn't I feel great? Am I fooling myself? Maybe my teenage years at Music and Art *weren't* so great. Often I felt like a second-rate violinist, basketball player, and intellectual, especially when compared to Bachner, who read books and could talk about them. I was a lousy communist, afraid to fight at May Day rallies, or speak up to my intellectual friends who knew all the answers and could talk rings around those capitalist slobs and apologists who ruled the world. We left-wingers, quasi and total communists, *knew*. We were the elite, the chosen, the martyrs and victims of the unfair capitalist system that destroyed the poor helpless proletariat we worshipped. We lived in a terrible social and economic system that only Marx, Engels, Lenin, Trotsky, and Stalin could fix. Luckily, these heroic leaders filled our landscape, bringing the hope of redemption to helpless communist souls lost, alone, and victimized by big business in a capitalist land.

I could go on and on, but I won't. Perhaps this is the reason I hate to look back, to explore or even talk about the past. Perhaps the High School of Music and Art and all those wonderful years at progressive camps weren't so wonderful after all. Have I been fooling myself? Is the "new" me, the tough, entrepreneurial, business-type rebel—the "real" me? Is it the better, tougher, freer one? Were those teenage years clouded over by repression?

I used to express myself through unthreatening forms like classical music and basketball. I dared not stand up for what I wanted. Such actions were "bad." Maybe I wasn't ready to stand up for myself simply because I didn't know who "myself" was. Which self would I stand up for? The first time I ever stood up was in my junior year at the University of Rochester when I decided to leave college and spend a year studying at the University of Aix-en-Provence in France. That was my first adventure, my first act of personal heroism.

Power and Strength

One of the joys of leadership is power! It's time I admitted it. In the past, I've associated the word with evil and negativism: You shouldn't be powerful; you should be humble, modest, and sweet.

What about strength? Same thing. Strength and power go together inseparably.

I don't know why I have had such negative feelings towards my own power and strength. It could be due to a communist upbringing. Under Marxist philosophy it is wrong and evil to own anything. Thus, it is also wrong to own your personal power and strength. Better to merge with the collective and be equal. Choose equality over freedom even if it kills you in the process. This is the heart of public collectivism and private rejection of personal desires and demands. In this sense, it is similar to Christianity and orthodox Judaism. Perhaps my family was orthodox after all, but orthodox communist, not Jewish.

In any case, rather than exploring the roots of why I am who I am, I'd rather explore the idea of personal power and strength. I love the words; but even as I say them, I feel guilty. Why? I want to suppress them. But I'm changing. I'm ready to dive into the pool. What better place to start than in Budapest as a tour leader, and with the California girls?

The Highest Achievement Is Inspiring Others

Our tour group is staying at the Hotel Korona in Budapest. I tried writing with a pen in the lobby. It felt so slow, primitive, and strange. The letters form so sluggishly. Writing by hand is dying; the computer moves at about the speed of my thoughts—or vice versa. I can use handwriting for calligraphy, Hebrew, or Russian.

I told Bob Gutin about my fears and guilt at exercising my power. He says he has no such fears. I responded by saying, "Perhaps you have a kinder unconscious." Mine may be too full of destructive urges and wishes. But I've just realized I don't have to be afraid of my power if I use it in the service of the Good. Making money is good. Serving others is even better. Serving, helping, inspiring, uplifting, are the highest good man can do on earth. By concentrating on that, money will come as a by-product. Running tours, teaching folk dancing, organizing weekends, are in the service of this higher good. I only have to recognize and admit it. I'm on the right track and have been all along.

Does that sound arrogant? If it does, I'll have to get used to it. It may be the way to go until I accept my own strength. Once I do, I'll be able to modulate my "arrogance" to "normal."

Selling a New Tour Program: Tours to My Mind

Are all accidents signs? If so, what do they mean?

I was so exhausted walking the streets of Prague on Sunday that I decided to return to our hotel to spend the rest of the day in bed. When I headed for the metro at *Václavske Namesti*, I passed a sign that read *Tunisair*. Why not explore it? I went to the front door, found it closed for the weekend, and was about to leave when a man came up behind me, took out a key, identified himself as the sales manager, and invited me upstairs for a drink of Sprite and a talk about Tunisia!

Was this an accident? A sign? Does it mean I'll run a tour to Tunisia in 1996? I'm thinking about it. First of all, it's one of the few safe Arab countries; second, I'd like to explore the ancient home of the Phoenicians, who invented the alphabet, and meet some of their descendants. Third, I'd like to study Arabic writing again; this will give me a good excuse. Fourth, since it's a country I know nothing about, it will give me a chance to do research on Carthaginian history. I'll be one of the first Americans to run a tour there. It might also be a good beach destination for February, a good substitute for the Canary Islands, Caribbean, or Eilat.

I used to think Egypt would be a warm place to get away from the cold, but I got too sick there, and the rise in terrorism will make it hard to get customers. The Middle East is always a problem. My tours to Israel never get enough people to be financially worth running. Yet Israel is a beautiful destination for the soul.

Tunisia might be worth exploring.

I am so tired today. I slept God's sleep for over an hour this afternoon, had some espresso, took a short walk, came back to the hotel to write, and, at the end of all this, I'm just as tired as when I started. I should spend the rest of the day writing, reading Indian philosophy, doing yoga, and sleeping.

Am I really so tired? Or do I need a new thought to occupy my mind, which, like a monkey, will jump all over if it's not tied down. I'm in a state of limbo, between tours. The Budapest/Prague tour structure kept my mind focused. Now I need a new focus to lift up my energies. Otherwise I become sad, logy, depressed, and sluggish. When I'm focused, I'm energetic, happy, buoyant, and upbeat; accomplishing something is almost secondary. I need to put my genie on a pole. Otherwise he'll drive me mad and eat me up.

Beyond Tunisia my New Leaf writing project is best. What better goal than to publish it when I get back? The process of writing is a good-in-itself. Can the publication process become one as well?

Two ways come to mind: first there is the satisfaction of carving an as-close-to-perfect writing work as possible. But a major motivating force is having others read, praise, love, and be transformed by it. Ah, could transformation be the goal of my desire to publish? I want my work to affect people, change their minds, rock them in their seats, force them to shout "Wow!" I want them to take part in my Cheerios experience, share my vision of the Ultimate. I feel like a prophet in secular clothing, a miniature Moses on the loose. I want to take my clay tablets out of their hidden place in my computer, go public with them, uplift others through the power of my hand.

Is it hubris to have such thoughts? Truly, higher powers feed me my best lines. Through my fingers they are transfered to the page, then to others. They are a gift to me, and I want to give them to the public. Is that a good reason to publish? Well, why not? What other reason could I have? The only thing stopping me from thinking this way is the old fear of my power and strength. To say my writing is worth reading and worthy is to take a stand on the value of my most personal, private, and important possession. I see my world view developing and clarifying itself across these pages. Let me give it to others.

Writing is a fascinating tour of my inner landscape, full of surprises, excitement, visions of paradise, and mistakes born in hell. Why not promote and sell it with my other tours?

Study as a Good-In-Itself

As I sat on the toilet reading the *History of Czechoslovakia in Outline*, how the Labe River is called the Elbe River in German and comes from the Celtic "Albion," I realized I wanted to study more about the Czech language, culture, and history. Then I thought, Why bother? After all, I'll soon be dead. Why clog up my mind with new information? How and where will I use it? Look at all the knowledge I have in my head already. Why learn more? I know enough already—how to survive on tour, how to get along in life. New learning won't help business, prolong my life, or make me healthier and happier.

Where does such a terrible attitude come from? I love gathering knowledge. I also love using it in the service of future benefits. I studied language and history to improve my chances of tour survival, and get better control of my itineraries, destinations, and tourists. Now that I've developed some travel skills, I don't need any more foreign language or history to improve my tours. Guides and travel agencies take care of that. Through acquired skills I have freed myself from some of the old burdens, mastered the skill of running a tour, even of getting customers. Increasing my knowledge of language and history will not improve my ability to do either. So why bother?

It's a question of means-to-an-end versus end-in-itself. Knowledge has been used to bolster my self-confidence and increase my power and strength. But now that I *have* them, my old purpose for acquiring knowledge has passed away.

I'll have to find another reason for studying Czech language and history; my days of studying as a means to self-improvement and tour survival are on the way out. If I don't find a new reason, I won't study at all. Yet studying has always been one of my great pleasures. It's time to see study as a end-in-itself.

MONEY AND ITS BRETHREN

Money: Practicing the Art of Nonworry

Most of my diseases are psychological in origin. I got my cold, cough, and sore throat after doing too many squats. A few days ago, on Tuesday, I practiced yoga for an hour and a half. That's much more than usual. Overuse may well have been the origin of my sickness. But a second thought occurs to me: I am facing my usual pretravel fears. I'm worried about leaving the house, my safe secure sanctuary, and flying off to Budapest and Prague. How will I survive there? What about my writing, yoga, guitar, reading, running, my miracle schedule? I'll have to give most of it up. Leaving the house is a hardship; traveling to Budapest and Prague is even harder.

My only consolation is that I'll make lots of money. Why do I even *want* lots of money? To relieve myself from the anxiety of financial worries. But mainly to fool myself. Somehow I believe that having lots of money will make me stop worrying about money —beyond that, that it will make me stop worrying about life and its problems.

I know, intellectually, this philosophy is ridiculous, that worrying about money does only one thing: creates more worries about money. Worrying, in general, simply creates more worry. If you want to worry, then worry you will, and when the problems created by your worries are solved, you'll create new ones. If the worry route is the one you want to travel, worries will never end.

Worrying will never lead me to freedom and self-liberation. The only way to give up worries is to stand firm and say, No! This is not my route. I must find a different one.

I've know this all along. Doing it is another matter. Still, I must start someplace, even if it is over and over again each day. So I'll start over right now.

Somehow I have to approach my Budapest and Prague tour with a different attitude; I also have to approach disease, sickness, bad back, sore throat, coughing, chills, sniffles and sneezes with another attitude: the nonworry attitude. It wouldn't hurt to make this a daily practice, a religious ritual. I practice the art of writing, the art of guitar. Now I'll practice the art of nonworry.

PERFORMANCE

Lessons

It all started when Gagik Karapetian gave his Armenian dance workshop last week. He taught a dance, *Shoorch Bar* (Circle Dance), which he choreographed using traditional Armenian steps. When he moved to the right on the second step, he borrowed one of the women and turned this step briefly into one for couples. He raised his right arm straight up high while his left went sidewards, parallel to the floor. He added beautiful hand movements. I loved it, tried it, and realized over a period of a week that I didn't know what I was doing. Gagik said this arm movement was a traditional Armenian one. Joyce Tamasian said a similar movement was used in ballet. So I decided to study some ballet: Maybe I could take beginner classes somewhere. I could use the foundation. Then, last night, Bernice taught me the arm positions. I struggled, became exhausted, realized how much I needed lessons, loved being taught, and how difficult it is to learn. Paradox in action: How discouraging and elevating learning is, how wonderful to have someone teach and lead me, how relaxing and inspiring putting myself into the hands of a capable teacher, realizing I don't have to know everything but can once again open my mind, heart, and body to learning.

I haven't taken lessons, learned any new skill, since I took yoga with Rama last summer. Lessons are traumatic for me. It takes days to recover and absorb them. Why they are so hard? I don't know, or care. The point is, I need and love them.

BUSINESS

Working with Steve

Last night's folk dance workshop with Steve was my first with him. Excellent. I had heard about his reputation as a talented but irresponsible drunk who rarely showed up for his teaching engagements. Last night only his talent showed. Maybe he's changed since he got married and had two kids. Whatever the reason, I learned an exciting Bulgarian dance, *Graovsko*, from West Bulgaria in the style of *Kjustendilska Ruchenitsa*. It reminded me of how wonderful Bulgarian folklore is. This tiny country has worldwide treasures. Not many know about them, but someday they will recognize the beauty, uniqueness, and excitement of Bulgarian dancing.

Perhaps my 1995 Tour to Bulgaria will be the beginning. What a tour we have lined up! Our bus will travel with three dancers and one musician—a constant folk school, our own personal festival. I'm writing up the flier today.

The one-week flurry of Bulgarian tour development has come to an end. I accomplished many things. I passed through the "success syndrome" and cut my mailing list from fifteen hundred to six hundred. Now I'm ready to move on.

Bernice said I have so many people touring with me this year because I am actively selling. It's true. I am *convincing* people to go on them. My enthusiasm is showing.

Use my belief in Weekends to promote and enthusiastically say to others: "It is just too good! You *must* go! You cannot *afford* to stay home!"

Tours

I've spent the last week creating two new tours. May 1996 to Bohemia, Moravia, Slovakia, and Poland has a great itinerary! It's the "complete former Czechoslovakia plus." To my knowledge, no one in America is doing it except me. We've got great guides, great itinerary, and a great program. Same with the August 1996 Romania tour: great itinerary, good program—which I hope to upgrade to great—and hopefully, good guides (I will have to research and find them). Both tours are winners. I just have to get customers.

Same with my 1995 tours. The March Budapest and Prague tour is a proven winner. August in Bulgaria is a winner with its festival, and musicians and dancers traveling with us on the bus, performing, singing, and teaching us dances while we travel. A first for us. What a coup! I love it! My concern, at the moment, is our Greek tour. I know I'm discouraged because we just had four cancellations. I'm also concerned because it might turn out like Turkey, a great tour but not much folk dancing. We'll have dancing with the Dora Stratou dancers in Athens, but beyond that, I don't know. During the five-day classical tour, I don't know what kind of groups we'll find, if any, and, as for the island cruise, if there is no dancing on ship with the crew, there won't be any dancing at all. Thus, Greece, so far, has little dancing. That's a negative. On the positive side, we have a great itinerary. Also, I might be lucky and find some folk dancing after all.

Greece is a new tour. I don't think my doubts about the dancing prevent people from registering. Until last week we had good registration. It's just my luck changed and I lost four. However, there is a big financial factor here. I need twenty people minimum to make any money on this tour. If I get under twenty, I'll make about a thousand dollars. If I get over twenty, I could make close to ten thousand! That's quite a difference for just a few people.

In retrospect, I see what I did "wrong." I offered a lower tour price on the hope that I'd attract more people and reach my goal of twenty. This is the only tour I've ever priced this way, and it's because the Greek Island Cruise raised the total net price about nine hundred dollars. It's an expensive trip to begin with, and, in order to make money on it I would have to make it even more expensive. I didn't want to take a chance on having no registration, so I took a chance on a lower price. As a result, I probably won't make any money at all.

Tours 2

This morning I woke up feeling low. I haven't felt low for ages. Why now? It could be that in the last few weeks, in spite of Arlene's great article in the *Bergen Record*, I've gotten five tour cancellations and no registrations. It's starting to get me down.

Let's talk about this. I'll talk to my computer, who happily listens to everything I say and doesn't talk back.

The haunting clouds that swirl around my head are all due to planning my next tour season: Turkey, Budapest, Prague, Romania, Slovakia, many questions about organizing and planning. It takes lots of work; it will keep haunting me until I get it right. Once I do, I'll feel better and can move on. I just about have next year planned: Budapest and Prague for March. Maybe I should plan to make all my money in the March Budapest and Prague tours. That way I can rationalize running a May tour to Eastern Turkey even though very few people, if any, will go on it. Let my adventures in the Budapest and Prague tours come from making money. These are areas I really know about and may be easier to sell. My adventure in Turkey will come from visiting new places. Romania, too. My August tour there should do well, but you never know. Besides, it is a new tour and an unexplored destination. Budapest and Prague, Hungary and the Czech Republic, can be seen as my potential money makers for 1996; Eastern Turkey is for personal sport and adventure, and so is Romania.

I like this attitude. A good balance between realism and dreams, the known and the unknown. It feeds my need and desire for adventure. Money-making adventures in Budapest and Prague, new destination adventures in Eastern Turkey and Romania.

Slovakia could be seen as an experiment in market exploration to find out if there is any interest among my clients for travel to Slovakia.

I have no desire to edit what I've just written. It's more like writing out a business plan than writing a journal. But perhaps my journal *is* my business plan.

Value in Tour Cancellations

I picked up my phone messages and found another tour cancellation. That's the seventh in three weeks. My Greek tour has gone from nineteen registrants to twelve. I've never had so many cancellations in my life. Why is this happening to me?

When I call Cally, my tour representative at Cloud Tours, and tell her, I'll feel like a fool. Only a month ago I told her I had nineteen people. Hold twenty-five, even thirty places for the tour, I said. I was so enthusiastic and optimistic. Now, a month later, it's all falling apart. In retrospect, my optimism and enthusiasm seem so foolish. How could I have been so deluded by possibilities, mere hopes for the future without realizations? Don't I know that registrations are only promises, not real commitments? How could I have been so naive? Why did I have to raise Cally's hopes and my own as well? I've had years of experience running tours. Shouldn't I have been "smarter?"

Looking back, it's easy to be "realistic," to "see" how tour registration can fall apart. But a month ago it was a completely different situation. I had reason to be optimistic. Proof in the form of registrations was coming in every day. Who wouldn't be enthusiastic? Conversely, who wouldn't be depressed about this business reversal? Suddenly, from a full registration and the hope of making mucho money, I've gone to a poor registration and the possibility of losing money.

Does enthusiasm and optimism cloud my judgement? Probably. On the other hand, doesn't this morning's pessimism, anger, depression, and disappointment over these cancellations cloud my judgement as well? Probably. The only way to improve my judgement is to rise above my emotions. Easy to say, hard to do, but nevertheless, a worthy pursuit.

Is there a lesson in all this? Why did God lift me so high, then drop me, if not into the gutter, at least near it? What was the purpose of putting me on the up-and-down emotional roller coaster? It must have something to do with *values*.

What does the Bhagavad Gita say? What does Vivekananda repeat? What are the lessons of karma yoga? Work as hard as you can without attachment to the fruits of your labor. Work is your salvation. Period. You can never know or predict the results of your work. Work that is wonderful may, in spite of your desires, hurt or destroy someone. Work that is terrible may end up helping others. Results can never be known exactly. But you can know the nature of your work. Thus, the best thing is to work as hard as you can, and forget about the results. Results are in God's hands.

This is a great lesson.

Will I remember it?

This year started when I decided to give up worrying about money in order to concentrate on doing the best job I could. My tours started filling up; so did my folk dance classes. As I succeeded, slowly my mind turned from the work itself into visualizing the results of my work, namely, more tour registrants and mucho money pouring into my coffers. As my thoughts evolved—-or rather, devolved—from the work process to its results, my registrations started drifting away.

Does mind create the world? Do my vibrations affect the world by subtly drawing tour registrants towards me when I am concentrating on my work, and by subtly repelling them when I am concentrating only on results? Do values create my destiny?

I must admit that, during the past few weeks, my values have disintegrated. I could feel them falling apart as I wrestled with the concepts of success. The beauty, wonder, and awe I felt as I wrote this summer and as I calmly looked at the world without desire for fame or fortune slowly faded as fame and fortune started coming my way. There's certainly nothing wrong with fame or fortune. The only problem is *believing in it*. Such belief can destroy you.

Perhaps I am lucky so many people cancelled. Their cancellations may be saving me from an even worse fate.

Work is a good-in-itself. Results that come from work are "accidents." Some are happy accidents; some are sad accidents. But whatever they are, whichever way they turn out, they are beyond your control. It is noxious to focus your mind on results. Attachment to results is a great source of misery. Work, work, work. Give up the fruits of your labor. This is helpful attitude, healthy, beautiful, and blissful.

I have been sending out poor vibrations. Perhaps these negative vibrations are creating tour cancellations. Strangely, even paradoxically, these cancellations are putting me back on track.

Money as a Warm Cuddly

I love the warm cuddly feeling of having money, the security of seeing high numbers in my check book. Too bad I see my money disappearing. As one tour cancellation after another rolls in, my profits for my Greek tour dwindling, first to nothing then to below zero, I realize what a lovely, unrealistic cocoon I have been living in during the last few months. I've been holding thousands of dollars of other people's money in my checking account.

After awhile I began believing it belonged to me. How sad that the due date is coming and I'll have to mail it all to Cloud Tours. I've gone from a fat but imaginary bank account back to the zero, where I started last October. Truly, it is depressing to have worked so hard, put in so much effort, ridden on so many high tour hopes, only to see them all dribble slowly back to a primal state of financial nothingness.

The nothingness reminds me of my love for the security, warmth, and power money gives me. How easy it is to hire world-renowned dance teachers like Gagik Karapetian, head choreographer of the Armenian State Folk Ensemble in Yerevan, or Alexander Antouchine, former lead dancer of the Moiseyev Dance Company, or Istvan Szabo Kovacs, formerly of the Hungarian State Folk Ensemble. Their fees are so low compared to the thousands that once sat in my coffers. It was so easy to pay my bills. Hundreds of dollars in rent bills, insurance costs, advertising and printing costs, mailings and postage, and food and entertainment didn't look like much compared it to the thousands sitting in my checkbook. Too bad it wasn't my money.

But that phase is over. I'm paying my bills. I'm mailing the money off to Cloud Tours. I'm back to the beginning again. Only the "feeling" of wealth remains. I would love that feeling to continue on some basis, but I don't know how.

Perhaps an idea will come along.

Pain Stimulant

Pain wakes you up, acts as a stimulant. A little pain never hurts. It increases your concentration and helps you focus. In so doing, it may even save you from more pain. What future pains can I look forward to?

I complain about tours; their worries and problems haunt my mind. Yet I keep running them. Why? There must be something in them that I want and need. I remember a few years ago I gave up tours in disgust. I can't take it anymore, I said. Too many problems, too many worries. I quit. I'm devoting myself to work based at home. To my surprise, I got depressed. I had given up my worries, but I had also given up my dream of adventure. Perhaps pain and adventure go together. I returned to running tours.

Perhaps I can find a middle ground, a new way of running tours. I don't want to suffer in the old ways, but I still want the excitement and stimulation. Is it possible to have both, excitement without pain, stimulation without risk? I doubt it. But maybe if I cannot eliminate the blows, I can soften them.

What kind of tour challenge am I looking for? I have dealt with accommodations, itineraries bathrooms, money, and challenges beyond challenges I can't think of right now.

Perhaps I should look for a supra-tour challenge; perhaps it is time to challenge my mind and see if I can have two concentrations at once—one on the tour, the other on fulfilling my miracle schedule with its focus on transcendence.

Facing the Fun Factor in the Tour Business

Last night after reading about Henry Miller I realized I no longer needed to worship or even agree with him. His importance had diminished. I was now my own hero. A gain, but a loss, too.

I also realized I was holding something back. Yes, I have to admit it: I love my tours! I love the excitement of putting them together, the adventure of leading them, visiting foreign places, learning languages, being part of an international community, meeting folk dance and music groups in their native settings. My tours are just plain fun!

How much fun can I stand? That is the question I should ask. Perhaps I throw up roadblocks in the guise of potential problems to block off my mounting feelings of excitement, adventure, and fun. Will my puritan past allow me to face the brilliant blinding light of the fun factor?

Focus on Details Brings Peace of Mind

Complaining is an art form. Perhaps it can free me and bring me peace.

First of all, my whole Bulgarian tour has to be changed. The stupid fucking Bulgarian government suddenly decided to run the Koprivshtitsa Folk Festival after all. This after I've mailed out all my brochures, fliers, and itineraries, put ads in journals and newspapers announcing the Bulgarian tour *without* the festival. Now suddenly there *is* one. I have to change the program, change the dates, change the advertising, write a new flier, call customers. . .what the fuck is the matter with that government? Couldn't they have waited until *next* year and done it right, with enough lead time? No. They have to mess it up *this* year. In two days I'll be off to Budapest. I have to rush through a whole new Bulgarian itinerary before I go.

My Greek itinerary has been changed, too. We've added an extra day in Athens. That's no big deal, and I'm making some money because of the changes. Still, it's an annoyance on top of another annoyance.

Then there is the annoyance of leaving for Budapest and Prague.

While I complain I realize I have lost sight of the higher forces—not only that they exist, but that I know where to find them. I'm wallowing in the dirt of the present, the endless mix-ups that constitute running tours.

Yet a part of me loves it. Which part, I'm not sure. I love the money and potential money it can bring. Recently I've learned to like the organizational aspect, too. Once again, I must remember that, although He is well hidden, God lives in the organizational aspect of tourism. He'll be on tour with me. The only question is where. In a seat on the bus? At the airport? On the line in front of me? All those and more. In the minds of my tour participants, too. He is shining in their excited eyes.

In Budapest and Prague, I want to focus on the fear of *my own strength*, which comes in many forms—in my body with its strength to run, do push-ups, dance, and lifts heavy weights; in my mind, with its strength of intellect, organization, creation, analysis, and judgement. But knowing them does not give me the kind of strength *I* am looking for, the everlasting unbreakable strength that brings utter and complete confidence. This can only come from *spiritual* strength, the strength of vision manifested when I experience visits from The Higher One, which, although they only come in spurts, are reminders of my relationship to the Highest Self and the ultimate manifestation of my power. Mental and physical strengths are derivatives of this. Intellect can never bring the bliss that resides in the indwelling spirit. But I fear my Higher Self; in order to experience It, I must obliterate my ego. I'm going to think about this in Budapest and Prague.

Wonderful, wonderful! I'm sitting in my underwear in my room at the Korona Hotel in Budapest, facing the street. It's 7:00 a.m. and I'm *writing on my computer!* First time *ever!* I've brought high tech with me and gotten it to work. I plugged it in correctly, put all the parts together, and they *fit*. Now I can write every morning!

Is it smart to keep my computer set up in my room, open and on display all day while I'm gone? Will it be stolen? It's a royal annoyance to put it together and dismantle it every time I use it. Yet I have to do it this way until I get used to it. Perhaps eventually I'll just "accept" the fact it might be stolen and move on from there. I'll ask the control and security people at the desk what they think.

Meanwhile, what an absolute pleasure. I can't get over the thrill of it! I've brought an important part of home with me.

This year's Budapest group is wonderful. I know almost everyone, like almost everyone, and they all seem to fit and flow together—all except for our three "California girls." They make me nervous. I don't know anything about them. Do they fit in? *Will* they?

When I met Linda and Michala at the airport, Linda seemed nice. My initial reservations about her melted away. Still, I sense an insecurity there, and a distance. Her friend Michala is beautiful and friendly enough, but standing next to her feels like standing next to an ice pack. Later, in Budapest, I met Tera, the third of the trio. She is movie-star beautiful blonde, the kind of woman you can't take your eyes off. When we sat in our introductory circle in the Korona lobby on opening night and introduced ourselves, she said she was a therapist and a minister. Of the three, she feels the softest. Beautiful as she is, though, I sense a vulnerability about her: "Please don't hurt me just because I'm beautiful."

Why am I analyzing these newcomers to our group? Usually I reserve this journal for self-revelations and discoveries and rarely think about observing others. But last night, Anand said, "These California women have a problem. They're stand-offish." At first I told him he was wrong, that he should give them a chance. They're new and feel uneasy with our group. But he disagreed. "They're still stand-offish," he repeated. Sadly, I had to agree. He said they were disappointed because our group was older and they were looking for younger men. That may be his own projection. It may also be true. I'm afraid to look at the three of them too closely, because I so much want to win them over, to have them become part of us and not break the unity feeling. Group unity is a reflection of my own inner desire for unity, the need to pull the disparate parts together. But that may be impossible. All you can do is your best. You can't change others.

Rebirth of Reasons to Run My Tours

Great night of dancing last night at Kalamajka Dance House at Belvárosi Ifjúsági Ház on 9 Molnár Utca, just four blocks from our hotel.

We arrived at 8:00. The room was packed already. *A tanár*, the teacher, was demonstrating a couple dance. We got into the circle and learned in the Hungarian way. The dancing got hotter and hotter, better and better. Parts of our group of twenty faded out as the evening progressed. Finally, about one a.m., a hardy seven of us left at closing time.

What a great night! I loved the dancers. I loved our group. Most are enthusiasts—except for the "California girls," who didn't show up. I suppose they'll go on the day tours and disappear for the folk dancing. But I could be wrong. Yesterday they improved, and so did I. Still, they are not folk dance enthusiasts, so I guess they'll stay "on the outside." I think they want it that way, too, and that's okay; they've faded a bit from my mind as the tour and my brain coalesce.

More pointings towards Romania and Transylvania for next year: Our teacher, Julia Redo, gave me a flier for a folk dance camp in Transylvania this summer. Perhaps someday I might go. More important, though, is what Bill, George, and Terry asked: "Why don't you teach them in America?" Then George added, "Why not get more Hungarian dance teachers to introduce Hungarian dances to our group?"

I like it! New horizons and possibilities. I could start by inviting Kálmán Magyar to do a June workshop. Second, I could try to learn the Transylvanian virtuoso dances like Mezöségi and Kalotaszegi Legényes—the "Lad's Dance"—for my own development and personal satisfaction. I'll probably never teach them, but I'll love doing them. This is something to think about. Folk dancing *is* the central theme of my folk tours. That's why I run tours in the first place. I want to make money, too, but money is not the foundation of my existence; there is a purpose beyond, which goes back to my original vision to learn about the folk dances of the country.

We must have folk dance workshops on these tours. Not only is it good for our tour participants, publicity, and business, but beyond that, it is good for my moral, mental, physical, folk dance, artistic, and spiritual development. Folk dance and music are the pillars, the foundations, of my tours. Whenever I ask myself, Why am I going to so much trouble to put these tours together? the answer comes down to my love of music and folk dancing. That's the bottom line. In America it is impossible to have folk dance nights like the one we had last night at Molnár Utca. The *tanc ház*—folk dance house—atmosphere exists only in Hungary among Hungarians. Therefore, I must go and be part of it. I must bring others with me too, because I like their company. The fact that they pay and are part of my tour and my business is really secondary, the earthly reflection of the heavenly force. Heavenly forces are manifested in this activity; the earthly incarnations exist in my tour participants' and our folk dance—and other—experiences on these tours.

I could not have discovered and verbalized such a wonderful concept without bringing my computer with me on tour.

New Tour Plans for 1996, Plus Hungarian Study Program

Another great night of dancing. Last night it was Greek "in the Hungarian manner" at Almassy Tér in the Szabadidö Központ (Free Time Center). We got there for the teaching around 6:30 p.m. Our group faded around 10:00, so we headed back to the Korona Hotel. It was raining. Half the folks took a taxi. The other half continued walking. On the way we stopped to explore another *tanz ház*, the Jószefvárosi Ifúsági, off Blaha Lusza Tér on Somogyi Béla utca. We arrived in time to sit down for a short concert by an amateur singing group, then left. On the way, I "trained" Peggy to say, "Hol van a Muszeum utca?" ("Where is Museum Street?") to help us find our way back to Kalvin Tér, where the Korona Hotel was located. Finally, she got it. We saw three men on the corner and decided to try it on them, but they were Turkish and didn't understand a word.

When we got back to the hotel, Martha said, "We're competing to see who's had the best time so far. Jim, the dancing is fantastic. It's your job to tell people America about this."

This gave me an idea: Next year I'll organize two tours to the Budapest Spring Festival, Weeks One and Two, or a combination of Weeks One and Two. Three choices, Week One, Week Two, or Weeks One and Two (Two Weeks). Each choice would be followed by an optional extension to Prague. This is a great idea and a challenge. It would add purpose and meaning to the upcoming year. I could start promoting and selling it right now. Next year I could also study Hungarian. I'll be planning for two weeks in Budapest plus our summer tour to Romania and Transylvania. In Transylvania, we'll spend much of our time among the Hungarian-speaking ethnic communities. My Hungarian will come in handy.

Sense of Humor Breeds High Tolerance for Humiliation

It's 5:30 in the afternoon, and I'm sitting in my hotel room, writing on my computer. What a luxury! Thank you, computer and all technological advances.

I just spoke with Károly Falvay. I'm meeting him at his house on

Gyarmat utca tomorrow at 11:00 a.m. To get there, I'll have to take the bus alone, meet him alone, then spend the day alone until the evening, when I'll plan dinner at the Matyas Pincer Restaurant for our group. Alone, alone—another luxury. How I love it—another chance to write and think.

I got the tickets for Shiffie's air flight from Budapest to Prague. No problem. Things were so *difficult* under communism. Now, with the service economy, even Czech Airlines is trying to please me by forking over a ticket.

I met Ann in the halls. She said, "You must have the patience of a saint to handle all these 'unusual' people on our tour." I like that diplomatic word for pain-in-the-ass, crazy, annoying (and the countless other adjectives I use) to describe the complainers I sometimes get. But so far, this tour has had almost none.

Do I have the patience of a saint? If I do, how do I do it? *A sense of the absurd*. It gives me a priceless protective screen: Humor confers a high toleration for humiliation.

One key to success as tour leader is tolerance. Since I take so many chances on these tours, I often make mistakes. People tell me I am wrong, and I agree. How can I face them after I told them to turn right on the next corner but, when we arrive there, I see we should have turned left? What can you do when the concert you promised them is cancelled, your tour guide never shows up, your hotel has no washcloths after you promised they did, and on and on? All I can do is laugh at the absurdities of leadership—often a case of the less blind leading the more blind. Not that I mind. Leading the blind is an adventure that opens many of your own blind spots. Often leadership is a case of covering and recovering from public mistakes. Luckily, in the long run, people forget most of what I say anyway. Then only the sparks of enthusiasm remain, and, ultimately, it is enthusiasm that creates these tours.

The word of God, my Silent Partner, is: Be Enthusiastic. It certainly beats running my tours alone.

Calm at the End of the Tour

Tomorrow we leave Budapest. I'm sad our tour is over but not as sad as usual. Not as happy, either. Just calm.

This one was easier because of my mental state, coupled with some good people. We had some on our first tour, in 1984, but it was a mental disaster for me. What a difference eleven years of experience makes. I handle people better; I'm seasoned.

Today I plan to search for the *Kalyi Jag cigány* tapes. I'm buying other gypsy and Hungarian folk music and dance tapes to sell in America. The blouse and vest business of our boutique is slowly fading. Prices have gone up too much in Hungary to make a profit. I'll buy a few to keep up a good display, raise the prices, and hope for the best.

Tour Groups and the Cheerios Experience

Did Moses lead a tour group out of Egypt?

On my last day in Budapest I usually I take a good-bye walk.

As I did, I realized good action can create harm and bad action can create good. Witness the Monday night concert at *Almassy Tér,* a splendid serendipity and highlight of our tour. My group loved it. But Lucinda didn't come. She told me afterward that I "should have known" the concert was going to be great. But it was as much of surprise to me as to everyone else. Nevertheless, she insisted it "had been my job as leader" to know, and that, if I did not know, I should have found out.

Lucinda is mad because she missed the greatest event of the tour. I don't blame her for being mad, although I do fault her for blaming me. How can I possibly predict serendipity? If I could, it wouldn't *be* serendipitous. Still, Lucinda's remarks have haunted me ever since she said them. They must have a kernel of truth in them. But what kernel? I think about how even the best of deeds, the most fortunate of unanticipated discoveries and most uplifting and wondrous of circumstances and events, can and often do end up hurting you.

What can you conclude from this not-so-obvious truth? That work must be a good-in-itself. That, even though work by its nature creates results, I must never work *for* results, only for the inspiration and illumination inherent in the process.

But that's why, as I've said before, I run tours. Beyond money, something else is driving me. Despite the headaches, heartaches, backaches, and stomach aches running tours produces, it is also a good-in-itself.

How? What do I like, even love, about running tours? I've become a good leader and developed skills. But we're not talking about results; we're talking about sparks, the holy fire, the Kabbalah.

Could it be that tour participants, miserable as some are, can merge their sparks and together create a rising *tikkun* of flame? Can a tour group rise to a higher plane?

Are tour groups miniature *tikkunnim?* Are they centers of energy, stars uniting and creating a rising flame in the universe? If they are, can the union of my tour members replicate the apocalyptic vision of my Cheerios experience?

Is running a tour like writing a book, playing a guitar piece, or performing a Beethoven symphony? Could my work be to collect the holy sparks of tourists and raise them up in a restoration? Is it possible that I cannot rise without them, that I need them in order to raise myself? Does the restoration of the world take place every day in small tourist groups?

Why was Moses afraid to take God's commandments? "Me run a tour?" he asked. "Am I worthy? Do I have the strength, power, vision, and ability?" God answered, "Any problems, call Me. I'll be with you. Just follow my commandments and shut up."

Maybe I should do the same thing. My tour groups may be modern Hebrews on the march. Instead of walking across the Red Sea, we fly the Atlantic. When we land in foreign airports we feel lost in the desert. Instead of forty years it may take forty minutes, four hours, or four days. But the feeling is the same.

We reached Prague yesterday, met our guide, Rosa Biskova, at the airport, and took our bus to the Hotel Panorama while Rosa told us about the history of Bohemia, the Czechs, and Prague. As we passed an ornate Baroque edifice, she noted, "On our left we have the largest circus in Europe. Our parliament." When we passed a monotonous socialist-realism apartment house put up during the communist period, she remarked, "On our right is an example of Socialist Brutalism."

We settled into our hotel. I met Jasan Bonus at 4:00 p.m. in the lobby. A former high school gym teacher, he now teaches folk dancing—mainly American contra dancing—and runs his own tour agency, Bonus Travel. Over espresso coffee and orange juice we set up a trip for next July, including Bohemia, Moravia, Slovakia—with the Vichodnya Folk Festival, and Poland (Cracow).

I'm reconsidering the August 1995 Romania tour. So far everyone except Andrew says Romania is terrible. Jasan said that, when his tour buses pass through Romania, they need two drivers—one to stay awake on the bus all night to guard it from being stolen. I keep hearing how unsafe the place is.

Should I be the first Columbus who runs a tour there? Could it really be that bad?

Last night we had a terrific night of contra dancing at *Kulturni dum Barikadniku* (Barricade Cultural House). American contra dancing is the rage in Prague and in much of the Czech Republic. It started during the communist period, when anything American tasted of the forbidden, the counter-revolutionary, the anticommunist, the anti-Russian. Young people flocked to it. Once communism ended, contra dancing grew even more. Over a hundred Czechs danced with us last night. Jasan himself called and taught the dances in Czech and in English for our benefit. How strange to hear do-si-do, swing your partner, and promenade in Czech. Everyone had a great time. The Czechs were so friendly, smiling, and gracious, with a lovely kind of innocence similar to that of the Hungarians we danced with in Budapest. When we took the metro, young men got up to offer their seats to the older women on our tour: so different from what has become the boorish American manner. I'm sure there is more beneath the surface, but the surface looks very good.

Late-Afternoon Ramblings

Our tour is ending. Tonight's folklore event with Jasan, an evening of Bohemian and Moravian folk songs and dancing, is our last organized activity. Tomorrow is a free day. On Sunday we're having a farewell dinner; Monday at eleven we're flying back to New York.

I feel the same sense of sadness I felt in Budapest a few days ago. Then I realized I wasn't sad because the tour was ending but because I was giving up my tour *structure*. Perhaps a tour ending is neither an ending nor a beginning but a combination of both. All beginnings and endings blend into one big circle. Where does a circle begin or end?

My room in the Panorama Hotel is dreary and mechanical. I face, not a wall, but a mirror when I write. Whenever I look up I see myself. They're also doing construction above me. Every few moments I hear the sound of drilling and hammering.

We're having our farewell dinner at *U Bumbrlicka,* a restaurant on Vodickova Ulice. What better babbling name could I find?

I met Jirinia Smejkalova at the contra dance last night and talked to Dr. Kristian Svoboda, who told me *szabad,* "freedom" in Hungarian, comes from the Slavic root for freedom: *svoboda.*

On the bus, Rosa told us that under communism, people asked: "Do you work, or are you employed?"

Foreign words are creeping into my journal. So are descriptions and conversations with real people. Historical facts may be next. Why not? Anything is possible.

The California girls still make me feel strange. I break into a cold sweat in their presence. I don't know why. I don't even *want* to, not yet anyway.

Bill made me nervous last night, but for a completely different reason. Someone complimented him on his dancing, and he deflected it by saying, "I'm no good, I've got a lot to learn." I told him it's hard to take a compliment, but that, instead of deprecating himself, he should say, "Thank you." A compliment is like a gift. It is impolite to refuse one. By deprecating yourself, you are rejecting it and hurting the person who compliments you.

Bill thought about it and agreed. Then he said, "I ought to take lessons about life from you." I said I understood how difficult it was to take a compliment and told him the problems I had with them. Again he said he should take lessons with me, learn about life from me. I backed away. Then I realized I was backing away from my own power. Bill was complimenting me by wanting my advice and ideas.

I *have* good advice, and mucho experience. Why not stand up proudly and give it? He wants it; I like giving it. What's the problem? The usual walking-away-from-strength-and-power problem. Now that I see it, I won't do it again.

Is it the same with the California girls? Why do I freeze up, break into a cold sweat in their presence, and try to avoid them? Does it have something to do with the obligation and responsibility I feel towards them as participants on my tour? Part of me wants to be welcoming and be a good host, to improve my business by winning new customers. Yet I feel the California girls are basically impossible. I can't stand them. I detest their arrogance and stand-offishness, though I tell myself I must somehow integrate them into the group. A conflict. Perhaps I'm afraid I'll slip and accidently tell them how I *really* feel about them.

Malá Ceská Musika

Last night's program was so beautiful. Our bus picked us up at the hotel at 7:00 p.m. and brought us to a music school. We walked upstairs to a long, carpeted concert hall—our own private concert hall—where we were met by

Jitka Bonus and the *Malá Ceská Muzika* folk orchestra, consisting of bass, two violins, clarinetist, and flute player. A beautiful evening. Chelley said, "I felt like royalty—our own private orchestra and music room!" The people in our group *loved* it, and I loved them *for* loving it.

An education for me. How the Czech music from South Bohemia—like the Moravian music I heard a few years ago in Straznica—makes me cry.

Hungarian music and dance is filled with excitement, fire, and *paprikas,* like the Hungarian personality.

Czech music breaks down your walls and makes you cry. No wonder my favorite Czech composer has always been Dvorak. Perhaps the Czech—Bohemian and Moravian—personality is mellow and calming, too.

Such an interesting trip. *Malá Ceská Muzika* introduced me to South Bohemian music and Bohemian couple dancing as well. The polka originated in South Bohemia and spread all over the world. Much to learn here. I've got something good going between Hungary and the new Czech Republic of Bohemia and Moravia. Next year we'll explore Slovakia and Crakow in Poland, too.

Today I'll look for books in Prague on history, language, folklore, and whatever; they can be in English or Czech. Music and dance have once again opened up my world. *Malá Ceská Muzika* did it. I also liked their green vests.

How to Have Fun in a Sea of Responsibility

I have a slight headache this morning.

My desire to please on this tour, to have happy tourists, to run a successful operation with well-appreciated events, is getting in the way of my appreciation, not only for what I have accomplished, but for all the beauty around me. This attitude problem is probably the biggest personal challenge I have in running tours: not letting the fickle and ever-changing moods of my tourists get in the way of my own vision, my own appreciation and enjoyment.

On the surface, I am in this business to please my customers. But beneath—and not too far beneath—I'm in it *to please myself.* How can I remember this? It's difficult when I have so much flak thrown at me in the form of tourists' demands and desires. I can't blame them for wanting something, from the tour and from me—that's why they came in the first place. We both want pleasures, and some, like me, want higher visions. The only difference between my tourists and me is that *I feel responsible* for them, for their visions and pleasures, and that, somehow, if they're not having good ones, I have to make them better. That is the bottom-line problem for me. It may even be the bottom-line reason why the California girls make me uncomfortable. I wasn't sure if my tour could please them. As it's turned out, it has.

Somehow I have to live in two worlds, upper and lower. Upper consists of my own vision, the inner freedom to appreciate the beauty I create around me; lower comprises my personal responsibility—particulars, conflicts, problems. *I can't escape from the lower world, but I should always remember the upper.*

Intensity of Concentration: Budapest and Prague

I'm recovering from the glory of Budapest and Prague. Marvelous trip! What dancing and concerts! My brain is still singing. *Focus has been the lesson of that tour.* For ten straight days I concentrated on my group, tour, and program. I didn't—couldn't—even read a book. I didn't—couldn't —even look at a word of Hungarian or Czech until the last day. Concentration on my tour was total. I achieved a oneness, unity, an inner peace I hadn't expected.

Now that I'm back, my mind is fixed on tours. Not a bad place to be. A fascinating profession. Admitting it is part of my newfound strength. I loved the intense concentration. I moved in and out of the turmoil and struggles. With one foot planted in the tour itself—the external material world—and the other in heaven transcending the tour, intense concentration on the moment, symbolized in focus on tour details, became my instrument and gateway to quiet strength.

Now I'm back home. I'd like to continue this pattern. How? My mind scatters in many directions. Fix it on one. I'm preparing for the Greek tour in May. I can, then, devote myself completely to Greece: Greek language, history, and geography.

April-June 1995

WRITING

Roots of Angst and Disbelief

What am I going to do with all these pages of writing, with all my books and boutique items piled up in the basement? I'm stockpiling them to sell in some distant future.

Why do I resist selling them?

Could it be disbelief in my own goodness? Is *that* the foundation of my desire to escape, and, expanding that idea, from selling my dance classes, weekends, guitar concerts, and tours?

How can I believe in my own goodness?

If I am not good, no matter how hard I try, how many accomplishments I collect, records I break, awards I win, I cannot change my basic nature. Deeds can never wipe away the permanent blemish. I am condemned to live always in shadow. No wonder I hesitate. I don't want to be dishonest. How can I enthusiastically promote and sell myself when I believe the self I sell is not-good? My mouth tells others to buy, but my inner self, resounding deep in its cavernous maw, talks about darkness, arctic cold, Aeolian winds howling across bitter plains of snow and ice, ice storms, being clawed at by polar bears, freezing beneath fish-eating Teutonic and Nordic monsters who, in their spare time, rip my flesh, suck my brains, and destroy my soul.

I can touch, feel, and smell not-goodness; I believe I even relish in it. It is a disease no medical plan can cure. Nor do I want it cured. I cluck and giggle whenever I rip myself up. I am a happy sadomasochist beginning each day with a search for exciting new forms of self-destruction. I've developed self-punishing skills to such a high degree I'm practically a professional. Perhaps I should give others guidance. I get a kick out of destruction. No wonder I'm enjoying reading the blood-drenched Greek myths. They may be just the stimulant I need to begin each day with a new batch of self-flagellation.

If punishment is my elixir of life, then maybe a new punishment would be to edit my New Leaf journals. What an exquisite form of self-torture it would be to discover they're good!

Is this sick? Of course. But sickness inspires and drives me on. It is only health, goodness, and a shining sun that make me cautious.

Beside the Point

I read an article about Horton Foote and his life in Texas. Mr. Foote is, evidently, a well-known writer, although I've never heard of him. What I liked was the picture of him sitting in an armchair, pen and paper in hand, staring calmly into the camera with the caption: *Writing by hand after seventy-nine years.* It reminded me of the beauty of writing.

It also reminded me that, although Horton Foote is famous and has published many books, my own published books are sitting in my basement, forgotten and mostly unread; plus I am producing an endless journal which may never even get published. My work just sits and there seems to be nothing I can do about it. I love and need to write. But I seem helpless to publish it. What to *do* with all that? It seems a shame to leave it in my basement. But once my books are written, their purpose of clearing and cleaning my mind is accomplished. I no longer need them.

Writing cleanses and purifies me. Publishing, although good, seems beside the point.

I can't believe what I just said: *beside the point.* Can it be true? I need the process of writing; but is the product, the publication and dissemination of what I have written really beside the point?

Part of me hopes beside-the-point will free me from the editing burden. Then I can let my work stay in the basement forever. It will be destroyed when I am destroyed.

But I know about the death and rebirth. My work can never be permanently destroyed. In any case, the destructive process does nothing to answer the question of why I can't publish, or even review, what I write.

Beside-the-point has many sides to it: One is the total freeing of mind from product. If I need to purify myself by writing, to purge all sticky cobwebs cluttering up my mind, then this need is fulfilled by writing daily in my journal. This cleansing process is definitely *not* beside the point. It is bottom-line, an ultimate self-expression. I am forced by an inner calling to write every day.

But as for publishing. . .I have a vague desire to do it, a kind of "it would be nice" feeling. But that isn't strong enough to push me into action.

One of my motivations for having a business is to make money. I love the wonderful sense of security it brings. But writing does not dwell in security. Rather, it is an adventure in insecurity, travel into unexplored realms. Money has nothing to do with it. Neither does publishing. Publishing and money go hand in hand. True, I also like working for money; it has its own worldly high. But it can't compare to sitting alone before the computer and letting my mind wander freely across the infinity of my inner universe. Those few moments, be they minutes or hours, give spring to my day, feed my purpose, lift my spirit, and bring the light into the dark muddy hole that often is my mind.

I've just hit on something. If money-making is my main motivation for leaving the house—and I need to leave the house periodically, not only to survive financially, but to touch base with real human beings in real-life situations, then perhaps I should think about how my writing can make money. That will be the only way I get my books out of the basement.

If this is the purpose of money, if it pushes me reluctantly but necessarily into the world, perhaps I should say, *God bless money, money making, and my need to make it!* Without that desire, I might turn into the hermit of my dreams or walk off the cliff of insanity. Love of money keeps me balanced, holds me steady between the spiritual and material worlds. Just as I married to balance my life, so I need to earn money.

What would happen if I were suddenly rich, if I no longer needed to work? In the light of what I've just written, wealth would be a tragedy. Or perhaps I would discover that money is just a symbol, a metaphor for the need to move beyond ego.

But why wait for wealth?

Through writing I've already found it!

Santa Fe Sunday

I'm sitting in the dining room in Santa Fe, suffocating from altitude sickness and writing. Lots of noise here, but with my notebook computer I am feigning off my sickness by creating a lunatic asylum of premiere order.

My lunasphere of babble writings is on hold. Days of rational, comprehensible writing have been followed by more days of rational and comprehensible writing. Why am I getting so understandable? Is this a development, retreat, or holding pattern? What has happened to my psychobabblantic flow of aural, oral, and acoustic images? Am I becoming more concrete? Are my feet stuck? Is the wet sticky substance sinking my imagination into a practical morass of the understandable?

I could be starting a new path of ancient and modern Greek, coupled with ancient Roman and modern Italian. I'm reading Robert Graves's *The*

Greek Myths, along with Greek history and Greek language. I'll follow up our tour of Greece in May with Roman and Italian studies in preparation for our tour of Italy in August. We plan to visit Rome, Florence, and Venice. I doubt if I'll study modern Italian history, but certainly I'll be studying Italian along with ancient Roman history and, in the future, Latin. I see the Greek tour and Greek studies as a three-year project. It takes at least that long to feel comfortable in a country. I'll study modern Greek and, in the future, ancient Greek. This will be combined with Greek history and mythology, and Greek literature: plays of Aristophanes, Sophocles, Euripides, and Homer's Odyssey and Iliad. I'll read these both in English and ancient Greek.

The same will eventually happen with Italian. I'll begin a three-to-five year study of ancient Roman history and Latin, and couple it with Italian. A three-to-five year project. Aim for three, then add an extra two.

Am I still a musician and guitarist? Last night, at the Santa Fe party, I met some of David's friends, who'd heard I was a classical guitarist. My first reaction was to deny it. I'm in retirement, I said. That didn't sound right. Bernice reminded me, I'm still a musician and guitarist. It's part of my identity and will be until I die. I haven't given up playing guitar, only performing. Even this may be temporary. Who knows? I may get back to performing someday.

How essential writing is to my psyche! It's so important that I write and study every day. These wonderful activities clear my mind, give me inner peace and balance.

Could I give them up?

No. I can live without other people for awhile, but I can't live without writing and studies. However, I keep it a secret, hesitating to tell anyone how important they are. Today I study Greek history, language, and mythology; tomorrow it will be Latin and Italian; I may return to Hebrew, the bible, Yoga, Indian philosophy, Bulgarian mysticism, or Turkish geography, history, and language. The subjects of my writing and studies keep changing. The one constant is: *writing and studies.* They are my foundations.

One last question: Why should I bother with this three-to-five year Greek and Roman learning project if eventually I am going to die anyway?

This question can easily be answered with Rama's "mind-on-a-pole" story. I need to occupy my mind, hang it on a pole, give it something to do, control it. If I don't, my mind with eat me up, destroy me. The mind operates beneath spirit. Touching the spirit is the only experience of unity and happiness.

It is not achieved through direct work but rather parenthetically, on the side, by serendipity. You cannot aim for union and oneness. Its revelation shines down by accident, through surprise, astonishment, and amazement, as a sudden gift offering from God Himself. Healthy, beautiful, fulfilling activities like writing, studies, athletics, and the arts put your mind on a pole and thus prevent the evil, destructive genie of wandering mind from devouring you.

As an extra bonus, the activities are all good-in-themselves.

Secretly I Have Always Believed in My Power and Strength

I have no desire to write.

But it's not stopping me from writing.

I'll just write without desire.

I'll write on empty, with the hope that the process will kick off a brainstorm and I will be redeemed for the day.

Yesterday I read an article about the psychologist James Hillman in the *New York Times* magazine section. A good article about psychology and the soul. However, what struck me most was that, after some kind of middle-aged breakdown, Hillman re-examined his approach to psychology, discovered a new approach and *started a publishing company to promote it*. In the last thirty years this company has produced seventy books, many of them by Hillman himself.

A publishing company: now there's a thought I like. I may soon be ready for it. The question of what to do with my writings is always in the back of my mind. It is a sin to leave them, both published and unpublished, in my basement. I want to give them, share them, force them, anything them onto other people. I want readers! I want my writings to be recognized, read, purchased; I want them to influence others, to have an effect on their lives in the same way that my writing has an effect on *my* life.

Is that ego talking? No doubt. An ego mixed with a desire to blend with a higher form of self.

I can use moral rage to begin this process. I feel outrage welling up inside of me, a sense of waste: all my work sits in my basement unread and unused. Such uselessness. I put so much time, effort, and love into writing those books; now they lie in the graveyard below the house, jewels in a treasure chest, buried at the bottom of my private lake.

The crime of waste. Do I feel enough moral outrage about this crime to do something about it? Do I even know that I'm mad? Until now, probably not. I've been sad, resigned, sluggish, waiting for someone to discover my work, waiting for some mysterious person to call me up and say, "Yes, we heard about the marvelous books in your basement. Thank God you've written them. Finally, we have discovered you. We want you. The world wants you!"

I am waiting for mythical people to call. Maybe they will, maybe they won't. In the meantime, my writings gather dust and dampness, protected only by a humidifier.

Perhaps that call will not come from without but from within. Someday I may call myself. That day may be close at hand.

Before I get the call, I have to learn my power-and-strength lesson.

Lack of belief may be what's keeping my writing in the basement. I don't have the confidence to take it upstairs and show it to others.

After years of running my tours, suddenly, last summer, they fell together and I believed in them. I was ready to sell them. Perhaps the same epiphany will come for my writing, too.

Should I start my own publishing company like Hillman? I already have my own publishing company, just as I already have a tour company. If I could promote my books like my tour company, I might even make money from them.

I believe in my talents and skills but an inner sense of "modesty" of "humility" is holding me back. A secret voice says, "I know my work is good, but I don't want to tell anyone else about it. That would be boasting. It is better to appear modest and humble."

Where did I get such a crazy idea? If it is true—and it is— then I believe in myself. I am proud of what I have done. *Secretly I believe in my power and strength.* I just hate to proclaim it publicly. I'm more comfortable keeping it a secret. Why? The words "modesty" and "humility" and "boasting" come to mind. My mother never used these words. I don't remember ever hearing them in my family. Where did I pick them up?

Perhaps I am beyond "where." It is time to recognize I have this problem. It is now holding me back. What a revelation to discover I secretly believe in myself. Power, strength, and pride in myself is nothing new. I have had intimations of it all my life. Sometimes these secrets reside so far down in my being I don't even recognize them in the privacy of my own thoughts. But no doubt they are there. They have always been there. Home of my hatred of humiliation, of my quiet toughness, and dignity. It is what gave me the confidence to conduct the senior orchestra in the High School of Music and Art, and to leave the University of Rochester after two years to spend a year abroad in Aix-en-Provence, France.

Confidence, guts, inner vision, power and strength have evidently been with me a long time. They are the hard rock at the bottom of my personality. How strange is my hesitation to talk about them or show them to others.

Pushing and promoting my writing and my publishing company would be the final expression of my power and strength.

The Birth of Specifics

As I write I'm thinking about two things:
First: intensity and concentration.
Second: Sticking to specifics.

Yesterday afternoon I drove to Greenwich, Connecticut, for my last night of folk dance teaching at the First Congregational Church. I always arrive at my classes a few hours early to meditate, study, and listen to talk radio. Yesterday, after picking up a chicken sandwich on a bagel, chocolate croissant, and cup of tasteless coffee at the Greenwich Diner, I drove to the parking lot of the church, parked my car in the corner, ate my bagel and croissant, drank my coffee as I listened to talk radio, and slept about ten minutes as I digested. Then I got out of the car and took a pleasant walk around the graveyard in back of the church. The well-planned layout of the gravestones, combined with the well-groomed grass and traditional architecture of some of the small granite tombs and floral patterns adorning many of the plaques, made it a pleasant place to walk. I strolled through the pathways and thought: what a good place to study. I returned to my car, took out *Teach Yourself Greek,* and the *History of Greece* and, as I strolled through the graveyard again, I remembered the intensity of concentration I had generated, and the records I had broken with my 152 squats yesterday and 150 sit-ups this morning. Perhaps I could apply this kind of intensity and concentration to learning Greek. I began by taking one word, *mporo*—"I can" (pronounced *boro*, I believe), and repeated it over and over, hoping to reach 150. I began repetitions of other words, and, as I strolled past gravestone after gravestone, Greek book in hand, I practiced the present tense verb forms: *mporo, mporeis, mporei, mporoume, mporeite, mporoun* ("I can," "you can," "he can," etc.), and *gelo, gelas, gela, gelame, gelate, geloun,* ("I laugh," "you laugh," "he laughs," etc.). I tried other Greek verbs and a few sentences. I improved my Greek in that hour. More important, I saw once again how the intensity-and-concentration method breaks down my barriers and self-imposed limitations.

In describing the above I used my second thought of the morning: sticking to particulars as I write. The rule is: *be specific*. "Not car, but Cadillac; not fruit, but apple; not bird, but wren." This according to Natalie Goldberg, whose writing book, *Wild Mind*, I am reading. I tried being specific when I not only described the Greek verbs but wrote down the specific *mporo* verb I was learning. *Wild Mind* is a real inspiration. I discovered Goldberg's book in a Santa Fe Health Food Store as I leafed through the magazine rack, where I found an article on her writing workshops. Yesterday I went to Barnes and Noble on Route 17 and bought *Wild Mind,* and *Writing Down the Bones. Wild Mind* was published five years after *Writing Down the Bones.* I like it better; it feels more mature. But both her books are good. I like her "How to write " concepts like "keep your hand moving," "lose control," and "be specific." Being specific is something "new." It opens up a richness of writing possibilities. Specifics will ground my writing and give it lots of juice. A good practice.

Later: I'm lying on the brown couch in our living room, reading further in Natalie Goldberg's *Wild Mind.* I love it. It makes me cry. She has so many good ideas about writing: like ten minute writing bouts, and reading to others. Most of all, she talks about the wonder, beauty, self-discovery, and importance of the writing process. I hate to tell myself how much I love the writing process. It frightens me.

What about a community of writers and writing friends? I like her idea of meeting a friend for lunch and writing together. Imagine writing with someone else, sitting together, and, at the same time, doing something as private and personal as writing. Then imagine reading it to someone else and sharing the drama and love and importance of the writing process. That's what I like about Barry's class: we are all gathered together because we love writing. Those people are like me. We are together in this wonderful and miserable struggle, fighting for the beauty of the printed word.

But, most of all, I like the community of writers. When I go to Barry's class there is an unspoken understanding of common values, of shared love of writing. We don't have to say anything about it, we speak not a word. In that way, the love grows even more powerful. Why say what is obvious especially when it permeates everything?

Writing

Today is not my day for writing. I may decide to throw out the entire paragraph after I edit it. But at least I'll have put words down on paper. Something is moving. Again Goldberg's dictum: "keep your hand moving." I like that kind of language. I say, "keep the words flowing." The most important thing is to just write. Never mind what comes out, never mind my moods and doubts and all the other things I have on my mind. The important thing is to keep the flow, the words coming, the truck rolling, the river flowing. Blow up the dams. Release the waters of the first flush.

Feeling like a Genius

I'm sitting in my room facing the courtyard of the beautiful Hotel Acrogiali on the Aegean island of Mykonos. Our hotel faces the ocean, and when you go downstairs you walk right onto a sandy beach. This place is close to paradise, especially when you consider that at 6:30 a.m. they serve coffee! That means I can start my writing program early and with a bang. Coffee, my morning drug of choice, once again performs its wonders. This steamy wondrous brown liquid dumps vast amounts of energy cream into the stockyards of my empty yet eager mind, helping to pour flame-throwing words upon the utopian fields of my fallow mentalia.

Once again I think of how streams of conscious and unconscious writing may be dangerous. Although Barry never says my writing is "bad"—still, he throws out most of my babble. I don't disagree with him. I just hate to throw away any of the pearls I create. Also, writing these golden streams *feels* so good. As these pre-nuptial words and dream-sounds flow through my mind, past my fingers, and disappear behind the computer screen, I *feel like a genius*, a mental giant in midget form, a pre-screened Karl Marx creating the manifesto for all mankind. I become a gift from heaven as the Lord Himself hands me word after word sanctifying His name through my nimble fingers.

But I must distinguish between the wild creative process, and the small editor's mind choosing between good and bad, right hand wrong.

This morning I feel the first urge to write.

Thank you, God, for visiting me. Even though Your angels come down in the form of writing depression, at least they visit. What would happen if You didn't visit me at all? I would be alone with only my limited human condition to talk about.

No Peace for the Pursued

No peace for the pursued.

I will never be free of the avenging furies of creation, those buzzing bees, stinging wasps, and crawling ants. Insect repellant won't work. These avengers will follow me even beyond the realm of Hades. Is this the fate of all humans? Or is it only mine?

This morning I began reading Homer's *Odyssey*. I spent an hour looking up mythological characters, checking ancient maps for locations of Homeric cities, rivers, and towns, rereading books on the Thracians and Cicones and their town of Ismarus, attacked by Odysseus and his men. During this research, I could not rid myself of that gnawing feeling: I am avoiding writing. Even though I was in touch with the history and traditions of the ages, of thousands of years of scholarship, with the fathers and forefathers of my own past and the ideas that propelled and created Western civilization, I still had a worm gnawing at my conscience, a gnat buzzing around my head, a vulture screaming in my ear: "Write, Write!"

Peace may come in small bunches. But it will come only after I write and give in to the call of the vultures. If I deny their call, pay no attention in the hope they will go away, their dizzying Dionysian screams only get worse. A heaviness descends upon me, a soggy half-bursting water cloud telling me I'm wasting my life. Only writing will resurrect me. It is difficult to write, but it is more difficult *not* to write. If I don't, the poisons pile up inside, ulcerate my body, and soon make me sick. The process of writing drains the poisons and slowly purifies me. What kind of pain do I prefer to live with: the unfulfilling pain of not writing, which leads to more pains, or the pain of writing, which leads to release?

I'd better write. . .or else!

Writing

My other revelation was in writing. During my Greek trip I produced forty pages of journal. I was going to hand it in to Barry, but as I read it in class, I crossed out large portions. Why hand in such a mess? I decided to keep it for another week and edit it. Yesterday as I reread it, I realized *I enjoyed reading my journal!* Not only did it bring back memories of my Greek tour, but the reading of it gave me pleasure as well. I have always denied myself pleasure in rereading my words thinking that "giving in" to enjoyment would inhibit my critical facility. Being critical meant finding mistakes, discovering what is *wrong* with my writing. I looked for the weak points, not the strengths. But now, I'm seeing power in my writing. What pleasure it gives me! Imagine, reading and editing my work and enjoying it! A *major breakthrough*.

Why I Write

I write to learn about myself. Period. That's it. There is no other reason I can think of. Oh sure, I like approval, positive audience reaction; I like fame and fortune. But my desire for these is not strong enough to motivate me to write. Only the search for self-knowledge pushes me to the computer every day to turn out pages of self-discovery, wait for the Muse to hit me squarely in the eye, and unearth a truth about existence I would never discover any other way.

Voices Beyond My Ego

I am a fan of writers.
One of my favorite writers is me.
I am a fan of me.
Yesterday Barry read my journal to the class. They loved it. So did I. How thoughtful, refreshing, philosophical, easy and readable it has become. In fact, when Barry reads my work in class, I don't recognize myself. Who is it? It must be somebody else. Whoever it is, I love what he writes. I want to buy his books and read them. Such wisdom, foresight, and insight; he expresses everything I've thought about so *clearly*. That writer is one of my favorites. Then, I realize that writer is *me!* What a shock.

How can I worship the writer that is me, put him on a pedestal, make his lifestyle a model I want to live up to, make him one of my heros? Hey, it's "just" me. I know him so well. He goes to the bathroom, eats lunch at Louie's, yells, curses, laughs, worries about money, dumps the garbage, does all the things most normal people do. How can I worship such a commoner? I want my gods to be higher than I am.

I can't get far enough beyond my ego to appreciate me. My writing is the kind of writing I have always admired in others, the kind I search for in bookstores and libraries.

Why am I so afraid of recognizing myself, taking credit, and accepting the beautiful writing I have done?

Am I afraid of *my voices?* Am I afraid of "going crazy" in private?

Moses felt inadequate. He didn't want God calling, didn't want to be chosen as a leader. "How can I take charge?" he asked. "I have a stutter. People won't listen to me. I don't have the power or authority to lead."

God said, "Do what I tell you. When I say lead, just open your mouth. I'll put the words in. Don't worry about a thing. I'm in charge."

Moses did as he was told. He gave up control; he gave in. He got good results, too.

I feel the same way. Voices are taking over my mind; voices are speaking to me, forcing me to write "their" words, to commit to paper thoughts I never knew I had or was worthy of having. Someone is speaking to me through my fingers. It's part of what I call my "higher self," but it doesn't feel like any part of my "self" at all. It feels like a stranger has invaded—lofty, with high ideals, beautiful word formations, and a talent for insight, philosophy, and thoughtful meditation on life.

When I write, I give in to this voice. I step aside and let it speak. The more freedom I give it, the better my writing gets. This voice is not part of the "me" I or others know. It comes from another world. I love hearing it but can't recognize the author or even take credit for it. "Someone else" wrote it. Yet I also know the "someone else" is me. What a puzzle.

My puny egoistic powers have been pushed aside, usurped, and replaced temporarily by the writing gods. I am being "forced" to write almost against my will. In fact, will and will power have little to do with it. When I use my will, I usually end up writing garbage. I have to put it aside along with my desires, hopes, plans, and private concerns. I simply give in to the process. Give in to my gods. Let my writing gods do the work. I'll just move my fingers.

Is it loss of control I fear? When Barry reads, he is giving a public demonstration of my private loss of control. Even though members of the class admire it and so do I, it's still embarrassing.

I feel more comfortable, thinking someone else is doing the writing for me, that a god speaks through me. I cannot associate my writing with the little ego I live with all day.

I need a new and wider definition of myself. If I don't find it, I'll have to keep living as a schizophrenic, bumping along in the lower world while inhabitants from the upper one periodically visit me.

If I am my best writer and the gods are speaking to me through my fingers, then I should read my writing to get instructions and directions about how to live my life. The best advice about how to live my life is in my own writings. Why should I look for advice on self-betterment in the works of others? The instructions I have written to myself are better and more personal.

Writing My Guide Book

A leader is a guide.
Who is my leader?
Who is my guide?
I am my leader.
I am my guide.
How do I discover this?
Through the process of writing.

When I write, I give myself directions. Often they are the best directions I can get, even better than other great guide books like the bible, Dante's Inferno, Homer's Odyssey, books on eastern philosophy, or those by Henry Miller and Paul Brunton. My instincts and intuition give me direct and indirect guidance, in language I understand. I know myself best. I give myself the best directions.

These guidelines and lifestyle ideas are handed down to me when I write in my journal. Thus, my New Leaf Journal is my personal guidebook to the twists and vicissitudes of life. That's why it is so important to read and study it.

My journal is my teacher. The higher power within hands down ideas and directions. By writing them down, I clarify them, make them visible.

I am leading a tour through my life. New Leaf Journal is my guidebook.

I haven't written yet today. Self-disgust is mounting. I'd better write. Such is the power of self-disgust that, if I don't, I may vomit in my soup.

Yesterday I had a private yoga lesson with Rama. We talked about how difficult it is to change an old habit and start a new one.

I'd like to make a habit of practicing yoga breathing exercises first thing in the morning. I'd like to give up my morning craving for, and dependence on, coffee. We'll see if I can.

Today I'm going to the Walnut Avenue School to give my World of Guitar program. I've twisted and turned so many times to get out of this one.

Yesterday I even called the school and made up a story about breaking my wrist when I fell during a hike on the weekend and that I couldn't do the show. They sounded so sad and disappointed—all the children were waiting for the show—that I couldn't continue this lie. I back-tracked, said I had an appointment with the doctor this morning, and I'd call them in the afternoon to tell them what he'd said. As you can see, I'd do just about anything *not* to do this show! But I couldn't follow through with my lie. I called them in a few hours later and said I would do it. We'll see where this leads.

Morning Writing Before Coffee: An Experiment

This morning I'm trying an experiment: writing *before* coffee! I got up, urinated, brushed my teeth, washed my face, combed my hair, did some stomach rotations, had a glass of grapefruit juice, read a Bulgarian sentence in *A Course in Modern Bulgarian* book, read another sentence in *the Artist's Way: A Spiritual Path to Higher Creativity*, by Julia Cameron, turned on the computer and did my radical deed: I wrote *before coffee!*

Why is this such a big deal? I'm not sure. It started with my yoga lesson with Rama. We talked about bad habits and how to change them. Specifically we spoke about *my habits*, how to get up in the morning and avoid or cut back on coffee. Rama begins his mornings with breathing exercises. I tried it once but never continued. My yoga session inspired me to try it again. I lasted two days; another failed attempt. Morning breathing exercises are just not my way—at least not yet. I knew I couldn't just give up coffee but would have to replace it with something. The Artist's Way suggested writing—Julia Cameron's morning pages. She's given them a spiritual, religious, meditative emphasis. Exactly what I believe. Before writing, I tried breath- movements. These are yoga-like exercises I've invented. You do them after getting out of bed. They are extremely easy and combine breathing with movement. Perhaps they are my answer to how to get out of bed, wake up my body and mind, start moving, and ultimately, begin my meditative morning pages of writing.

I begin by rotating my right arm. Slowly I breathe in and out. I do the same with my left arm. Then I raise my right leg as I inhale, lowering it on exhalation; same with my left. Not only do these exercise combine breathing and movement, but they are creative and original. They fit my calling. I invented them; I created them. That means they were sent by a higher force to teach me how to conduct my life.

Now I'll stop writing, have my coffee, read the newspaper, then return to writing.

Writing as Meditation

Artist's Way, by Julia Cameron, is boring me. It is an excellent book for someone else. I've already been through her program, discovered many of her truths. The *Artist's Way* is a "how to write" book. I've already found out how to write. I didn't buy the book to learn how to write but, rather, how to meditate—more specifically, how to meditate early in the morning and avoid coffee. Well, I've solved that problem. I see that writing is my morning meditation. Julia Cameron calls it her *morning pages*. I like that term. Her book, with its creative references to God, spirituality, meditation, and exploratory stream of consciousness writing, says everything I believe in. I'm reading my own work written by someone else. It's an excellent book for a blocked writer, a beginning writer, but not for me.

Summer free-time mode. I've got almost four months off to write. June, July, parts of August, and most of September. Four months.

I've also solved my meditation problem. I've been trying to meditate ever since I started yoga thirty years ago. The few times I've succeeded in sitting still, concentrating on my breath and on the Universal Self within me, have been memorable. But I hardly ever do it.

Perhaps I have not succeeded because traditional meditation is not my way. I have developed an alternative meditation method: writing.

Writing as meditation is very simple: just sit down and write. That's all. I don't have to read books about how to be creative or study great literature of the past. The way to learn writing as meditation is by writing. End of discussion.

Thus I'm "meditating" every day. It's part of my miracle schedule. I only have to follow it. It is my personal road to health, vitality, and fitness.

Road of Intensity

I began with a bang. The road of intensity opened before me.

First, I pulverized the blocks of granite in my known petrified universe. Down into the abyss I went, passions aimed towards the center of the earth. Knife-wielding intensity cutting away the foreskin in a true soul-cleansing *bris*.

In the morning, I broke through. My guitar relaxation pose cracked. I played the Alhambra. It worked! I smashed through callisthenics and yoga, pushing stretches and squats beyond normal boundaries with frightening intensity..Then I ate breakfast.

I got nauseous.

I'm still nauseous.

The screaming of eagles mystifies my mind.

I'm writing poetry. Or is it pottery?

Intensity feeds the solar plexus flow. My fluid sails past volcanic Santorini heading towards the Nile cataracts.

Intensity opens doors to stews beyond meat.

Intensity piles up the words. Meaning will come later.

Creation: The Last Gasp of Ego

Can I accept a higher force working through me when I write? On the other hand, how can I not accept it?

Yet admitting it feels like a sin. My ego keeps asking is: Am I worthy? When it steps aside, a river of power runs through my fingers, filling the pages with verbal music. When the "I" steps aside, angels rush in to fill the vacuum.

Many artists speak of a higher power, "someone" or "something" working through them, using their hands, arms, voice, whatever, as a medium, an intermediary to transfer ideas and visions from above. If it's true for others, why not me?

It is true for me.

But I hesitate to admit it.

Humiliation, weakness, embarrassment, shame, fear, and hubris are *creations of my ego*. The crying before beauty is the meltdown of ego as forces of the higher Self flow in to cleanse and purify.

This is my creative process. As I write, ego slowly releases its hold and falls away. Streams of wisdom flow through the reed of my being; beautiful music spreads across the empty pages.

LANGUAGES

Verbs

I'm at the farm. After a beautiful ten hours of sleep, I woke up well rested.

After coffee, I sat down in our living room and started studying Greek verbs, writing them down in my Hand Written Journal. Soon I moved to Greek breathings, the smooth and the rough, then began writing words like "Hydra" and "Hygiene," in Greek.

How much simpler verbs seem today. For years I have been unable to understand them. I still can't understand tenses, moods, imperatives, conditionals, Greek aorists, and inflections even though I have been studying and involved with languages for years. I have no trouble understanding nouns, adjectives, adverbs, or articles. Even gender is not a problem. Only verbs. Strange, isn't it?

I've had a thirty-year block against learning them.

The block is crumbling.

I don't know why.

Perhaps my time has come.

The Quiet Power of Withdrawal: Resisting Oppression Through Verbs

As a child I stood up for my power and strength by *resisting my mother's teachings on verbs*. I've been doing it ever since. Independence from her was based on dependence. I learned to say *yes!* by saying *no*.

Slowly I acquired my own quiet power of withdrawal. I still use it today to stand up against oppression.

I'm determined to conquer Bulgarian one syllable at a time. It's tough and slow.

Writing every day is the same struggle. But as long as I keep my fingers moving, keep the flow going, eventually something interesting will come out. Even though my writing warm ups sound essentially the same, nevertheless, faith and confidence rest in my daily attempts.

This morning I studied Bulgarian demonstrative pronouns. What is a demonstrative pronoun after all, but a "this" and a "that."

LIFE

Service

The purpose of this journal is to help me remember who I am.

I took a substantial leap in this direction during last week's tour of Budapest and Prague.

Service: I have always rebelled against the word. It smelled of subservience, giving up my dreams in favor of pleasing others, of collapsing into a prune-flavored doormat.

But that image changed during the Budapest–Prague tour. Somehow I realized that service to others brought me a inner peace, a temporary *samadhi*. I toured and transcended simultaneously.

As tour leader I was a creative server, developing and managing a program that made my customers happy. Maybe I unwittingly helped them transcend. But in focusing on their needs, I helped myself transcend ego.

Focus-on-group became its own mantra. How could I have been so lucky to discover this? After running tours for many years I have finally achieved a level of skill and competence. I can "relax" and focus on my program and the tour participants. Is inner peace good? Yes. But for me it is best achieved in a dynamic way. *Dynamic inner peace*: It comes through working fervently in the world, using work as an instrument to reach the divine. Help others. I see how this mantra can make you forget ego.

Miracle Schedule Revisited

Focus brings happiness.

Lack of focus leads to unhappiness.

No wonder I have been so miserable these past few days: I lost my focus. Not only have I given up my miracle schedule, I have given up *focus* on it. My concentration is leaking in every direction.

We've spent the last two days chauffering. I ended up exhausted. In the process, I "gave up my focus" on miracle schedule and its importance. True, I wrote a few lines each morning, studied a few pages of Greek and read some Greek mythology. But in my mind, I had given up. I let events and vicissitudes carry me away.

Giving up my miracle schedule, even for a short time, makes me a little miserable. Giving it up for a long time makes me *absolutely* miserable. I must accept its importance. Discovering it was a miracle I should not take lightly. This schedule may be the most important discovery of my life! It is source of ninety-five percent of my happiness, fulfillment, mental and physical balance, even my transcendence. It should not be discarded lightly. In fact, it should not be forgotten at all.

Miracle schedule is my personal Ten Commandments. Somehow I climbed Mount Sinai to receive it. Fires from the burning bush incinerated my ego. In the ensuing vacuum, God handed me the tablets. I carried them down the mountain to use as a guide for daily life.

The commandments are only for me. Others need not follow them. Should they?

Perhaps. If following them gives me balance, organization, satisfaction, fulfillment, happiness, and even transcendence, why shouldn't others follow, too? Instead of fighting others, they can use their energies in the struggle to fulfill their own miracle schedules. Everyone has one. They only need to find theirs. My discovery will help them.

It takes courage to fulfill the miracle schedule in spite of the conflicts and demands of the daily world. But fulfilling it gives perspective and inner peace.

Am I denying my own power and strength by keeping the power and strength of my miracle schedule to myself? My hesitation to tell others comes from my desire not to "impose." I want them to make their own decisions. But is this "explanation" really an excuse in disguise? Shouldn't I be telling them about my discovery?

What is the different between teaching my miracle schedule and teaching folk dancing? Aren't they related?

Is it "selfish" to keep it to myself? Doesn't the word "selfish" really show a lack of confidence in my own ideas? I believe in the vision of my own "selfishness." Shouldn't I tell others about it? I may not want or even be able to impose it on anybody, but, at least, I can tell them about it. The telling *is* my teaching.

Could telling and teaching be part of an expanded folk dance teaching program? Just as weekends and folk tours are expansions of my business and its vision of folk dancing, why shouldn't the miracle schedule be included in this expansion?

Lots to think about here.

Imposing the miracle schedule on myself is my way of imposing discipline and order on a chaotic world. Self-imposed discipline and order is good for me. It's good for others, too.

Accepting Power and Strength: A Transition

Somewhere near the beginning of my life—perhaps in my teenage years—I decided I needed a mechanism to "put me in my place," "make me humble," and protect me from hubris and the dangers of standing out. Ma had something to do with this, too, but I'm not so sure about these so-called psychological truths anymore. They are very simplistic. In any case, there is no doubt that my mind decided to take this route by defining a "lesser me." I swam in a school with the same fish, crawled with the same worms, grazed with the same sheep. I did not stand out, excel too much; I did well but not my best; I didn't aim for the bottom, but I didn't strive for the top either.

I created walls, drew the cover, built the strangulation box.

But now I have run out of excuses, explanations, and rationalizations; I have run out of terrors. Suppression doesn't work anymore. Ghosts are losing power. I am moving out of prison into freedom.

But the transition takes more time than I could ever imagine. Simply recognizing the problem has taken decades. Now I must strip off the old skin and don a new one. Each day a small stripping occurs, but it is slow, slow. An example: last night we met Larry and Marilyn for supper. I talked about politics and my "new" views. At first, everyone disagreed with me, and we started an argument, which didn't last long. I stopped it by withdrawing. Why argue? I thought; it rarely gets you anywhere. Better to just wait for the right moment and, if it comes, speak your mind. Soon that moment came. We adjourned to the hotel lobby. Larry and I sat down in separate chairs. I started talking about the personal and the political. After about a half an hour, to my surprise, he understood my point of view and even agreed with it! I had "won." My first political victory, and it took place calmly, at the right moment, and without much effort.

How did I react to this victory? As I left the hotel, I felt sad and empty. Why? I had won, had "crushed" the opposition, which fell willingly and gladly at my feet; my ideas had influenced someone. All victories of the premier order. My reaction? Instead of happiness and exhilaration, I felt sadness and emptiness.

An old reaction, one I have had for years. My old self popping up again, refusing to die easily. To my credit, this time I recognized it and quickly stopped the spreading of its poison. No, I said, I will no longer submit to such self-destruction and denial of my resources. I won this battle. Instead of slinking off the field, retreating from the wonder and mystical epiphany of victory, I am going to face it squarely. If I can't luxuriate in it yet, at least I can realize, that some day, I will. Some day I'll be ready to move even higher.

Use power and strength for good, giving service to others. But the word "service" sounds so slavish; it lacks the characteristics of rugged individualism, artistic creativity, and entrepreneurial adventure; it lacks the *shining* of self. When I see "service," I see peasants groveling at the feet of a king, or bureaucrats crawling in front of a senior official. No self-respecting creative, independent, gutsy, rugged individualist would ever give such bland, self-denying service. Instead, they would shine before people, radiate their strength, energize others through the power of inspiration. That's the way a tough love guy does it: he shines, glows, radiates, emits the striking halo of a godlike image and, through presence and life example, inspires others to higher effort and aspiration. That, in my mind, is real "service." I wouldn't actually call it "service" either, but rather "electricity." My goal is to give others an electric bulb that will light up their lives.

Of course, whether you use the word "service" or "electricity," the meaning is the same: Use power and strength for the good works. Radiate inspiration. Connect with God.

Wisdom Through Squats

This morning I did 152 squats!

I broke through a psychological barrier.

I've wanted to squat well, because I wanted to do Russian dance squats—the height of masculinity. I've been trying on and off for years. Usually I try too hard, injure myself, give up, come back and try again, reinjure myself, give up, and try once more. I've never given up completely, but I've never succeeded either.

I started a new squatting adventure two years ago when Vivian gave me the chi kong squatting exercises. Three months ago I had a yoga session with Rama who told me about the ritualistic 108 squats sometimes used as prayer in Hindu temples. The 108 was based on the mystical number 3. I started practicing. I built up to 82.

Of course, I didn't do all these squats in a row. I did them in groups of

9 and 18 until I eventually reached 82. But this morning, after reaching 82, I continued in groups of 9, 12, 15, and 18 until I reached 152!

That is an incredible number of squats, more than I have ever done in my life. It borders on the unbelievable. I broke not only a psychological barrier, but my personal record as well.

It is scary to break records and pass a psychological barrier. What does this say about limitations and freedom?

I create my limitations.

I build my barriers.

I create my own physical and psychological limits.

What does breaking the squat barrier say about me and about the future? What does it say about possibilities? I'm afraid to even think. My possibilities border on infinity; they are incredible, unbelievable. All I have to do is focus completely, concentrate my mental and physical resources, remove the barriers, and aim high. That's a tall order, but it works.

If I remove the barriers, who knows what I can accomplish in running, money making, yoga, languages, and writing? It makes my mind spin.

The 152-squat psychological breakthrough forces me to rethink who I am. It pushes me beyond my limits into wisdom.

After I did the squats, I practiced slowly getting into a full lotus position. Then, as I got out of my final lotus I lost my concentration and felt a sudden pain in my knee. Once again I realized the power of mind. By focusing completely I was not only able to do 152 squats, but able to do my lotus posture without pain. When I lost my concentration, I opened the door to pain. This means that, by focusing on one thing—one thing as a symbol of Oneness— I was able, not only to accomplish a great deal, but to *bypass pain*. This is an amazing discovery. For a moment, I had stepped out of, not only my body, but my mind as well. I viewed them both from a distance. I could see the future: my body and mind were dying. Yet that space from which I was watching did not die. That space was an eternal spot, the home of my personal connection with Oneness.

I began this thought process about six o'clock this morning as I sat in the kitchen wondering why had so little energy or desire to do anything today. I thought back to my Budapest-Prague tour. During that time I focused on my tour for the ten days, I not only did a great job, but achieved a peace of mind never achieved on any former tour. This is a good way to think for the next three weeks. Concentrate totally on my Greek tour, on pleasing and caring for my tourists, as well as aspects of Greek culture, language, history, geography, philosophy, art, literature, and mythology. In other words, for the next three weeks I shall try to achieve the same union, the same oneness by concentrating all my efforts on Greece, that I did when I ran my Budapest-Prague tour. During that tour I also discovered an answer to life's pains and travails: total concentration.

I finished *History of Greece* by A.R. Burn last night. Although the early chapters on ancient Greece—Mycenae, Homer, the early city states, Ionian coast—were okay, the later section on the rise of Athens, the Persian Wars, and the Peloponnesian War were so confusing and miserable that I ended feeling my reading was a waste of time. On top of that there is the empty feeling of "finishing my Greek projects." Yes, I've read the history books, the mythology books, and I have no comprehensive knowledge or information that I want to gain on Greece. There is no Greek philosophy I want to take with me, no Greek yoga, Zen, or religion I want to be a part of. The only things that come to mind are the Eleusinian Mysteries, the name Pythagoras, and parts of the Ionian coast, names Heraclitus of Ephesus, Thales of Miletus, and perhaps Herodotus of Halicarnassus. I also like the descent and invasion of the Doric tribes, and, on the side, the Aeolian and Ionian. These names hold something of a mystery for me. I always liked the idea of Thales thinking the world was made of water. Actually, more than that, I liked the idea that he *thought*. One of the first thinkers, a philosopher. Heraclitis, too. "You can't put your foot in the same stream twice." All is change. I like that, too. Again, a philosopher. As for the invasion of the Dorian tribes, that has the mists and dreams of a time long gone, it has the vague contours of a distant, ancient dream world. All these tribes, Aeloian, Doric, Ionian, attacking the indigenous population of mainland Greece long ago, in the nether times, has that halo of ancientness, distance, mystery. Even Odysseus has it at a later time, and certainly the mythology is full of it. But when I get up to fifth-century Athens and even Sparta, all becomes rational, political, organized, easily visualizing, and boring. No sparks fly when I think of the Athenian constitution, or even the playwrights. Athens never had any sparks for me.

In any case, this is a long way of saying I'm moving on to the next phase. And that is, I'm just about ready to leave for Greece. I'd like to have some good book to read on the way over, some philosophic project during the next two weeks, but, truth is, I have none. I should focus on learning Greek.

I'm also annoyed at reading Natalie Goldberg's *Writing Down the Bones*. Here is a book about writing and how to write. Why am I bothering to read it? I already know how to write. The reason I liked her books in the first place is because she says exactly what I say about writing. Plus she has added *specifics*. But I hate being told how to write even by a book I agree with. The very concept that I have to think twice, first about what I want to write, then about following the precepts of writing in her book—even ones that I agree with—turns me off. That's another reason I'm both low and a little mad this morning—this dual fascination with Goldberg's books.

Perhaps, by trying to follow the "rules" in Goldberg's writing books, I am trying to deny my own power and strength.

That is why I felt low this morning. I first gave myself over to *The History of Greece*. Then I tried to "become intellectual" by reviewing what I didn't like about the book. That's okay, but I also "tried to use specifics," in this case, specific facts about ancient Greece; I tried to "follow the rules, the specifics" cited in Natalie Goldberg's book. It's fine to experiment, but to give up my own power and strength to follow her rules is simply a slow death for me. Actually, I even wonder if it is fine to experiment. Maybe it isn't. Maybe experimenting with writing technique is simply another subtle way of running from myself. After all, I've been writing long enough. I know how to write; I know how to let loose, let it all hang out, go for the jugular, do all the things Goldberg prescribes in her books. Why should I even bother listening to her? I could have written her book myself. That's probably why I liked it in the first place. In any case, following her rules are no longer a good way for me to go. Instead, I'm return to my own vision.

What about the simmering disagreement with Sally? Here's a situation where I "know I'm right" and know she is being trivial and petty. Yet she insists of staying mad at me. It is the Dallas syndrome all over again. I do something minor, petty, and my action "hurts her," and she goes on for days, weeks, sometimes months, castigating and criticizing me for doing it and for being me. I used to apologize, "try to understand," especially when she would complain about "not caring about her feelings." This was a cry that could go on forever. What does "caring about her feelings" mean, anyway? Even if I do care about them—and to a certain extent, I do—how can I convince her? It's impossible. No matter what I say, she comes back to tell me I don't care about her. She *wants* to believe I don't care about her. Anything I say to defend myself is besides the point. I am running into her rock-bottom beliefs, her image of herself as being used by others in general and men in particular. No matter how I explain myself, I cannot dent her vision. And defense or explanation of why I do what I do enflames her more, throws gas on the fire. The Dallas incident went on for years. It even forced me to go into therapy to find out why this simple problem became a never-ending source of friction. In therapy I basically discovered how to stand up for myself, how to agree when I was right, how to stand up for my own power and strength. It was a great lesson. It didn't get Sally to agree with me, but it ultimately gave me a new technique in handling her: the technique of silence.

Yes, I have developed a new relationship technique, and I must admit, it works. When Sally and I get into a disagreement about something, I simply state my position, my thoughts and my feelings. Then I listen to what she has to say, I do it *once,* and that's it. For then on, I maintain silence. But it is not a passive silence; it is an *active silence.* I concentrate on my position, think about what is right and wrong, and, while holding my position in silence, try to communicate my thoughts *telepathically.* As long as I do this, our fighting slows, then stops. She may remain angry at me, but as long as I do not respond to unfounded accusations, the fires are not fed, and, over a period of time—it may be weeks, even months—the problem subsides. I doubt if it ever goes away completely—I cannot change Sally's basic views about herself—but it subsides to a liveable level.

Am I Responsible for the Feelings of Others?

Power-and-strength may well be the bottom-line problem of my life. I'm going to need many books to deal with it.

A new example of dealing with it came yesterday. I was arguing with Judka about what I will now call the Seattle experience. This is similar in kind but certainly not in intensity to the Dallas experience. In both, I somehow hurt her feelings by doing what I thought was right for myself. In Dallas, I left her a few times to go off on my own; in Seattle I wrote and ran for an extra two hours while she baby sat. Both experiences drove her crazy. Seattle almost ended our friendship. She said she wouldn't see me again unless I went into therapy to "solve my problem." Finally, I did, and it did help solve my problem. I discovered my denial of power and strength problem. Whenever I exhibited it during my childhood, I was put down and threatened with extinction. During the first ten years of our marriage, Jutka took care of our children, Andras, and Susie. My main job was to make money to support us. I put all my effort into this work, slowly building up my concerts until I was making a living at them. When Jutka overprotected the kids I said nothing. Once when Andras came home late from a peace march down Fifth Avenue, she flew into a rage. I've rarely seen such fury—and over what I considered to be a minor misjudgment. She screamed and even hit him. He was only ten. I couldn't see what the big deal was. A few hours late might cause worry, but not this insane overreaction. However, it did "warn" me about what would happen to me if I ever spoke up. If I ever expressed an original idea about child-rearing or stood up to her about what I thought was right for the kids, her rage would be turned on me. So I remained quiet for years.

Then came the Dallas experience. I went into therapy with Dr. McNutley. He was first rate. Slowly, I unraveled parts of my childhood. McNutley pointed out strengths in my character which I had either denied or refused to recognize. The process took about two years. At the end of it, I emerged stronger and wiser. I also accepted the fact that, if I stood up for myself, Jutka might leave me.

Slowly, over the next few years, our marriage improved. Then two weeks ago came the Seattle experience. Soon we were arguing again: the Dallas experience revisited. But this time, I vowed things would be different. The "cause" of our problem was, I wrote and ran two hours longer than I expected. Jutka took care of the kids an extra two hours. True, I underestimated my time and apologized for it. Still, I couldn't see why it was such a big deal. Jutka *made* it a big deal. Soon it developed into a mountain. In my view, I had done nothing wrong except misjudge my time. She, however, soon went into her rage, complaining and accusing me of being irresponsible, and shouting about how miserable I was, etc. I've heard all this before; it's been her complaint for years.

Jutka blamed me for her feelings and emotions. She told me I was the cause of all her pain, I was the reason she had to take care of the kids, I didn't understand or care about her feelings. The usual stuff.

But this time, I'd had enough. No more Dallas syndromes for me. Then I had my realization: *I was not responsible for Jutka's feelings.* They were hers and hers alone. She, creative person that she is, had created them. She could have created other feelings, positive feelings about how wonderful I am, how creative and dedicated I am to writing and running, how kind I was to give her some independence in Dallas. But instead, she chose to create *negative* feelings, to feel misery and fright, and to blame them on me. Of course she can feel whatever she wants and blame her feelings on whomever she wants. But should I accept the blame? Am I really responsible for her feelings? My big realization was: No.

No! A great step forward for me. A liberating observation and realization. It frees me from self-blame and guilt; it even frees me from fighting back when Jutka blames me. After all, most of my fighting back comes from believing her negative feelings are my fault. I fight back to protect myself from her accusations. But why fight back if her accusations are mere paper illusions and ghosts? Why fight back if I am not responsible for her feelings, if I am not to blame in the first place?

Here is another reaction I had. It made me understand once again how deeply my power-and-strength denial problem goes. After I saw I was not to blame for Jutka's feeling, I got depressed, sad, and heavy. How strange. But not strange for me. I had just had a major realization, gained a major insight and victory, and, instead of shouting for joy and running down the street in jubilation, I felt sad. An old reaction. I had it with the Larry's political victory a few days ago. I've had it countless times with victories in the past. The sadness is part of my denial of victory, a denial of my own power and strength. An old habit I am slowly breaking.

To know I am not responsible for other people's feelings is a major knowing, a major league victory over myself.

It goes beyond Jutka. When people complain on tour, on weekends, in folk dance class, or in general, if I can help them, fine. But if I can't resolve their complaints and they remain unhappy, it is wonderful to know I am not *responsible for their feelings.*

I love freeing myself from the blame syndrome!

The Positive Effects of Lying

Here's a good way to deal with Jutka: lie. In Seattle she wanted me to commit myself to two hours of writing and running a day. I told her I would try but was not sure I could always do it. Some days I might need more time, some days less, some days even no time at all. How much time I need is often situational and cannot be completely predicted in advance. However, this nuance, this subtlety, is not easily understood. Usually only leaders in general and tour leaders in particular can understand how to play the drifts and subtle changes that occur during each moment. This idea of playing the situational drift is often beyond the experience of most normal people. Jutka is quite normal. It is I that admire, appreciate, and even respect the abnormal as reflected in the subtleties and serendipities of the moment.

Jutka wanted me to make a commitment. When I make one I cannot usually make it in concrete. I used to try, and the result was a retreat from reality rather than a union with it. But Jutka wants a firm commitment. Whenever I tell her how my commitments depend on *judgement,* she doesn't want to hear about it. She calls me irresponsible. I want to tell the truth and be straight with her. After all, she is my wife, the one closest to me. She should be able to hear my truth and accept the nuances. Right? Wrong. She cannot. She is like many members of my tour groups. Just as I must often lie, stretch, twist, and change the truth to fit the moment to create a successful tour experience, so I will have to lie, stretch, twist, and change the truth to fit the Jutka experience. Thus I'll commit to two hours and see what the future will bring. Who knows, it might work out. Or it might not, which will prove me a liar.

Truth may be true, but it is often like a razor blade leaving the receptor bloody and miserable; a well-placed, well-told lie, on the other hand, can really smooth the way. Perhaps truth isn't so good after all. How could it be if it hurts so much? Lies often sweeten the path. They get people to relax, be soft, accept, dream, and move ahead. Truth may be a sledgehammer pounding and cracking the cement of real cities, but lies help create new cities in which you can love and dwell.

It is time to reconsider the positive effect of lying.

More on the Art of Lying

Jutka and I are back together again. This proves that lying works. My two big realizations created our reunion: first was knowing I am not to be responsible for other people's feelings; second, that lying is an excellent lubricant to help smooth life's path.

The lies I am talking about are not harmful lies, not black lies, but white ones, or at least gray. The word "lying" has a negative ring to it, an immoral tone. Nevertheless, I like the tone. I like the forbidden quality to it, the feeling that I am breaking a law in a smart, macho way. How clever I am to lie and get away with it. It's the delicious cleverness-slightly-tainted-with-evil feeling.

This journal is about power and strength. What does lying have to do with power and strength? Is lying a weakness? The exaggerations and twists on truth, the permutations and combinations I create, swelling it beyond realistic proportions, changing truth slowly into little gray lies, show the strength of my creativity. To know what I am saying isn't exactly true. To keep this secret to myself is an expression of personal power. Why tell the truth, anyway? Most times it is only to absolve myself of the responsibilities that come with lying. It's hard to lie. It's even harder to maintain a lie over a long period of time, days, months, even years. Maintaining and living a lie is an act of major creative importance. Liars rule the world; their illusions are what makes society expand and stick together. Most people in society *want* to believe in lies. They yearn for something higher than themselves; they need great lie-givers, the prophets and leaders dressed in the removable clothing of truth. Their creative lies pour down from the mountain, flood society, and cement people together through the creative bonds of falsehood and illusion. Is that so bad? It's been going on since God invented man. Who knows, God may be the supreme liar, feeding us illusion after illusion, amusing Himself while He watches us try to function in the dim corridors of fantasy and dreams, beneath His good lie, in order to raise their sights, expand, and inspire them to grow. Most people will not take responsibility for lying. But they're happy to ascribe the lie they are living to someone else. A chosen few don't mind facing their lies as long as they don't have to face them too squarely. But most don't want to face them at all. It's easier to believe you are living a true, good, and fair life, following the universal virtues of goodness and truth. If you like believing such an illusion, fine. But the mighty ones, the rulers of the earth, live under the half-lights of truth.

   If leaders and prophets can do it, why can't I? If God does it and sanctions it, why can't I? Doesn't lying connect me more intimately to God? As I lubricate my path of marriage, business, and personal relationships through the creative use of lies, am I not ultimately doing good in this world? Who cares if I lie or not, as long as I can smooth the way? Besides, it may be years before the people I lie to find out about it. They may never find out at all. During this period of time my lies are helping them lead fruitful and productive lives. If, after many months or years, they discover their beliefs have been illusions, well, so what?

   Plus, there's always the possibility that the lies they live, the illusions and fantasies they believe in, are not illusions after all. Could two illusions equal one reality, two lies equal one truth? It's possible. After all, in the mathematical world of illusion, one and one often make three.

***

Last night I read an article in *Runner's World* by Uta Pippig, the women's New York and Boston marathon champion. Inspiring. Much wisdom, too. She talks about the beauty of the marathon. It made me want to get back to running. My running has fallen off the past few months. I miss it. I have replaced it with yoga and my one hundred eight squatting, sit-up, and push-up goals. Still, I want to get back to it.

Running on Mykonos

Last night, about eight o'clock, Aaron and I took a beautiful run from our Hotel Acrogiali into the town of Mykonos. We started out slowly, fatigue and high winds buffeting my tightened, cruise-lined body. We puffed up a small mountain, over roads squeezed by cars and motor bikes. Soon we arrived at the historic Mykonos windmill pictured in the travel newspapers and ads. We turned back, ran in descending darkness, dodged cars more motor bikes, up and down hills, until we got back to our hotel. The run took an hour and ten minutes. Great! While running the hills I felt passing pains in my Achilles tendon; I started to worry about tearing it. Visions of Dr. McNierney and his warnings crossed my mind: An older body running up hills takes many chances. I could see my dance career ending as I tore my tendon. I tried relaxing it, slowly, slowly, concentrating on the muscle. Back at the hotel I stretched it mucho.

Does running warrant such Achilles tendon worries? Am I overdoing it? Dr. McNierney said, stretch a lot, but *do not* stop running. Care is a good thing, but too much worry perhaps is not.

When I touch the edges of my notebook computer I get a shock. Is that normal? Or is something wrong with my computer? Could it be coming apart from too much transportation, bumping, and moving around? I'll have to check it out. Meanwhile I'll try to avoid touching that area. I'll ask Aaron about it.

How disturbing. I may need another computer.

After our Paros experience the idea of *taking notes* occurred to me. Notes could be names of people I meet, or names of places I visit. I would use them in my journal. Witness Paros: names of Nikos, Marilyn and Petros Metaxa, Maria Tripolitsiotis, etc. Thus, carry a notebook.

In fact, I'm now copying notes and writings from my handwritten notebook into my journal. Here's something I wrote while waiting for the bus to town of Myconos:

"I've been waiting for a bus forty-five minutes, thirty of which were at the wrong stop. I started out tired, a bag of windless gas, but now *my anger has energized me!*

"I'm rearing to go into town; my mental waves are searing me with vitality. Even my vision has improved. Madness in the form of anger is an aphrodisiac for the soul."

Aaron just fixed my computer. It seems I was grounding it. My socks had gotten wet when I walked into the bathroom this morning. When I turned on the computer, I became a ground as electricity passed through my body. Not enough to electrocute me but enough to shock me.

What a relief to know my computer's not broken! It will live to see another day of writing.

We're leaving our Acrogiali Hotel this afternoon to continue our cruise on the Epirotiki Cruise line. It's too noisy to concentrate or write in the lobby where we're sitting. Instead I'll read Dora Stratou's book on Greek folk dancing or *The World of Greek Dance* by Alkis Raftis.

I did yogasthenics (I still can't figure out a good name for it) in a fine manner late in the afternoon. First I did one hundred sixty three push-ups—in series of nine times three, equaling the Hebrew *chai, plus* one eighteen-times-three equaling fifty-four. Then I did the same number combinations with sit-ups. Between both these series, equaling one hundred sixty-three, I did yoga stretches. (I was too tired to add the squat routines.) During the lotus exercises I noted once again the power of concentration. When I give the exercises my *full* attention, I can do many more sit-ups and push-ups than if my concentration wanders. In fact, when my concentration wanders in the lotus position, I feel pain in my knee, a pain which goes away when I'm warmed up and fully concentrating. As I broke through exercise barriers, I felt some fear, then pain. It is amazing how fear and pain, concentration and conquest, work together.

Heraklion Revisited

El Greco and Nikos Kazantzakis were born in Crete. Once their names thrilled me; I fell to my knees in worship of these gods. I also worshipped Kahlil Gibran, Herman Hesse, and the classical music gods like Beethoven,

Mozart, and Mendelssohn. But today, when I heard their names, nothing happened to my soul. Why is that? Has my soul outgrown them? Have these gods served their purpose in my quest of self-discovery?

I have incorporated my gods. They have been swallowed, digested, and redistributed throughout the need-channels of my body. I have made a direct connection with *their* God who is *my* God, the God of artists, musicians, intellectuals, and people who are part of my tradition and upbringing. Who will support me if I no longer have my gods? They have become a part of me. Where do I go from here? Back to Athens, of course.

Stocks

Although the stock market is shooting up every day and has gone up over four hundred points in the past few months, my stocks have gone absolutely nowhere. Bernice's mutual funds are flying and she asks me why I don't sell all my losers and buy mutual funds. In the world of reason, she is probably right. However, who operates in the world of reason?

Patmos

The Greek island of Patmos off the Turkish coast haunts me. A beautiful spiritual island. I read in a brochure how Saint John had been exiled to Patmos by the Romans, how he lived in a cave for years where he wrote his Revelations. When we visited the island, after my shopping spree in Kusadasi, my mind had been on making money by running successful tours. But I sensed something different about Patmos. It gave me a feeling of contentment. Visions of higher thoughts increased as our tour bus drove up the twisting road to the monastery at the top of the mountain. The view of the Aegean grew even more spectacular. We visited John's cave, where a monastery had been built in the 12th century. In this cave, at the age of ninety-five, St. John had dictated his revelations to a scribe. These revelations, so incomprehensible, mystical, and beautiful, are close to my heart. They reminded me of Ezekiel, another prophet I can't understand.

John and I

This morning as I was studying Greek, I went downstairs, picked the New Testament out of my basement library, opened up to Revelations, and tried reading it in the original Greek. I didn't get very far. But I understood something: the first word, "apocalypse." The sound of the word in Greek reminded me of Patmos and how close I'd come to John. So close I became him.

Alone in my vision, I was he.

Backache on the Farm: Power and Strength Go to Sleep

I woke up with a backache on my birthday. When it aches, I'm usually mad at something. What could it be?

Yesterday I went out for a long run under perfect weather conditions, did some post-run stretches, ate breakfast, rested, read Homer, wrote, and played guitar. Again before supper I did a few good stretches and squats.

Miki, Bernice, and I drove into East Kortright for our birthday supper. From the moment we left things started going downhill. Miki drove. I was starving; I couldn't wait to eat supper. But the fancy Hidden Valley Inn restaurant in Kortright turned out to be a forty-five minute drive away. We got there late for our reservation. We had to wait another fifteen minutes to be seated. We ordered our dinner, had a few appetizers, and waited still another hour. I was about to walk out in rage, frustration, and disgust when our food finally came. By then I had lost my appetite. Still I ate, hoping that the piles of fettucini Alfredo I stuffed down, then drowned with Zinfandel rosé wine, would help me forget my anger. It didn't work.

After supper we drove Bernice to the emergency ward in Delhi to treat a gnat sting. The nurse filled out fifteen forms of useless information in duplicate and triplicate. Then the doctor took an hour to treat this major insect emergency. When we drove home, just outside of Delhi, a half-drunken idiot stood on the road and waved us down. He wanted a lift to the nearest police station. Miki told him Delhi was just behind us and he should walk. He said, "It's cold out," but we drove on anyway. I thought such things only happen in New York.

Instead of getting a good night's sleep, the annoyances of our birthday dinner made me toss and turn on a full fettucini Alfredo stomach all night. In the morning, I woke up stiff and tired, had coffee, and studied Greek. Then I felt a pain in my lower back.

Why the pain? It's obvious.

Isn't this similar to the feeling I had on board the cruise ship *Odysseus* on our Greek tour? I had "decided" my responsibilities as tour leader were over. I gave up leadership—and got depressed. I soon realized how important leadership was to my psyche, and decided to resume my leadership. Rather than giving up control, I decided to take control again, to reassert my power and strength. I immediately felt better.

Had I been running a tour, I would have written off last night's annoyances and left it at that. But because I decided to give up control over myself, to "take a vacation," my vacation turned into a backache.

It is deadly to give up my power and strength. Every time I do, I prove it over again. Last night was another example.

A backache means I have drifted away from my center.

New Mind, New Body

Yesterday I had three visions for this summer. Here they are in descending order:

1. Blow my guitar world apart.
2. Blow my linguistic-verbal world apart.
3. Add "literature of imagination" to my repertoire.

I have made three new beginnings.

How do I feel about this? Lousy.

My body aches. I am constantly tired, fatigued, and can hardly move. All I want to do is sleep. I have no drive or desire to do anything physical. My inactivity only makes my aches and pains worse.

What is the meaning of this?

I believe God is in the process of *changing my body to fit my mind*. He is creating a new container for my new thoughts. Aches and pains signify the destruction of my old body and its gradual replacement. My attitudes are changing.. I am on the road to a new way of guitar thinking, linguistic and verbal thinking, even literary thinking. The old body was created for an old way of thinking; the new one will be created for a new way.

What a radical thought! Such an optimistic view of aches and pains! Imagine, creating my own pain and destruction, burning my old instrument, then building a new one above the ashes. Phoenix rising.

I must clear my house of old furniture before filling it with new pieces. How can I put in a new armchair when the old one is in the way? I need the Divine Garbage Man knocking on my door. He offers me new ideas and directions. This includes a thorough house cleaning at no extra cost. It will be difficult to throw out old furniture: I've become attached to it over the years. The Divine Garbage Man makes me an offer difficult to refuse. Of course, I am free to reject the new. But if I do, my old furniture will start annoying me. It keeps decaying. Soon I won't want to live in my house anymore. I'd better accept the offer. If I don't, I'll end up moving out anyway—and without furniture. I'll end up homeless. So, I'm accepting. Come in, Mr. Garbage man. Clean my house. Throw out my furniture. Bring in the new furniture with its shining surfaces and fresh well-built interiors. I know it's superior.

Still it hurts to see my favorite rocker, armchair, sofa, desk, and chair, being carted away.

Changing is tough. But not changing is even tougher. I've got "no choice" but to accept a new mind along with my new body.

Spirit: The Source of Power and Strength

An unhealthy influence hit me. How quickly I slid downhill.

When did it start? Yesterday? Day before yesterday? Is it Jutka's trip to the emergency room or a retreat from the good things I did—the tours and folk dance teaching?

Whatever it is, my mental and physical health has fallen apart in the past few days. It seems only a week ago I was filled with hope, wit, and happiness. Now I am down in the dumps and dumpettes, thinking about death and the shortness of life. Along with these negatives thoughts comes the "Why bother?" feeling.

I've been through this many times before. The only solution I have ever found to the "Why bother?" feeling is understanding it as an illusion: *The "Why bother?" feeling is a trick my minds uses to deny my power and strength!*

Could it be that simple? Is the core of my life a simple swinging between the antipodes: power and strength on one side; denial of power and strength on the other?

The emotional life of man fluctuating between feeling good and bad. That goes for moral, intellectual, artistic, physical, and others lives I can't even think about. The world, as a moral, mental, and emotional construct, fluctuates between these opposites. So do the value systems of Western and Eastern civilization. Good and bad are a big deal everywhere.

I am walking above the secrets. One of them lies in the words "power and strength." *Plug into power and strength and you feel good; pull out the plug and you feel bad.*

Is it really so simple? Of course, anything simple is difficult to do. The simpler it is, the more difficult it becomes. The simplest thing is to realize you are one and part of the One. We all know how difficult is it to have this experience of unity.

I have arrived at a doorway of wisdom; I may even have passed through it. "Power and strength" is a "simple" truth. Perhaps it is the central theme of my entire New Leaf Journal, even the central theme of my life. How to find it, how to remember it, how to keep it? What is power and strength? It is, ultimately, the God connection. The self and Self are connected. One cannot exist without the other? Mr. Self is the big guy. Little self is an offshoot, a projection of Him. Mr. Big Self needs little self the same way a father needs a son. The roots of power and strength comes from Mr. Big Self. Without His wisdom and electrical energy, little self would disappear. It's nice if Mr. Big Self thinks about litle self. But it is imperative that little self think about Mr. Big.

Jews believe that Big Self and little self have a personal relationship. They need each other. Eastern philosophers, yoga masters, believe there is ultimately no difference or distinction between Big Self and little self; they are really the same thing. A union; a Oneness. Jewish philosophy puts more emphasis on the dichotomy and its personal responsibility; Eastern philosophers and mystics stress the union and oneness.

Will power and strength live beyond my death? Indeed they will. Are they at the core of my motivation? Indeed they are. Is Mr. Death my most powerful enemy? Indeed he is. I have met the devil. He is me. I have met evil. He is me. The twin partners, death and evil, live in good housing inside my brain. They will never leave. They will always try tricking me into denying my own strengths. It is in their best interest to make me weak and helpless. When I am, I focus on them, give meaning to their existence, and make them happy. But when I remember my strengths, they are forgotten; they wilt from neglect. They can survive only if I keep recreating them by giving them work to do. Their work is to destroy me and everything I create.

What can I do about them? Awareness is my only solution. Awareness, and constant vigilance.

Mr. Fear

There is nothing like a visit to the hospital emergency room to give Mr. Fear something to do. He thrives in hospitals, rehabilitations centers, grievances centers, and funeral parlors. My visit to the emergency room with Jutka knocked the legs off my power and strength. I looked tough and in control, but burst a blood vessel in my eye: a physical manifestation of my fear of losing Jutka to sickness or death. It's sure to happen some day. A big fear.

It is possible to forget about such fears. But it is probably impossible never to have them.

Maybe fear has a higher purpose. It gives you something to work against. You build up anti-fear muscles which strengthen you in the fight to discover and maintain your power.

You can't have friction without a rubbing stone.

Fear is a rubbing stone.

From the friction come the sparks to light the fire of power and strength.

Effort and Hard Work Bring a Vision of Paradise

Yesterday I had an excellent one-and-a-half-hour run, going up two short mountains, and down a long back road. When I returned, I did a few stretches, then had a memorable yogic vision: I saw how to step out of the endless cycles of existence, to escape from the avenging furies of creativity that pursued and haunt me. My activities, desires, thoughts, and goals are *products of my mind*. That in itself is no great realization. But somehow, after the run, I was able to step out of the mind trap, to become, for a brief moment, part of the endless and timeless world of spirit. Lovely. I saw how all-encompassing mind is. If you don't keep it busy, it will eat you up. There is no way of escaping the endless movements of mind. I can only escape once in awhile. I'll just have to accept that.

However, a realm exists beyond mind. It is called freedom.

As I experienced it for a brief memorable moment, I saw guitar playing, folk dancing, touring, running, yoga, reading, language study, family, friends, everything I do and think about all passing before me. A great peace descending. I stepped away from mental constructs; I put aside the structures of my ceaselessly creative mind. Suddenly, I was "free." A higher world beckoned; I had moved beyond prison into the magic circle of spirit. Wonderful. I hope I can remember it.

How did I achieve it? Could it have been from pushing myself hard during my run, especially on the hills? I pushed time, too, beyond the usual hour. Such extended effort released the hold of mind over ego; it broke down the gates, allowing me to enter, although briefly, the world of heaven.

Yes! Entering paradise, the spiritual world, can be briefly achieved by making a great effort; pushing, trying, and working *very hard*. That is work's ultimate reward. It can break barriers of ego and propel you upwards into the *good-in-itself* world of relentless attempts and ceaseless pushing. The kind of work you do doesn't matter. The important thing is to do it with terrific intensity, total focus, and heart-breaking concentration.

I'll try it again when I play guitar.

Jumping Mind as a Warm-up to Paradise

I'm doing too many things at once this morning. As I write my mind is on yoga; as I'm doing yoga, my mind is on writing. This is no way to do things, to work, especially when I realized yesterday that my Nirvana-paradise approach to life is based on intensity and focus. Work hard to get beyond the body, the ego, and little self; focus hard to enter the higher world of power and strength. That's all there is to know; all I should know, all I want to know. Everything else is footnote.

When jumping mind jumps around, I'm not focused yet. I'm "warming up." It is a necessary prelude to focus, but it is nowhere near the Garden of Eden I'm aiming at.

Focus and intensity on work is, as the monks in Meteora say, the means to enter the Holy Spirit. *Focus puts you on the road to heaven.*

I Am a Soul

The desire for self-improvement is a lower goal.

A higher goal, the highest goal, is realizing you are a soul.

My effort, work, and exercises are not for the goal of self-improvement (that happens anyway as a by-product). Rather they are *means* to self-knowledge and the realization: I am a soul.

Walnut School

My performance at Walnut School relaxed me. Instead of worrying, sweating through stage fright, pacing nervously, wondering whether I'd please the audience, or get hired again, I focused, concentrated... and relaxed. This is a major development. I am ready for *work as relaxation;* I experienced it at Walnut School. Once you walk through the door there is no going back. Yes, I can step outside for awhile, but not for long. From now on, I'll always know what's behind the door of work as relaxation.

This morning I am leading folk dancing at the Kauke bar mitzvah. I shall apply this new principle to my Kauke bar mitzvah job. Simply knowing *the secret of relaxation: concentration and focus,* will help me experience it.

Relaxation in work through focus and concentration assumes power. You can't focus unless you believe in your self and your ability to control, guide, and conquer your audience. My job is to focus. God will take care of the rest.

Yesterday afternoon I studied Bulgarian for a solid hour. Difficult. My brain felt like sand; I pushed through humidity, heat, and sleepiness. At the end of an hour of Bulgarian concentration I felt so healthy and fine! My mental muscles had been exercised to their fullest. What a charge! So much better than the passive watching of TV or a movie. Most passive activities are just plain boring. There is nothing better than calling up your energy to meet a challenge, to push, try, and give all you've got to a good cause. Bulgarian is my good cause. As I sat in my lawn chair in our backyard, coffee in hand, Bulgarian grammar on my lap, I fought, and finally conquered the chapter on Bulgarian personal pronouns.

Outside work as relaxation. Until now I have only seen *inside work as relaxation.* Writing, guitar practicing, yoga, running, reading, studying languages, the "inside" activities, are my personal forms of prayer and meditation, personal paths to salvation. But none of them ever applied to the outside world. There I found haunting doubts: What people would say? Would they hire me again? Financial security was on the line with every job. How could I relax when future work depended totally on today's performance? This was not work as relaxation, but work as a *means to freedom,* a way to get money to buy my freedom. Then, later, once obtained, I could use my time studying, writing, playing guitar, doing the "important things" unpolluted by fears of audience and financial failure.

But for some reason that has changed. Could it be the money I am making on the Bulgarian tour? The idea that running tours can pay such good money frees me from depending on bookings and folk dance teaching for a living. Thus I am more free to relax when I do them.

The monies from tourism have partly liberated me. But not completely. Business goes in cycles. What happens when tour registration starts downhill again? Will I return to my old fears? Will I be unable to do my outside work as relaxation? Or is this step into freedom an irrevocable one? I don't want to slide back into the old neighborhood.

Focus is the key to relaxation. . . and freedom. I'm starting down this road. It's a new tour.

The Summer Soul-Release Program

A ring of terror screamed through my body. But the chill didn't last long. After I finished my desk work, paid a few bills and faxed the list of Bulgarian tour names to Cezary at Balkan Holidays, I looked at the calendar and realized: I have no more work to do. *I am finished for the summer!*

An emptiness came over me. Then panic. What am I going to do with all this free time? I've always wanted free time. Now I've got it. But my vacuum didn't last. Soon I thought about projects, programs, and all the ways I could use this wonderful new freedom. My situation is similar to last summer's. After my Turkish tour was cancelled, I saw three empty months ahead on the calendar. Instead of focusing on all the money I'd lost because of the failed tour, I thought, Why not see this new time as a gift and use it to fulfill a few dreams? So I poured myself into writing and ended up creating beautiful new pages in my New Leaf Journal.

The added plus to this summer's free time is that, for the first time in years, I'm out of debt.

What will I do now with my summer? I have no new interests. I am happy to do the miracle schedule things I love for the rest of my life. What could be better than spending days writing, playing guitar, running, practicing yoga, studying languages, reading history, or Greek literature? That alone is heaven. When I add an occasional tour, weekend, folk dance class, or guitar assembly program, I have to admit: there is no better life for me.

What will I do? I'll do what I love to do, only more of it. I can't wait to start. I don't even have to wait. I've already started. I've been following my miracle schedule ever since I discovered it last year. Sure there are a ups and downs, starts and stops, but that happens with every program. Besides, a few bumps in the road help keep you in tune.

Imperfections Make My Day

God and I are partners. Why look for gurus when the ultimate guru is the Me in me?

I'm thankful for my imperfections. They create sparks. They are sharp edges, shards that prick, wake me up, and fire me into action. Without my imperfections I might sleep all day. The snore of the perfected, life in the perfect tense. Luckily, there is no hope of that.

Who cares about my perfections? What else can be said about them?

Imperfections are most interesting. They drive me on. Luckily, I have lots of them, so I'll have something to work on for the rest of my life.

Life is fire. Friction creates fire. By rubbing my imperfections together I create fire and ride it upwards. Rising Fire Road is not perfection but the *path* to perfection. It ends on the mountain top. There I glimpse of eternity and the expansions of my soul. But soon I move—or is it slide?—off the mountain into the next valley where I begin my imperfect ascent all over again.

Imperfections make my day. Life would be dull without them.

A Massage

Yesterday I got my first massage from Fran. I left euphoric, stunned, and metamorphosed.

What happened?

After leaving the Massage Center, I seemed to walk in a normal fashion. I went out the door, drove home, answered my mail, made a phone call, then picked up my Mitsubishi at Mario's.

When I got back, I fell asleep on the couch. I slept over an hour. I awoke with no energy, pep, vim, or vigor. A lump, a thing, a clod.

This morning I have a headache.

Was it the massage?

Fran's massage rearranged my molecules. Her skilled hands moved my parts in all directions. When I got up from the massage table, I got up as someone else. I don't even recognize myself this morning. But if massage is good for me, why do I have a headache?

Fran's massaged away my cares. Worries, frustrations, and problems disappeared. I emerged relaxed and problem free. Not a concern in the world. Lost in my own sensuality, in the hedonistic feel of wonderful hands moving all over my sweet-smelling oil-covered body, I returned briefly to the sensuality of a bygone childlike existence.

Why did I wake up with a headache? Part of me hated to give up problems and worries. I embrace frustration. It energizes me. The arms, legs, and torso that I carry into my worry-ridden world were kneaded into a smooth, well-rounded lump of protoplasm. Such pleasure caused me to lose my boundaries. Do I want this? Will I be reborn on a higher level, or simply end up wallowing in the horizontal?

I must like my worries. Otherwise why would I struggle so hard not to give them up? Maybe "worries" isn't the right word; "challenges" is better.

Fran's massage knocked the challenges right out of me. Challenge wake me, draw my faculties into a dynamic ball of concentration; it raises me out of my body. It seems the massage did just the opposite. My concentration descended into my body. I ended up thinking only about it. Is that what I want? Doesn't happiness consist of forgetting the body, surmounting ego, and transcending self? Am I right to "mistrust" massage because it will take away all the things I am working for?

But it feels so good. Should such pleasure be painful? Or should pain be pleasure in disguise?

I abhor the destabilization of my personality that massage seems to cause. I hate giving in so much that I throw myself away. And yet, if I keep control, won't I lose the pleasure of giving myself over, of "putting myself into someone else's hands?"

Perhaps it is different from putting soul, mind, and brain in their hands.

Could power and strength be separate from the body?

As I walked down the street after my massage, I did see my body moving separately from my soul. I saw an amorphous mass of inchoate protoplasm gliding blissfully along the street while my soul sat outside, enjoying the view. On one level—the highest level—body, soul, and world are One. But on another level, the Teaneck massage level, body and soul are separate. Massage highlights this separation.

Quantity Leads to Quality

Last year at this time I discovered my miracle schedule. Revelations were falling from the sky almost every day. It was a brilliant period. That period is over. Once again I have a free summer. What shall I do? Last summer my mental archeological dig uncovered Miracle Schedule City. As Columbus said on his way back from America: "Now what?" Then he made two more trips.

I'm at the same place. I've discovered my America. I can't think of anything better than my miracle schedule. I guess I'll follow it again.

Will this summer repeat last summer? I can't get that excited about a repeat. But it's not bad either. *Not bad either?* When I say that, I know something is missing. I want to reach new heights, find a new planet, be thrilled again. Can't I find something new to write about? I don't want "the same old thing." over again.

I need a challenge to drench my guts and wrench my brains.

What will give me that?

Quantity.

I can't aim for quality. It comes from heaven after push, try, effort, breath, die, and then living again in the new flesh of rebirth. Quality rips the envelope on the tear sheets of quantity. I want to bend the rules of time, smash through the skin, bones, brains, and ideological freezings that descend upon me every night, cauterizing the wounds of my creations. Quality will appear as a gift if, every day, I fight for my freedom.

I am on the road searching. Intensity and quantity are my tools. Quality may emerge—or it may not. Intensity is my route. Scrapping the ever-present barnacles that stick to and stink up my ship, I cleanse myself before rising above the sewage creations of my defiled surroundings.

Write, write, write—I hope to reach a higher level. But any level will do, as long as it's a new level, one I've never seen before, crossing borders, beyond the level of levels, and leading to the heaven above all levels. Discover worlds beyond worlds, and even the giant Penelope-Plus star shining in the galactic borderland beyond the universe.

When I ran this morning I broke the mold of body. Stars and moons shone in broad daylight. I ran an hour and a half, pushing four hundred breathings, flying within the hypnotic counts of threes. Trees bent to kiss my knees. Now that's a run! I broke body's resistance. Standing in morning darkness, I entered the land of sunshine. What an accomplishment! Push, struggle, and try, not only on the run, but in every branch of miracle schedule; then chains will break and mountains will crumble. Then I'll catch collapsing giants and smile as they are stored in the graveyard behind me.

Exploring My Miracle Schedule in Depth

I spoke to Mayra at Ginger and Jim's party yesterday. I told her about my miracle schedule and what a good thing it was for me.

Her interest in my miracle schedule reminded me of its importance. I've got something good going here. Remember it, study it, follow it.

Yet even with this schedule, I feel lost this morning. Have I forgotten fundamental truths I discovered last year? Or is another creative voice rising from invisible pools, flying across my face, whispering in my ear: "Your miracle schedule has been reduced to a mere fact of life. Time to reclaim the wonder you once had, the mystery that filled last summer. Find something new to do, something different. The miracle schedule has lost its miraculous quality; it has become commonplace and ordinary."

But another voice is speaking: "Hold on! The miracle schedule is like a Torah dictated by God to Moses. It is an ethical, moral, and spiritual blue print for your life. That's why I sent down Angel Mayra to reestablish your faith in it. Do not listen to the false voice. Of course, you could choose to follow other creative paths, develop new skills, and spread yourself in a thousand directions. I didn't give you one talent, but many. But I also gave you the power of choice. Stretch yourself too thin across the horizons of choice, and you'll bend beyond the breaking point. You'll accomplish little, and the little you accomplish will have even less depth. Stick with the miracle schedule I sent you. Rather than find something new to do, a new art form, business, sport, craft, skill, or activity, *rededicate yourself* to the miracle schedule. That's what this summer is about: rededication. You didn't start reading Henry Miller's *The Colossus of Maroussi,* with its definite article in the title, for nothing. Your hero, Henry Miller himself, said that the Greeks have unique ability to create ferment in the present.

"For a Greek every event, no matter how stale, is always unique. He is always doing the same thing for the first time: he is curious, avidly curious, and experimental; he experiments for the sake of experimenting, not to establish a better or more efficient way of doing things."

There is my desire and philosophy in a nutshell: to see the miracle of creation fresh in every moment. Whether the Greeks are that way or not, I don't know. Maybe Henry Miller is that way himself and projects his beliefs onto the Greeks. But most important is the ability to find in the unique in the stale, daily, ever-repeated, present occurrence.

My miracle schedule is threatening to become a stale. Yet every time I experiment and improvise within it, I find something unique. Sure, I could study anatomy, art, and drawing the human body, or develop my calligraphy. There are many other things I could do, too. But my other voice is warning me: I'd better not. I've built a beautiful city at the edge of an everlasting cliff. God gave me land free of charge with building skills as well. But the devil is calling on me to destroy this city, pull it down, and find a new building adventure. I am sorely tempted. What a conflict!

If I stay, I can develop in depth. Why not just say, "Devil, I'm not giving in to your temptations. I'm sticking to the straight and narrow, the path of purification and illumination. I'm following the miracle schedule which your Older Brother sent me."

The devil will say, "Hell, man, that brother of mine is no part of dualism.

He's mono all the way. You want dualism, call me. I'm pulling you off the cliff and dragging you down into the abyss. That's where I live with all my friends. You'll have a good time here. Who cares if the only light you'll see down here comes from the fires of hell?"

I am choosing between God and the devil, between my miracle schedule, and the temptation of a thousand directions. Can the devil's path ever lead to heaven's green and fertile pastures? Will the straight and narrow path of cleansing and purification ever lead me astray?

I'm leaning towards the Higher. Writing has always been my haven; guitar and song my calming vistas; yoga and running speak to body and mind; study opens up new paths *within* the old. My folk dance-tour- weekend business is the foundation of my house. What else is there for me to do? Why tamper with these gifts?

I've been experimenting, traveling on many roads for a long time. The miracle schedule road is my personal road to salvation. Shouldn't I follow the only truth I know?

MONEY AND ITS BRETHREN

Bless My Depressions

Once I start writing, it's so delicious to see the cloud of depression lifting. Would I even bother to write without these heavy wet blankets hanging over my head? Probably not. Pleasure isn't enough. It takes a tough guy beaten down by a tough depression to break the inertia gathering, like polluted rain water, in my brain every morning. If I don't clean my pipes, the brain will get clogged.

Bless my depressions! They motivate me, push me out of bed, force me to write.

They started a week ago, when I finished work and realized I had a summer free to "do what I want."

Of course, I do what I want all year long anyway, so having summer free to do it is no big deal. Actually, I was facing emptiness after a grand business victory. My success depressed me.

What a Bulgarian tour I had! I calculated my profits. Wonderful! Add to this historic sums from my Hungarian tour and an acceptable pittance from my Greek tour and I've made mucho bucks from tours alone!

I've not only paid off my debts, but, for the first time since I started the tour business eleven years ago, I have a surplus in my account.

What a way to start the summer! I am ecstatic. I'm not used to such financial success. My habit is to worry about money, a worry which keeps my mind busy and motivates me to think up new means of survival.

Now, however, my economic survival is assured—at least for the summer. I'm not used to this kind of assurance. I don't even know if it's good for me. I've gained five pounds. Usually I worry my weight away. I never gain. During the summer I drink lots of water, so I gain some. But today, this extra weight feels like a symbol for mental sloth, a heaviness and dullness caused by lack of worry.

Money has freed me from my fears. But it raises a question: If I had enough money, what would I worry about? Health? Do I really want to live worry-free?

I've worked long and hard to reach this financial equilibrium. Yet success has caused a vacuum, an emptiness. If my mind doesn't worry, will it eat me up?

I must occupy my mind with something.

It's not success that's bothering me as much as emptiness. Ideas emerge with or without money when they are ready. It's just that right now, none are emerging.

This is the down-and-empty period after success with nothing to do but walk around the block, lie in the sun, relax, and wait for the next cloudburst.

PERFORMANCE

Power Among Family and Friends

I'm doing everything I can to escape from little Zoltan and the noise he is making, but so far I have been unsuccessful. All I want is peace and space to write. It's almost impossible in this house. I must have this writing hour alone. I'll be a happy person for the rest of the day if I take it; if I don't, I'll be miserable.

I'm taking the writing time. Little Zoltan is looking over my shoulder as I write. My escape has succeeded. I'm writing is spite of the frustrating family situation, and I'm happy.

Last night Jutka, Joan, and I went folk dancing. Fred and Mary are the leaders of the Santa Fe group. They run a friendly class. We had a great time.

When we came home Jutka told me one of the dancers had said: Please come back. We need more life in this group. Then once again I realized I had denied my power. That our presence added life to the group is not unusual. What is unusual is my hesitation and denial of it. But, of course, hesitation and denial are lifetime habits. I'm just beginning to recognize and love power and strength. The more I recognize it, the more recognizable it will be. And the more I will love and accept it. I just need more practice.

What are the benefits of such recognition? Numerous surprises and amazements. Amazements come when I look at my ability to effect and affect a folk dance class or simply a room full of people. I do it by standing there and silently radiating throughout the room. It is the conscious exercise of unconscious power. Amazing and astonishing.

I could also use it with my family. Until now, at home, I usually sink back and "relax" into a passive mode. Do I still want to do that? Shouldn't I use my power everywhere? It could be used both in the public world outside and in the inner "public" world of family, relatives, and friends.

Family power is something new for me. Think about it, then practice it.

Why is folk dancing like going to the laundery? Because it cleanses your soul.

Joyce Harris Was Right

Joyce Harris was right: I see her face when I play the guitar. She said, "Play guitar only for yourself."

What did it mean?

No performing, no career, no thoughts of the audience. Only for myself. Imagine playing the guitar for the so-called "myself?"

Suppose I expanded the Joyce Harris Approach to singing... and writing? This would be a radical qualitative change.

The Guitar God Lives in my Right Arm Near the Shoulder

I made beautiful progress on my guitar this morning. The movement of my fingers across the strings reminds me of my tourists scurrying back on forth on the Greek tour: when I pay *total* attention only to them, I am lost. But when I remember who I am, who He is, and my relationship to Him, then *add* my tourists to this equation, I become centered. I become peaceful; priorities are in order; I make good decisions.

It is always a case of remembering who I am. This morning when I played guitar, I concentrated on my right arm near the shoulder; I let my fingers move as I centered my mind on that heavenly space. As long as I focused on that space where God lives missing some notes didn't matter. My focused approach to playing caused me to play beautifully. This is the answer to my years of searching. It is the right attitude, not only towards guitar, but towards everything I do.

Remember priorities.

Remember who I am.

A New Look at Performing: World of Guitar Revisited

On Saturday afternoon I sat alone on the porch at Solway House in Saugerties, New York, playing the guitar, enjoying the relaxation improvements a la Joyce Harris. I was playing Gaspar Sanz's Pavane when Sam Diamond came out of his cabin, said hello, and sat down in a chair about twenty yards away from me. Although he sat quietly and unobtrusively, reading his book, my performing reflexes returned. I started thinking of Sam as if I were "performing" for him.

I cannot "play alone" with others present. Relaxing with my guitar can only be done alone. As long as someone appears, I start performing for them.

Obviously there is a qualitative difference between playing the guitar alone and in the presence of others. No amount of practicing, meditation, or Joyce Harris approaches is going to change that.

An old and new realization: When the audience is present I will never escape from them!

I saw it again Saturday night. I decided to give a mini-concert to my group of twelve people. All of them love my weekend and accept me. But as soon as I sat down to play, my performing instincts took over again: same nervousness, same split focus on both audience and guitar, same tightness.

Thus, in spite of meditation, years of guitar practice, leaving the performing field, returning to it, trying to rip the audience out of my mind, trying to forget about them and concentrate on "playing for myself," relaxation, and higher forms, *nothing has changed!* I am still thinking and feeling the same way

I did thirty years ago!

Oh sure, my techniques have improved. But that is a quantitative thing. Qualitatively nothing has changed. Last night I was nervous before an audience of twelve. I used to play before audiences of hundreds. Same nervousness. Even practicing the guitar near Sam while he read made me nervous.

Years of effort to change my feelings. Result: I am the same person.

What is going on here?

After the performance last night, I had a powerful thought: perhaps my original World of Guitar concert program, combining classical, flamencan, and folk guitar with stories and songs, is my best approach. Perhaps it has always been my best approach and was good all along.

I made a living out of guitar concerts for years. Others knew I was good. I was the only one with all the doubts.

This means I was on the right track to begin with. All along, I have been on a quest, not necessarily to improve my program and guitar playing, but rather to find my power and strength. Evidently this power and strength existed all along in The World of Guitar. My problem was not in the program, but in denying my power.

It has always been *so easy* for me to get up in front of an audience, sing a folk song, and especially *talk*. That is my talent. Playing classical guitar is also a talent, but a secondary one. However, for many years I have been using my classical guitar playing as a shield to deny my talent, to deny my strength. I've used it as a battery ram to hit myself over the head, beat myself down, keep me weak before my omnipotent audience.

Last night those thoughts came to an end. Now I have to reevaluate my approach to guitar playing and performance. I'll have to admit I'm good at talking and singing, and later, perhaps, classical guitar. My program is good. I can't deny it anymore. I'll look back on my old program with a new attitude.

Imagine going back to my past performances and seeing most of them as good? I might even begin to like memories, looking at old photographs, rereading old writings, talking about old times, etc. Who can tell where this will lead?

Beyond Inferiority at Walnut School: Performing with Inner Peace

I gave my World of Guitar performance at Walnut School. Joan Melvin, the principal, calmed the kids, watched their every move, kept them in her viselike grip while I played my Pavanes, Granados' Spanish Dance No. 5, and Zapateados. Then I sang songs and told stories.

I did the same show I always do. That's one of the reasons I quit performing in the first place: I couldn't get out of the "rut" I was in. After many years of trails and experiments, I'd finally put together a good show. How could I change it, especially when schools were paying me all that money? My answer was: I couldn't. Slowly my creativity died. I gave up performing.

But somehow, yesterday's show was different. When I finished I felt a quiet satisfaction. Some of this peace of mind was because the pain of performance had ended. But yesterday, at Walnut School, something else was new. This time I *accepted the peace*. I realized, not only did I have a good show, but I would probably never change the show. My show was fixed and more or less final. The *pressure to be creative was off*.

I don't know if this is good or bad, but I did feel peaceful when it was over. I even thought about doing more shows in the future. No-sweat shows, simply repeating the show I already know. No pressure to perform "Alhambra" or pieces I can't play well, no pressure to prove myself or feelings of inadequacy expressed by the attitude: I'm only playing my "Pavanes," "Granados," and "Zapateado" because I can't play the "Alhambra," "Leyenda," and all the great tremolo pieces.

In other words, I am performing *without* a sense of inferiority.

Wow, what did I just say? *Performing without a sense of inferiority.* Have my power and strength explorations reached such a point? If they have, it is a great accomplishment. Imagine performing without a sense of inferiority. I can't. That's how far removed such an experience is. Every performance I have ever given has been with a sense of inferiority. I've always done so under the threat of impending doom and the bordering-on-panic fear that, at any moment, the audience might rise up and throw things at me because they have finally seen through my fraud and realized I'm no good.

No wonder I have stage fright.

The result of performing without inferiority is not elation or excitement but, rather, inner peace. I've sometimes had this feeling after a performance but have never accorded it much importance. Now it may be the only feeling left to recognize in my performance repertoire.

The pressure I have always put on myself to be creative derives, in part, from a sense of inferiority. I must constantly "prove" that I'm worthy, that I'm talented and creative. Since I never believe it no matter how many times I "prove" it, no matter how many people tell me how good I am, I have been doomed to never accept who I am and what talents I have. I've been doing this most of my life, and it has never worked. Once you get into the habit of beating yourself over the head, it is very difficult to stop.

I have reached the stopping point. My self-abuse chapter is ending.

New Performing Adventure: Ending the Self- Improvement Flagellation Mode

I love breakthroughs.

I am at the beginning of a new breakthrough.

The new road began at Walnut School. Walnut School is the wall-nut I cracked, the wall of nuts that has surrounded my guitar performances and musical life for years.

Suddenly, performing *feels so easy!* All the struggles to rise, improve, grow as a performer and guitarist, have fallen away. My egg fell off the wall; the shell cracked. Now yolks are running wild all over the place; even the shells are having a good time. I can't believe it. But I must admit, I can see new yolks on every corner.

I can play the same pieces over and over again for the rest of my life, and nobody will criticize me. Best of all, *I* won't criticize me. What a relief to be rid of my ever-present and ever-pounding censor! Suddenly, he just dropped out the window. I don't know what garbage can he fell in, but I'm glad to get rid of him. He's been hanging around for years. No mental or physical trick I tried could get rid of him. Finally, I gave up trying to chase him away. I changed directions, found new roads, gave up performing, gave up trying to prove I could play guitar, gave up competing with the greats—the Segovias, Sabicases, and Julian Breams of this world.

But this morning, I'm settling, comfortable and happy, into my corner of the world—the children's corner. No sweat. I like performing for children. They are so uncritical, accepting, open to humor, sound, light, and movement. Of course, their openness in no way effects my self-image. I could play in front of them for years and nothing would change unless I changed *my view of myself*. An outside audience can do little to change a self-image. Oh sure, they can encouragement you and shout approval. That's nice. But it doesn't have much effect on self-image. No matter how good they say I am, I still don't believe it. Standing ovations, audiences screaming love and approval, didn't make much of a dent in my view of myself. In fact, all their screaming usually gives me a headache. Don't they see how many mistakes I make playing guitar? Don't they know how nervous I am singing those songs? How can their perception of me be so off? And if they're so stupid, why should I believe them when they cheer me? The cognoscenti, the wise and smart, the true art critics, will criticize me in a second because they know my mistakes and weaknesses.

How could I have believed in this shit for so many years? Amazing, isn't it? But I did. The steam of self-loathing, lack of confidence, and self-flagellation went on and on. Perhaps one of my missions on earth was to climb over this mountain of self-disapproval, to crack the prison wall of self-doubt.

In the last few days, for some unexplainable reason, I've taken a gigantic step on my life's mission. Perhaps it's age, or simply so many years of improvement drops falling on my mistake stone. Who knows? But, whatever it is, it's here now, and I'm here with it.

What will happen to my folk dancing, my weekends, my tours if I return to performing? How will I look at them? How much work will I put into them? We'll see. But this summer marks the beginning of a performing adventure.

BUSINESS

Heavy and Tired This Morning

Woke up this morning heavy and tired. Why? Deborah and Larry on my mind. Mostly Debby. She is the truck driving through the night of my dreams, pulverizing flowers beneath her nonstop talker wheels. I made a mistake taking her on my Bulgarian tour. But how could I have known? Larry is okay, but he's quiet. Deborah is the mouth and force behind the plastic throne.

After going with us to Bulgaria, they wanted me to book a tour to Turkey.

My first thought was, I wish they would book with someone else. But I'm stuck with them. Then I rationalized that having them on tour might be a challenge, though I've learned that putting in lots of special effort for demanding clients often turns out to be a waste of time. I make arrangements, phone calls to find out about flights and hotels, and, in the end, they often cancel. This may well happen with Debby and Larry. So I've decided to set my own limits. First of all, I will hope they cancel their tour. That hope frees me from working tirelessly to fulfill their petty demands. Within limits, I will do what I can to help them; I will not make a superhuman effort.

I spoke to them for a half hour last night. Luckily it was their phone bill. We planned a tour of Turkey.

Telepathy

I feel a little rushed this morning: we're leaving for Santa Fe in an hour. I want to put a few words down, brief and scant as they may be.

Yesterday I taught folk dancing at the Doade bat mitzvah. It was a down experience, even though everyone loved it. Why? My mind created the down.

Once again I denied my power.

It began when I drove through South Orange. I looked at the beautiful homes, some of them mansions, and they touched off the following inferiority-complex train of thought: *I'll be leading dancing for rich people who have more money and live in nicer houses than I do. They are better than I am.* After this little bout of self-depreciation, I drove into the Temple Beth El parking lot. Packed with cars. *Wow, I thought, hundreds of rich people here. How am I going to please this superior class?* I entered to find the congregation just finishing services. I set up my minimal equipment and waited for Mitch Kahn and his orchestra to arrive. When he did, I said hello, moved my coat to my "office" backstage— a mere chair—then left the room to "feel out the crowd," milling around the hors d'oeuvres and cocktails table in the lobby. As I entered, I stood on a promontory about five steps above the crowd. I put my hands against a railing, leaned on it, and surveyed them. Then it happened. As I stood there I thought: *Here is my crowd. I have to somehow get them to dance. How will I do it? Through the power of mind: I will consciously use the power of telepathy to project my thoughts and personal power into each individual. Soon, subtly and unbeknownst to them, they will be unconsciously under my control. Then, when I tell them to dance, they will obey without resistance. They will have been subtly and unconsciously hyp-*

notized through the power of my telepathy.

Now this is a great thought, a great idea. It is the ultimate exercise in personal power to use over a crowd. It works, too. When I focus my concentration on them, it strengthens my bonds with each person in the room. I have done this countless times before, with tour groups, weekend groups, but I have never felt the concept of power rush through me with as much clarity as it did when I stood on that promontory.

Then I denied it. I said, *Who am I to think such thoughts? Isn't it hubris? After all, these rich people are better than I am.* Then I retreated to my old "humble" self and spent the rest of the afternoon in semi-denial.

It wasn't until the bat mitzvah was over and I was driving home that I realized what I had done. That was why I felt so exhausted after the bat mitzvah. I spent those three bat mitzvah hours mentally driving with my brakes on. Though the people loved my folk dance leading, I doubted myself. All afternoon I was wondering what to do next. Well, that's part of my job. But exhausting myself in self-doubt is not.

Hopefully, never again. The power thoughts I felt at the top of the promontory were the right ones. My power is right and true. I use it for good. Controlling people by getting them to dance is an undeniable good.

When I say "controlling people," a negative kicks in: controlling anyone is bad; better to give them their freedom. But this negative thinking comes from my upbringing, my desires to free myself from Big Ma. It is a childish fantasy, and I have outgrown it. Power, in itself, is neither good nor bad; it depends how it is used.

I accomplished a lot this week. I put together next year's tour programs: I wrote the flier for Budapest/Prague, March 1996, and for Bohemia-Moravia-Slovakia-Poland, July 1996. I did most of my packing for Greece, visited Cloud Tours to put the final touches on our May Greek tour, then visited Balkan Tourist, put some almost final touches on our August Bulgarian tour; I drove to Darien, CT, and found another room for our Friday night folk dance group. One good thing after another popped and clicked into place during this week. As I drove out of Darien on Thursday afternoon I said to myself, "I'm so lucky. People are signing up for my tours, I found a beautiful folk dance room, I even had a great cup of coffee in Darien's Arcadia Coffee shop." Last week in Santa Fe was also a pleasure. I stood up for myself and conducted a lovely Seder. *Hakol beseder*—all is in order. Victories for my power and strength. A hot week.

I stand under the sun enjoying the dazzle of light on my face.

An Ending

Most of my work is done. I've been going almost nonstop since the beginning of March. I ran my tour to Budapest and Prague, put together my May Greece and August Bulgaria tours; then I put together as much of next years tours as I could: Budapest and Prague in March; the Bohemia, Moravia, Slovakia, and Poland for July; and I'll know about next May after this May's tour to Greece. I even found a lovely folk dance room in Darien, for our Friday night group. We went to Santa Fe for a week, visited the kids, and had a good time. All the tour ads are out; so are the brochures and fliers. I've got a few mop-up operations yet: pack for Greece, send out the Bulgarian bills, etc. but, basically, most of my work is done.

Done! Hard to believe. I'm stunned—and deflated, too. An ending. But every ending is a new beginning.

Last night's Russian dance workshop with Alexander "Sasha" Antchoutine was an incredible hit. People loved him. I felt happy and proud to have "discovered" and booked him.

But my main mood these days is exhaustion bordering on I don't know what. Most of my mind is on tourism. At the moment, nothing seems more exciting than finding tour customers, and visiting new and exciting places like Iceland, Tunisia, Italy, Greek Macedonia, and who knows where.

Is that the problem? Once, having a workshop with a Moiseyev dancer like Sasha would have once been the thrill of my life. Today, however, I feel I have passed through the Russian dance and Moiseyev phase of my life and am moving on. I have "been through these forms already." Last nights's happiness came more from seeing so many people enjoy Sasha rather than from what I actually learned; my happiness came from bringing others something I knew was beautiful, from introducing them to the incredible thrills and beauty of the Russian-Moiseyev and now Alexander Antchoutine experience.

Service to others: I did it again.

I keep thinking of the satisfaction of getting people to join my tours. I say "satisfaction" rather than "joy." Satisfaction feels like a more level experience; joy is pointed and sharp; "joy" feels more personal, whereas "satisfaction" includes others.

Will thinking-only-of-self no longer work? Or are these specious distinctions? Has the separation between self and other only been in my mind? My work helps others. Perhaps the distinction between self and other is a false, "Western-type" distinction and never really existed in the first place.

Every living creature in this world gives to others even though it may simply be exhalations of carbon dioxide.

Reading the Waves

I feel like a fool. Ever since I went into Balkan Tours last Friday and told them that I might get forty, even fifty people for my Bulgarian tour, I've been either standing still or backsliding. Today my first cancellation came in the mail. It reminded me of the Greek tour when I lost almost half my registrants through cancellations. I hope the same things doesn't happen with Bulgaria—but it could.

It seems that the peaks of my excitement come just as the crest of the wave is forming. My excitements are followed by either a leveling off or a downward slide. Just like a personal stock market. *Perhaps my moods are secret signals, mystical signs that my fortunes are about to change.* Excitements—and depressions—are my secret and personal communications system. If I'm too excited, they tell me it's time to cool down; if I'm depressed, they tell me the market will soon heat up. I must be careful when I see my fortunes rising to infinity. It usually means I'm about to move in the other direction.

My fortunes may well be read in opposites: extreme excitement and expectations lead to a flattening, backsliding, and depression; extreme depression and lack of expectations lead first to flattening, then to a rising market, hope, and higher expectations. It is very difficult to interpret these emotional waves correctly. Unfortunately—or fortunately—I suffer from human qualities like delusions of grandeur, superman complex, extreme fears of failure, depression, and more. Still, the signals within the waves may have miracles hidden within them. Some day I may even be able to interpret them correctly.

It's 5:45 a.m. and I'm sitting in the Philippos Hotel on Mitseon Street in Athens, writing the first pages of New Leaf 3 in my second New Leaf Journal. The writing conditions aren't particularly good. Coffee in the lobby won't be ready for another half hour. Writing without coffee is a miserable experience. Also my room at the Philippos, although small and charming, with well-designed indirect lighting and pink walls, and extremely clean, has no writing desk. I'm sitting crunched in a corner, leaning over my computer, and writing. I have little time this morning. At 7:15 our tour bus leaves on the Classical Tour, beginning with the Peloponnese.

Our tour group has wonderful people. I'm lucky. Last night we had a delicious meal at the Socrates Prison Restaurant. I'm not much at describing things this morning, though. Without coffee I can hardly function. Nevertheless, I want to write a few words to keep the flow flowing.

So far this trip feels remarkably easy. Even the jet lag isn't much of a problem.

I'm grateful for the few moments of writing time I have this morning. I went down to get some coffee, said the magic words to George: *Einai archigos stin to grup Amerika*—I am the leader of the American group, and he gave me a pot of coffee, hot milk, and a tray. I piled on a sandwich and an orange—more food than I expected—and went happily back to my room to write. I passed by the front desk, practiced my Greek by saying, "*Thelo na plirano to logorismo. Domatio hilia sarantepente.*" (I want to pay my bill. Room 145) and paid my bill. My Greek may not be exactly right, but it's close.

I'd forgotten to save my seat on the bus. I had to sit way in back away from my group. I asked our guide, Zoe, to announce a seat rotation tomorrow. Will people give up their front seats? The front people are my group. I want them to keep the best seats for the tour's duration. I don't care about being fair, but if it's forced on me, I'll take it.

I'm watching the clock as I write. These are the "timed writings" Natalie Goldberg was talking about in *Writing Down the Bones* and repeated in *Wild Mind*. I'm grabbing the small time available. Rush, rush, rush. I don't like it, but I have no choice. Our bus leaves at 8:00 a.m.

Actually, I do have a choice, but I don't know what it is.

Nice People

The people on this tour are nice. Not only the ones on our bus, but on the other buses as well.

Why are the people so nice?

Are they so nice?

Or is it me?

Last night the people were miserable. I had a headache and hardly slept.

Sunstroke or the tour, I'm not sure. But this morning, after coffee and breakfast, the people looked nice.

Maybe the people are nice. On the other hand, maybe it is my *vision* of them. After all, this journal is about power and strength. If I'm radiating power, then no wonder everyone looks nice. Since I create the world through my perception of it, if I'm feeling good why shouldn't I project my good feelings onto everyone else? A simple witness of the coffee phenomenon bears this out: before morning coffee, the world and its inhabitants look miserable; but after coffee, an incredible transformation takes place: They improve with each sip until, by the time I reach the bottom of the cup, the world and its people look wonderful.

Is that subjective? You betcha. But the world is subjective—with an objective tilt. I must give myself credit. It is my vision that has created these nice people around me. I'd love to give them some credit, too, but I doubt if I can. Even if they themselves are nice, I wouldn't notice it unless it were true of me, too.

Thus it is right and fitting—and nice, too—that Lorene gave me a T-shirt. Did my good vibrations create her giving of the T-shirt? Could be.

Another thought. Are the rest of the people on our bus nice partly because of the influence and positive vibrations our group creates? We were the original group on the bus; we set the tone. Is my group nice because of *me*? Partly and possibly. If that is so, then *I* am setting the tone of this tour or at least much of it. It's the telepathic-vision-of-power from the promontory at the South Orange bat mitzvah all over again.

Is this too egoistic a vision, too hubristic? Am I giving myself too much credit? Do I really have such power? Or by these very questions am I backing off, stepping back from my powers because they are too frightening? I don't know whether I have these powers, but certainly it is possible for me to *believe* in my powers. Believing in them is frightening. Imagine, does the power of my telepathic vision actually influence and partially control this tour? It's scary to think so. Am I becoming too grandiose?

But what else can I think? What else do I have but my vision? Maybe I am right. Certainly I'm walking at the edge of the cliff. It is frightening.

Last night Arlene said I should take the mike from Zoe, stand at the front of the bus, and announce to all forty-five people that I'm running a tour to Hungary and the former Czechoslovakia next year, and if they would like to come or be on my mailing list they should speak to me. Then she also said I should make a T-shirt saying *"Moravia, Bohemia (Czech Republic), Slovakia, Poland, and Hungary in 1996"* and wear it on my Bulgarian tour in August. After that, Selma said Arlene should be my marketing person. I told her she was. Selma said she should also market my books.

This created quit a stir in my brain. First, I showed everyone at the table what Arlene had created—my brochure, her article in the *Bergen Record*, even the *New York Times* article she hadn't written, but had put together. It was so easy praising Arlene as compared with praising myself. I cringed at the idea of announcing my tours in front of the bus. So brassy, so pushy, I couldn't do it. It had *poor taste* written all over it. Yet I knew it would be a good idea. It probably has nothing to do with poor taste, anyway, just my own personality and "approachless approach" to marketing. However, the way I so quickly and happily wanted to demean myself in front of the group did not speak well of me as a leader. Why put doubts in their hearts? It only cuts their confidence in me. Better to keep quiet. But I didn't—although I sensed I should (that's progress, anyway). I retreated into the old world of denying my strength. To my credit, I caught myself in time to soften the blows. An hour later I was back on my feet, berating myself in private for slipping backwards again.

Let's look at some of Arlene's ideas: first, regarding book promotion, she flatly told me she couldn't do it. She has no knowledge or feel for the specialized world of book promotions. So much for that. *An interesting "personal" project would be: how to promote my own books.* Perhaps I could mail out *Mad Shoes, Handfuls of Air, and Crusaders Tours* to various agents and publishers, offer them the rights, and see what happens.

Regarding T-shirt advertising: I like it. *Creating a specific-goal advertising T-shirt like the 1996 tour one is a good to excellent idea.* Maybe I'll do it.

Regarding announcements on the bus: I doubt if it's for me. But Arlene's idea did make me think about talking privately to people on the bus, telling them about my tours, and that *I am a specialist in Hungary, the Czech Republic, Slovakia, and Bulgaria.* Then I can tell them about next year's trip and see if I perk their interest. These countries are rarely visited, and most who have been to Prague and Budapest have never gone into the countryside. No question I have a specialty going there. (I could talk about Turkey, too, or Israel. But I'm not running tours there next year. I think the Eastern European countries are a better hook.)

As you can see, I'm introducing parenthesis. Perhaps they'll become more prevalent as my thoughts lead to subthoughts.

In any case, Arlene had some good ideas.

How and When?

I only have ten minutes to write before our bus leaves.

We're going to Meteora today, a monastery city of great personal significance. I love the solitude of monasteries. But this morning my mind is in such a rush I don't know what to put down. Ten minutes certainly creates a different kind of pressure on you. Perhaps ten-minute bouts are a good way to write: It gets the juices going immediately.

Next year I'll bring my own coffee maker to Greece. There's no coffee in the hotels until 7:00 a.m. I get up much earlier than that. This morning I got up at 6:00. Since there was no coffee, I did my yoga stretches for twenty minutes. Not a bad way to start the morning. *A pre-coffee yoga-stretch beginning, a new habit in the making?* Maybe.

Last night at the dinner table, Mike and Maureen got me vaguely interested in running a tour to Australia to see, among other things, aboriginal dancing plus a side trip to the Fiji Islands. Something to consider for my outer life.

For my inner life, I had Joyce Harris sitting next to me. A beautiful smile and something special about her. She said, *"You have to get back to playing guitar, but for yourself. It will bring you peace. It's an integral part of your soul. You need it."* It's hard to describe *how* she said it, and, more importantly, *when* she said it. The confluence of how and when brought me a subtle kind of epiphany. I've been trying to play the guitar "for myself" for years. I've just about given up trying. Something about the timing of Joyce's statement, and the way she said it, touched me. She told me she belongs to a society of psychics that meet periodically.

I'll be thinking about what she said for a long time. Where the eruptions will lead and rains of peace will fall, I do not know.

The Glory of It All!

We arrived in Athens early in the evening, settled in our hotel, then went out to eat supper in the Plaka. I can't get over how high the prices are and how much money I'm spending. I'm almost out of cash and I've still got half the tour to go. I'd better get a cash infusion soon.

We discovered several folk music and dance tavernas with excellent folk dance performing groups. Athens has lots of good dancing. It's worth staying here an extra day or two. Just be prepared to spend a lot of money.

I am grateful for having free time to reflect on my tour. My first thought is *the glory of it all!* When I step back a moment, beyond the daily changing of hotels, the miles of driving and sitting on the bus, the blur of seeing so many sites of incredible physical, historic, and spiritual beauty; when I comprehend that, in my lifetime, I am able to see and experience all this, it fills me with awe.

I realize it when I have a moment alone to reflect.

Leadership, Meteora, Local Folk Dance Groups, and Union with the Holy Spirit

On the bus driving back to Athens from Meteora, I had a terrible headache. Usually I average two or three headaches per tour. I slept on the bus for about two hours as we drove through Thessaly and Boeotia. My headache began to diminish when Bob Salem, who sat behind me, tapped my shoulder and said: "You're very good with your people. You run a fine tour. I saw it right away at the beginning of the tour, but I wondered just how long you would last. Well, five days have gone by, and it's still lasting." Bob teaches English at Brookdale Community College in south Jersey; he is also a travel consultant and has been leading his own tour groups for about fifteen years. I was very moved by what he said. It's nice to get recognition from a fellow professional. I started "explaining" how my mind works on a tour, the twists and turns of my thought processes, how focusing all my attention on my group is a kind of meditation for me. I soon realized by "explaining" my actions I was trying to escape the beauty of his compliment. He had recognized my power and strength. To my credit, my denial didn't last long. I realized what I was doing, stopped "explaining", and instead thanked him. He said, no reason to thank me, it's true. I agreed.

Bob's compliment caused me to start rethinking my role as leader. What is leadership? What am I leading when I lead a tour? What am I offering people that is different when they sign up for a tour with me? Why should they choose me in the first place?

In dealing with these questions, I am dealing with my personal view of leadership. Thanks to Bob's question, that view is expanding. Until now, I've felt I must give my tour participants folk dancing and meetings with local folk groups in order to justify my "folk" tour and their reason for going with me. Without these meetings, I've felt my tours are failing their expectations. On this Greek tour, we've hardly danced at all so far. The folk dance performance in Olympia was great, but it was a performance given for all the tour groups, not ours alone. After dancing every night in Budapest and Prague, this Greek trip has little dancing. Not that anyone in my group is complaining. They love it so far. Still, I feel—or have felt—that I have to justify the folk tour concept.

After hearing Bob's compliment I realized that, not only am I a good leader, but there is more to my leadership than folk dancing. I could run a tour without one moment of folk dancing and it would still be a good one. My skill in leadership is due to my caring and attention to my people. I have a leadership talent. Leading folk dancing is part of it. But now I have revealed a new level of leadership, a more expansive leadership with a broader-based appeal. Caring, attention to detail, trying to satisfy individual needs of my customers, constitutes a leadership beyond. It is true that without folk dancing I probably wouldn't even want to lead a tour. Whenever I ask the question, Why bother organizing these tours? the answer is to meet and dance with local folk dance groups. The experience combines the worldly and ecstatic, reminding me of the union between group, country, and universal spirit. As the monks at Meteora said, "All the penances, services, songs, and good works we do are but means to an end: union with the Holy Spirit."

That is my goal: Union with the Holy Spirit. It happens when we dance with local folk groups. So I'd better keep meeting these groups, for the good of my own group, and for myself: to remind me of who I am. It is, ultimately, an identity question: I am my smaller self, the individualized, isolated island of my ego; but I am also part of the universal Self, part of the Holy Spirit.

Anything I do to help remind me of this truth should be fed.

Promises

The folk dancing at the Morea Taverna was so beautiful that I promised the smiling Morea owner I'd bring my tour group tomorrow night. He promised to hold a table at the front for us. Then we went further up the street and found another excellent dance group at the Sissofos Taverna. The smiling Sissofos owner offered us free drinks and baklava if we would only sit on his rooftop restaurant. We accepted his offer. Later I promised him I'd bring my group to the Sissofos tomorrow night. Next night when we passed the Morea, when the owner saw us I told him we couldn't come tonight. He cursed us, our American ways, and our shit-word promises. I tried to explain how badly I felt about the 'betrayal" of my promise, how I would make it up to him in the future, how my group wanted to eat at the Sissofos and how I had to do what they wanted, but he paid no attention to my excuses. He simply cursed me and piled on the guilt. I had broken my promise. I agreed with him.

What can I learn from this miserable experience? I know from leading many tours how subject to change my promises can be. I believe I'll do the things I say. But situations change, sometimes instantaneously, and often I must do exactly the opposite of what I decided to do a few moments earlier. I make spur-of-the-moment decisions and changes based on my survival instincts. Some of these changes lead to wonderful serendipitous results; others lead to miserable ones. I rely on my own judgement. I cannot base them on a restauranteur's desires or even my own once-given promises. What I have learned, however, is *not to give my promises lightly*.

I don't blame the Morea owner for trying to get our business. If the Morea owner believes in the absolute promises of group leaders or any other customers, he is either stupid or naive. I *know* he is neither. He is a salesman selling his restaurant.

So why did I feel guilty? Because I had promised to return *so sincerely*. (As Betty Comora says, sincerity is the most important thing, and once you've learned how to fake that, you can do anything.) I loved the folk dancing in his restaurant. At the time I believed I would return. But the future proved me wrong. All I could do was apologize to him, tell him "I owe him." I did that: I apologized and promised him my future business. He could have been gracious and accepted my apologies. However, he chose the "lower" route of anger and guilt. That is not good salesmanship—at least for me. It may even be *bad* salesmanship. Now I will feel uncomfortable returning to his restaurant. Truth is, I owe him nothing. He simply has a dance group that I want. He should not let his his feelings get in the way of how he handles his customers. How often I have felt that sense of betrayal with my own customers; how often they promise me they will go on my tours, join my dance classes or weekends, only to find I never see or hear from them again? This happens all the time. It's part of business. Sure, it hurts and make me mad. But I don't tell them how I feel. That's the only difference between me and the

Morea owner. I do not reveal my hurt feelings except in my journal or in private with a friend. I hope that by shutting my mouth, I will get these customers back in the future. My way feels smoother than that of the Morea owner, but both of us tread the same worldly path of sales.

I'm sitting on our Triton cruise ship on our way to Mykonos. The peace of the sea has been broken by the cackling noises of tourists sitting in front of me, laughing about their bathing suits. I've just awoken from a beautiful sleep. I went to the uppermost deck, put down a mat, and slept the sleep of Poseidon. I don't know how Poseidon would sleep, but I imagine he'd sleep like me. I dreamed about the history of naps during the Mycenean period.

More and more tourists keep sitting near me, chattering, shouting, laughing, talking, and ruining my peace. This is exactly what I *do not* want on a cruise. But I'm stuck here, since I promised Peggy and Arlene I'd guard their bags while they took a nap. It's the history of napping all over again.

I thank God for the existence of my notebook computer! How glorious to write wherever I want. A technological marvel. Maybe I'll bring it to the island of Paros with when we sail there tomorrow to meet the local folk dance group.

We're passing many islands, but I don't know which ones they are. I heard there are over eleven hundred islands in the Aegean, only a few of which are inhabited.

I marvel over the words I'm pouring out. The flow seems endless. But it's just been broken by another sharp announcement, this time for bingo. I am sitting beneath a speaker, which adds to all the noise around me. When an announcement is made, it comes not only in English, but is followed by French, German, Spanish, Portuguese, and Japanese. Those are the nationalities on board so far.

Someone said that at three o'clock there would be Greek folk dance lessons on board. I hope they're right. It's ten after three now and still no announcement. We'll be pulling into Mykonos around four-thirty. I'll be glad when we do.

Folk Dancing on the Island of Paros: The Metaxa Experience

Yesterday the weather looked bad for sailing. High winds. We didn't know if our boat would leave for Paros. By morning half our group decided not to go. Arlene went as far as the boat but decided to cancel at the last minute. Only a hardy six remained: myself, Lynn, Selma, Peggy and Aaron, and Hilda who, in her diabetic, arthritic, and multi-other-diseased state is hardy of soul if not of body. The six of us sailed to Paros in heavy seas.

Step-lift-heave is the dance step I choreographed to help combat seasickness and nausea.

Our visit to Paros turned out to be the most memorable day on our tour. Words alone cannot describe it. Nevertheless, I'll give it a shot: we were met at the Paros dock by Marilyn Metaxa who comes from Seattle but settled on Paros with her architect husband, Petros, about fifteen years ago. Dmitri from Meridian tours was also there. We transferred via "flying taxi," dashing around curving roads to the lovely artistic and picturesque town of Naoussa. From there we went to Marilyn's house, a beautiful white-walled creation built by Petros. As we sat in her yard with its swimming pool and fountain, members of the American community of Paros began to appear along with parents of the folk dancers in the children's dance troupe who were going to perform for us. In a gorgeous hospitality of wine, cheese, bread, olives, and sweets, we met them all: Gregorio and Katarina Altamirano, jewelers from Berkeley, California, who own their own Labyrinth Jewelry shop, Alice, a water color painter, and Patricia Donnelly, friend and one-month visitor from Wyckoff, New Jersey. Soon the children's folk dance troupe of Paros appeared. They danced an hour program in full costume. This was followed by a sumptuous meal of moussaka, salads, lamb, breads, wine, olives, more dancing, dance lessons, a discussion about the origins of Greek folk dancing, and walnut cake and coffee. I showed some of the children in the folk dance troupe my magic coin tricks, then talked with Nikos Gavallas, an English teacher and the dance leader from Pensacola, Florida who had now settled in Paros. He invited us to see the older group's rehearsal late that afternoon. Why did we have late afternoon free? Our return trip to Mikonos had been cancelled due to high winds. We were to take the next ship leaving at three a.m. So we had lots of time. After a short walking tour of Naoussa, some of us sat down for coffee while Marilyn took me to see the Svoronos Bungalows. I particularly liked room 37, which I plan to take for myself when our group returns to Paros next year. Bungalows are hardly a good word for this beautiful architected, white-walled, antique-decorated hotel. Better "suites."

We attended the dance rehearsal lead by Maria Tripolitsiotis, the founder of the group. She dynamically shouted: *"Ena, thio (dio), tri, tessera; ena, thio, tri, tessera; mpros (bros), piso, dexeia, aristera!"* (One, two, three, four; one, two, three, four; forward, back, right, left!") At the end of the rehearsal, she gave us brochures, posters, and a book about the Paros folk dance group. The group is not only self-supporting through its concerts and dues membership, but has over two hundred dancers ranging in age from six to fifty.

By seven o'clock everyone was exhausted. We booked a hotel in Perachia (Paros) a few hundred feet from the dock. I took a solo walk through the town's winding streets, looking for a new shoulder bag, since my shoulder strap was frayed and about to break. I couldn't find one and went to sleep strapless. We awoke at two-thirty a.m. to catch the three a.m. boat back to Mykonos. When we arrived two hours later, Meridian tours had miraculously arranged a transfer back to our Acrogiali Beach Hotel.

Odysseus

I sit in my cabin V30 on board the cruise ship *Odysseus*. We've just arrived in the harbor of Kusadasi in Turkey. While my tourists go on the Ephesus excursion I am going to visit the town of Kusadasi. I keep thinking of Selim and our previous tours of Turkey. Both times we visited Kusadasi. The first time we toured Ephesus on a broiling hot August day. I did some good shopping there, bought lots of blouses for our boutique. The second time, I visited the town alone and I bought Turkish pants. Perhaps I ought to do the same today.

I have a nice room on board ship. Room service even brings me coffee! For members of the Coffee Addiction Class, this is a large bit of heaven. My cabin steward's name is Thanasis. He hardly speaks any English. Most of the staff on the Odysseus hardly speak any English. This is good; it is a chance for me to practice and learn some Greek! I have personal Greek teachers in the form of stewards on board. I'll practice with them each morning. Practicing in Athens is frustrating because when I ask someone a question in Greek they answer me in English.

The hard part of my tour is over. Why? First of all, I'm safely ensconced in my room, computer all set up, books in order. I even have a wide exercise floor for calliyogathenics. I can continue most of my miracle schedule. The fact I can write without hindrance is a gift from heaven.

I don't have much more to say this morning. My mind is on Kusadasi. I am also somewhat in a state of shock. I don't know why. I have to get used to my new surroundings on board ship. There is so much eating here: six feedings a day. Two troughs run into my room just above the bed. During each of the six feedings, food is funneled through the troughs into my waiting mouth. There's even a machine to push my jaws up and down just in case I'm too tired to chew.

Mucho food. I can't get into the swing of things. Is it the claustrophobic feeling of being in such a small cabin? No. Perhaps I'm just excited about going to Kusadasi again. I have so many good memories from my previous tour of Turkey.

But there is no rush to disembark. Stores don't even open until 9:30 or 10:00 o'clock.

I spent the morning in Kusadasi looking for blouses and Turkish pantaloons to sell in our boutique. I wandered through the labyrinthine back streets searching for stores I had visited two years ago. I couldn't find them. I was about to give up, when a rug salesman asked me if I was Turkish. I told him, American. *Blouses istyorum."* (I want blouses), I said. He said his friend had blouses, then led me to another store where I ended up spending three hundred fifty dollars on blouses, pantaloons, and scarves. Then I visited his rug store for tea before returning to the ship.

I did yoga in my cabin, went on deck for a huge buffet lunch, lay in the sun for awhile, then returned to my cabin for another half-hour of sleep.

I awoke with a question: why have I been feeling low since I got on this cruise ship? Is it because my group has scattered and my leadership skills are not needed as much? Is it because my cabin is dark and dungeonlike? Is it because I'm a prisoner on a cruise ship? Perhaps it is the feeling that I have exchanged the land of Greece for a floating hotel filled with American and foreign tourists. So far, I can find absolutely nothing of interest on this ship. I can't run. My cabin is cramped, tight, stuffy, and uninspirational for yoga. What am I doing here? A cruise may not be for me. The only thing I "look forward to" is writing on my computer, and perhaps reading a bit.

I liked the Nile River cruise in Egypt. Why? We stopped at Luxor, Aswan, and some small sites. I loved the serenity and peace of that cruise, sitting in my lovely light cabin, looking out the window, watching the biblical Egyptian scenes glide by. We sat on deck under the brilliant Egyptian sun, and visited many ancient and mysterious ruins.

Now I am sitting in a lounge on one of the upper decks of the cruise ship *Odysseus*. It is comfortable, spacious, light, and almost empty. It is peaceful and serene. Still I miss the mystery and awe of splendid mountain sites of the Peloponnese and the Greek mainland, and the passionate Greek dancing. Will it happen again?

Perhaps I have to get used to the slow, leisurely mood on a cruise ship. Perhaps it is too early to judge.

I Need to Lead

Now I know why I got depressed as soon as stepped on the Odysseus: I had given up my leadership role. It was a personal decision—and a step backwards.

Leading calls up my energies, my powers and strengths. It is just plain good for me—and others, too.

I have always been a natural leader. I sensed it ever since second grade when I led the boys against the girls at Barnard School for Girls. When I attended P.S. 7 I lost it for awhile. I regained some in high school, especially when I conducted the senior orchestra, and then still more when I became the social director at Chait's Hotel in Accord, New York at the age of nineteen. Others must have noticed it. Why else would they have followed me, listened to me when I organized a chorus, offered me the job of social director usually reserved for adults twice my age? Everyone knew I had leadership qualities but me. I acted like a leader, my enthusiastic eyes shone like a leader's—bright-eyed Athena was my goddess—and my movements and gestures were those of a leader. Only my thoughts were not. I didn't deem myself worthy. Even though instinctively I took charge of things, an inner voice kept commanding me to hold back, be still, don't push too hard, be a nice guy, don't offend others. It was the voice of weakness I have been struggling with most of my life, the hidden voice of my mother saying she'll love me as long as I remain modest, sweet, and inoffensive. Perhaps it was not my mother, but someone else. Whoever it was, I remained divided between the voices of strength and weakness.

Onward and upward! I'm taking the reins of group leadership again. I will become their leader because I *need to*. I will assume command even if only ants follow. A leader needs followers. Suppose my customers decide *not* to follow me? It doesn't matter. Someone, something, is bound to, even if it is only the clouds, wind, or nurses from the Peloponnesian auxiliary. Followers will come. Just think *leadership*.

Apocalypse at Patmos: The Revelations of St. John

Three more days to go—or is it four? I'll be glad when this tour is over. I've had enough. Four days on cruise feel like four days at the Paramount Hotel in Parksville, New York, except my room at the Paramount Hotel is better.

Yesterday we visited Patmos, where St. John wrote his Revelations. A beautiful island. Lovely feeling to it. Spiritually, it is the best so far.

We visited the cave in which St. John wrote his book at age ninety-five. It is now part of a monastery. I bought books about Patmos and John's apocalyptic experience. Then I thought, what's the big deal about Revelations, anyway? I have revelations all the time. I write as clearly as John. Plus, my allusions are not as incomprehensible—except, of course, for my babble writings. There is nothing so strange or mysterious about Revelations, the New Testament, or even the Old Testament. Personal visits from God, visions of the apocalypse, are not uncommon. Experiencing them as I write, dance, play guitar, meet with folk dance groups on tour, or whatever, is always unforgettable. They feel brilliant, unique, overwhelming, and universal. I don't see much difference in quality between John's vision and my own.

Does that sound blasphemous? Does it demean the historic revelations and powerful visions of the apostles? Is it tainted with hubris? Perhaps. But upon further reflection, I have to answer: no. Simple acceptance of my spiritual visions is another step upward, an expansion of my power and strength. John's visions are similar in kind to my own—unique but at the same time universal.

I have them, too.

I am part of the Bible and the religious vision of ethical monotheism that began sweeping the Western world four thousand years ago.

At first, when I realized this in John's cave, I felt sad and lonely. If I have my own visions and they are similar to those of great men such as St. John, Moses, and Christ, to whom will I look for guidance? Who will lead *me?* The answer sounded loud and clear across the island of Patmos: only my own power and strength, given and filtered through me by God. No human being can give me any more than I have already. All the important revelations and apocalyptic visions already exists within myself. John had it, I have it, my tour members have it, everyone has it. It must only be rediscovered.

We visited the island of Rhodes this morning. First our tour bus drove to Lindos, a beautiful but tourist-packed town on Rhodes's eastern shore. We climbed through narrow streets, past shops selling jewelry, leather, rugs, T-shirts, tablecloths, blouses, souvlaki, and more; we passed restaurants and tavernas. Women selling tablecloths, blouses, and scarves were lined right up to the Lindos acropolis, a magnificent location for views, crusader protection, and more sales. I ended up buying two white blouses and asking our guide about the unique sounds in the Greek language. She wasn't so sure about them. Greek is the only language I know with so much frontal quality, lots of tongue near, on, and in front of the upper molars.

I wandered around the old town of Rhodes in the afternoon. Hundreds of shops. Tourism has invaded not only Rhodes but all of Greece. It's the 5th-century Persian invasion all over again. The quality of the merchandise is good. It's hard to find a Greek experience beyond sales, though. That's why our folk dance meeting at Paros is becoming more memorable with each passing day.

Tonight I had my first stab of sadness and excitement as I realized our tour was soon ending. Tomorrow is the last day of our cruise. The following day we'll disembark at Athens, spent a day there, then, on Saturday we'll take the plane back to New York. It's been a good tour. Still I'll be glad when it's over.

I found the exercise room, beauty shop, and massage room on the top deck of the ship. I looked at the massage table with longing. How wonderful it would be to get a massage! I deserve it and I'd love it. When I met the masseuse, a beautiful blonde from Scotland, I was afraid that, if she massaged me, my desire might expand beyond a massage. So I chickened out. I hate chickening out. Why can't I just appreciate the wonderful touches, pressing, and squeezing of my body? I've always liked the massages I've gotten, but they were given by men. I hate to fear a wonderful massage given to me by a beautiful woman. When I get back to Teaneck maybe I can "practice" massage by getting one. It's such a good reward for running a tour.

I've finished reading Alkis Raftis's, *The World of Greek Dance*. What did I learn? It is impossible to separate folk dancing from the traditions in which it is born, impossible to capture the flavor and "meaning" of folk dancing by removing it from the situations where it fulfills its purpose. People milling about, live musicians playing, drinks, smells, background noises, people sitting at a table eating, drinking, and talking, children playing in the corner, a few people dancing. The *atmosphere* in which the creation of the dance takes place is such an integral and important part of the dance itself; *Real folk dancing* cannot be separated from its environment. But that is precisely what I do in America, what every folk dance teacher does—separate the dance from the village and community in which it was born. It is impossible to do otherwise. We do not teach "real" folk dancing, but a new kind of creation: we teach folk dances based on folk dance situations. We teach a hybrid kind of dance. In reality, it is a new dance form. Folk dancing is the wrong word for it. We are creating our own unique community based on traditional dances of foreign countries.

This shows how important it is to educate myself by going on my folk tours. It's important for the dancers I teach as well. Nothing beats dancing with the natives of a foreign country. They teach you the way no teacher can.

This Greek tour has been an incredible education for me. It will take months to fathom all I have learned. But one thing I have learned is some *limits of improvisations* within the Greek folk dance forms. I can now make of my own additions, improvisations, and choreographies. Naturally, they cannot and will not be exactly from the village traditions. Rather, they will be creations from my own Teaneck village based on the knowledge I have of Greek dancing.

One of my tour quests is to see how much I can improvise within the bounds of a tradition.

Ecstasy: the True Nature of Man

We're leaving Athens in a few hours and flying back to New York.

This morning I learned how to say, "I would like to thank you," in Greek: *"Tha ithela na sas efharisto."* A very important phrase.

I failed to write one word yesterday. I certainly could have written one word—I can always write *one word*. But I "excused myself" by saying I was too busy. *No more excuses! Writing one word is one hundred percent better than writing no words.*

I got two good ideas talking to Peggy yesterday. One: have a sit-down *culture corner* before folk dance classes where I can teach about essentials such as rhythm, meter, geography with maps, and history. This is an earthquake idea, a new approach to folk dance teaching. Whether I'll ever do it remains to be seen. But it is in the same class of earthquake ideas as the classic guitar relaxation idea I heard from Joyce at the Amalia Hotel supper in Meteora.

Two: Peggy felt conflicted. She didn't want to buy presents in Greece for her friends and relatives, but if she didn't, they would be disappointed.

When you strip away life's problems, all the causes, explanations, and rationalizations for its joys and pains, the bottom-line revelation is *ecstasy*. Folk dancing with others is really *collective ecstasy*. The ecstatic experience teaches you the ultimate teaching. It reveals the essence of the world when God touches man. When you experience ecstasy, you end the search for the meaning of your existence.

But ecstasy can also be dangerous, even life-threatening. If you are not ready to receive it, it can destroy you. Thus, we protect ourselves against it. Defenses come in countless shapes and forms. Most common are negative defenses: "I am no good. I am selfish, I don't want to give people presents, I don't earn enough money, I earn too much money, I am a capitalist, a communist, a racist, a pervert, a womanizer, a non-womanizer, an extrovert, an introvert, too aggressive, too bashful, too greedy, I don't care about others, on and on. The explanations, reasons, and rationalizations to support your "I am no good" protective armor are as myriad and creative as man is myriad and creative. But their basis is always the same: an escape from our essential ecstatic nature, an attempt to run away from our higher reality by holding on to our ego with all its fears, desires, and frustrations, our little self living within the material bounds of the finite and temporal world.

Thus Peggy, a former teacher of classics in Brooklyn College, by focusing on the gifts she does not want to buy for her friends and relatives, has figured out a wonderfully creative way to dampen the joy and adventure of her Greek trip, a trip she wanted to take all her life.

It seems we will do almost anything to escape from our true nature.

Tourist Loss Syndrome and Writer's Melancholy

As I speak these words, I start feeling less lonely. I am suffering from tourist loss syndrome, a disease afflicting tour leaders at the end of their tours. All the excitement of running the tour, the responsibility of leadership, the kudos, complaints, and admiration received not only from your tour members, but from the agents, hotel managers, guides, bus drivers, and support staff I meet along the way, all the people who look to me as leader and symbol of authority, disappear at the end of a tour. Suddenly, I am sitting home alone, just another Teaneck resident remembering my tour.

It takes awhile to readjust to my new state. The first sign of readjustment is the return of my lovely writing depression. The word *depression* has a negative ring; it has been used and abused too much by our national psychotherapy industry.

I don't want to be cured of my depressions: they are my guides in negative feeling form. I need another word for depression. Perhaps *melancholy* is a better. How's *writer's melancholy?*

Walnut School

The Joyce Harris guitar approach is slowly being realized. As I played guitar this morning I decided *not* to perform at Walnut School in Cranford, to cancel my job and give up the $350.00 fee. I'm amazing at myself. First, giving up $350 is no sneeze; second, the irresponsibility of cancelling a performance is something I have never done in my life. I'm going to tell them I broke a finger. This cancellation signifies *the end of my guitar career as I know it*. It is probably the "final" step towards making the guitar "my own" again. How will I feel once I have decided never to perform again? Will I regain that lovely attitude I had when I first started playing guitar, or when I played violin in my room during high school? Then I loved playing, worshiped at the feet of soaring notes, divine melodies, and godlike performing artists. But for many years my interest in guitar performing has been going downhill. I cannot get out of the "professional musician trap" I have created for myself. Every time I play I see an audience. Then desire to please them invades my being. I cannot get back to the simple joy of playing "for myself." I'm hoping that canceling my Walnut School job will be a big step towards rebirth of performing enjoyment. The Joyce Harris vision. I've still got a few days to think about this. We'll see what happens.

Fear, Awe, and the Dawn of Creation: Folk Dancing at the JCC

Last night as I approached the Paramus Jewish Community Center for my Tuesday night folk dance class, fear and nausea hit me again. Here I was on top of the world, a successful Greek tour under my belt, a successful upcoming Bulgarian tour in August—thirty-five registrants—and, God-willing, if things go right, I'll even have lots of money when it's over; all these good things coming up and having been completed and yet, as I approached the JCC of Paramus, I feel that tremor of fear before the beginning of my folk dance class.

The old primordial terror churns my stomach. The strange, wild call originating deep in the cave of my soul, the dark recesses of an antique world I will never completely know but only graze with each creative effort. Fear rides my tail, and rightly so. I came to the JCC feeling rich, successful, and competent in the extreme, with hopes of my rising tour business rising even further, rosy coffers filling with beautiful money, financial worries disappearing, security and happiness up ahead. Still I'm just as nervous as ever before my folk dance class.

Does this nervousness say something about the creative process, and about life? Indeed, it does. It says in the realm of creativity, past accomplishments mean nothing. Nor do future hopes. Only the present reigns supreme. It shines in its omnipotence, shielded from past and future in a sheen of bright protective armor. It is challenging, fear-inspired, awe-driven, stomach-churning, soul-nourishing creativity, a smashing breakthrough to the towering creation of new, never-to-be-seen-again, never-to-be-forgotten-again celestial forms.

Each creation is a minor trauma. And well it should be. Whether it is tonight's folk dance class, next month's tour, this morning's writing, my guitar performance at Walnut School, leading folk dancing at a bar mitzvah, whatever. In awe and wonder, I stand at the doorway of each creation. Then I enter the haunting habit of the unknown where hairy screaming monsters, twisted serpents, and winged Avenging Furies steer my creative efforts across uncharted seas.

There is no rest. Success or failure mean nothing. Terrors will still pursue me, standing forever in the doorway of creation, barring entry to all those who refuse obeisance to their heart-piercing, terror-belching, soul-drenching, sweat-engulfing demands. Whenever I face them I face the hope that fruits from paradise will fall upon me. Indeed they will fall, but only after I have ploughed, planted, sweated through back-breaking labor, given my all to the garden; they will fall but only after I have fallen on my knees, spent and exhausted in the full-throated expansion of every kernel and screaming cell of my puny body and finite mind. Then and only then, as I lie breathless, prostrate, and beyond exhaustion, will the golden fruit of Paradise fall into my waiting, thirsty, beyond-panting, Tantalus-driven mouth.

There is no escape from the creative process. There is only denial. Even death is followed by rebirth. As the flesh clothes the body, it is, once again, visited by the wing-carriers of creation, those Avenging Furies flying straight out of Greek mythology, screaming in my ears, scraping out my eyes with sharp-scissored, poison claws, stuffing my throat with molten rock from the lava pits of volcanic Santorini. Then my brain is flooded with water from the Lethe River of Forgetfulness. I will forget the bombardments and catastrophes. I will start again; I will create anew.

The Lethe River of Forgetfulness conquers ancient enemies, washes away pains of self-destruction, dries old fears, and prepares the earth for the flood of the Fire River. Then, sparkling light floats in from a kabbalistic heaven, illuminating folk dancers dancing at the JCC of Paramus every Tuesday night.

"Slow" Stimulates My Imagination: A Source of Power and Strength

I am in mourning for my Greek tour. No more leadership, no more highs of Greece. There is no escape from this down, this energy low. All I can do is ride, feel, and experience it, and see where it leads. I do not lead my energy cycles. They lead me.

There is room in the world for many levels. On the highest level there is only One God. Beneath Him is the realm of many gods. These gods act as intermediaries between the Chief and man himself. Greek polytheism and Judaeo-Christian monotheism can co-exist, even thrive together.

I'm still reading the *Odyssey*. How slowly I read.

I have never been a fast reader. I always admired people who could read fast, speed readers. "Can you comprehend it, too?" I'd ask. Of course they could. They'd read straight down the middle of the page, gobbling up book after book in a few hours or less, and they remembered most if not all of what they read. Photographic minds. Power minds. They made me feel inferior.

I read slowly...very slowly. I comprehend slowly...very slowly. Is there strength in my reading? Is there a hidden power in reading slowly, and comprehending slowly?

Reading slowly frees my imagination. Slowly I sound out each word, picturing the event or image in my mind, I experience the words, the sounds, the images as I read. That's how they make a deep, lasting effect on me. Speed reading leaves me with little or no memory of what I've read; it also pressures me to finish my books, killing my enjoyment and cutting out my imagination. Thus, *slow reading is a source of power and strength*. It feeds my imagination.

Yesterday I picked up my Augustine Lo Prinzi guitar from Tom Doyle. He spend six months fixing the cracks and refinishing it, putting on twenty-seven coats of lacquer—or was it varnish? I started playing my guitar pieces on it and was amazed to see how easy they felt. Even the Alhambra and Leyenda: easy. Why? I was playing them *slowly*. No pressure to move my fingers fast, no pressure to fly and impress an invisible audience. Slow going, easy, freeing my imagination to create new rhythms, rubatos, fermatas, fast and slows, and more. Even Bach, my old nemesis, slowed down and became my friend.

How can I apply power and strength to my guitar? Slow playing. In one sense, it is a short jump. I have been playing under the same guitar ceiling for years. I have finally broken through the ceiling. It is a big break, but not a long distance. Only a few inches to move through the ceiling to the next floor. I have cracked the ceiling. My future playing will take place on the second floor.

Slow reading and slow guitar playing are goods-in-themselves. They open new doors of imagination.

I'm ready to admit it.

Soon I'll dine, then digest its delicious fruits.

The Kauke Bar Mitzvah

Doing the Kauke bar mitzvah yesterday was so tough. Why? It seems at bar mitzvahs I'm paid more for not dancing than dancing. Most of my time is spent waiting, trying to decide when to move into the crowd and start dancing. It's stop-start, stop—start, and it's exhausting. I'm constantly making decisions and judgements. No wonder I'm paid a lot. Plus, there is the ever-present feeling I'm not doing my job. What am I doing there anyway? Aren't people supposed to be dancing during the bar mitzvah? They're paying me all this money, and all I'm doing is sitting around waiting. It makes me feel guilty and useless. Then, when I do teach, I worry and wonder: will the people get up to dance? When I take a bar mitzvah job, I spend lots of time walking around at the edge of humiliation. At least the Hester Street band can keep playing—which they did. Whether people listened or not, they could choose to play. They played almost four hours. Quantitatively, it's easy to see they're worth the money. It's obvious they are doing their job: four hours of moving their fingers, filling the room with music and song.

What about me? That's another story. I just sit in the corner and wait. I ended up teaching a total of about twenty-five minutes. I did it in three sessions. The first lasted about six minutes. The band played a hora. Most people got up to dance. That was a good sign. They danced to the left, formed a second circle, lifted the bar mitzvah boy on a chair and carried him around the room. After that they lifted his mother, then his father, and his brother on the same chair and carried them around the room. I joined the circle, tried to dance unobtrusively and slowly, always watching for an opportunity to lead or continue doing nothing. I danced in "brake mode." Finally, I saw an opportunity and gently nudged the people forward and back into the circle. It was a gentle and subtle exercise of authority—and masterful, too. But it only lasted a few minutes, and that was that. Everyone sat down. Uncle Sammy then cut the challah.

Salad was served. I got a few people up, and we did about four Israeli dances, including Mayim and Zemer Atik. This was good; people enjoyed it. I even worked up a small sweat. At least I felt I was doing a job.

The main dish was served. When people finished eating, I tried to start more dancing. I went around the room encouraging people to join me, but not one got up. How discouraging, humiliating, frustrating—and, yes, enraging. What the hell was I doing there, anyway? How could I do my job if no one would even get up? The Hester Street Band kept playing. No problem for them. Only for me. Finally, I found two people who said they'd join me: Ron Hollander and his wife. We were about to start when Barbara Kauke, the woman who had hired me to do the bar mitzvah, asked me to try getting the children involved. Ron and I went outside to look but couldn't find them. That killed the dance mood. I wound up my engine and tried again. This time we found a few people to join us for the Miserlou. This grew into a medley of dances followed by an improvised dance routine, short but truly wonderful. It lasted only fifteen minutes, but it made the bar mitzvah for me. That was the end of the dancing for the afternoon. Even though it was only three o'clock and my job was supposed to last until four, I was finished.

The main problem with leading dancing at bar mitzvahs, weddings, is that I spend most of my time feeling so useless. Intellectually, I know it's not true. Even though a diamond is small everyone knows its value. When I teach dancing for a few minutes at a bar mitzvah, those few minutes often end up being the highlight of the bar mitzvah. People love it! I know this. Yet every time I lead the dancing, I have to start all over again—the same concerns and judgements, the same walking on the edges of humiliation, the same hopes that people will dance when I ask them. Doubts about mastering these situations never end. Past successes do not make success in the present. The present must be won anew whenever it appears. And it appears whenever I do a bar mitzvah.

That's why books like the Artist's Way are so frustrating. They make creation seem so easy, so possible. Just follow the few rules, exercises, and ideas laid down in the book, and your creative child will rise up in affirmation. But the torture of creation is impossible to conceive of and describe. It never ends; you never conquer it. Psychotherapy doesn't help. Neither do countless successes. The battlefield is always fresh and waiting for new blood; opponents wear new colors; yesterday's battles are history, surviving only as ghosts in a memory. The Trojan War must be fought daily. The Iliad comes alive every morning.

Leading my Group of Black Sea Coast Explorers

During the past few weeks I've been worrying about our Black Sea Coast Extension. What am I going to with all my people for six days?

I'm faced with a unique situation. Instead of the original three day extension—which would have been just the right amount of time to relax, do nothing, and snooze on the beaches, we have been "upgraded" to six days. I'm disappointed by the windfall of extra days at no extra pay. Of course, my tourists love it. Why not? Who wouldn't like three free days on the Black Sea? But I'd like less days. The way it stands now I'm taking a chance: six days at the Black Sea may be too much and that my customers will be bored.

I'll make the best of a "bad" situation.

What kind of adventures do I want to find on the Black Sea Coast?

I'll need a different relationship to my group. Instead of leading them, I'll include them in a partnership: we'll search for adventures together. I'll still be their leader, but I'll be leading a research team instead of a "tourist" group or "participants." The latter names are bland, passive, and abstract. Better to have our group of individual brains create an adventure of the Black Sea coast.

I like it. It's adventurous. I'll be making decisions for a group of adventurers.

I Need a New Business Vision

My jobs have ended. Slow time is here. I'm wallowing in the slag heaps of depression like a pig swirling and stewing in the narrow confines of my sty.

I haven't traveled this miserable, rainy, windswept route for many months. Before I stepped on the bus to this nearly forgotten land I had been rolling past sewage heaps and landfills, vomiting half-digested morsels of high cholesterol products. I've returned to that turnpike of misery. Enough! I'm sick of it.

The quiet two months are upon me.

I'm *too* relaxed. As Vivekananda says, I need to work, work, work. Work without concern for results; do my duty without concern for the future.

Religious gurus ask, How can I serve? But service is not my way. I can't stand the thought of serving others. How can I become a yogi or a saint when the thought of serving others repels me? Impossible, you say. Perhaps. My only hope is that it isn't true. Why do I want to become a saint or a yogi in the first place? I'll tell you why: because I've got nothing better to do. The idea of service to others is out. I only want to serve myself, even though I know that serving myself is the quickest way to misery and inward toenail growth. But "serving myself" isn't the right term. Serving my Self is what I'm talking about. I know about pushing my ego aside; I know about cornering my little self, stamping on it, crushing it underfoot with my heel. I know it's important to forget this little critter in order to recognize big Mr. Self. I know that, by serving Mr. Self, I'll be serving the small-fry humans as well. But my first thought has to be: Find Mr. Self. Look for his invisible form hidden behind the illusion of my body and the illusion of the material world which I create and recreate each day.

Tough stuff. Can I do it? I don't know. But I'm mad as hell, sick of moping around, wallowing in mud while I wait under heavy-gathering black clouds. No, no! It's not me anymore. Goodbye you miserable wretches, piss-laden clouds of intestinal vomit. I'm through with you. I'm moving on to vermin-crawling, wasp-filled action that bites, stings, and rolls across the tank-fields of today's dipped-in-future vision.

I'm stepping into concrete; I'm stiffening myself, donning the iron jacket, returning to the straight-and-narrow, one-Bulgarian-word-at-a-time lifestyle, the do, do, do, and do-do-do.

Forget results.

I've been thinking about thirty-seven Bulgaria tourists too long. I'm stuck, attached to the details of my tour and the money I will make. I'm forgetting about the big picture. Ninety-nine percent of my Bulgarian tour is now in God's hands. There's nothing more to do except send out tickets, take care of minor programming details, and wait for it all to happen. A day's work.

Not only is Bulgarian tour set up finished, but so are all my tours for the next season. Only details remain. Weekends and folk dance classes are set up for next season, too. I am set up, finished. No wonder I'm bored.

Mini-Business

Mind abhors a vacuum.

I am been faced with a mental vacuum: classes and tour work have ended; next year's schedule is completed. Here comes two months of "free time." It's driving me crazy.

If my mind is not kept busy it will eat me up.

I must pour myself into something during these two months to keep myself from going crazy. These are the only two months I have during the year where I can pull back and do something different.

Return to writing with a vengeance? Throw myself into it several hours a day? Prepare works for publication? Cull, gather a few good pieces from my journal, send them out to magazines?

I have been through these questions before. What is different now? I'm looking for a two-month mini-business. Do writing, preparing manuscripts for publication, and sending them to magazines fit the bill? They may.

INVENTIONS

On "Word Salads"

Barry and most of the class agrees that my word salads are incomprehensible. Most, but not all.

I consider the word salads I write to follow in the tradition of James Joyce's *Ulysses* and *Finnegan's Wake*. It is true I hate those books. Yet I write in their style. This is understandable. If I hate something with enough passion, I usually end up doing it.

Word salads may be a necessary evil for me, but the key word here is *necessary*. Writing them loosens me up. When I am in a certain mood, they are exactly what I need to write. This strange word-salad babble may descend from a divine source or ascend from mining pits beneath the earth or roll towards me from the trucks of Ambrose Buldo, our Teaneck garbage collector. But, no matter where they come from, I need them. More than that, I love writing them.

Why give up such a pleasure simply because it may be incomprehensible? Plus, there is always the chance it isn't. I may be knocking on a strange new door. Someday it may open; a wealth of beautiful writings and new ideas will pour out.

GOD

Standing Alone with your Values and God

God helps you stand alone without being lonely.

He was present in our family of atheists, communists, secularists, and socialists, but not in His traditional form. Traditional religious worship of any kind was anathema. The intelligentsia, the chosen secular communists, never worshipped in traditional religious forms. We flowered in anti-religious fields.

But God still lived in our home—only in disguise. He lived in the form of ethics, in the coming of the messiah, in the future communist millennium; He lived in our love of the arts, learning, and culture. Ours was a strange kind of atheistic worship in the form of passionate attachment to earthly ideals, passionate atheism, passionate communism, and even passionate hatred of God.

July–September 1995

WRITING

Writing in the White Whirlwind

Yesterday's production was, quantitatively, the most I've done in months. I spent almost the whole day on it. Beginning around seven in the morning, I wrote about five pages, took a break, came back, added two more, took another break, then returned and edited all the pages in two or three sittings. By the time I turned off my computer it was one-thirty in the afternoon.

As soon as I start writing, my depressions fade away.

They do when I play the guitar too, or run, do yoga, focus on Bulgarian, philosophy, or, for that matter, anything outside myself. Perhaps they are expressions of inertia, heaviness, the sleep factor. Perhaps I will never know *what* they are but will spend my hours trying to chase them away by creating new thoughts. In any case, they have caused me to write all these morning pages. I become my own master.

Still, I am ashamed of my depressions. Why can't I get rid of them? What's wrong with me? Why don't I go to a therapist, a psychologist, an analyst? They can "cure" me. Isn't it time I grew up and stopped being depressed? How long can I go on whining and complaining?

I suffer from the disease of creation, from having a mind that runs me wild, that leads me into dangerous holes filled with mud slides or inexplicable darknesses that no searchlight can penetrate.

Unfortunately, my mind is my master. I cannot control the damn thing. It is such an independent cuss, jumping first to valley, then to mountain, then scurrying off to worry about money. It is so damn *fickle*. No sooner do I have it nailed and focused on a project than it suddenly jumps ship and hydrofoils to another destination.

What is depression, after all, but a movement of the mind?

I try to keep it busy; if I don't, it keeps *itself* busy by plaguing me. Its wasps, hornets, and bees buzz in my head, sting me when I'm asleep, prod me with an unending whirr when I'm awake. Constant work and focus are the only answer to the wandering mind. If I struggle to focus until utterly exhausted, I get some relief, though not much. As soon as my energy returns, my mind starts wandering again.

Would I bother acting if I counted my blessings? Or would I simply fall asleep?

In Praise of Babylonian Babble Writing

Deep in the auricular caverns of my semi-demi-hemi circular canals I hear the deep-combing of boustrophedonous languages running to and fro, back and forth, up and down across the page. Why be a prisoner of sense when you can be part of the Non-Sense Work Release Program? Open the brain cells for a few moments. Total alphabet release!

It's nice to know that Judaism has lots to offer beyond the synagogue, where I'll probably never go. A direct hit by the Original Luminescence could become a daily occurrence. How will it happen? Focus on Hebrew letters or the boustrophedous writings of the ancient Greeks; write journal backwards. How nice to pull down a basket of words from *rakia* ceiling or yank the firmament chain, and see the pinata of treasures falling into my eager lap.

Shall I practice neck relaxation as I write? Let my unconscious percolate across pages useless to mankind. Babble on in Babylonian, Semi-Semitic, Neo-Babylonian, Psycho-Akkadian, Meso-Chaldian, or even Magyar Sumerian. Write it! It feels *so* good! Could anything be wrong? Bablyonian writing may be babble writing in modern disguise. I may be creating a language, incomprehensible to the modern listener, but in perfect communion with ancient Babylonian Jewish ancestors. Who can tell what I am writing? Just because I don't understand it, doesn't mean it is not understandable. Perhaps, because I don't understand it, it may even be better! That's something to think about.

I feel better this morning. There's nothing like a good write, followed by good yoga, good run, good meal, good company, and a good read.

This trip to Florida is turning out much better than I expected. Ellie's house is so peacefully decorated.

I read the *Colossus of Maroussi* yesterday, marveling at Henry Miller's wonderful use of language. "Why can't I write like him?" I asked. "Why can't I be as verbal, brilliant, funny, and wise?"

Explorers

I am reading *The Heavenly Ladder* by Edward Hoffman, a beautiful book about the kabbalah. He talks about Jacob's dream of a ladder with angels ascended and descended from heaven. God stood at the top. Jacob's ladder: the Jewish image of transcendence. Hoffman is the clearest spokesman for the kabbalah that I know. He made me recognize many characteristics in myself that might originate from being Jewish. I belong. It's nice to know.

My writing has been approaching truth like a hawk circling its prey. What truth? *Babble writing* truth. Although useless, it is *so much fun!* My imagination runs wild. I travel to foreign lands of thoughts and fantasy, mysterious verbal destinations on my inner globe I never knew existed. I am well beyond Miller, Hesse, and Gibran. I think of Ezra Pound. Now there's a writer I hardly know. I have only read a few incomprehensible lines of his *Cantos*. Yet for some reason, he pops into my head as a fine creator of babble writing. Strange. Ezra Pound stands for something. Perhaps it is insanity. Aspects of insanity attract me. There is much wisdom and daring in it. But danger, too. You're walking along the edge of a cliff. At any moment you can slip, lose your balance, and fall into the abyss. But there is also the possibility that, instead of following the laws of gravity and descending at rapid speed, you might defy natural law, rise, gain wings, and fly upward, mounting rung after rung of Jacob's ladder. By walking at the edge of the abyss and flirting with demons, you encourage chance meetings with heavenly angels, higher knowledge, and the wolf-face of wisdom itself. Explorers take risks. Otherwise they would just stay at home and drink coffee.

The Necessary Clean-up Work

Drained and empty with nothing to say. Only the habit of writing sits me down and forces me to write. Good. I've got to keep the engines greased. I'll feel miserable if I don't. I may end up throwing out ninety to a hundred percent, but at least I'm starting up the engine.

Edward Hoffman's *Heavenly Ladder* makes me reevaluate, not only Judaism, but also my relationship to it. There's more in Judaism that meets my eye. Edward Hoffman is opening my eyes.

Today's writing is a tribute to grit, determination, habit, and crawling on my belly through sewers and camouflaged landfills, hoping to come upon a fresh morsel to eat or a spark to warm me. Hell or heaven, I don't care. A spark, please, give me a spark! I want a celestial angel descending Jacob's ladder two rungs at a time to bang on my soul. "Wake up, wake up!" she'll cry. "Time for breakfast, but not in bed. Sit only at the computer, eat nutritious verbiage, burrow through time's tunnel to find deliverance and internal rewards."

I can't find my issues. I'm skirting around a blind spot, waiting catlike to pounce. But I don't know where my mouse is or what it looks like. This waiting period may last for days. There's no rushing a good meal.

I'm in a hiatus-hernia mood. Perhaps it's because it's clean-up time. Before I can move on I must edit the last fifty pages. Tomorrow and the next may be editing days, too. It's clean-up work before the next garden can be planted.

Search for a New Reason to Publish

I like beginnings and fresh starts. I'm back to the beginning again. Not a bad place to be, even though it feels awful.

Why am I lost this morning? Perhaps it has something to do with Alice Hamburg. She called me yesterday and wanted a personal conference. I went over to her house. It turned out she had headaches and thought I, as a yoga teacher, could help her. I told her I wasn't a yoga teacher but that I hired yoga teachers for our weekends. (I *have* been doing self-taught yoga for about thirty years.) We talked for awhile. Then her daughter came in and said she had found my *Handfuls of Air* in the library. Both of them liked my books. "I'd love to read more of them," Alice said. Her daughter did, too. I said that I didn't have time or interest in publishing them, that writing was really an inner exercise, that I'd be better off promoting and selling my tours, weekends, and dance classes because that's where I could make money. An old story. I "explained" all this under a cloud of self-denial surrounded by a mist of sadness. As I blabbered on about why I didn't promote my books and writings, I kept hearing the word "rationalization" ringing in my mind. How long am I going to make these excuses for myself? I asked. How long am I going to fool myself with this nonpublishing crap, hiding behind "higher forms," "art of writing," and "self-exploring journal?" When will I get so sick of hiding, so nauseated by my procrastination and lack of action that I will tackle the project of looking for agents, editors, and publishers? When will I face that world of selling, rejection, and wonderful potentiality?

I don't know. I've been asking this question for years. Is it a lack of confidence? Am I not ready to start sending out my work? Do I need a different approach and reason to do so?

Probably all of the above. Let's look at them. First, lack of confidence. I'm dealing with that every day and am slowly making progress on it. Second, as for "readiness," I'm as ready as I'll ever be. Plus, the recent entries in my *New Leaf Journal* are new and different enough to try sending them out. But so is the writing from my three previous books. I've been ready for years.

Third, I haven't wanted to face all the time, effort, work, and rejection that will come with trying to publish my writing. My rationalization—which, up to now I have believed—is that I should spend my time selling products and services that will make money. Money has been in the forefront of my mind for years. Paradoxically, I have been in debt for years, all in the service of trying to free myself from financial fears.

However, last September I concluded that financing debt and being in the stock market was no way to get rich. After many years of losing money, I finally realized the best way for me to make money was to work. I decided to invest my money in myself by promoting my business. I inaugurated that process last September. It was followed by my most successful tour year ever. Consequently, now I am out of debt and even have extra cash left over in my account. I haven't been in this kind of financial situation for years. I hope it means a new direction and life style.

I had always wanted to make money in order to support my unremunerative habits of writing, running, and study. Wealth was a means to an end, a way to buy my freedom. My search for it led to incredible financial losses. Had I simply put my money in the bank and forgotten about it, I might be able to retire on my income by now. But all that is over. Searching for wealth in itself does not work; the thought process is not good for me.

Perhaps I'm ready to explore a new road, to try selling my writing again.

But I can no longer say I want to publish to earn money or become famous. In publishing three books, money and fame have been stricken from my vocabulary. I can earn money from my business; fame, too.

What then will inspire me to travel the publication route?

If not for confidence, fame, or money, what?

I need another reason.

What is it?

Cure Myself by Giving It My All

I'm at the bottom this morning—and I like it. It feels as if all my worlds are falling apart. Everything of importance.

Why do I like falling apart? Why do I welcome the destruction of everything dear to me, of all the building blocks on my miracle schedule?

Destruction signifies a new beginning, my favorite place in the creative cycle. I hate endings. They signify, not only completion and success—which

I don't mind—but also an end of the energy cycle. I am left alone and triumphant, empty and successful, at the end of the road. A few moments of transient glory, a lion's roar of victory, shouting at the top of my lungs. Then the victory party is over, participants go home to bed, and I am left wondering: Now what?

Why do I need to find something new? "New" brings a burst of energy to my being; it puts me closer to heaven, one rung up on Jacob's Ladder. *I lose myself in purpose.*

I like that line. Imagine, I created it! A wise gift from heaven. I'd like to take credit for it, and will, but the most credit will come when I forget I invented it and lose myself in the purpose itself.

So I'm here at the bottom of the drainage bin, waiting for a signal, a sign, a direction, from above or within. I'll keep waiting. If you lie down with open mouth beneath the apple tree, eventually one of those golden ones is bound to fall in.

Meanwhile, I read a wonderful line from the Baal Shem Tov: "Forgetfulness is exile. Remembrance is redemption." Also one by his great-grandson, Rabbi Nachman of Bratislav: "Man includes all worlds. Nothing is beyond his ability." He also said that *our greatest barrier to self-development lies in our tendency to belittle ourselves.* I couldn't agree more.

My downward slide began Friday night at Goldens Bridge, when I taught my folk dancing with left foot pain. This in itself is nothing new. However, *I held back* when I taught. Teaching with the brakes on is the worst way to teach. It takes all the joy out of it. I hate it and myself for teaching that way.

Of course, I have the excuse: I must hold back in order to cure my foot. If I give it my all, I'll reinjure it and it will never get better. I also worry that it may get *worse,* that I'll put myself on the long downward slide to cripplehood. Soon, instead of simply hobbling, I won't be able to dance at all.

Are these realistic fears? Who can say? A doctor? Suppose nobody can; suppose I am an experiment of one and, in an experimental mode, must find all this out for myself. What role does the mind play, after all? The word "experimental" has, hidden with it, the word "mental." When I experi-ment, I experience experi-mentality, I start an adventure into the unknown world of mind.

Could it be possible that, if I give my all to folk dance teaching even with an injured left foot, I will release enough endorphins to not only make me forget my left foot pain, but *actually cure it?* That would indeed be a discovery!

Is my left foot pain resistence in disguise?

I am hovering between restraint and release. Which path should I take? My instinct, and certainly my desire, are to let loose and give my all to dance teaching, hoping my foot will cure itself on its own time.

Am I not my best doctor? I have an intuition that "someone living somewhere in me" knows the answer to my problem even better than my podiatrist, Dr. McNutly. Certainly this is my wish. Does wishing hint at some kind of inner truth? I'd like to think so.

"Never Again!"

It is amazing how pain in my heel has caused me to forgot all my learning and experience. What happened to power and strength? Forgotten. What about my views on leadership, folk dancing from the promontory at South Orange, business skills, tours skills, philosophic writings, meetings with the Higher Forces, transcendence, sparkle, wit, wisdom, and my miracle schedule? All forgotten. My heel pain has cleaned every positive thought from my brain.

I heard a story on the radio. The devil was having a yard sale. Among the items on the table was discouragement. It carried the highest price tag. When asked why, the devil answered, "It's one of my best tools!"

I know my heel pain has been caused by overuse. But on a higher level, the level of vision above the maze, what purpose does it serve? It shows how easy it is to forget my talents, transcendental experiences, meetings with the Higher Forces, and everything good I have done. The supreme moments in which I "saw" didn't last long, but they were memorable; they shaped my vision and gave meaning to everything I did.

The higher purpose of pain is to teach the importance of remembering.

I hear the cry, "Never again!" Of course my heel pain cannot be compared to the Holocaust. Yet, on another level, pain is pain. Levels are different. A fly's pain hurts, too. My heel pain, like the fly's, is worthy on a lesser level.

The Editor's Call: Remembrance

Suppose my heel pain is saying: Stop! You have been moving long enough. It is time to take stock of yourself, to review, reevaluate, and organize New Leaf. The editing process I have so long feared may have finally arrived. Naturally, it does not arrive without stabbing, wisdom-creating heel pain.

Slowly I am moving towards this gigantic editing project. The best way is to start making *categories*. During the last eighteen months I have written close to three thousand pages of New Leaf. I'll be spending the next years editing and organizing it.

Barry reminded me that editing is part of writing. I can still do the morning meditation writing I have always done. I'll keep the best of both worlds: morning writing meditations *and* New Leaf editing.

How will I find time for both? I don't know. But if it is important enough, I'll find the time.

Barry read my New Leaf in class. When I heard its beauty I nearly cried. Imagine, I did that! Where did I get such ideas from? Who was the "I" who "did it"? That's the "I" to remember, the great *neshamah* circling my brain, residing beyond my ego, the "I" of self-remembrance and connection to the divine.

Torah, Mishnah, and the Writing Process

I'm reading the *Mishnah* this morning. It is quite satisfying and says exactly what I want to say. It is even replacing my need to write.

This is an amazing and frightening experience.

I write to find myself. Lost and depressed are my two biggest motivators. I have to thank them; without them I would probably never write at all. They may not feel good, but I would otherwise lose the joy of writing. This speaks well for the so-called negative states; it shows their positive contributions.

Suppose, by studying Torah or Mishnah, I find the same fulfillment and joy I find in writing?

When I write I often find spark and inspiration; I reestablish myself in creation and in Creation. I start out lost and end up found. Since I have a short memory, I have to reestablish these contacts almost daily. This gives birth to my writing process.

But Torah and Mishnah are "found" books. They speak immediately, directly, and always about Creation and the Creator. They go directly to the heart of my lost state. In reading them, I am immediately found. Not only that, I become part of a long, incredible tradition of Jews who wake up every morning feeling lost, read Torah or Mishnah, and soon are found and whole again. It means I am not alone in this world. Others are lost, too. They have found the Torah method of self-discovery. By reading Torah and Mishnah, I can be part of it.

It's nice to belong to a tradition, to touch Creation every day, to have a Teaching as a place of refuge I can visit.

Studying Torah and Mishnah is a good-in-itself, *lish'mah*. Writing is a means to an end, the end being to reestablish myself in creation and in Creation. Are Torah and Mishnah also means to an end? Certainly the *act* of study Torah is a good-in-itself, but can you call the Torah and Mishnah good-in-themselves? After all, they are only books with words, the symbols of Creation but not its actuality. Only through the act of study, doing the deeds, thinking the thoughts, does the spirit of heaven descend into the human soul. Torah and Mishnah are means to an end. Only their study is an end-in-itself, a good-in-itself, a *lish'mah*.

Nevertheless, could anything ever replace my writing? Or is this a passing phase?

Is it guilt? Fear? Both?

Whatever it is, I must write something. I don't know why, but I must—whether writing is a haunting, a disease, a blessing, a whirlwind. Why bother questioning it? Obviously I was born to do it.

But even more important than writing is creation itself.

This morning I ran thirty miserable minutes, read Hebrew and Mishna, tried a touch of scales and "Alhambra" on the guitar, a few minutes of yoga, and some newspaper reading. But it was all hopeless. As I floated through these sundry disciplines without any discipline or direction, I realized I was simply using them to avoid writing. I dreamed up every excuse I knew, but avoidance was the bottom line.

When I try avoiding the writing process, it haunts and follows me like avenging furies. The only cure is to sit down at my computer and write. Why try to explain it? Trying to simply gives me more excuses for not writing. No matter how many times you explain why the sun comes up, it keeps rising every day. Writing is like that. I simply have to do it to clear my mind, touch my soul, and put the plate of purpose and direction before me.

It doesn't matter if I write about writing, the sun, moon, stars, why, where, when, or whom. It only matters that I write. Any excuse I use to make me do it is a good one. I need incentives and/or fences around my writing program. Sit at the computer; promise to write ten minutes. Anyone can do it. It's easy. It gets me started.

I have come back from Europe with two writing projects. First: daily pour out those health-filled words in my journal to cleanse and purify my body and mind; second: start organizing my journal writings, preparing them for publication. This is a giant project and may take years to complete. I'll add this burden to my writing schedule.

First I must put my *New Leaf Journal* into book form. Barry has suggested categories as a good way to start. I started writing categories before I left for Bulgaria. Now that I'm back and have a mountain of "free time" ahead of me, plus the commitment to organize and eventually publish my work, I can start further exploring the category idea. Maybe in the process I'll find something better. Or maybe categories is the best way to go. I don't know yet. . . but I'm starting down the path.

What will I call this vast work ahead of me? Paul Brunton calls his: *The Notebooks of Paul Brunton*. Mine could be *Journals of Jim Gold*, or *New Leaf Journal*, or some other title I haven't thought of yet. In any case, I'll start organizing it.

I'd also like to get back to guitar playing.

Lots to do. My main problem is: too many activities. Perhaps it's not a problem but a strength. I've always done many things in short bursts. That's my way.

Thinking "vast work ahead of me" pressures and even frightens me. Should I be "frightened?" Naw, I don't need fears, nervousness, anxieties, and worries to motivate me. Love of work is enough. Getting out of debt and putting some money in the bank has freed me from much anxiety. Both are symbols of a more stable life style. I no longer have to play the anxiety game; I no longer need the possibility of an upcoming catastrophes to motivate me.

Self-Editing New Leaf Journal as an Exercise in Self-Worth

If I don't believe in myself, who will?

Paradoxically, if I believe in myself, then everyone will.

Self-appreciation leads to better editing.

I realized this when I read the "On Language" entry in the last volume of my journal. How beautiful it was! How poetic, lilting, and wise! I wrote that beautiful piece over a year ago. I have enough personal distance from it to appreciate its worth. Imagine, I wrote it! Why is it so strange, incomprehensible, even impossible that I did? Where did I get such a low concept of self? I can go back into therapy for some clues, a few hidden home places that I have yet to uncover. But no matter how long I search for the "Why?", no matter how long I try to find the "Who, Where, and How?", I'll still never find a satisfactory answer. What is a satisfactory answer? One that dispels my illusion of an unworthy self. Perhaps the illusion is part of the human condition. Everyone fights this monster in his or her own way. Sometimes people climb to great heights and, for a short time, forget their unworthiness. But it often returns during quiet moments of reflection.

Editing my journal is an exercise in self-worth.

Remembering Reincarnation

Wouldn't it be strange if I had been a writer in a former life and I am now simply continuing the process? If this is true, what's the rush to write? If I don't finish now, I'll finish in the next life. Reincarnation takes the pressure off. Perhaps I was a musician in my former life. Or a runner, yogi, athlete, or linguist in former lives; perhaps an intellectual, rabbi, teacher, mystic, recluse, or monk. Why not? My inclinations hint at what I was. Could they have been handed down from former lives as memories of former existences?

Chronology Versus Subject

Yesterday I thought some more about organizing *New Leaf*. I'll put each Category on a separate disk.

Do time and date matter? If they do, then my Categories will be listed and organized in the chronological order of their creation. If time and date are not important—if subject is more important than chronology—then I can shift my entries into Categories whenever I write them. I could put today's writing in a Category right away!

I am thinking out loud. Part of me wants to put down words and fill up my four-page quota. Nonstop writing keeps my fingers moving, wakes me up, and keeps the juices flowing. I'm afraid to stop and think too much. I may stop the word flow and not be able to write at all. I want to keep the process going and hopefully, come up with some good ideas.

Chronology versus Subject: My feeling is to move in the direction of Subject. After all, in my journal, the content of my thoughts, experiences, and ideas is more important than when they occurred. I'm leaning towards Subject, away from Chronology.

If I choose Subject, then I will be radically altering my lifestyle, writing style, and organizational style. I like that. Dramatic, memorable, cataclysmic, a wonder in the making, a miracle about to happen—I love the thrill and power of such potential events. Give myself the luxury of accepting them. Sure, choosing Subject will radically alter my lifestyle. Instead of simply pounding out journal entry after journal entry and letting them simply sit there in chronological order—namely, no order at all—I'll now be taking charge of organizing on a daily basis. Every entry will have its place, and it will be put into that place on that day! If that isn't a radical lifestyle change, I don't know what is. Why deny the power of my vision? Why not admit that, every time I get an idea, not matter how small it may seem, it is a miracle in the making, a wonder appearing before my eyes. Imagine, an idea! How exciting! Amazing! Extraordinary! And it is my idea! Oh sure, it came from a distant place, funneled through my mind by a divine force. Still, when I die and look back on my life at my biggest regrets, one of them will be lack of faith in myself and my vision. God gave me talents. He intended that I use them to the best of my ability and even beyond. He intended that I contribute something to this world, improve the place, leave some better creations behind that weren't there before I entered. What better creations can I leave behind than the fruits of my talent? I can't take credit for my talent. That's a gift. But I sure can take responsibility for what I *do* with it, how I use it, view it, and deal with and accept my personal world-view vision.

I believe my best thoughts and ideas, the best of me, are expressed in my journal. Other people should read it; it would be good for them. Accept it. Love it. Admit you have the power and strength.

Writing. . . and Robert Graves

Robert Graves wrote always. I want to write always.

When Graves wrote, he detached himself, composed himself, put himself in order.

Me, too.

Travel and Writing

Last night, Sid, Phoebe, Bernice, and I went out to dinner. We talked about my Bulgarian tour. Phoebe and Sid thought it would be a good idea to send each client a little Bulgarian "fact sheet" with basic information such as weather, currency, geography, etc. I offered strong resistance. I don't want to write "information articles" that anyone can find by themselves in bookstores or libraries. But I realized the stronger my resistance, the stronger my attraction. Perhaps it is a good idea after all.

My first thought is to include such writing in my journal, make it part of my New Leaf Categories, a Travel Category. I might write about Bulgarian history, giving it a personal touch.

Writing on travel would be a challenge. But it may also be a passing fantasy.

Perhaps I should pay someone else to do it.

I hate to take time from my journal writing; it puts me in touch with angels and inspired representatives from Upstairs. God heads and god bodies leap from my pores, spark the surrounding atmosphere and make it vibrate. Why should I write travel articles when the best help I can give anyone is to write for myself?

Organizing New Leaf

I'm thinking about replacing the word "Categories" with the word "Books": The Book of Writing, Book of Folk Dance, Book of Travel, Book of Health, Book of Miscellaneous, Book of Babble, etc.

I may have many books hidden in my New Leaf Journal.

Writing, Meditation; Publication and Obscurity

My writing is not to be published until I am called.

What does that mean?

It is similar to my feeling about my guitar programs and performances. I have given them up. However, if someone calls, if a booking comes, if a school, club, organization, or whomever calls, then I will come. I will not turn away a calling; I will not turn away work; I will do the job.

You may ask, Who will call?

There is almost no chance of anyone calling me to publish my writing. Either they don't know I exist, or, if they do, they don't have the power or interest to publish me.

This may change someday.

I'm going to have to find writing happiness beyond publishing.

This may not be hard to accept. My pleasure comes from the act of writing. It's only when I sit back feeling neglected or blessed that I think others should read what I've written.

But something is stopping me.

Writing melts my depressions, frees me from my demons, opens up new mysterious worlds of worth, confidence, vision, power, and strength. Every day my guts, brains, and other hidden aspects of myself spill across the pages. That alone is enough. Why pressure myself to publish?

Word of mouth from humans or God may bring my writing to someone's attention. Until that happens I have to accept the possibility I may never be published. And that possibility is all right. Writing is a good-in-itself.

Can I accept obscurity?

To detach myself from the fruits of my labor, I must accept it.

Finished-Unfinished; Work-in-Progress: A Family Tradition, and a Legacy from Jim Lechay

Last night we visited my uncle Jim. He said all his paintings are "finished-unfinished."

He works them over for years, changing some, throwing others out, adding new elements, deleting old ones. His paintings, even when he sells them or after they are exhibited, are always subject to changes.

Each painting is a finished-unfinished work-in-progress.

I could look at my writing the same way. My eighty-eight-year-old Uncle Jim paints this way.

It is a family tradition.

LANGUAGES

Studying Language in the Morning

I woke up at four-thirty a.m., had coffee, and studied Bulgarian. It was slow going. I looked up word after word. But by the time I finished I had made progress. More important, I'd done something useful with that beautiful first hour in the morning.

How about making the first hour of the morning time language study time?

This would be a wonderful habit. True, I can find no use in studying Bulgarian or any other language. It won't increase my tour registration, make me wiser or more intelligent; it won't earn me more money or get me more respect. But it is, in itself, satisfying and fulfilling. It will do for me what writing does, mainly nothing. Nothing for the world, that is, but plenty for me. Studying language is an intellectual luxury similar to developing the skill of playing the violin. Language study is a good-in-itself, just as reading the newspaper in the morning is a misery, a waste-in-itself.

LIFE

God, Heel, and Death: A Visit to Florida

My brother-in-law, Walter, died in his sleep a week ago. He was Ellie's fourth husband. They lived in Ocala, Florida. We are visiting them over the Fourth of July Weekend.

I hardly knew Walter. Bernice hardly ever sees her sister. Yet family ties run deep. Bernice was one of the first people Ellie called after he died.

I taught folk dancing at Goldens Bridge Saturday night. Opening night of the summer season was great, some of the best dancing I've done in ages. A young crowd; many knew how to dance. I taught *Hora Jerusalayem* and *Kopanitza*. They learned the steps quickly, and we danced with joy and abandon. What fun!

At the end of the evening my left heel hurt. I'm not quite sure what this problem is. It began when I increased my squat exercises a few months ago and added the forward hamstring stretches. The pain started slowly over a period of weeks. I handled it by denying it. Now it's gotten worse.

Today it hurts so much I'll have to start paying attention. Is it a heel spur? Something else? I'll see what Dr. McNutly thinks. It's going to take a while to cure it, probably six months to a year. I'll have to "watch it," concentrate my mind more carefully on it when I dance, walk, or run.

I am writing about my heel to heal myself. Will writing help? It always does.

Why does my heel bother me more today than other days? Could it be this trip to Florida? I am pissed that Walter died. What miserable timing. I have to drop the important things of my life and visit Ellie in Ocala. This whole death thing is a pain in the ass! Why do people bother dying, anyway? I get home from teaching dancing at Goldens Bridge one in the morning, stretch, eat a bit, listen to the radio, go to bed two-thirty a.m., get up at five, dress, pack, wash, and catch the seven-thirty flight from Newark to Orlando and stay at Ellie's house in Ocala for two nights. I even believe in this obligation. It is important, not only that Bernice visit her sister, but that I go with her for moral support. Still, it's a pain in the ass.

I am focusing my fear of death on heel pain, transmuting my loathing of life's ending, transfiguring the sorrow that someday everything I love will be taken away from me. In this world, you can hold on to nothing. Death is here again. Its visit is to remind me how ultimately unimportant are ninety-nine percent of my ideas, worries, attractions, goals, desires, and fears. The preacher was right about vanity. All the effort I put into my work will ultimately amount to nothing. They'll be washed away and purified by death. The grim reaper is the ultimate pain in the ass.

The only cure is to stay in touch with the higher forces, to see Magnificence everywhere and in everything. Since this is true, why not see Magnificence in my left heel pain? Hasn't this pain been sent to me to as a teacher? Through the pain in my heel I may learn something about the universe and its forces. No pain is useless; it is only painful.

As I limp from living room to kitchen to bathroom and back to bed, I might try learning from my pain instead of cursing it.

Well, I have no choice. The pain is not going away. Neither is death. Or God. Perhaps the four of us can work together on this problem.

Remembering: My Search for Self Is over

After graduating from college and moving to Greenwich Village, my search for self began. Before that I didn't even know what a "self" was.

I had no problem with self in elementary and high school. I simply played baseball, basketball, rolled in the dirt, soaked myself at the water fountain, and squashed ants. During high school I discovered the glories of playing violin and orchestral conducting. "Self" was never my concern. My parents took care of it.

But after graduating college I said good-bye to my parents. It was the adult thing to do. I shouldn't get my identity from them, anyway. Rather, I must find it within me, in the—you guessed it—"self."

The search began.

What was my lost self? Where was it hiding?

In truth, I never "lost" anything. I just kept forgetting. My "self" has made appearances throughout my life, peeking in and out from behind a cloud, pointing out a beauty spot before disappearing behind another cloud. This shining essence has been with me since I've been born. I just never realized what it was called.

It first appeared to me in the bedroom where I practiced my violin. Often it came on Saturday morning. I remember warming up with scales and arpeggios before moving to the big pieces, the Mendelssohns, Lalos, Wienawskis, Bruchs, Bachs, and Vivaldis. During these practice sessions the sun would shine through the window behind me, flooding, not only the pages on my music stand, but all of my bedroom, with light. An incredible sense of well-being came over me. How glorious! My fingers flew, the pieces sang; I conquered space and time; the sonatas and concertos danced under my fingers. Little did I realize *this* was the famous "self," the very essence appearing before my eyes. I just bathed myself in the "Wow, this is glorious!" and left it at that.

In Greenwich Village, I hoped to become a writer. Thus began many years traveling the up-down, elation-depression highway. In the search to find myself, I paradoxically forgot those stellar violin-playing moments.

You can search for years, wait for years, but cannot rush the unfolding of the self. At the proper time, it will emerge. No sooner, no later. You just have to work patiently, endlessly, hoping some day your time will come. It usually does. Only you can't tell when it will be.

Last year, when I found and followed my miracle schedule, I discovered the self that knew what was best for me. Often it had spoken to me in the past, but I hadn't had the courage or experience to listen.

This gut realization signifies that I am no longer moving on a path *towards* something. I am already *there*. My problem is not finding a new light but remembering the old one.

No more reading books to find my life plan or searching for teachers to show my direction. Books and teachers are pleasant—but secondary. I know the truth. I only have to admit it and remember it. It's a big "only." But I'm ready to do it.

It's not a question of hubris. It's not even that new. It's a matter of recognizing that, all my life, I have entertained visitations from forms of higher truth. But I was afraid of them. I sensed they would force me to abandon my ego, give up my addiction to the up-down, elation-depression cycle. I labored under the illusion I needed pain to spur me on, force me to work and function in the world. I feared that, if I accepted the shining truth within me, the material world would become irrelevant. I would retreat into the world of "crazies," sitting in sublime passivity, meditating on wonders. Yes, I was truly afraid of going crazy. This was a primal fear.

The truth was simply too powerful for me to take.

But I am stronger now. My celestial visions are tempered with the work ethic. My business keeps me anchored to the earth. I will not fly away or retreat to a monastery or mountain cave. Evidently, I am not the type to leave the world. I am a doer. I must move. I am a typical karma yogi living in the world of doing, the Hebrew *assiyah*. This is nice to know. Now I can be crazy and grounded at the same time. Perhaps that is why I can now afford to recognize, welcome, and live with my truth.

My job is to *remember*, to bring my truth with me in deed and shining eyes.

I am not moving horizontally but upward. Sideward movements will no longer get me anywhere. Vertically is the way to go—up Jacob's ladder, one rung at a time. Once you start climbing, the search is over.

Self-Discipline and Eating Out

I am disgusted with my lack of self-discipline. I finished off a heavy meal at the Binghamton with a cup of espresso and couldn't sleep last night. I went to bed about three-thirty a.m. and awoke this morning in a foul mood.

I am still in one. Why? I'm mad at myself for my lack of eating control at dinner. I wasn't even that hungry in the first place, yet I ordered the biggest meal possible, along with dessert. I left the table stuffed. The result is self-disgust, anger, and a miserable, sleepless night.

I keep thinking of the Eubie diet, how good I feel when I follow it, and how miserable when I don't.

What I did at the Binghamton was a prime example of *not* following it.

I'd like to learn and practice different dining habits. That's what I'm mad at. If I want to feel good, watch out for my tendency towards overindulgence.

Spark

To spark or not to spark: That is the question.

Spark makes my day worthwhile. If it is extinguished, so am I.

This morning I rolled out of bed in an uninspired, flat, state. I can find many reasons why. But reasons are not important. I can always find reasons to feel miserable, depressed, flat, uninspired—reasons why life is not worthwhile.

Part of me enjoys a low state; it shows creativity, the ability to create my own misery.

The only cure for the low is the *tikkun* spark of restoration, the eternal, universal, God-created spark that filled the Zohar with beautiful verbal music and clean-wiped the faces of the 16th-century Safed saints. It rescues and raises me from morning doldrums and puts daily life on an exalted plane.

I read Jewish history this morning, about the Commonwealths from 586 B.C. to 70 A.D., the prophets, philosophers, and saints, the warriors and statesmen. These facts left me flat. No connection; no spark. How do these ancient events touch my life? I thought. Why is history so important after all? What effect does it have on my life today? How wonderful it would be if I could see a connection between myself and historical events, the rise and fall of the ancient Judean state, myself and my group, myself as an ontogeny recapitulating phylogeny.

"God chose the Judeans as His instrument in a great human experiment." That's what I read this morning. I like the phrase. If God chose the Judeans, that means He also chose me. I am part of the experiment. Why do I like the phrase so much?

The only connection I can see between myself and such a phrase is through spark. The spark is my connection to the Jews of historic Judea, the Age of the Patriarchs, Abraham, Isaac, and Jacob; the First Commonwealth, from 1200 B.C. to the Temple destruction in 586 B.C.; the Second Commonwealth, the final Temple destruction by the Romans in 70 A.D.; the *Tannaim,* Judah *ha Nasi*—the Prince—and his writing of the Mishnah, Palestinian Jews adding their Gemara, Babylonian Jews in Parthia and Persia developing the Talmud, Jews of the European Middle Ages, Eastern European Jewry, and present post-Enlightenment Jews. Only spark holds these historical periods together and gives them meaning.

Every morning, I try to resurrect my spark. There is nothing else for me to do. Without it, I am a hollow corpse, with it a vibrant being, inspired, functioning, useful, and filled with a fervent desire to live.

Wearing New Shoes

My heel pain hangs on and on. Saturday it got worse. Monday saw slight improvement, but then I started Russian dancing and *bango*, back to square one. It's killing my dancing pleasure, to say nothing of the wonderful "improvements" I made in squats and running.

How about applying some of the God-sends-pain-in-order-to teach-philosophy to myself? What has the Creator taught me so far?

First, watch out for "self-improvement." Ninety-eight percent of my injuries have come from attempts at self-improvement. Invariably I go too far. I try too hard, and the overuse syndrome kicks in, causing injury. Sometimes the injuries last days, sometimes months. This heel injury feels like a "months" injury.

I am prone to psychosomatic ailments. Could hidden fears be feeding my heel pain? I'd like to think so. If it's true, the right psychological insight can make it disappear immediately.

Could pre-Bulgarian tour anxiety be feeding my heel pain? We have forty-one people on this tour, yet I am remarkably "anxiety free." Forty-one is a record! Can I handle it? Will things go well? Have my fears disappeared in a new revitalized self-confidence? Or have they been transplanted into my left heel?

I'm worried about not being worried. In the past, worry pushed me to prepare every detail. Now I'm still preparing every detail, but I'm not worried. Can I handle things if I don't worry?

Does my heel pain reflect and "express" this "worry-free" state of mind? Am I fooling myself?

No. There is a qualitative difference in this tour approach. My new power and strength are reflected in my approach to this Bulgarian tour.

I have to get used to a new self-image. It's like putting on a new pair of shoes. Breaking them in creates temporary foot pain. But once they are broken in, they'll feel comfortable and I'll walk even better.

Heel pain is my old crippling voice of worn-out habits and ancient fears. That voice, although dying, still has some fight in it. It almost speaks from beyond the grave, a fading monument to a once-powerful civilization of personal fear.

My new voice is rising strong and confident in my back yard. Old and new voices are meeting on the Bulgarian Tour battleground. There they will fight for control of my soul. Old voice is armed with heel pain, new voice with confidence, power, and strength. Old voice won't give up without a fight. My Bulgarian tour is the first battle.

This morning my body parts all seem to be falling apart. My heel hasn't gotten better; yesterday I got a stiff neck. I hate functioning like this, but what can I do? Minor afflictions are visiting me for a reason—but I don't know what it is yet.

I'm tired of pain. On my upcoming Bulgarian tour, we'll be traveling on two buses. That's a new one for me, but it's all an *organizational* problem. That's what I should study. But I even know organization. The money is rolling in, too. What is left to do? My dreams have been realized: money in the bank, a successful upcoming tour; my folk dance jobs are paying a bit more; yesterday even my stocks went up.

I am a success. Usually success depresses me. But I can't even say that anymore. I've said it so often I'm getting bored with it. The best way to describe my state is somewhere between bewilderment, wonder, stuck, and semi-comatose. Actually, I wish I *was* depressed. A deep, satisfying depression might inspire me to find something new. But since I'm not depressed—or even elated—I don't know what to do. Perhaps I'm approaching that limbo state which occurs just before a tour begins.

Follow the Commandments, Or Else!

Another day. Busy, busy. No time to write. I have myriad excuses to keep me from my computer. The main one is: no time. How easy it is to start the slow, soft descent into oblivion, to slide down the trail to the bottom of the abyss. That's why I have to build tough fences around my personal Torah, to protect my interests by writing every day even though some days it absolutely kills me. I've followed every excuse I can think of, tried everything I can to avoid writing. The upcoming Bulgarian tour fills my mind with countless details, gives me endless reasons why I can't and shouldn't write. No time, no time! I can excuse myself forever. Straying, slipping, forgetting the straight and narrow writing path is so easy. Before I know it, hours have slipped into days and I've done nothing. It happens in other areas, too. I found my personal Torah, the rule book of my life, in my personal mitzvah miracle schedule. The tablets were handed down to me in my Teaneck-Mount Sinai living room. Fulfill their dictates, and I am happy; forget them, and I am miserable. There is also the in-between dribbling state where I fill up my time with useless activities, when I watch the sandy grains of my life sift through the hourglass and disappear into nothingness.

One day my Maker will ask: "What have you done with your life? Have you followed my commandments? Have you followed *your* commandments?" What will I answer? I followed a few some of the time? The fence around my personal Torah had lots of holes in it? The world marched in, stole my time, then drowned me in an ocean of trivia? Eventually I *forgot* about commandments and wasted precious moments eating pizza and drinking Coke?

It's hard keeping the fence maintained.

Be wise, study, and fear God. I like that. What does "fear God" mean? Tremble in awe and wonder before the miracle of this world; tremble at the difficulty of following the commandments. Laws have been handed down to me; they are planted so deeply in my brain that they form the core of my being. I am an ontological Torah, its personal truth imbedded in the mud of my cerebral hemispheres. I'd better follow my commandments. . . or else!

Heel Spur

It is amazing how a heel spur can destroy hope, confidence, even optimism.

Dr. McNutly said I have two heel spurs, one in each heel. Only the left one bothers me. I can't run or do squats; I can't even dance. Well, I can *do* them, but Dr. McNutly says they'll only make my heel worse. It takes about a year for a heel spur to get cured. I'll have to operate with the brakes on for a year. Depressing, indeed.

Prime Motivators

Here's a good line from a commentary on the *Pirkei Avot*: "Preparation to learn Torah includes willingness to forego luxuries and comforts which often deter one from study. . . .

He must free himself from every concern that could interfere with his Torah study, such as exaggerated worry about health or finances."

I cannot agree more!

Slow Yoga: Exercise to the Sun!

Slowly, listening to every nuance of sound, feeling the slightest finger movements even down to the vibrations and flow of red blood corpuscles from brain through body and into the fingers: A good meditation between morning Bulgarian and writing.

Who Am I?

When I fall asleep at night I have no trouble remembering who I am.

When I am snoozing, snoring, or sleeping peacefully through the night, dreaming only of darkness or light, I have no trouble remembering who I am.

It is only when I wake up that I can't remembering. Who am I, anyway? Have I forgotten? Or did I simply never know? Hard to say. But there is no doubt sleep is free of identity problems whereas my waking state is filled with self-searching. When I wake up I immediately start looking for an identity. Am I a folk dance teacher, tour leader, guitarist, writer, runner, Jew, yogi, father, husband? Am I Jim Gold, James Gold, James R. Gold, Jimenez del Oro, Sylvan Woods, or any other of the characters I invent? Am I the only one present in my journal, the upbeat "I" teaching my dance class, the depressed miserable "I" when my stocks go down? Am I all these identities or none of them?

How did I discover this identity—or lack of identity? I took my nap this afternoon and I woke up after fifteen minutes. Instead of returning to my desk, I turned over and slept another half hour. Towards the end of my sleep I tossed and turned, half-dreaming about who I would or wouldn't be when I woke up. When I finally got up, I still couldn't figure out who I was. I panicked. Frantically, I started searching my mind: Who am I? Who was I? Who will I be? What will the "who am I" and "who was I" do when I find out who they are? Are there phone calls to make, letters to answer, bills to pay, contacts to contact, customers to track down? My mind centered on business and money making, that is, thoughts of security. But I sensed that money and business would not solve my problem. I was merely escaping in my waking state, clinging to the debris of transient forms, slipping slowly into the abyss of nothingness where all my identities eventually drain. I was going down with them, sliding into oblivion. I caught any identity I could find to save myself: folk dance teacher, tour leader, businessman, artist, it didn't matter as long as I had something. Without an identity to hold onto, I felt like nothing.

And truly, while I slept, I *was* nothing. My ego had vanished. I dwelt in the sublime state of universal bliss. I abandoned the torturous creations of my ego. I dwelt, ever so briefly, in that sweet state.

Too bad I have to fall asleep to do it. Is it possible to be egoless while awake? I'd love to give it a try. But even if I success, I can't stay egoless too long. I don't have the skills yet.

Did I say "yet?" Do I have the hope that someday I may, through greater understanding, stay longer? Hours, days, weeks, years? Do I have to die to stay there forever? Does the concept of "forever" disappear when you are egoless? Can I find it while I am still on earth? If I do, will it matter much whether I am alive or dead? After all, "alive" or "dead" are mental concepts created by the ego. If I have no ego, if I can dwell in the eternal and infinite, and can achieve what the Tibetans call the "wisdom of egolessness," will it matter much whether my body and mind are around?

Answers are easy.

Practice is difficult.

A Grasping Attitude

How can I simplify my life?

My first thoughts were: cut back. Then I realized my life is simple enough. I am down to the bare bones already. I can think of no better way to live than the way I am living now. I like my life style.

So why am I dissatisfied? Why am I searching for something better? Why do I still want to "improve?"

A grasping attitude is the reason for unhappiness.

How can I conquer grasping attitude? By *simplifying my mind*.

Easier said than done. My mind is imprisoned in a cell of hope.

Cosmic Manager

I want a partnership with God.

I'll give Him my folk dance groups, tours, weekends, guitar programs, writing, yoga, running, reading, family, friends, house, car, books, windows, parking lot, thoughts, intuitions, reasons, rationalizations, plans, hopes, winnings, losings, angers, hurts, rages, passions, loves, desires, rejections, anticipations, fears.

If I do this, I'll be moving in the right direction. And that right direction is nowhere. I have gone everywhere already. It has led me to the center of the world, which is the Great Nowhere, the Cosmic Vacuum, the Mystic Gap.

Where else is there to go? I've visited all the places I need to visit, heard the sounds, seen the sights, felt the feelings. I am tired of these transient visions.

It is time to step out of prison. I want a conference with the Cosmic Manager.

If I tell others about this, they'll say I'm rejecting Marxism and dialectical materialism. They're right. When I grew up, all "thinking" people were atheists, Marxists, communists, socialists, or true believers in the "science" of dialectical materialism. Anyone who thought otherwise was dismissed as a fool. Such deluded religious simpletons were simply not worth the bother. "Spiritual" was not part of our vocabulary. Anyone using such a word was one step away from the insane asylum.

I stayed quiet, hiding in my room, playing my violin and secretly soaring to indescribable heights, reaching planes of existence I could never verbalize or discuss with anyone. Intuitively, I knew if I tried, an unsympathetic audience would dump mud on my vision. I would be crushed. Also I feared verbalizing these experiences would diminish them.

Poetry and beauty are my entrances to the divine. Original turns of phrases rushing out of the Nowhere Pool are essences breathing juice into my life.

I often forget about the hidden fortress within. Scattered and transient thoughts militate against remembrance of Unity. Beneath the daily drama of life One Stream flows.

The new and the old, tomorrows and yesterdays, blend into the Stream.

I sit on my kitchen chair witnessing the spectacle. I write to remember it. Witness, Spectator, One. A trinity of words. Descriptions of the indescribable.

MONEY AND ITS BRETHREN

Calm

A calm has come over me.

Hardly a check has come in the mail, or a registration for weekends, tours, or dance classes.

The phone has not rung.

September business has been dead.

I keep waiting for a rush of anxiety to flood my being, waiting for the fear-ridden, anxiety-prone, worry-worry to return. But it doesn't. . . and hasn't. The calm remains.

Are all my readings and thoughts about yoga, meditation, universal self, God, Judaism, Witness, reincarnation, Higher Powers, beginning to pay off?

Karl's publicity arrived in the mail. Usually, when I read about his tours, weekends, and dance classes, I get sick with jealousy. But this time, I felt weary. . .and calm.

BUSINESS

A New Vision of Business

This summer I've added business to my miracle schedule. That in itself is a miracle.

Lifetime conflicts about business suddenly slipped away. How did this happen? Why? I don't know. Perhaps it was simply a case of fruit ripening, ready to fall.

Gradually, I have stepped away from seeing business as a means to an end of making money and producing wealth. I never liked the means-to-an-end philosophy. It always felt completely wrong. I've never been able to put my finger on why. Perhaps the haunting fear of financial ruin helped cloud my vision. Financial doubts have plagued me since marriage. Even periods of financial success didn't help. I needed grace from above to cancel my worries.

Grace has come in two stages: first, the "Somehow I'll make it" philosophy; second, the gut-wrenching realization that *business is a meditation on service*.

This idea is not new. I've been reading about it for years. But suddenly, this week, for whatever reason, *I believed it*.

What an incredible blessing! I can only fall on my knees and thank the higher powers. Imagine, "relaxing" in business by finding the same beauty, harmony, and peace there that I find in music, writing, yoga, dancing, and studies. If I forget about my money, bank accounts, and bills, and *focus on serving others*, not only do I free myself of financial worries, but I feel a peace inside as well. Business becomes *an instrument,* a means to an end. It is like a guitar, writing keyboard, or the body with which I dance—a tool of service to others.

When I serve others, I forget my ego.

Naturally, in serving others I serve myself. No one profits greater than I.

I've spent the past few days on the phone with Norma, discussing her Black Sea Coast extension. She was grateful that I took the time to "think it through on the phone" with her. What a beautiful, peaceful, fulfilling feeling it gave me. My service to her made me happy. Even though I knew I'd lose money if she cancelled her Black Sea Coast extension, I still gave her the pros and cons. I even offered to share the expenses of the extra night she'd have to stay in a New York hotel to make her return plane connections to Atlanta. Finally, after many calls and much thought, she decided to cancel. Fine. She was happy with her decision. By serving her, I had not only helped her but won a new customer for future tours.

If I think of service to others, money will come by itself. Service is an orange tree; money, my orange. Plant the tree, the fruit will grow.

Arlene had a cancerous kidney removed. She's okay at present although in mucho pain.

What is the future for Arlene—and for me? Will she live? Will she continue doing PR work? Will she moved to Florida next year?

In the future, I will lose Arlene either through cancer, sickness, or to Florida. Through all our clashes in personal style, now that I'm threatened with losing her, I see how important she has been. Slowly her press releases have had their effect. So have her brochures, publicity, PR campaigns, and private consultations. Arlene and I have the same attitude about people. She has been a business ear for me.

If I lose her, I'm losing my right-hand business woman. Losing her to cancer—if that happens—is even more depressing. But what can I do? At this point, weeping and whining only cut my power and strength. They won't help her either. I'd better expect nothing, assume the worst, and move ahead. I'll plan my fall schedule and future without her. Then, if she improves and can still work for me, all the better.

Arlene's PR has helped make our Russian Dance Class with Alexander Antchoutine a big success. It brought in Dionysius Bellas, a Greek folk dance teacher who'll give us a Greek dance workshop in January. Tuesday nights have drawn big crowds. My 1996 tours are ninety percent in place. Business is good and in order.

Yesterday, Marilyn said, "You gained some weight." I was shocked. Me? I never gain weight. But I knew it was true. What bothered me was that someone else would *notice* it. I told her I'd gained five pounds and couldn't seem to get rid of it. As we spoke, I realized my weight gain began with my successful Bulgarian tour registrations after I got back from Greece about two months ago. Money rolling in has softened my financial fears and, with them, the seething worry that always churns my stomach. That churning always created weight stability; worry burned off all the extra calories I ingested. Now I'm not worried. Instead, a heavy, bloated feeling has invaded my stomach and perhaps even my brain. It manifests itself in extra eating and extra weight. Even though I am glad to have a successful tour, I'm not happy with my "satisfied" condition. A fat stomach and a fat body signify a fat mind whose ideas are also fat. I've arrived at the top of the Fat Mountain with its twin peaks of Success and Saturation. I am full. I can't say it is a wonderful feeling. It's more like a pig who has found some fine mud to roll in. For a pig, I'm happy; for a human being. . . well, not so great.

Success is like a shooting star: a few moments of stellar glory, then darkness. I'm in the darkness now, wallowing in mud and the murky waters of a hidden new project. What could that new project be? I want it to fill me with biblical awe, reverence, and fear.

I want to worship something greater than myself.

I want something larger and everlasting to consume me.

Nervousness Blocks Mounting Excitement

My Bulgarian tour begins Friday. I'm nervous.

But nervousness, emotional upheaval, and conflict are motivators. Without them I might not even bother running a tour. So I'd like to thank my sleepless nights, churning stomach and periodic headaches. While I'm at it, I'll even thank my heel spur and the pain in my neck.

Pains are often blessings in disguise, secret messages from above, hidden teachings clothed in the removable garb of annoyance.

The only things left are nervousness and motivation. Nervousness blocks mounting excitement. Wow, what a positive and beautiful explanation of stage fright! Pre-tour anxiety is motivation in disguise.

Bulgarian Beginnings

I'm having a great time.

Great nights of dancing. I can't describe what we're doing, but so far the trip has turned out to be so much better than I expected. I can't get over the people and how I'm handling them.

Something qualitative has changed. Could it be wrapped up in the wonderful way I am handling the Linsk-Klauss phenomenon? They are symbols of what used to be my worst tour fears. Debbie is a whirlwind of misery and trouble. Yet I am even beginning to like her a little. She makes me laugh.

What new ideas are being born? Perhaps we should travel with dancers and musicians on the bus. Or return to Bulgaria more often. Or aim to get better tourists—like the ones on this tour. Most of them are folk dancers. I know them. But I have little control over who will register for a tour.

Perhaps I'm just becoming a better tour leader. Now *that* is something I have control over. I get lots of personal satisfaction from self-improvement. I handle people and situations much better now; I can foresee problems and act to prevent or forestall them almost immediately. I'm more experienced.

I'm sitting in my Sandanski Hotel room, writing in the late afternoon Bulgarian heat. I'm tired because I only had two hours of sleep last night.

Why? Ognian Alexiev, our traveling choreographer, gave me a Bulgarian costume worth at least six hundred dollars. Before that he had given us our first Bulgarian dance workshop in a giant conference room at the Sandanski Hotel. The room was filled with an enormous table. We squeezed in nevertheless and had a good evening of dancing with Ognian, his partner, Tanya, and their gaida and accordion player, Bobi. All three of them are traveling with us. On our bus I sit in front next to Ognian, who doesn't speak any English. I break my head trying to speak Bulgarian with him. It's lots of pressure on me, but I'm learning fast.

After the workshop I went back to my room, did an hour of yoga stretches, and tried falling asleep. I failed. About 12:30 a.m. I took a late walk through the town of Sandanski to find something to eat. A hundred yards from the hotel was a small cafe. I went in, and there were Ognian, Tanya, and Bobi sitting at the table. Ognian invited me over and asked what I wanted to eat. I told him kababshi, and he ordered a whole meal for me with beer. Naturally, he paid. I say "naturally" because, since he joined our group, he has been inviting me for coffee, meals, food, and paying for everything. He is an excellent host and gracious, too, not only to me but to everyone in the group.

After we ate he wanted to show me a tape of his choreographic school's graduation performance. The cafe had a video, so at 2:00 a.m. I saw an hour and a half performance of the best Bulgarian dancing I have ever seen! Ognian's choreography and the training of his dancers is absolutely fantastic—he's a real Moiseyev. As it turns out he knows, not only Moiseyev, but every top choreographer and performing group in Eastern Europe. This guy is a find, perhaps a genius. How did I get such a top person on my tour? Why is he so gracious and hospitable to me, not only insisting he pay for my coffees and meals, but giving me such a costly folk costume? I didn't know what to make of it, how to handle it, or how to accept it. Naturally I accepted it with grace and charm, because I'm a professional at accepting. But why is he doing this? Does he want something from me? A tour of America for his performing group? What else could it be?

Perhaps there is no reason for giving it to me other than he likes me and is a good host. Maybe our tour group is a new experience for him. Or he just has a good heart. Perhaps I'm wrong in trying to find all kinds of hidden reasons for his actions. I am somewhat overwhelmed by his gift. It makes me feel both indebted to him, grateful, and moved.

Perhaps he simply believes in doing mitzvahs for people like me. His hobby is cooking. At the table in the cafe he put some garlic cloves in the tongue they served, mixed them together with some vegetables, put them on a fork, and fed me like a mother feeding a child. Very touching. A nice gesture, and I was moved.

Perhaps part of the problem is the resurrection of the old question: Am I worthy of all this? Do I have the power and strength to accept it?

My Bulgarian is so limited, his English almost nonexistent, and Tanya, who translates for him, is very weak in English—all and all, an uncomfortable but beautiful experience. Perhaps I am meant to be uncomfortable on this tour in order to grow.

I am growing! The Ognian experience could open up a whole new tour idea of traveling on the bus with musicians. But it's still too early to tell what's happening, and I'm still too much in shock from running this tour to make any long-term decisions or even assessments. Evidently God sent Ognian to me for a reason. What it is I do not know, but it shall be revealed when it is ready.

Meanwhile our guide, Albena Stoykova, is absolutely first rate. She is the best Bulgarian guide I have ever had. The quality of *all* the people on this tour is excellent. When David Levy put on the folk dance tapes at the end of our Bulgarian workshop, and everyone danced "our" dances—that is, the ones they knew—it was the culmination of the evening. I may well reconsider bringing folk dance tapes and tape recorder on tour—an excellent way to bring our group together and even put on a show for the other people at the hotel.

Using Others and Myself Being Used

I couldn't sleep again last night. I went to bed with a headache and awoke at four in the morning after a nightmare where I was stuck in the corner of my room behind a big black cement mixer. I was about to be suffocated and broke out in a cold sweat. That's my situation on this tour. I am suffocating and stuck behind a big black truck. Part of my truck was Ognian. Having him on tour with us has put a lot more pressure on me, not only to speak Bulgarian but mainly to be his host. Imagine, he is giving me all these presents, yet I am his host.

Then I understood my conflict and why I had a headache. I didn't want to be his host; I wanted to use him. How could I both use him and "be kind to him" as a host should be? Then I realized the best way to be kind to him is to use him. That's why he's here: He wants to be used.

I want to use everybody on this tour, and in life. But the word "use" has gotten bad press, a bad name. "Use" has been confused with "abuse."

I love using people, especially for a higher purpose. What is that purpose? On one level, it is to please myself. But on a higher one, it is to fulfill a cosmic plan. God wants people to be used. It is not necessarily comfortable to be used. But just because it is uncomfortable does not mean it is bad. Running this tour is certainly not comfortable, but by being in this very uncomfortable position I can grow. And indeed I do. One grows more through suffering and discomfort than through ease and pleasure. This is not an absolute rule, but is usually true.

I use Ognian. I am also *being* used by him and my tourists, and by the Creator, master of the higher forces, to fulfill His plan. My purpose is to bring unity and adventure to my tourist group. Ognian, Albena, our driver, Balkan Holidays, and I are serving my tourists. We are working together to fulfill the higher purpose, the larger plan.

The idea of using others and myself to fulfill a higher purpose of the

Creator is a beautiful idea. Realizing it will remove my headache. Instead of placing all awesome responsibilities on me, I now have a partner upstairs.

He is sending helpers to work with me.

I can't verbalize this idea too well this morning. It is still too fresh. Yet it is the central idea of this tour. It gives me power and strength.

This could all be a comedy of errors, although it doesn't feel like it. Last night was, in many respects, a horrible night. I again awoke this morning with a nightmare. Two orphans, about six years old, appeared in my dream. They were dirty, ragged, and old, and one had dirty legs with thick muscles. I had the choice of whether to kill them or not. Sadly and regretfully, I decided they should be killed. There was no other choice. Then I awoke.

I recognized those thick, muscular legs as belonging to Ognian. I suppose it is time to kill him. But I can't get angry with him either. That's the sad part. As I say, last night *may* have been a comedy of errors.

It began at the Novotel in Plovdiv when I invited an Israeli tour group to attend our Bulgarian folk dance workshop. At first they said only a few would come. Then they asked if their whole group of thirty-five people could come. I knew it was too much but okayed it anyway. When they piled into our workshop Ognian's face fell. He insisted they go. I had to ask them to leave to save my workshop. I did it while he and the whole class waited. It was an embarrassing and humiliating moment, because I had invited them and now had to insist they leave. I had sensed that my original decision to invite them all would lead to trouble—but I'd done it anyway. I'm mad at Ognian for throwing them out, but I can't really blame him. On the other hand, he could have been more gracious about it. Maybe that's what most bothers me.

This event left a bad taste in my mouth for the entire evening. Whose fault was this? It is my group, and I can invite whomever I wish. But Ognian is the teacher and, in fairness, deserves to be consulted about those attending his class. That I didn't do it is my error. He called me on it. Maybe that's why I'm mad.

Later we had another "misunderstanding." I wanted to buy a two-hundred dollar gaida for Hal Brandmaier. He said a professional gaida costs five or six hundred, but an average one two hundred. I told him in Bulgarian to buy me an average gaida. But he brought me the expensive professional one.

He said I had asked him for a professional five-hundred-dollar gaida. Doing the transaction in Bulgarian may have created the misunderstanding. On the other hand, he could have simply sold me something I don't want in order to make money. I sense it is the latter, but I cannot be absolutely sure.

Spending all this "unnecessary" money is annoying but not as annoying as all the so-called "misunderstandings" that are going around.

Add to this Bernice Goldmark's disappointment with the workshops; she wanted more advanced ones. I can't disagree with her, and I'm trying to get one for this afternoon. Still, it put more pressure on the pot.

The bottom line is, I'm mad, but I can't get too mad at these misunderstandings and miscommunications. Why do I feel so badly? Could it be because my customers and dance teacher are right? Or am I simply denying my powers of intuition once again?

One thing good about buying this possibly overpriced gaida— it removes my guilt about receiving Ognian's six-hundred-dollar costume gift.

We're going to Koprivshtitsa today.

A bit sick in throat this morning.

I'm getting sick of leading this tour. Perhaps that is the "symbolic value" of my sore throat.

I'm at the Koprivshtitsa Festival—the "Big K"—and feeling no pain. At least I felt no pain last night after the family I'm staying with gave me some vodka. Otherwise, *all* I'm feeling is pain—especially in my heel.

My body is falling apart on this tour. I started it with a heel spur. It calmed down until I put on my costume in Plovdiv and danced without an orthotic. The next day I could hardly walk. Added to that was an oncoming sore throat and my lower back pain which hasn't gone away since the tour started.

I'm used to lower back pain: I can handle it. My real worry was that my sore throat would develop into strep or something even more serious. That hasn't happened, and this morning, after a good night's sleep, the throat feels much better. The chills have gone way.

But my heel spur has gotten worse. It is not life-threatening, but certainly is a pain in the heel. Yesterday I led my group up the mountain to the Festival site. On the way down the mountain my heel was killing me. I could hardly walk. I kept stopping to stretch it and finally made it to the town center.

Today I'm leading another group up the mountain; then I have to walk around the festival, be on my feet most of the day, and perhaps go up and down that big hill a few times. And this with my left heel spur practically making me a cripple. I must walk slowly, hesitantly, carefully, and with lots of concentration. Maybe if I stretch a lot it will get me through the day.

It's so disappointing and frustrating. I was looking forward to the Koprivshtitsa Festival—to freedom, fun, and walking up and down the mountain. Instead I am a virtual cripple trapped in my heel spur.

We'll see how I survive the day.

It is almost impossible to write on this tour. Too much to think about, too much to do. On the Greek tour most details were taken care of. My mind was somewhat free, and I could write a bit. But on this tour every moment is taken up with some small problem or other. I won't be free until we reach Varna. I might as well accept it and give in.

Certainly nothing rational will come out of my mind. I even have to give up my morning shits in this "hotel." So be it. There is only one more day left.

My heel feels a bit better. Perhaps there is hope after all. . . but it moves so slowly.

Will I Start a New Business?

Hardly anyone reads my writing.
Why does this bother me?
Probably because today I almost gave it up.
Yesterday we arrived in Varna. I was exhausted. After a fair night's sleep, I got up and had early-morning coffee for the first time since our tour started. While I sat on the pleasant terrace overlooking the swimming pool in front of me and the Black Sea beyond, I studied Bulgarian. I wrote some practice sentences in Cyrillic in my hand-written notebook, then talked to the waitress in Bulgarian, in which I'm making progress. It felt good.

Then I had a lethal thought: Why not give up writing on tours? Why bother bringing my computer, which I have to worry about losing or breaking? Wouldn't it be better to use the small amounts of time and energy I have on tour to learn the language of the country? After all, I write all year long. I spend two weeks in three or four countries a year. At most it's two months away from home. Would it hurt if I took this time to practice my languages?

When I'm in a foreign country I'm inspired to speak its language. Writing retreats into the background. What use is it on my trips, anyway?

I continued to rationalize until Joyce Weissman said her son was coming to visit her this Friday. He is a Slavic scholar living in Prague and is having a tough time finding work in his field. She told me he is discouraged. Would I talk to him? With great pleasure, I said. Slavic studies and scholars are close to my heart. What will I say to him? I'll tell him to hang in there, stick to it, never give up. He has something special, something many people would envy him for: love and passion for Slavic studies. That passion is a secret gift filled with beauty and pain. The pain comes in the struggle to maintain the love, to keep the passion alive amidst almost constant discouragement and rejection from the outside world. Yet if you give in to the pessimism and discouragement, the rocks strewn along the path, you are dead. You cannot give up your dream. It is why you were put on earth. It is one of your most worthy attributes. You have to fight even to the death to keep it alive.

That's what I would say to him.

As I walked away from my conversation with Joyce I started to feel a slight headache and depression. Aha, the old signal!—I myself had not followed my dream; I had given away my dream of writing, traded it in for language study.

Where was the writing I had expected to do on this tour? Answer: There wasn't any.

I realized it right away. I started writing on my computer this afternoon. I am following my own dream once again and feeling some inner peace.

Some, I say, but not a lot. Something new happened, and it happened in the first sentence: "Hardly anyone reads my writing." What does such a sentence mean? That I need to start selling my writing. I need to do for writing what I am doing for my folk dancing, weekends, and folk tours. I need to find an audience.

It's not my folk dance audience. True, some of my dancers read my books and like them. But they are basically folk dancers and follow me because of my folk dance interest. They are *not* primarily readers of my books. Just as my books have been a "sideline" for me, so they are a sideline for my folk dancers.

Wouldn't it be incredible if I return to America with an actual interest in selling my books?

I would have to make a different commitment, search for a new audience.

I would have to start an entirely new business.

Am I ready? Will I do it? Time to walk around the Varna block and take a think.

This is the first morning I've felt good since the tour began. Why? Probably because it's all over, the pressure is off, and I'm back to my old routines again. But there could be other reasons, too.

I have to thank Ruth Diamond for suggesting, nay, pushing me into teaching dancing last night. I taught Bulgarian dancing for an hour and a half, came home, got a fan for my room, did yoga stretches, had a great night's sleep, got up this morning to study Bulgarian for an hour over coffee in the dining room, came back to my room, did a few light yogas, and began writing in my journal. It all feels good. Even my room, which is small and located in back of the hotel, seems better. I'm glad we had to book these extra days of so-called "rest" in Varna. They're starting to pay off.

I especially liked studying Bulgarian in the morning at the breakfast table and practicing it on the waiters. I practice it on almost every Bulgarian I meet. I love the progress I'm making in speaking Bulgarian. That's my personalized "Torah study" for this tour.

A State of the Spirit

"A state of the spirit"—that's what the Bulgarian monks created in the 9th century. Higher education, higher learning, evangelizing the Slavs in south and south eastern Europe, creating a mood, an atmosphere, of learning and admiration of the spirit which would survive whether a Bulgarian state survived or not.

I can believe in a state of the spirit.

I cannot believe in the state itself. Too brief, temporary, transient.

Even the Roman State, the Empire, lasted only five hundred years. After its death, it lingered on in the medieval minds for another five hundred. A "temporary" millennium in the larger scheme of things. I'm looking for the Big Lasting, the Long-Term Commitments like infinity and transcendent. Don't bother me with small potatoes like states, empires, and dynasties. The squabbling of these peewees only lasts a few lifetimes—petty cash in the universal banking system. But a state as a reflection of the spirit—now that is something to consider.

The medieval Bulgarian state was a reflection of the medieval Bulgarian spirit. States and governments in general are the coagulation of many minds into a semiamorphous whole. They are minuscule compared to spirit. But to the human voyager passing through in a rowboat, canoe, ship, freighter, or even ocean liner, these passing states may loom large indeed, especially if there seem to be no higher forms of nourishment in the ocean; these objects in the water may seem to be the ocean itself. This is the height of blindness exemplified by the communist system, whose destructive day in Bulgaria is slowly dying, although remnants remain. The Bulgarian Floating Potato Party is still active but it is a shadow of its former self. New potatoes, home fries, french fries, and others are rising. Hopefully they will embrace the potato of the spirit as well.

Today is my last writing day in Bulgaria. Tomorrow morning at eight a.m. our bus will transport us from the Prostor Hotel and Lebed Hotel, where we have been staying in Varna, to the airport. I'll be packing today.

I'll be coming back to America with a new writing business plan. I don't quite know what this means yet. Still it is something to get excited about. Somehow I'm going to turn my writing into a business which will eventually make money. I don't know how but I'm going to do it, but I am. It is my new business direction.

This is the first time I am approaching business without panic. I see it as both a strength and a weakness: a strength because I'll be calm and strong in the face of the many upcoming rejections I can expect; a weakness because I'm not sure I'll put in my maximum effort if I'm not fueled by panic or fear. But I could be wrong. Maybe without panic or fear I'll put in even more effort. Wouldn't that be something? Fear and panic may have held me back rather than propelled me forward. Maybe without them I'll fulfill my potential on an even higher level. We'll see. At the moment, my writing business is new territory to explore.

It's exciting; I'm starting to churn. How do you start a writing business? What do I do? New and good questions. A fresh fight and a bright challenge is brewing.

I wonder if there is any relationship between my heel spur and the unfolding idea of a writing business? I know God works in mysterious ways. At the moment I can see absolutely no relationship. But I like the idea anyway. Therefore, it must have some credence. Only I don't know how, what, or where. This may all unfold in the future. I know there is a relationship in the symbolism and metaphor of a heel spur. Is the pain driving me on? Will its crippling effects force me even further into the sedentary activity of writing? Is it a prediction and preparation for a future non-dancing state? These are certainly negative views but sometimes the positive is couched and camouflaged by the negative.

On the other hand, my heel spur could be metaphorically "spurring me on." It is, after all in my *left* heel, the side of deceit, darkness, and my unconscious. Long ago, in Aix-en-Provence, it was my left side that became half-paralyzed by loss, grief, anger, and rage over losing Claudia, my first love. True, the situation was hopeless, and nothing but grief could have come from getting married at the age of nineteen. But that is the *rational* side. Our breakup crushed me. I was vulnerable, virginal, and new to such pain. I didn't know anything about the hidden powers of anger, rage, resentment, and hatred that could tear up my body and, if not understood and aimed in the right direction, actually paralyze and destroy me. It almost did. My half-paralysis lasted two months. Finally it passed after I visited a neurologist who told me it was my nerves. I left his office wiser and more guarded. My pain transformations had all taken place on my left side, the unconscious, raging, feeling side of my body.

My heel spur is on my left side. Could it be part of the same syndrome?

I'm already missing Bulgaria. Too bad I can't return with another tour next year, but I'm too booked up: Budapest and Prague in March, Greece in May, Czech Republic, Slovakia, Poland in July, and Turkey in August. Still, it may be possible to return to Bulgaria next year in some form. If not with me, with someone else.

I am hinting again at expansion, at my original idea of running tours with other people leading them? Am I ready to try it again?

Or am I kidding myself? Something to think about.

Jim Gold Pride Day

It's Sunday morning, and we're leaving the Lebed and Prostor Hotels, driving to the airport, flying out of Varna to Sofia at ten o'clock, and flying from Sofia to New York at 3:55 p.m. It will be a long day. I'm in my usual preflight state of limbo.

I've managed to write twenty-five pages on a difficult tour, half during the movement-infested first ten days, the other half during our six-day "vacation" in Varna. I managed to continue writing under poor conditions. That is a victory. I should be proud of myself. My tour is over. I should also be proud of myself for running such a good tour with difficult people under moderate-to-poor physical conditions.

Pride of accomplishment is the highest prize I can receive for running my tour, writing my journal, and any other good deeds I have done. It is impolite to reject such a gift. I must learn politeness, not only towards others, but towards myself as well.

October–December 1995

WRITING

I Am Part of the Ocean

I feel lost. I cannot find the center or even the sideline. "I've done it before" and "Why bother?" mood are attacking in full force. Their hidden and disparate germs beat my sides, drill and pulverize my hopes, and generally rend and wobble my appetites. Their gentle but insistent wormlike gnawings slowly tear away my insides, and I am left empty, sluggish, energyless, hopeless. It is the invasion of the "Less."

What can I do about such attacks? Nothing I can think of. Simply wait them out, ride the waves. High crests always lead to troughs.

A child is being born. I am riding turbulent winds in the process. As I organize my New Leaves, my wild mind gallops in all directions, looking for a home.

Old tracks have faded. Lost, lonely, forlorn, whacked down, living under the sodden cloud of the black axe, I wander along bent borders. I can think of no way to raise my spirits. Best is to accept bottom crawling. Although unpleasant and maddening, in its lava straight-jacketing there is no other way. Could it be I'm approaching the big question: after I edit and organize New Leaf into themes, will it be worth publishing? Or will I simply create another book to fill up my basement? Can anything get out of the basement without a push?

Then, even if all my books were recognized throughout the world, I would still ask: How long does fame last? A year? A lifetime? More? Eventually, even centuries of fame are forgotten. Why work for such a transient goal? How stupid can you get?

Why work so hard if death wipes accomplishments away? I may be remembered months, years, or even a millennium. But no matter how long memory lasts, it is still circumscribed by time, the mini-master.

To function or not to function, that is the question. Since neither seem to work, why not combine them both?

Perhaps I can transcend *by* functioning. Now that's a good idea. Questions of whether my writing is good, quests for fame, recognizing the inevitability of death, do not help. These questions are walls I create to protect and challenge myself. They are part of a game to make life more entertaining. They have no more long-term meaning than a sunrise or sunset.

Fickle, creative ego creates these slow-moving games of depression, sluggishness, and aimlessness, the whining over rejection and lack of recognition, the frightening game of upcoming death, the hopeful one of resurrection, the frustrating and endless circular cycle of death and rebirth.

The ego is like an ocean wave, rising and falling, undulating, ever changing its self-images.

Fears Are Friends Disguised as Enemies

A thick, murky, muddy cloud has been settling over me during the past week. I am not used to it.

One reason is I have stopped writing. The liberating epiphany of a guitar breakthrough put writing on hold for a week. When I don't write, I get confused. Simple as that.

Writing is my great organizing principle.

I keep complaining about the same things. Cycles repeat with slight changes, but not enough to make them revolutionary. I want to amaze my audience, but my writing is becoming "nothing new." They may think I'm running out of gas, unoriginal, uncreative, that I've lost it.

I need to write about anything that pops into my mind. Writing is gateway to the creation of a new world; the freshness and sparkle of tomorrow lies just beyond my finger tips.

But sparkle has been smothered. I feel pessimistic, not about my abilities, but rather my lack of desire for fame, fortune, and recognition. After seeing Bela Fleck perform in concert, I felt no jealousy or competition. I enjoyed his playing without the down feelings I usually get after hearing a concert by a fine guitar player. That is a major victory for me. I should be happy, right? Part of me is; the other part has lost its motivation. If I am not suffering, not jealous, competitive, angry, put down, sniveling, slobbering, miserably crawling in the gutter, chained to the foot of a glorious mountain, what will motivate me? If desire for fame and fortune is fading, why bother doing anything?

Another example is classical guitar. I'm ready to give a concert but I'm lukewarm about it. Worse, I feel I don't *need it*. I have no need to prove myself. By losing this "weaknesses" I've also lost my desire to thrust myself forward.

I'm happy to just play and relish in my victory.

Is there a motivation beyond fear? Bill Gates consciously tries to frighten himself and his employees with upcoming Microsoft competition.

Competition drives him on, pushes him to create new forms. But I doubt his motivation method is for me. I've spent too many years trying to free myself from fears. Now that I've succeeded, I'm confused. Fear and doubt were tremendous motivators.

You'd think I'd feel glorious because of my great guitar accomplishment, an eighteen-year-old fight concluding in victory. I did feel great about it last week. But this week I ask, What do I do next?

What will challenge me in the future? If I'm not challenged, I will sink into a postmortem, somnambulant, black soup that will make dying more pleasant than living.

Yesterday I wrote on a slip of paper: "The marketing challenge, the serving challenge." I put it on my desk to contemplate for my morning thought. But without fear to motivate me, the marketing or serving challenges seem dry.

It's a strange, confused state I'm in. I'm coming to it through strength and victory, not weakness and defeat. Successful tours, guitar breakthroughs, even a semblance of financial stability: Somehow focusing on these successes is sapping my future strength and motivation. Very strange, indeed.

What am I supposed to do with these victories? I'm tired of basking and glowing in their light. It is time to move on—but where? Did my search for a fearless state lead only to emptiness? Maybe I should reconsider fear. Bill Gates's Microsoft is on top of the world, and he is one of the world's richest men. Yet he's still "afraid." He creates fear to motivate himself and his Microsoft employees. Could he be onto something?

Could fear be a prime mover for success in this world?

Although the challenge of serving, the idea of working to serve others sounds good, it may not viscerally motivate. I don't think "serving others." My motivations come from selfish intentions. If, in the process, good deeds result from my selfish actions, so much the better.

One of my goals has been to live without fear. But perhaps I have overlooked a crucial ingredient: in order to conquer fear, I have to have fears to conquer. How can I rise above them if they do not exist? It is the dynamic struggle against them that creates something new.

Perhaps fears are friends but come disguised as enemies.

If that's the case, maybe I'd better start creating some new ones to push me forwards.

The Dream of a Writer

After an afternoon nap I sat down at our kitchen table, nibbled some Italian pastries, drank microwaved coffee, and read an interview with William Styron. He spoke about taking Prozac and other drugs for depression. The drugs neutered him, took away both his highs and his lows. He gave them up.

My drug of choice is coffee with Italian pastries. By ingesting and imbibing, I can often create a pastry-induced, coffee-inspired writer's high.

Of course, it has little to do with writing. I write not a word. Instead, I dream the beautiful dream of writing.

This afternoon's lofty writer's vision was unsullied by desire for fame, fortune, or recognition. Instead, honey bathed my body with a capital W. I saw the goddess of writing shining, dressed in translucent hand-me-down angel's clothing, perfected for earth-walking use.

Behind her I heard ethereal beauty breathing softly in a sea of blue silence. Bells tolled in the sky above, first fortissimo, then pianissimo. Finally. . .silence.

How lucky to immerse myself in this sea, to float as I survey my many selves rising and falling on majestic waves. The eerie silence of voluminous mountains, the power of waterfalls crashing into canyons, cerulean rocks hurled into dark ravines where golden crabs claw sunken wooden throats.

I am lucky for this vision.

Now I return to my world of pinion nuts, crackers, and vegetables.

Neck Pain Reborn

Neck pain returned a week ago when I did too many head stands, shoulder stands, and legs over my head. It was exacerbated by mucho guitar practice and sitting at the computer writing.

Can I work with pain? Yes. Moderate my practice. Go slow, soft, and less. I can do it. Matisse kept painting even as an arthritic cripple to the end of his life by holding his paint brush in his teeth. If necessary I can do the same.

Aha! I have been reading music on a music stand, pushing it to the left side, stretching and straining my neck as I look to the left. That is the origin of my neck pain. After all, I have been writing at the computer, doing head stands, shoulder stands, and legs over-the-head positions for months, and my neck has been fine. The only new added element has been the addition of reading guitar pieces from the music stand on my left. Thank you, writing process! Pain origin discovered!

Speaking

I've returned from years of meditation and contemplation experienced on my personalized Mount Sinai in Teaneck, New Jersey. After thinking in isolation for years about universal questions, suddenly, strange words are falling from my mouth. They feel awkward; none exactly fit my ideas. But I use them in spite of their limitations. Alone in my room, my ideas seem so clear, translucent—brilliant suns, radiant and blissful—but when I wrestle them down to earth, offering them to others through my inadequate tools of language, they feel heavy, unnatural, and stilted.

Sometimes language acts as a shield, preventing others from understanding me. Only through an intuitive leap can they jump over words and capture the essence.

Moses said, "God, I can't speak. I stutter. I feel so dumb." God said, "Don't worry. I'll put words in your mouth."

I feel dumb, too. Maybe I should wait for God to put words in my mouth. When I step out on the world stage, I'll pray that God speak through me.

LIFE

Sluggish

Since I returned from Cape Cod a month ago I've been sluggish. There I was engrossed in Eastern philosophy and books by Paul Brunton, Deepak Chopra, Sogyal Rinpoche, the Dalai Lama, on Hinduism, and thinking about death, afterlife, rebirth, and the "Gap of Oneness," I didn't pay much attention to sluggishness. Suddenly, it hit hard two days ago. Once I devoted myself to daily writing, committed myself to either four pages or one hour of writing a day. This kept my ghosts and demons at bay. But during the past month I've hardly written at all. Only edited. Editing does not clear the gates and bring heaven to my eyes.

Yesterday I took the first step toward organizing my heavens. I sat down at my computer. Now as I write spontaneous and fresh I can feel the fog lifting.

I'm coming back. Rebirth is here. I sure need it. What better way to start than through babble writing—to clear the gates?

With fingers lubricated, my horse gallops forth, leaving the barn behind. God, I love to ride. Thanks for the hay.

I Am an Artist

I am an artist. There is no other road for me. No matter how much I twist, turn, and try other directions, I always return to the source of who I am. Art is in my soul, my body, the world that I project around me. Whatever else I do is peripheral.

All my businesses have developed to support my art. Am I not expressed in them?

Perhaps they are secretly an art, too.

An artist needs an economic foundation. I have a good instinct for survival; I've developed ingenious ways of earning a living. When they succeed, I get excited about the money coming in. Conversely, when I'm broke, I'm afraid. My focus shifts radically from art to money. I lose my way on the twisted pathways. I forget who I am.

Art is the center of my soul. Remember that and I'm okay. . .but how often do I remember?

Usually I try to *forget*. My high school inferiority complex still haunts me.

But no matter how hard I try forgetting, truth keeps returning. This morning it's shining down on me in brilliant light.

During the past month I tried giving up art in favor of sainthood. I've been reading books on religion, transcendence, Eastern philosophy, Judaism, how to love others, be compassionate, help your neighbor, attain goodness, and achieve oneness with God. The ideas are sublime but terrible for me, especially when I believe them. Whenever I aim for sainthood I'm on the wrong path. These books are inspiring; but to truly find yourself you have to look within. Books give you confidence in your vision. But they cannot impose *their* vision. You can only find that yourself.

I have an artistic vision. It has always been so. I read about religion, transcendence, mysticism, and philosophy to find words, explanations, support for visions I already have. I am on the path of self-discovery, searching for a vocabulary to express them.

Most important is to remember who I am.

My Journal Is My Therapist

After writing the "I am an artist" piece, I reaffirmed my identity. Then the world opened up. Three people registered for our Yoga and Folk Dance Weekend; the Turkish tour materialized; other good things happened.

I am happy this morning. I'm not sure why. I rarely know why I am happy or not. If I am happy, then I make up an explanation why; if I am sad, I make up another explanation. First comes the feeling, then the reason. Perhaps it's an energy cycle. Outside events seem to have little effect beyond a temporary jolt of joy or misery. As soon as I realize how transient it all is, I move on.

Excitement returned as I started developing next year's tour of Turkey.

Happiness is that beautiful inner calm, the tear-soaked meltdown of body and mind that occurs when powerful waves of a Beethoven symphony sweep over me. Within that wondrous personality, disturbance is sublime happiness. When such fire fills my being, everything else feels like a footnote.

I Love

I love exploring the intricacies and subtle weavings of my mind.

I love talking about myself.

Is this selfish? You bet it is. Yet it also has its own glory.

I love the freedom of journal-writing. I can say anything I want. I don't have to worry about insulting anyone, considering their needs, or hurting their feelings. This is *my* journal. I am totally free to explore my thoughts, feelings, joys, hopes, depressions, emotional crests and troughs, whatever piles of garbage or nuggets of ecstasy happen to float through the universe of my mind.

What about the religious dictate to love your neighbor? What about helping others? Well, folks, I hate pressure. Tell me I should love my neighbor, and I usually end up hating him.

Actually, I probably do love my neighbor—as long as he doesn't bother me too much and gives me lots of free time. What will I do with my free time? Write my journal, of course.

Why do I have such a need to talk about myself? Could it be that I cannot find anyone else more interesting? Not that there are no other interesting people in the world. It's just I'm the one I know best.

Also I have no one else to talk to. My journal is my therapist.

A Tree Fell on Our House

During the storm last Saturday night a tree fell on our house. It destroyed our gutters, tore a couple of screen windows, and broke one of our protective bushes. The Teaneck Department of Public Works came quickly, removed the tree, and cut it up.

Yesterday afternoon, as sun streamed into my den and living room, I realized there was too much; we no longer have protective shade. Our house looks denuded and sunstruck; our privacy has been destroyed.

Why is this happening? What message is God trying to send through this minor annoyance? Is a falling tree a warning? How about our basement? We've decided to carpet and paint it. We removed all books on the shelves, then the shelves themselves. I've disrupted years of collections and collectibles. By rearranging our basement I am rearranging my mind. Mind rearrangement is true of our trees as well. Suddenly, we have to think about redesigning our entire front yard: buy new bushes, find new trees, rethink our approach to landscaping. I've never bothered thinking about trees in the past. They just existed, and that was that. Now I have to occupy myself with thoughts of trees, sun protection and privacy.

Is physical destruction symbolic destruction as well? Is it necessary in order to move on to a new level?

Remember: every problem is an opportunity in disguise. Destruction precedes creation. It is the law of karma and the life cycle. The physical destruction I see outside the window in my front yard has symbolic significance as well. Same with our basement reorganization. A new structure will be imposed: new basement and new landscaping. Opportunities are hidden within miseries. I'm just too annoyed to see them. Nevertheless, I sense they are there.

The basement and front lawn are symbols of my brain. All three are being rearranged.

Witness the word "breakthrough." Didn't the tree fall on our house and almost "break through" our roof? I got the message. I don't need a total catastrophe. A warning will do. I remember when I was ten years old and robbed mail boxes with my friend. My father caught me. He told me I was committing a federal offense. Then he said he would take me to jail. I got the message immediately. I knew that, punished or not, I would never rob mail boxes again. My father took me downstairs by the hand, put me in our car, and drove off. I was sure we were heading for jail. Instead he took me to a candy store for ice cream. I didn't cry at the time, but I sure could have. What a wise teacher my father was. He knew the letter and the spirit of the Law.

Our fallen tree and basement cleaning are symbols as well as warnings. They are also endings in disguise. Destructions and endings have within them seeds of new beginnings.

What are my new beginnings?

Back to the word "breakthrough." Guitar performance is one. I've decided to play the guitar at the upcoming Solway Yoga and Folk Dance Weekend. I sense something new is happening. Perhaps a tree has fallen on my old way of guitar thinking. It grazed my house, hit the ground with a thud. Shade has been removed; blinding sunlight streams in every afternoon. I used to crave sun, but now it is so brilliant I cringe beneath it. Could this be a new sun of guitar performance shining down? I have always wanted such a thing but now that it's here, I cringe before its power. Like basement cleaning, am I removing the old debris of past guitar performance thoughts and getting ready to replace them with new paint, a beautiful carpet, and a new basement organization? This collection of annoyances may be laying the foundation for an upcoming new self.

I've got to get back to writing, even if all I can say is I've got to get back to writing.

I was on the right track during the past couple of years when I wrote four pages a day in my journal, pouring out words of wisdom, babble, sense, and nonsense in a daily expurgation of demons. I chased away many fogs in those daily exercises. I developed writing skill too, even though I am not certain what use I can make of it. However, the miracle of daily writing is such that, just as I spoke, just as this sentence poured out, I realized how it served me. It teaches: have faith in the first thought, the one conceived in that millisecond between mental creation and its transference onto paper or into the material world of spoken reality. Writing creates confidence in spontaneity; it teaches not only to follow my muse, but to realize that ninety-nine percent of the time that initial "muse-ive" instinct, that "muse-ical" thought, is the right one.

The last couple of weeks have been blockbusters. All reactions, instincts, and habits developed during the past two years were suddenly washed away by my guitar breakthrough. This rush of guitar creativity has blown my brain apart; I've been thrown into a heaving sea of uncontrollable emotional waves, troughs of weeping alternating with crests of jubilation.

I can't believe the things I am saying. "I'm becoming a great guitarist!" and "This breakthrough is for good." I'm forgetting about Segovia, Bream, Montaya, Sabicas, and the other guitar icons of my youth. These haughty figures used to dominate my dreams and practice sessions, peering down at me from my ceiling or walls, mumbling how I'd never be able to play the gorgeous guitar pieces I loved so much. They were my ghosts of incapacity and inability, demons unexorcized, ever ready to strike me down. They hung out mostly around my right shoulder, but also settled in my right wrist and index finger.

Now, miraculously, they are gone! I hardly remember them. I can't believe I'm saying what I just said, but I am. I can't believe I believe it, but I do. I am coming into my own. I can't believe I just said that either, but I did.

Alexander Bellow taught me the wrist relaxation technique patterned after Segovia's playing; Rolando Valdes-Blaine told me to just relax and play it. Their personalities were opposite, yet both were right. It took eighteen years to actualize their teachings. Now this actualization is shaking my foundations.

I've broken the glass ceiling and am rising upwards. Heaven has poured its beautiful forms over my face; I bask in the pure white glow of celestial light. I'm not used to such beatific bathing. Rather, I'm accustomed to seeing a few stray rays of light while stung, stabbed, and lacerated by the darts of hell. This conflict is winding down. Thank God, and all my other teachers!

Prayer Forms: Building My Own Church

In the Middle Ages communities spent years, even centuries, building a church in an act of community worship.

In northern Greece, on the Thessalian rocks of Meteora, monks lifted one loving stone after another to build churches on these inaccessible mountain pillars. Each building stone put in place was an act of worship, a service to the Creator.

I'd like to build my own church; each brick and stone placement would be my act of worship. Construction itself might be ephemeral. Nevertheless, it would remind me of my greater self.

I am not going to build a stone church. Material constructions and visual creations are not necessarily my way. I delight in sound, vibrations of words, and music. I am an aural person. Thus the church I dedicate to the Higher

Power and build one brick at a time is made out of guitar playing. Also New Leaf Journal. Perhaps that is the reason I have little desire to play guitar publically or publish. Rather, guitar playing and writing are prayer forms, my own artistic style of worship. Through their daily rituals I build my church laying one brick at a time. Thus, by creating, I worship my Creator.

Thoughts of Cool Nights and Morning Death

"*Ee nichta eene droseri.*" The night is cool.

As I read this Greek phrase early in the morning, I realized I was trying to forget an all-important truth: I will die. I'm not suffering from a fatal disease; I don't expect an accident. Nevertheless, even with the best of luck, my time will soon be up, whether that soon is tomorrow, next year, or in fifty years.

The Tibetan philosophers say you should think about your death during every moment of the day. Let that ever-present thought shape your attitude towards life; it puts everything into perspective. By diminishing the importance of whatever you do, it eliminates hubris, false pride, even fear and hope. Nothing kills hope like death.

Should man live with hope? Is it a good thing? In *Tropic of Cancer*, Henry Miller says, "I have no hope. I am the happiest man in the world." I like Henry Miller. Perhaps the loss of hope is not a bad thing, especially if it helps you focus on the present.

There is a difference between living without hope and hopelessness, but it's hard to describe. Like the feeling I had this morning before reading my Greek phrase. I saw my mind moving from *ita* to *epsilon* and knowing the difference between these similar-sounding letters in the Greek alphabet. I saw how my mind, focusing on the letters, slowly moved away from my dark morning thoughts of death.

Death is followed by rebirth. This cycles dominates earthly existence like Greek letters appearing and disappearing, troughs and crests, waves on the ocean. I go through death and transfiguration once every six weeks.

Practicing Yoga as an Art Form

Yoga is turning into an art form. I'm practicing it like guitar or dance. I'm perfecting postures along with the attitudes needed to maintain them, namely, attempting to *rest* in them.

I am developing my own religious rituals, my own form of worship. The divine is everywhere and in everything. So why not worship through an object or process? I find it difficult to visualize God in all His manifestations. These abstractions, though lovely in concept, are too distant for me to feel *personally*. It is natural to worship through my own religious forms—guitar, singing, writing, folk dancing, running, and yoga. Through them I can express the joys, sorrows, frustrations, and peccadillos of my theatrical life.

What does God desire? He wants to play with forces of good and evil, ideas of right and wrong. His imagination runs wild on His cosmic stage, drawing curtains at will as He releases dreams across the world. He creates them in material form, lets them play out their life cycle, destroys them, then moves on to His next game.

I am part of His dream. As one of His reflections, I create and destroy my own dreams. All take place on my own stage, mirroring the play of the Creator.

Fsitchko e Edno: All Is One

The snow falls outside my window. It is cold and crisp—a perfect day to stay home, read, write, philosophize, play guitar, stretch, do quiet and meditative things. Today I have "permission" from Mother Above to do what I want. The outside world has been temporarily shut out; I am climbing one rung of stratosphere after another, reaching for higher things. If I am lucky, I'll reach the highest.

What is the highest? The *fsitchko e edno* experience. It means All-is-One in Bulgarian. I don't need religious or social organizations to experience *fsitchko e edno*. It can happen anytime, anywhere, alone or with others. This experience of mystical union suffuses meaning into everything I do. *Fsitchko e edno* makes other experiences seems like footnotes.

On life's path the best map is *fsitchko e edno*.

Angels of Challenge and Fear

It is amazing how fast hope can disappear—and reappear.

I am caught between an amazing lack of tour registration, and a readiness to move on to something else. I am waiting for something to happen. Meanwhile, I read, play guitar, write, and exercise.

It is astonishing how quickly registrants can flee from tours. Just a few months ago, they were packed. Now I am almost empty. I stand in awe of the vicissitudes of life. "Follow your passion, and the money will come." Well, I'm following it. Where's the money? What does money mean, anyway? Love? Security? Power? All three, no doubt, and more besides.

I'm forcing myself to write this morning to clean the cobwebs from the backside of my brain. In the process I hope inspiration will come. I want to be uplifted on the wings of a brilliant new idea. None is in sight at the moment.

Motivations have dribbled away. I'm left with *wanting to want* to give a concert, but with no reason to give it. It's the same as wanting to find a mystical tradition in Judaism, something to explain, exemplify, rectify, elicit, give birth to, affirm, and reaffirm my inspirational sparks. Where is the place I belong? What can I love as much as Beethoven's "Violin Concerto?" The *kabbalah* gives me glimpses. Its mystical tradition affirms the musical fire of enthusiasm I discovered as I stirred my Cheerios and listened to Beethoven's "Eroica Symphony." At age thirteen I had first experience of the ultimate.

I want to give a concert and feel the thrill of playing before others. But "why bother?" keeps returning. Why put myself in an uncomfortable position preparing for a concert? I'll get nervous. Why go to all that *trouble*?

In the past, hopes of fame, glory, and money drove me to the concert stage. I traveled to colleges, universities, and communities throughout America. Desire to support my family heaped mountains of worry on my back, squeezing my energy into a career path. Then the same thing happened in my second career of folk dancing, weekends, and tourism.

Now, even though business is slow, burning desire mixed with fear isn't there anymore. Is that true? Or do I simply not want to face stage fears again? Am I chickening out, hiding under a veiled lack of enthusiasm, rejecting the challenge, using lethargy and laziness to conveniently cover up old fears?

Fear is a great motivator. Do I need it in order to grow and progress? Are my fears gone? Have I really "conquered" them? Or are they simply being avoided because they disturb me too much? As long as I accept a challenge, fears will be part of it. In order to avoid them must I avoid challenges?

Time to reexamine fear.

Did God create it as a motivator to help me grow? Is there a "goodness" in it? The kabbalah says every blade of grass has two angels standing besides it like cheerleaders, encouraging it, enthusiastically calling out: "Grow, grow!"

Could one of my angels come in the form of fear? Does the unpleasant push me to do positive things?

Part of me refuses to be bullied by fear. I want to be a hero and stand unafraid before the challenges and problems of the world.

Is a hero someone who is unafraid? Or is it a frightened person who does not let fears prevent him from doing what is right? Maybe I *should* be afraid. Maybe I'm fooling myself saying I'm not, and by making conquering fears my goal. But fears are not my motivators, challenges are. Fear enters as a by-product of the challenge.

Challenge pushes one to grow. It is accompanied by a cheer-leading angel. But fear is also my angel. I have two: the angel of fear, and the angel of challenge. They work together, guiding me through twists and turns on the road to higher realms. Challenge angel pulls me; fear angel pushes me. Slowly, I ascend the ladder, my hands gripping every rung. Occasionally I glimpse the ecstatic worlds above.

Art as Religion

I have a warm spot in my heart for things Jewish. Yet I never go to temple; I have no interest in following the laws of the Jewish religion, keeping kosher, or observing the Sabbath.

Judaism may be my culture and ethnic identity, but art is my religion. Through the daily practice of artistic "rituals" like writing, music, and dancing, I discover ecstasy and mystical experience. These are my daily "Sabbaths."

I don't keep kosher. I keep "art."

I'm reading a fantastic book, *Healing Into Immortality*, by Dr. Gerald Epstein. It is subtitled: "A New Spiritual Medicine of Healing Stories and Imagery." This book takes a new look at the Ten Commandments. It sees their importance in terms of personal health.

I almost used reading it as an excuse for not writing. *Remember* this! Keep up the habit of daily writing! If I have nothing to say, write about nothingness. Keep fingers to the keyboard. This is my personal process of Healing Into Immortality. If I don't write, I don't heal myself and end up feeling like a heel, too.

Yesterday we went out for brunch with the Wanders. I started to tell them about the great books I'm reading about imagery, religion, mysticism, Judaism, Eastern philosophy, the bible, and the Ten Commandments. But as soon as I opened my mouth, dried up, dull, dead words fell out. I stood mute before my new books and new learning (too early to talk about them). I read, study, think about these things for days, weeks, even months. The gestation period is often so slow that, by the time the learning sinks in, I have forgotten where and from whom I've learned it.

How can I give credit to my sources if, by the time I absorb their influences, I've forgotten them? Epstein says that, by not giving credit, I am committing a form of murder and disobeying the sixth commandment. He is turning the Ten Commandments into a useful moral, social, and health doctrine. It may help me with my worship of false images and idols like expectations, hopes, and worries about the future.

Today is December 29. It would have been Mom's birthday. I remember her with much more love now. Even though I often struggled against her domination, she was my savior in many ways. Today I realize I am a lot like her. I have the same compulsive, driving qualities, and the same beliefs, too, especially the love of music with its mysterious sparks flying in all directions. I wonder if Ma was a closet mystic. Pop, too. Of course, during the '50s when I grew up, mystics were considered nut cases. Mysticism was far from our world-view—especially the communist, Marxist, dialectical materialist world view. "Mysticism" wasn't even part of our vocabulary. The word didn't exist, but the experience did. It took place privately in my room when I practiced violin. It also existed in perverted in the communist pipe dreams of hope for a perfect world in the here-and-now. After all, as Karl Marx thought: Why die before you meet the Messiah? Why not meet him here on earth in this life? The Messiah and his friends will be waiting for you at the door of our new communist paradise, located up ahead to the left of Time's road.

I hadn't planned to write about Ma this morning, but rather about the children's stories I told Zach and Zane. I have a talent for writing them. They're saleable, too. But I need children to inspire me.

After telling inspired bedtime stories to Zach and Zane, I had decided to give up journal writing in favor of writing for children. It was so wacky, imaginative, pleasant, and different to write in the third person again. But upon further reflection, I don't want to give up journal writing for children's stories.

But I don't want to give up children's stories either. Maybe I'll do both.

MONEY AND ITS BRETHREN

Sales Breakthrough

I've been telephoning GPs—good potentials—on my tour lists. These are the people who expressed interest in my tours. Calling them is, in itself, nothing new. What is new—and bordering on the miraculous—is that I liked it! Imagine, *me* liking a sales call. It has never happened before in my memory. Sales were always something I wanted to avoid, even though I was a good salesman and needed to be for my business.

I don't know why this breakthrough is happening now, "suddenly," after almost twenty-five years. But reasons are unnecessary. The point is: Keep your eye on the miraculous.

The best kind of sales, the most effective and in the long run cheapest, are telephone sales. When I call people, not only do they respond, but I gather information about their likes and dislikes I'd never find anywhere else. Telephone sales churn my mind. New ideas and directions come up just by talking to customers.

Another strange thing is happening: I am becoming interested in my customers as human beings. This is truly radical. It frees me from guilt. Part of me has always felt guilty calling customers, because I knew I was only after their money. I used them, turned them into fodder to be crushed and squeezed under the wheels of my money-making machine. That's probably the thing I hated most about sales. I felt forced to use people to insure my financial survival. Sales thus prevented me from doing my best. I sold "with my brakes on."

I hated myself for selling, too, for having to deal with people so inhumanly.

My priorities were screwed up. Sales are a form of service. Money, the result of sales, is secondary. Without service, money falls away: People won't pay.

It was my communist upbringing and left-wing philosophies that molded my sales attitude. According to the Marxist Fathers, only an evil person would sell. Sales were exactly what dirty capitalists did when they fooled people and forced them to part with their hard-earned money.

Panic or Love

Not one of the GPs on my Hungarian tour list wants to go to Hungary! That means I have only one registrant for the Budapest tour four months away. Last year at this time I had ten people; the year before, eight. Having one person bodes ill for the future. I'll have to face the possibility of having a small tour or no tour at all.

My spirit sagged. Then I panicked as hopes for sales dribbled to zero.

Yet how many times have I been through this before?

I promised myself that never again will my mood or attitude be pushed, butted, controlled, or whip-sawed by the vicissitudes of the market. I can't control the market, only my attitude, which right now consists of total disgust with myself. I am slipping backwards into the putrid, death-masked, health-rejecting, piss-inspired, beer-drowning attitude of the Wimp of Wobblehood, dribbling with tears. "Oh, no! How embarrassing! How humiliating! How financially frightening! Lose my tour? How will I support myself if my business goes down the drain? How will I manage?"

These fears are old. I am so tired of them, they're almost boring. (Almost, but not quite.) Still, I didn't slip on boredom's banana peel. I slipped because financial and emotional wind-scares howled against me and I fell over backwards.

Now that I'm aware of it, I won't let it happen again. I refuse to bend! *I refuse to give in to fear!* I'm not making sales calls anymore simply to allay my fears. Instead I'll read my new book on the Kabbalah, or play guitar, study Greek, read about the monks in the monasteries of Meteora, run two hours, practice calligraphy, or do yoga. Yes, there's lots of things I can do, but they will *not* include giving in to fear!

I'm going by the rule of love. If I can't love what I'm doing, and to whom I'm doing it, then fuck it all! I refuse to be bullied. I'd rather walk away and die.

It may happen. Maybe my weekends, tours, folk dance classes, and customers will simply dry up, wither away, and disappear. Such a possibility always exists. But I don't care. I *refuse to care* if caring means groveling in fear-filled cesspools or shitting in a pit of panic. Never, never, never! I wasn't put on this earth to be bullied by these lumps that want me to give up and roll over so they can roll over me. No, no, no! I won't let it happen. Never again!

I'd rather drift into the vast emptiness of the number zero, or hang by my finger tips from houses of prayer. I don't know what the Lord has in store but I do know that, if a squatting existence is what He planned for me, I am beginning my rebellion right now. I'm not moving from this spot until He sends a lighting bolt to either strike me dead or open a new door. Nevertheless, He'll no doubt do whatever He wants. Right now He's probably amusing Himself by testing me with miseries, tempting me to see whether I'll give in to inner pestilence or harden my resolve.

The Lord woke me up. I'm turning my back on Panic County. I've done that side trip already, and I didn't like it. I'd be crazy to tour those hell holes all over again.

I'm on the road of freedom and love.

I've been exploring freedom all my life; but love is new. I rarely use the word except when I say, "I love it!" I'm afraid of a such a vague yet powerful term; it has so many meanings that no one seems to know what it means.

There's "falling" in love. Frightening, indeed. I'm afraid to hand myself over to a goddess who will capture my heart and soul, then throw me away. I don't even mind being thrown away. That, at least, would give me back my freedom. But most of all, I'm afraid of my secret *desire* to give up my freedom, to exchange it for someone who will take care of me and make all my decisions, If that's "falling" in love, it scares me.

I hate falling. Yet it has a secret attraction.

Perhaps it's not love I'm afraid of but my tendency—even desire—to throw away everything I've worked for, to give myself up. But as I reexamine this tendency, I see there isn't much reason to be afraid. Truth is, I give myself up only for a short time. My need of freedom soon overwhelms my desire for slavery. I squirm loose.

Perhaps that is why I'm ready to use the word "love." My self-confidence has increased.

What is my business approach?
Do what I love to do, and hope money will follow.
It always has—although not exactly when I want it.
How do I know it will, that people will want what I create?

I don't. No one does. There is no proof. Even if I have succeeded countless times in the past, there are no guarantees of future success and earnings. Faith is the only answer. Create an excellent service you believe in. The rest is up to God and His sales people.

Knowing my services are good is not the problem. It is more a question of waiting out the quiet periods when no business comes in and bills pile up, those fearful times that sometimes make me forget my goals, projects, mission.

When I focus on money I distract myself from my projects and goals, the very juice, substance, and energy-giving source of any future sales.

One of my old attitudes was: Forget money, just work. It's time to revive it.

Can Sales Be Mitzvahs?

Yesterday I played guitar slowly and thoughtfully. As I played, I could see *focus on your passion* floating before my eyes. "Each note is making money," I thought. "Focus on my passion, and the money will come."

Can each note make money as I play it? Of course. But time creates an illusion.

People may not pay me the day I play. It may come days, months, even years later. But no one knows exactly when.

Indirectly, passion equals money. Passion brings money and money brings passion. All is One.

Sales

Getting paid is a mitzvah; it helps others equalize the world; it relieves other of guilt by allowing them to give you something, namely money, in return for services. Money and mitzvah work together. Mitzvah is man's connection to the divine through good deeds. Money connects man to mitzvah by helping him give service.

Sales are mitzvahs, too. Rabbis may not agree with me, but that doesn't matter. I'm inventing my own religion. God is the same everywhere. Why not invent my own rituals, traditions, and forms of worship? I already use running, writing, guitar, and dance for meditation and prayer. Why not add sales?

These forms are my passions. Except sales. Someday sales may become a passion, too. I sense that moment is getting close. I'm waiting.

PERFORMANCE

Guitar

Why not express universal thoughts *through* guitar playing? All the ideas and emotions I write about—transcendence, power, beauty, love, anger—could be expressed nonverbally on the guitar. *Leyenda* could express cosmic emptiness, darkness, and mystery.

My concerts could also be viewed as training grounds where I learn to fight the enemy within—fear of audience judgement. By focusing on guitar playing in public, I could strengthen my concentration muscles.

I Hear the Sound of Freedom Striking

This morning I brought my guitar to the Solway lounge to practice. While playing "Alhambra" I noticed one of the guests eating an early breakfast. Even though she was far away, I still imagined her listening to me. Suddenly, the old fear of performance returned. I have been through it countless times before. But this time I realized I will never be free of this performing fear—never, never, never! No matter how much I practice, how good my tremolo becomes, how excellent the "Alhambra" or works of Bach flow while practicing along in my room, as soon as I step on a public stage or even imagine the public listening to me, stage fright returns, freezing body and mind.

There is no escape for me—ever. For years I have been trying to prove myself through the classical guitar. It has never worked. It will never work in the future. For whatever reason, in this life I will never be free from performance anxiety. The best thing to do is give up trying. Playing classic guitar in private is fine; but in public, it is torture. Yet singing folk songs is no problem. Neither is ad libbing. Only playing classical guitar in front of an audience tortures me. Why not stop trying to prove myself with something I can't do? Why not *give in* to my natural talents? Maybe I'm finally ready to accept limits—and my natural abilities as well. I fooled myself into thinking I could give an anxiety-free classical guitar concert at Solway's on Saturday night. Instead I'll sing folk songs, which are easy. Somewhere in the distant future I may introduce a classical guitar piece. . .or I may not.

The Thirty-Year Utopian Search

Fear and performance anxiety will be my lifetime companions. Give them up, and I die inside. They are lifelong Enemies Within.

Could they also be my friends?

I twist and turn through a thousand philosophies trying to free myself. But there is no escape. Buddha was right. Life is suffering.

I give a concert, I suffer. I don't give a concert, I suffer, too. If I give a concert, I'll be squeezed, pulverized, pushed, twisted, and torn. But I won't die.

If I do not give a concert I'll be asphyxiated. Hope for conquest elation, and victory will die. Breath will be gone. Depression will win.

It's a false peace that comes from not fighting a challenge.

Whip-sawed: First, I give up; then comes rebirth of struggle.

What have I learned?

Fears will never leave. When—or if—they do, I'm dead.

I have been on a thirty-year utopian quest to conquer stage fright and performance anxiety. There is no escape.

I am an artist. The life of the artist is haunted, a never-ending struggle against never-ending fears. My cross is hewn from wood, footlights, and curtains. I am an artistic Jesus nailed to the stage. Monsters stalk every corner. Dangers lurk everywhere. But the artist marches on, ever assailed yet unassailable.

Desperation Makes Me Brave

When I got married, I searched desperately for work and money. Desperation made me brave.

By trying to escape my desperation, I put bravery in chains and heroism in shadows; questing after security and safety, I lost the vision and vitality of the struggle.

Luckily, I am getting desperate again. Tonight's concert is coming up.

I feel like the Democratic Party experimented with a new program to improve the world and ending up with a mess. Same thing with my guitar. Anyway, I'm back to the "right" track. There's no denying that suffering works.

Entering Guitar Heaven

Gorgeous!

I'm back.

It has taken eighteen years to break through. Once I recover from the shock, the incredible time it takes to move an inch, then it is no big deal. Look how long the Roman Empire lasted until it crumbled—and the Democratic Party, too. Ideas go on for years, even lifetimes. Suddenly, one day a realization occurs, and their history changes forever. Such a powerful revelation takes a few seconds: the nature of so-called reality shifts; you are faced with a radically new world-view. Earth shakes, mountains tremble, clouds dump a thousand-pound rain in seconds, the sun darkens before bursting into brilliant light. The world is reborn in a flash, your vision transformed. What have you done? Seemingly, nothing. An event has overwhelmed you, thrown you to the ground, instantly buried your old self. A shining new one, spanking and radiant, breathes upon the ancient molecules of your former existence. No doubt the seeds of such transformation were planted months, years, even lifetimes ago. You've long forgotten the planter and the plantee. You are only aware of a vague malaise; existence doesn't feel quite right. You lived in the vague middle, hoping for a reprieve though you've forgotten from what. But you kept fighting to lift the veil and free yourself from the invisible chains. Suddenly, one wondrous day, the lighting strikes, melts the chains, buries the corpse, and leaves a new and shining you in its place.

A miracle? Certainly. But miracles take place every day. It takes an enlightened soul to see them as they occur, as one moment shifts into the next, death shifting into birth, and vice versa.

Such is the story of my guitar playing—the miracle of the week. After years of dead-ends and frustrated ventures in countless new directions, suddenly, in a wave of sweat, piss-inspiring fear, gut-wrenching, bile-churning, stomach-turning revolution, a new guitar self was born. It happened on the Solway House Yoga and Folk Dance Weekend. It had nothing to do with the weekend itself, or Solway House, or our yoga teachers, my folk dance teaching, our guests, or any thing else I can think of. It happened because the time was right. In the beginning, when God created the world, He decided the exact time and place— October 20, 1995, in Saugerties, New York. On that day Jim Gold would have a guitar revelation, encounter a pathway revealed.

I decided to give the concert and face the vision of sweat and fire. I rejected the desiccating desert wind of retreat. Embracing visceral panic, I leaped into the concert fray. With palms sweating and poison streaming from my trembling body, I accepted the baptism on the musical cross and blasted my swinging, finger-plucking way into the star-filled heavens.

My fears vanished, transmuted into a heavenly ether. I traveled in the starry heavens of a guitar vision well beyond anything I could ever imagine. Indeed, I had touched these spots briefly in the past, but I had always retreated. (How could I, a mere Bronx-boy mortal, underling to the great violinists, pianists, conductors, guitarists, and musicians of past and present, dare to play so well?

Answer: I didn't! Every time I touched heaven, I crept back to my lowly, rat-filled existence. I was not meant to dwell with the gods or enter heaven in this life. I could only *glimpse* it. But that glimpse was enough to set me on the path, the long crawl, the hanging, rolling, striving, to peer through that crack of light up ahead. Hope and relentless practice were my instruments. Classic guitar music was my vehicle.

Eighteen years of frustration followed—or was it thirty?

But on the Solway Weekend the gates opened.

How do I know?

I had forgotten my rationalizations, my curses for mistakes, my catechism of self-blame for missed notes. Through some miracle of self-transformation, I had risen beyond my doubts. Their meaning and power had dwindled into insignificance. I didn't care about them.

Now I am running down the road freed from my devils, leaving them further behind with each step. And up ahead—even surrounding me now as I speak—pours the ineffable quality of those heavenly clouds in which I, for so many thankless, fruitless years, wished to clothe myself.

The Birth of Self-Confidence

Are there any conclusions I can draw from my excellent guitar playing? I think so. But before I explore them I must congratulate myself on making a qualitative leap by using the word "excellent." That I should even admit the word into my guitar vocabulary is the first plus. That I should use it without hesitation, no "perhaps," "maybe," "Could it be?", or any other qualifier is another sign of progress. Once tentative about superlatives, I am now definite.

I have touched excellent playing in the past but retreated from it. I wasn't ready for such self-confidence: the ability, skill, luck, and good fortune of being able to trust myself. In the beginning, I circled around my instincts, glancing, briefly embracing, before withdrawing. That was stage one. Stage two came when I embraced them more quickly. Stage three, excellence in guitar playing, comes with complete self-confidence, accepting the directives of my instincts.

Alexander Bellow said that relaxing my right wrist would give me greater power in guitar playing. Did I believe him? Yes and no. I believed his words but rarely felt his conclusions. Could I have been afraid of such power? Probably.

I wasn't ready. Now I am. As I played my scales this morning, relaxing my right wrist so that the strings touched a more inward part of my finger nail and rolled to my finger, I "knew" it was right.

I've suffered years of trial and error to realize Alexander Bellow's technique was correct.

I am lucky to have gained self-confidence in this lifetime.

Conquering Stage Fright: Jump over Speed; Focus on Feeling

I am at the door of my final guitar breakthrough.

It is occurring through two events.

We had our Thanksgiving dinner at Miki's house. My cousin, Jo, who lives in Montreal, and her daughter, Anika, were there. Jo is a professional dancer and has, over the years, together with her husband, Gene, a playwright, director, and former director of the Guthrie Theater in Minneapolis, put together the Jo Lechay Dance Company. Gene writes "plays" for Jo, which are dance performances using words and multimedia. Actually, I am not really sure what they are, since I have never seen her perform them.

In any case, because of her experiences in the art world, coupled with the fact that she is "in the art fight" as a professional dancer, when she asked me what's happening in my life, I told her about my guitar breakthrough. Usually I don't mention it to anyone, or, if I do, don't elaborate. I don't think most people will either understand it or be able to add anything helpful. But Jo is different. She told me that dealing with stage fright was her specialty. Both she and Gene specialize in this aspect of performance. I decided to call her the next day for a "phone session."

She said, "In order to conquer stage fright, you must focus on expressing a feeling, an emotion. All your focus must be on this. Forget the audience. A passion to express this most important idea, the most important feeling, must override everything you do."

Then she asked me such questions as why I play guitar, and what I want to express when I play it. These are basic questions but ones I hardly ever ask myself. They certainly started me thinking.

Then, last night after I played Leyenda slow and fast, I decided to glance through a wonderful book I first read over twenty-five years ago called *With the Artists*, which has interviews with many great violinists, violists, and cellists.

The first interview was with Mischa Elman. He said the problem in those days (the book was published in 1955) was an obsessive concern with *speed*. Young musicians were forgetting about content and feeling in the music, and instead focusing on velocity.

An addiction to speed has been my problem most of my professional guitar life. When I say "addiction to speed," I don't mean that I could *play* fast; only that I *yearned* to play fast, and my inability to play at amazing speeds—especially the arpeggio and scale passages in the pieces I loved—always hung over my head like an albatross, highlighting my deficiencies. The goal of my practice for years has been to acquire speed so I could overcome my speed inferiority complex. Now, here comes Misha Elman, one of the great violinists, saying that focus on speed is a wrong direction and detracts from the music.

I had thought about the above observations often over the years, but nothing had ever come of it. I always fell back into the same mold, trying to conquer slowness, trying to increase velocity so I could prove worthy of joining my musical heroes. I didn't expect to compete with Heifitz, Elman, etc. But I wanted to at least get up in front of an audience and play proudly and with confidence. I didn't want to live chained to speed and fear.

I did though—until today. Now the time is right for the next movement in my musical life, the third movement of my symphony. I am ready to jump over speed as the prime focus of my playing and replace it with *feeling*. That is a major, major step. It means admitting I *have* all the technique I need. It also means focusing on feelings whenever I play. *By focusing on feelings, I can eliminate stage fright.* Instead of focusing on my inadequacies and speed "weaknesses," which only serve to make me more nervous when I perform, I will focus on feelings. Who could question me when I express my feelings on the guitar? I am an absolute authority on them. I will be expressing something unique, something absolutely mine. Such an attitude can only bring me confidence, security, and ease when I perform on the stage.

Listening to the Notes

When I play guitar, I climb into the notes to see who they are. Why force my ego on them? They always resist. Ego fails when it fights. Why not relinquish it, turn it over to the notes? Let them tell me what to do; let them decide. I will be their servant. It's easier that way. Notes have answers and adventures I never dreamed of.

If I hand these notes my illusion cloth, does it really matter whether I play them fast or slow? Does it matter whether they play me fast or slow? Of course not. Slow and fast simply express moods and feelings.

It's such a pleasure to be free of musical ego. Maybe now I'll have some peace—and play well, too.

Fugue Feeling

I'm playing the Bach "Fugue in A minor." It's a piece I always manage to get through even though I cannot understand its structure. Somehow my fingers move automatically. If I don't think too much, I can play it.

As I practiced the piece this morning, I thought, What if I performed it in public and *forgot* it? How would I handle it?

My first thought is: If I give enough concerts, I am bound to forget once in awhile. Thus, accept forgetting.

But it is not so much forgetting that is the problem, but *the fear* of forgetting. What do I do about the fear?

Jo says, Focus on the feeling you want to express. Let your music and fingers take care of themselves. Total concentration on the emotion will carry you beyond the fear of forgetting.

It's a good approach.

What emotion am I trying to convey? I haven't thought much about that until now. I usually focus on the technique of playing the fugue rather than the emotion I am expressing.

Why do I play it? Do I ever know why I play anything? How about Villa-Lobos's "Prelude Number Four," Granados's "Spanish Dance Number Five," "Leyenda," "Alhambra," or any other piece? Having a reason to perform the piece doesn't seem to be the way I do things. I like discovering something new in every performance or practice session. My method, if you'd call it a method, is based on revelation. I want to experience awe and wonder when I play.

I want my moods, emotions, and slow-thinking thoughts to drip out slowly through my fingers as I press and caress the strings. I'm going on a tour. Each piece will be an adventure, new, different, and fresh. This spontaneous approach often brings me unity and peace.

Meeting the King

My ego knelt before the King. He poured music and symphony through my shoulders and down my spinal chord, flooding my heart with humbling supernal power. He stepped into my hands when I played the Bach "Fugue." His loving fingers caressed the notes, stroking them with the softness of his strength.

A knife of focused fingers cut through my brain.

He split my ego in half, chopped it up, and squeezed it through my eye.

Awe-struck, I left frightened and naked.

Mental Preparation for Guitar Concerts

I have decided to give a concert at the Paramount Hotel this New Year's Weekend. This is the first public flowering of my October guitar breakthrough. The physical aspects consist of concert preparation, of reviewing and practicing all the pieces I know. But I would like to add a new mental practice. Napoleon Hill, in *Think And Grow Rich*, speaks about the effect of the conscious mind on the unconscious mind. If you consciously repeat a phrase, day after day, month after month, year after year, the unconscious mind will accept it, and soon you will begin to believe it. This is true whether the conscious mind tells the truth or a lie.

Through constant repetition of a phrase, I can therefore hypnotize myself into believing whatever I want.

I might begin my mental preparation for my guitar concert, my new mental discipline, by telling myself every morning and during the day: "I play beautifully. It is impossible to make a mistake. The audience loves me." This new mental preparation approach is definitely worth a try. Apply the principles of *Think and Grow Rich* to guitar concerts.

A Healing Disaster

The best I can call last night's concert is a *healing disaster.*

I planned a classical guitar program. I got nervous and messed up my opening suite by Gaspar Sanz. I forgot his "Canarios" in the middle but managed to muddle my way to the end, embarrassed but unbowed. The next, Villa-Lobos's "Prelude Number 4" was better, and so was Bach's "Gavotte." As I progressively warmed up, I relaxed and my playing began flowing smoothly.

The concert itself was a public success. The audience loved it. Nervousness was my own contribution.

Follow the path of pain and you transform yourself. My evening concert felt like the end of a road.

For years I wanted to give a classical guitar concert in order to prove myself worthy. After a four-hour bout of depression and longing for suicide during the October Solway Weekend, I finally decided that, no matter how much torture it was to give a concert, it was better than killing myself. The concert I gave that night turned into a big personal success, leading to six weeks of incredible classical guitar playing. Then I decided to give a full classical guitar program on the New Year's Paramount Weekend.

I gave the concert, but nervousness killed my pleasure. I hated it, even though the audience loved it.

The answer may be to start with a group song. I'll use it to relax myself and the audience. After I'm relaxed, I can play classical guitar.

I am "healing myself in freedom." This format is easy and natural. Plus it's lots of fun. Imagine ad libbing freely in front of people, creating and improvising before them. It's like writing my journal in public.

I'm on to something. Travel a twisted trail of self-torture and concert misery and you can find yourself. It often leads you home, though it may take more than a lifetime to get there.

BUSINESS

Self-Publishing, Plus Three New Business Ideas

I made a decision this morning: follow the self-publishing route. Give up trying to find other companies. Of course, if another publishing company says they will publish me I might accept. But that possibility is very slight. Therefore I am putting no more effort into searching outside.

I've always followed the self-publishing route. Why should things be different now? I took that direction because it gave me control over my writing, my books, myself, and my destiny. Ten years ago, after failing to find a publisher, I decided to explore and learn the skill of self-publishing. Then I did it. Wonderful! What a feeling of power, strength, and control over my destiny! This morning as the desire to self-publish returned, so did the control-over-my-destiny feeling. That alone is a good reason to self-publish. Add to this my lack of desire, energy, and drive to find an outside publisher, and self-publishing my book is the best solution.

Most of the books I like have either been self-published or put out by some small press—which is almost the same thing as self-publishing. Look at the *Journals of Paul Brunton*, published by Larson Publications in upstate New York, or even books by the Dalai Lama, put out by Wisdom Press in Boston. All small presses. The difference between their small press and my Cumberland Press is that they have books of several authors in their sales catalogue. I have only mine. That might change some day. I may promote other books like Alkis Raftis's *The World Of Greek Dance*. I could have a separate section of my sales table reserved for books I believe in. Also tapes. Why not? There's a new business for me.

Sales of books and tapes. A business expansion. I like it. My own books, other people's books, tapes, someday perhaps even my own folk dance or guitar tapes. We'll see.

Love Versus Need

Yesterday I put in a fine day's work.

I sent out ads for the 1996 season to *Viltis, Gypsy Planner, Ontario Folk Dancer, Delaware Valley Folk Dancer*, and a couple of other magazines I can't remember. Then I called our Blue Grass gardener, Fred, told him I needed a landscape consultation, and ended up visiting his house in Teaneck to look at his Douglas fir tree. I didn't like it for our front lawn and ended up choosing a flowering pear. We'll plant it on the lawn in front of my den window; we'll also plant three Rose of Sharon trees between my den and Gopal's house next door. That's enough landscaping for awhile. It's the first step towards reclaiming our house and lawn from the maple tree that fell on it last Saturday night.

I also painted the basement.

I went to National Paints on West Englewood Avenue, bought two cans of white paint, a brush, roller, pole, and pan, returned home, and started work. I did most of the broads strokes, the ceiling and walls; Bernice did the details along the pipes, corners, and windows. It took about four hours of heavy, nonstop work. Then I cleaned the basement floor and put the books back on their shelves. All in all, I saved about $350 and had the satisfaction of a job well done.

Pride in labor: the ultimate payment for painting the basement. Perhaps I should think about doing some physical labor in the afternoons. Post-lunch time is physically and mentally a down time. I can hardly function until three or even four in the afternoon. How about a home project, something "mindless" but meaningful—like painting a room, cleaning a basement, or fixing something. A "relaxing" change of pace.

I came up with new thoughts on *New Leaf*: organize it like a book of prose-poems.

I also considered working backwards instead of forwards—a nonlinear approach to organization, poetic, indirect, based more on intuition than reason; it moves from "A" to "E" and even "P" rather than from "A" to "B" to "C".

I am overwhelmed by all the *New Leaf* pages I keep writing. They just keep coming. Most are pretty good, so I can't just throw them away. Should I use the *Handfuls of Air* approach—organize it in themes, categories?

Maybe for now I ought to drop the idea of organizing *New Leaf*. Evidently, I lack the motivation, the gut-wrenching need to edit it.

Fame, recognition, fortune, do not drive me with the same intensity they once did. I no longer suffer from the "Must do it before I die" approach. Now it still calls, but quietly.

Barry and the writing class will hear my writing. Even if they didn't, it wouldn't bother me much. Worse yet, it wouldn't bother me much if no one read it.

I am moving towards aloneship. Even that doesn't bother me. Outside rewards seem extraneous. Pleasure, satisfaction, and the personal rewards of writing itself seem enough.

I say this regretfully but with recognition.

I love the labor but feel indifferent to its fruits. Isn't this a high state? Maybe. But nevertheless, I remain a performer. Part of me feels guilty for not wanting to "share" my writings with others.

I don't "share" running or yoga with anyone. I have no desire or need to. I am even moving towards not "sharing" my guitar with anyone. Up to now, writing has remained in a "secret-sharing" category, an unvoiced hope that, some day, somehow, someone will read it, look into my heart with recognition and say I'm wonderful. But this need is also diminishing.

The more my need for recognition diminishes, the more my love of writing grows. Is there an inverse relationship between love and need? Must needs diminish *in order for* love to grow?

Babble at Nomad

We are attending the Nomad Festival. Paulician marksmanship was the premier order in store-bought Connecticut sphincter yesterday. Still, no reason to cant, cank, or victulate. All ordered surroundings prefigured the desire to speak Bulgarian to the walls. But Days Inn walls only understand Turkish.

So be it. Move on. Tear down vast forests filled with maple, elm, oak, and sugar trees, step on mammoth rocks piled deep in the brown-wet jungle, slip across mud flats and vast dumps of fetid vegetables and gigantic marble stumps. Flatland rocks are everywhere. Poetry in action. Great lumps of words wedded and wetted together, rising, fentlike and hover-filled, across barren plains while nomadic hordes side by side with hordes from NOMAD graze on, bifurcating grass before bisecting livers of adjacent neighbors. Yes, the air is fresh this morning.

Last night my dance class sang a preambulatory song on stage before a large crowd of purple onlookers. Delving then diving into the dance, not one fell off stage into the purple pit of people sea beyond. A miracle! The Lord, deep in His planning wisdom, kept the circle moving to the right, using me, His instrument, to push it along. I fulfilled the plan, smiling, crying, screaming, shouting, coaxing the mass of dangling feet and floppy legs sluggish to the right. They hobbled forwards, skipping, jumping, stumbling in the proper direction. While this minute, prelestial event took place, high above, in the celestial sphere, an Eye peered down upon us, bending to the left in humorous selection before winking at our proceedings.

David said I hadn't aged a bit in ten years. "No gray hairs? Do you dye your hair?" he asked.

"No," I answered. "I only lose it."

Meanwhile Leora's knees buckled. This stalwart wife of David spoke to me in Newtown High School hallway. Her words brought a wreath of God. Straight down it descended upon the marble floor whereon stood we. I bent my ear towards her, hoping to catch the sound of scribbling hope, but only a scratch appeared.

It's the last day of Nomad Festival.

Nice writing this morning. So long.

When we got back from Nomad Festival last night I found a fax from Cloud Tours with the 1996 Greek tour prices. So high! There goes my profit. Then I saw cuts I could make, places to negotiate, a smaller gross price, and a possibly successful tour after all.

The combination of returning from the exciting Nomad Festival to pedestrian home with further blows from bills and Cloud Tour prices sent me into a tailspin. This time, however, I could "witness" my tailspin, step aside and watch it "from a distance" as it took over my thoughts and clouded my mind. Part of me remained in positive vibrations of transcendence; another part fell into a mud pit.

"Witnessing" is progress.

The Nomad Festival gave birth to many new business ideas. One of them is printing name tags with my name, address, and phone in small print below. This could serve both as a business card and a personalized name tag I could design in calligraphy for each customer or potential customer. Such a card would be an excellent sales tool, a way of meeting, greeting, and talking to people, giving them a "lasting" and personal memory of my business. Plus doing names in calligraphy is so much fun!

Another idea is trying to find a contra dance teacher to join our summer tour to Czech Republic, Slovakia, and Poland next summer. The Czech Republic is a center of American contra dances. If I can't find a contra dance teacher to work with perhaps I can advertise in contra dance journals, magazines, or newsletters. I'll call the Contra Dance Society of New York to find out about their bulletins, etc.

Another idea is the Sue Fish Weekend combination at the Fallsview for November of 1996.

Another is consulting or even participating in the Balloon Festival Tour to Albuquerque and New Mexico in October of 1996.

Both of the above events have me working in conjunction with other groups, using my organizing skills, abilities, and knowledge both for their benefit and my own. I am becoming a consultant for these groups. My first reaction to them was, "Why don't you do it yourself and make some money? I'll guide you and be your consultant." But, strangely—or perhaps not so strangely—most people want more than consultation: They want me to actually participate, to take the burden of being responsible out of their hands. Evidently they are not entrepreneurial types. They don't want to develop a business. But I do. This new direction is lots of fun. It's easy, low pressure. I'm just doing what I know how to do. I like guiding and helping others. There is no desperation for money either. Living without desperation is new; a wonderful, calm feeling is beginning to envelop me. I have had it since September. I don't know why it has "suddenly" happened, but I won't destroy it with too much analysis. Suffice it to say I am consciously and unconsciously meditating on Deepak Chopra's advice: focus your mind on loving your work. Use it to serve humanity. Money and other rewards will then accrue to you by themselves.

Sales Calls Relax Me

Yesterday in the late afternoon I sat down at my desk, wrote four pages of babble. Then, released from my demons, decided to make some telephone sales calls.

I started calling. I asked my customers how they were and what was going on in their lives. Then I launched into my sales spiel. The spiel was easy, filled with subtle suggestions about why I'd called. I followed up each call with a personal note and included my brochure and fliers. It turned into a good hour of sales calls. Most important, I found them *relaxing*. The calls served a purpose similar to running and yoga. Following the intense concentration of writing, or even practicing guitar, I need an intense break, something so startlingly different it wrenches my mind away from previous attachments. Violent push-ups can be such a break; so can sit-ups, difficult yoga postures, or fast and focused running. Yesterday I discovered that telephone sales calls can also serve as such a break. Such a discovery helps round out my life. It's also good for business.

Defending My Tour Prices

I read the *Times* travel section this morning and saw Paul's ads. His prices to Budapest and Prague are low. Mine are higher.

I think about Fleurette. She wanted to join my tour to Budapest. She's a psychologist, nice but a bit flaky. When I called her she told me my prices were too high. I said they depend on the kind of hotel we use. Since ours are better, so our prices are higher. She countered by saying that the ABC Tour ad she'd read advertised four- and five-star hotels; yet even with these fine hotels, their prices were lower than mine. I didn't know what to say, so I said nothing and simply sent her a brochure.

I have to do better than that. I must defend my tour prices, not just with the "better hotel" description, but by explaining how and why my tours *are* different, by telling people what they get when they go with me. I should tell them what is included in the price. Actually the price is not higher. Rather, *it is different.* For what they are getting, *the price is fair.*

Wonderings

Thanksgiving is over. I have much to be thankful for—1995 was my best year yet. My tours made lots of money. I had a monumental guitar breakthrough, followed by three smaller ones in running, yoga, and telephone sales. But 1995 is ending. What now? November was the slowest business month all year. I used the time to consolidate my breakthroughs.

I'm not ready to move in my next direction. . .but I'm starting to get nervous.

I've had a wonderful day.

I began by practicing guitar for two hours in our newly renovated basement. I played the Bach "Fugue in A minor," Villa-Lobos's "Chorus," and "Leyenda." A wonderful, fully concentrated session—it reminded me of my high school violin-practice years, when I'd close the door to my room, shut out the world, draw my bow across the strings, and violin myself into ecstasy.

In the afternoon I went to Sam Ash on Route 4 to buy a music stand. I wandered into the classical guitar department. A guitarist sat playing in the corner. Young men milled around listening, talking softly, or glancing at the guitars hanging on the walls.

Then a miracle took place. For the first time in years I didn't feel inferior upon hearing a good guitar player. The jealousy, competition, and inferiority haunting me most of my guitar life had disappeared, somehow dribbled away. I luxuriated in the music and in the secure, serene, warm feeling of that Sam Ash guitar room, a striking difference to the oppressive, competitive, envious, kill-all-the-guitarists, jealous, hate-filled feelings of my past. What a blessing to have reached this state!

It's hard to describe the inner transformation I am experiencing. Language may only diminish the magnificence of my guitar release into freedom.

It is not necessary to tell the world about it. No one has to know about these revelations to understand or sympathize with me. My freedom feels unconditional.

I imagine, if I had no guitar, this experience would have happened anyway. It is a gift from above, an act of grace.

What is happening is beyond survival level. I have been visited by a heavenly force. My door has been opened to bliss incarnate.

How do you crack ice on a lake in winter?

You pick up an axe, a pick, and start picking. How thick the ice is, you don't know. You start picking anyway. Without the sun, spring weather, and cosmic forces, you might pick forever. But when these powers combined with the will and muscular power of your own picking, work together, soon you break the ice.

Just like my guitar breakthrough. For years I picked at the ice. Dead of winter. A spring thaw came, but things soon froze up again. Ice and cold everywhere. My sole protection was thick skin. Determination, and, hidden far away, the faint hope that someday I might break through and reach the flowing waters beneath.

I've been picking for years—thirty-six years—if I am to use the mystic kabbalistic number of double *chai*. It started when I graduated from the University of Chicago and moved into my St. Marks Street apartment in East Greenwich Village, New York. I started my new life as an aspiring writer and guitarist. I picked my way in and out, married, picked my way through New Jersey and Teaneck, through a concert guitar career, folk dancing and tourism. All the while I practiced my guitar.

This year the sun came up. The weather changed, the ice broke. I slipped into the clear flowing waters below. Drifting blissfully downward, experiencing a revelation every day or two. These are not the volcanic eruptions of primal October but pleasant vibrations of realization, dips and descents into deeper levels of fluidity.

I am taking another look at my musical past. I've reopened books in my basement library I never thought I would read again, books on music theory and harmony, and the lives of composers, pianists, violinists, and other musicians. I even put the Bach "Chaconne" on my music stand. Astonishing.

I read a book about Casals last night. He speaks of Bach's religious mysticism and how it is expressed so perfectly in his music. Bach a *mystic?* I never thought of him that way. I saw him only as a blockage, a gigantic technical obstacle I had to surmount to prove myself worthy.

But now I'm moving on, taking a fresh look, revisiting former music lessons and teachers along with former perceptions and conceptions. I'm reviewing Bach. I've been playing him all these years because, hidden deep down in my soul beneath crusts of camouflage, unknown and unrecognized by the superficial egotistic me, I "knew" he was a brother, that some day I would understand and appreciate his excellence. Perhaps I needed thirty-six double-*"chai"*ed years to see the true face of Bach.

Something else happened during those thirty-six years: I matured. I developed my own philosophy of life. During my early violin and guitar years, I tried out the philosophies of other musicians and composers. Some fit, but none fit well. I needed to find my own.

Now I have. Water is flowing in my lovely lake. I'm picking up my guitar and I'm diving to the bottom for another look.

Music and Writing: My Form of Giving

I went through my entire classical guitar music collection, picked out twenty pieces I once played, put them on my music stand, and spent a week going through them. By a slow process of elimination I ended up with "Venezuelan Waltz" by A. Lauro, "Campanas del Alba" by Eduardo S. de la Mata, and Villa-Lobos's "Étude Number Eleven." I'll also bring back "El Colibri" (The Hummingbird) by Sagreras and Emilio Pujol's "El Abejorro" (The Bumblebee). I decided against working on Paganinni's "Moto Perpetuo," since I doubt I'll ever play it in public. I even put the Bach "Chaconne in D minor" on my music stand but decided against learning it for now.

I've set myself up with a long-range guitar-playing project. During the past six weeks I have been carving out a new musical path, represented by new pieces. New paths take a long time to travel. I'm taking my first steps.

Playing in public again? Public performance never leaves my mind. For years I have been practicing to "be good enough." Recently I've been luxuriating in the happiness of being "good enough." Now, with new pieces and new direction, I am fast approaching the next stage.

Could it be my desire to perform will never die? Has it been on hold for years? In my gut I know this is true. My performing urge will not go away. Perhaps it is one of the mitzvah forms I was put on earth to do, to perform. Perhaps it is my "responsibility" to offer the fruits of my talents to others no matter how torturously difficult the giving process may be.

Deep down I know performing is one of my purposes. I'm just trying to avoid it.

Yoga and running have also crystallized in new forms—yoga as an art form, running with its Steve Berall schedule. In the list of priorities, music is at the top along with writing—which I consider an expression of music.

Business has been terrible during the last few weeks. I have been exiled from my Tour Registration Garden of Eden. There is always a reason for exile, even though I'm not sure what it is. I'm getting nauseous thinking about all this. Visceral stomach pains often point towards new quests, directions, and transitions.

Music and writing are my mitzvah forms of giving.

Birth of My Business Leaf

I answered the phone message, hoping it would be a Budapest customer. It wasn't. My low mental state continued. I started whining about how miserable business is and how my Hungarian tour will probably be cancelled.

I asked my wife if I could whine to her. She said fine. I was about to unload all the familiar complaints about how no one calls and how quickly my Budapest tour has collapsed, but something stopped me: It's not manly to whine and complain.

Then I realized my vacation was over.

I have been on a three-month extended relaxation spree since my tours ended in September. During this period my mind has been at "play," with such side pursuits as guitar, reading, yoga, running (though, strangely, not writing). I love them all, but none make money. To be sure, as a cosmic aid, the phone hardly rang and registrations stopped coming in. It's as if God didn't want me disturbed with any future business, wanted to give me time to focus on guitar breakthroughs, yoga, running, and reevaluating my past. I've had a lot of free time during these past six weeks, the duration of my "period."

It's time to move on to. . . business.

I get frustrated, mad, and disgusted with no phone calls, no sales, and no registration. This, plus my disappointment over only one registrant for my Budapest tour, are all warning signals.

My 1996 brochure is coming out; my brain is coming out; I'm coming out. But my only *creations* in business this year have been cutbacks. Wednesday night folk dance class was cut to once-a-month meetings; weekends have been cut to four a year. (Tours have remained stable.)

Thus my business "accomplishments" this season have consisted mostly of diminishments, treading water, and the expenditure of minimum mental effort. I'm not complaining. I needed this resting state to reevaluate past and settle old scores.

Searching for "Fsitchko e Edno" in Business: The Role of Time

What is business? How important is it to me? How do I do it? How and why should I get customers? How important is money? What is the real meaning of money? Should I get more of it? How do creativity and business go together?

My mornings consist of guitar practice, writing, study, yoga, or running. When I fill the best and freshest time of my day with these wonderful pursuits I feel I have made my day and life worthwhile.

But I spend afternoons and evenings paying with alienated labor for my morning fulfillment. Is that a good deal? Once again I see the same dichotomy, the same flight from Oneness. This division between life and labor is exactly what I am trying to escape from. My goal is *fsitchko e edno—all is One*.

I can no longer see my mornings as separate from business. Conversely, I can no longer see business as separate from what brings me joy. How can I bridge the gap, connect fulfilling labors with alienated ones? How can I weld these opposites into a cohesive philosophic mosaic?

Here's the answer: my pleasures someday may make money! They may be part of my business. They are Jim Gold International's R & D department. It often takes years to develop a product or service; twenty or thirty is not unusual. When I practice guitar, write, study, do yoga, or run, I am in a long-range process of product and service development. Thus there really is no division between business and nonbusiness. The division between my leisure and work is one of time, not of essence.

In the morning I am planting seeds, tilling my garden. Somewhere in the future, services and products will grow. When they are fully ripe, I can offer them on the open market.

I often feel selfish when I work alone, creating world after world. What will I do with them? Who will profit? Is there benefit to what I am doing beyond self-satisfaction and personal growth? What about service to others? Am I really just selfish, narcissistic, and self-involved?

Good questions. But no matter how selfish and self-involved I may feel in the short run, I am creating products and services for others long-term, since, in the end, all service to oneself is service to others—and vice versa.

For the past six weeks business has been pretty bad. My phone has stopped ringing, hardly any registrations have come in for either weekends or tours, and my Budapest tour may be cancelled for the first time. Short-term, business has slowed to a virtual standstill. But long-term, perhaps it hasn't: For the past two months I have also been practicing guitar—a future service. I also keep turning out pages in my journal, another future service. I don't know where yoga, running, or kabbalistic study come in. Perhaps someday they will be part of my business, too.

Short-range thinking prevents me from seeing that.

The weather report predicted a blizzard, eighteen inches of snow over the next two days. Barry cancelled his class. I'll cancel tonight's folk my dance class. Winter is here with its fierce folk dance-cancelling power. Barry said he agreed with me: His business is slow, too. "How do you know what I think?" I asked. He said he'd read it in my journal. Barry knows me better than anyone else. He reads every entry in my journal—and that writing is the best of me.

Business is *slower* than slow. This may be a year with small tours and tour cancellations. The money I'm spending on Barbara Tapa's design of my new brochure may be a waste. But I planned it, so I might as well follow through and worry about the debts it incurs later.

I predict a slow year. I hope I'm wrong. It might only be a temporary lull. We'll see. I can't predict the future; I can only imagine, think, and worry about it.

November and December killed my expectation for a money-making New Year's and put a damper on a money-making 1996 tour season.

I'm retreating from the world. There is a new annoyance in my voice when I talk to people. Conversations bother me; I resent the time I have to spend with others. I don't mind talking to them about business or registration or about how their dollars can support my study habits. I feel like staying home for days, weeks, months, years, to practice guitar, study bible, read philosophy, and learn the secrets of self, God, and the universe. After my 1995 blow-out best-year ever, I want a retreat where I can sit in my armchair and concentrate on my interior existence. I'm on an adventure exploring who I am, where I belong, where I'm going, what my purpose is, my self, what its relationship is to the Self, where I stand with Judaism, religion, spirituality, mysticism, Kabbalah, and the outside world. It seems the only way I can find out what is outdoors is to retreat indoors. I dwell in my house of study and prayer, the meditation-study cave of my personal *beth hamikdosh*. My living room, basement, and bedroom comprise a monastic cell. I sit at my desk, in my armchair, on the sofa or floor, studying by sunlight or lamplight, delving into the mysteries of life. It's back to school, college revisited. Only this time I'm attending the University of Cumberland Avenue in Teaneck, New Jersey. Campus grounds no longer include meadow and field, fraternity buildings, dormitories, and science centers. My teachers live in books, or they visit me via telepathy in disembodied spiritual forms. I have little desire to leave my *beth hamikdosh*. I have food in the refrigerator, a running road outside, stretching rug lying at my feet, a computer at my desk, and a beautiful Ramirez guitar to play on. It's cozy. Sure I'd be glad if some business came in and I made some money. But this may not be the right time. There may be a cosmic reason for this business slowdown. It gives me free time to evaluate my life and my place in the world. I can sit, a good Yiddish *zets*, and meditate, doing my personal "upanishad" under my bodhi tree.

I am researching future projects—part of my cosmic business plan encompassing all aspects of life, from the microscopic study of gestating cells in my being to the visible products and services I shall create for others.

INVENTIONS

Crankyville

When the sun rose in Crankyville, locals cried. As it rose higher in the clear blue sky, warming the good earth, they sat in their backyards and wailed.

In the evenings, sitting before delicious steaks, rich wines, and succulent desserts, they moaned.

They were not a happy lot.

The day came after 9.3 months of incubation: Lawrence and Emily Cranky gave birth to the Sam child. "He is strange," noted Mrs. Cranky. "See how his eyes shine." Sure enough, when Sam saw the sun rise, his eyes lit up. He crawled around his crib singing. By noontime he giggled. In the evening, he breast-fed with happy gusto gurgles.

Mrs. Cranky shook her head. "A strange child. What is wrong with him?"

"We can't have him go around *smiling* all day" said Mr. Cranky. "What will the neighbors think? We should bring him to Leslie Pissencure, the sad therapist."

"You're right, Lawrence. It's a down day in Crankyville when you see a child smile. And our own son! How embarrassing! It's just too much to *bear*." Mrs. Cranky broke down in a grin.

Mr. Cranky took her hand. "Don't worry, dear" he said. "Dr. Pissencure is an excellent doctor. She'll fix our Sam so he'll never smile again."

"You're wonderful," sighed Mrs. Cranky. "What would I do without you? If there is one thing I can't stand it's a happy child."

The Crankies took Sam to Teary Wing of Lachrymose Hospital, specializing in cases of public happiness. They gave him misery miracle drugs and depressive talk therapy for two years. But even these powerful modern techniques couldn't stop the baby from gurgling, smiling at the doctors, and rocking with excitement when the sun came up.

"He is a danger to the community," said Dr. Wilbur Chronickrank, the hospital's chief surgeon. "If he keeps laughing, we'll all be out of *business*. We need something drastic like the scalding rag. We'll dip it in boiling oil and wipe that smile off his face."

They wiped Sam's face with the rag. But he kept smiling. Then he laughed.

A that moment the hospital fell down.

Tom and the Hebrew Letters

Tom, a seven-hundred-foot giant, was born with feathers on his legs. Yet he couldn't fly because he suffered from stupidity.

Tom was ashamed of his condition. He decided to find a teacher to guide him up the Smart and Self-Improvement Ladder. Deep in his undeveloped brain, he realized he could use his body as a springboard to a higher state. The only question was how.

On Monday morning he visited Mrs. Dolan's Landslide Academy of Torah, Talmud, Calligraphy, and Hebrew Letters. She took him by the hand, smoothed his ruffled leg feathers, and taught him to draw the Hebrew letter *aleph* on the school yard using a hundred-foot Bentworth shovel-tipped pen. Tom towered above the Academy as he drew the first diagonal line of *aleph*. He added hooked curves on the upper right and lower left.

Suddenly, the *aleph* burst into flame! Smoke and fire shot out in all directions. The entire letter rocketed into the sky, zoomed in concentric circles around a cloud before turning around and, in a paralyzing line descent, headed straight for Tom's head! With a flash of blinding light, it entered his left ear, burned in the center of his brain, inflamed his cerebellum, cerebrum, and medulla, and lit his eyes with a fiery passion.

"Good for *you*, Tom!" encouraged Mrs. Dolan. "Now you understand the nature of aleph." She loaded three cookies on a derrick and hoisted them up to his eager mouth. "These sweets are your temporary reward, a small pleasure. But no pleasure can compare to the joy of learning a Hebrew letter! Next we'll try *beth*."

Tom painted *beth* on the schoolyard pavement. When he finished, *beth* burst into flame and rocketed into the sky. Tom gaped with amazement as *beth* circled and somersaulted on the American Airlines air path. Suddenly, it turned around, and in a paralyzing line descent, headed straight for Tom's head! *Splat!* Beth landed in his mouth! It burned his tongue, singed his esophagus, charred his throat, and peppered his stomach with burning ash before heading to his brain, where it vibrated next to the *aleph*. His eyes shone with *beth* light of white letter-learning passion.

Next came *gimel*. Tom painted it in the schoolyard with his Bentworth shovel-tipped pen. But *gimel* didn't catch fire. It froze in place, hardened into iron, and sank through the concrete. He watched it disappear under the schoolyard. Suddenly, he heard the rumble of an earthquake! The schoolyard burst open and *gimel,* covered with molten lava, shot skyward. It rocketed through the sky, searching for a landing place. It spied Tom. Like a falling star, *gimel* shot straight down, zinged through his right eye, filling his brain with molten lava, electricity, and magnetism before nestling next to *aleph* and *beth*.

Every day Tom painted another Hebrew letter. After twenty-two days he mastered the entire alphabet. At night fire from the Hebrew letters in his eyes lit up the town. Like a light house, it shone for miles around.

Mrs. Dolan was pleased with her student's progress. So was Tom, who had gone from dumb to smart in twenty-two days. On the twenty-third day the feathers on his legs moved to his arms. He flapped them like wings; his giant body began to soar. Ascending skyward, he flew through space, passed American Airlines, and headed towards a higher cloud of Hebrew sentences.

The Laughing Turnip

Tom planned a vegetable garden in his back yard. He planted rows of tomatoes, corns, potatoes, asparagus, Swiss chard, carrots, cucumbers, onions, and turnips.

At the end of the summer, he started picking. He filled his basket with corn, carrots, asparagus, tomatoes, cucumbers, and turnips.

"Ha, ha, ha!"

Who was laughing? No one else was in the garden. He picked more vegetables.

"Ha, ha, ha!"

He looked in his basket.

"Ha, ha, ha!"

It was the *turnip*!

Tom had never heard a laughing turnip before. But soon his confusion turned into an idea. Ma and Pa needed cash for their failing dry cleaning business. No one had ever heard of a laughing turnip. With proper promotion, he might be able to make some money.

Next day, Tom took the turnip to Pathmark. At the check-out counter, he placed it besides his purchases. The turnip laughed. The check-out man eyed Tom. "Young man, are you laughing at me?"

"No," answered Tom. "It's my turnip."

"You think I'm stupid, young man?"

"No, no. I've got a laughing turnip." Tom pointed. "There it is on the counter." The turnip laughed again.

"Watch out, kid. Anyone laughs at me gets smacked in the head."

"It's not me. It's my—"

The turnip laughed again.

The check-out man grabbed a broom and started swinging it wildly. "Get *out!*" he shouted. Tom grabbed his turnip and ran out the door.

He went to the hardware store. The turnip laughed again. "Sorry," Tom said to the manager. "It's my turnip."

"Just pay for the hammer." The manager sighed. "Why do I get all the nut cases?"

Tom began doubting himself as left the store. "Who will believe me?" he asked. "How can I make money on this turnip?"

He walked for several miles deep in thought. Suddenly, he cried out: How about TV stations? *They'd* believe it!

He went to the local WBBB-TV director and showed his turnip. Management loved it. "No other station has one," said the director, rubbing his hands with glee. "Our ratings will *soar*!"

"Yeah, but we can't put a naked turnip on TV," said the head sales manager. "Dress him up." They put a shirt, tie, and jacket on the turnip, then fitted him with pants and shoes. He looked quite handsome. They started him off with his own talk show.

Audiences loved the Laughing Turnip. He answered all questions with a laugh. As his speaking ability improved, he expanded his answers, commenting on politics, human relations, sex, and the weather. He punctuated every answer with a healthy laugh.

Management changed his name to Ted Turnip. Soon Ted made so much money he gave up talk shows and bought the TV station. At that point he gave up laughing altogether.

Ted Turnip didn't need Tom anymore. He gave him $14 for his service as a talent scout and told him to kiss off.

Meanwhile Tom's parents' dry cleaning business had reached near bankruptcy. But Tom wouldn't give up. The following spring he planted another garden. Fourteen laughing turnips came up. Using them as talk show hosts, reporters, actors, and ad reps, he started his own TV station. Soon Tom's Turnip Network raked in millions. He saved the dry cleaning business with a quick infusion of cash.

January–December 1996

WRITING

Two Hats

I met Sid Norinsky for lunch yesterday. He told me he is sending out his writing, looking for an agent and publication. Why am I not doing the same thing?

I am afraid of losing my vision among the rejections and attractions of the market place. Then I'll get so angry and frustrated I'll forget my larger purpose: the creation of beauty.

It's an old fear.

Yesterday I slipped. I was about to give up my tour business in disgust. Low registration had prompted me to throw in the towel. Then I thought: "What about the beautiful tours I worked so hard to create? Should I give them up just because the market is not responding? I want registrants. Instead, the market is rejecting me. Should I give up what I love simply because I am enraged and disgusted? Or should I struggle onwards, undaunted by market vicissitudes, following my dreams regardless of how the market may react?

Struggle on! Dreams are my life blood. Giving them up leads to darkness, then death.

Trouble is currency: anything good costs trouble. The better it is, the more trouble it costs. Fight for customers! Fight against dream destruction. Guard against distractions. Never give up on the dream.

Create, create, create! I am created in the image of the Creator. If He created, why shouldn't I? But I also might mention He didn't have to worry about sales.

Faith is knowing I will pursue my dreams *no matter what*. But how to get customers?

Sid Norinsky says he wears his writing hat in the morning and his marketing hat in the afternoon.

Two hats: something to think about.

Love

I love teaching dance class, writing, playing guitar, running tours, and doing my exercises.

But that love frightens me. What could I be afraid of? Love? Is that why I often gravitate towards the black hole? Am I more afraid of light than darkness, of fresh air than dank, dim life in a cave? Or is it "merely" a habit of retreat—escaping to familiar darkness in order to avoid the ecstatic light of the sun?

Bob Baumol called last night. Talking to him reminded me I haven't written for about a week. A long time for me.

This morning I awoke with an energy burst disguised as a feeling of disgust. Definitely a signal. I hadn't written for over a *week?* What twisted visions had besieged my mind on its bumpy ride over the hills, valleys, stones, and broken glass of maya?

All I can think of is tourism, tourism, tourism. The word reverber ates in my brain. Where the hell are my clients? Where are the registrants who should be signing up for my wonderful tours?

Hiding, no doubt. They're playing God. The Torah, the Kabbalah, the *Teaneck Gazette,* all say that God exists but that He hides himself in alleys, clouds, trees, human bodies, ant hills, and more, waiting for others to be ready for revelation. Open your eyes and, voilá, there is God. He waits in the sod and in the *sod* (Hebrew for "hidden").

Well, that's exactly where my tourists are. Evidently they are not ready to be revealed, especially to me. Perhaps I should run tours with hidden tourists. I can show up with a busload of invisible registrants, then take them to hidden places.

My disgust is aimed at the tourist industry in general and at my absent registrants in particular. Nothing new here. Just another morning of anger, frustration, and peevishness. Naturally this doesn't mean I am leaving the tourist industry or giving up. As running guru, George Sheehan says, the purpose of a race is not to beat others but to fight against the small voice inside you that wants to quit.

I am not quitting. In fact, during the past week I have explored two new programs for 1997. I am thinking about tours to Sicily in May and Romania in August. I called the Italian tourist bureau. They are sending me information about folk festivals throughout Italy. I am particularly looking at one in Agrigento, Sicily. I never knew there *were* folk festivals in Italy. If I find one, I'll organize a tour around it.

Also, Joyce Dalton gave me the name of a new tour company in Portland,

Oregon, that specializes in Romania. I called them and spoke to the director. He is sending me all kinds of information. They're even running a FAM tour there in May. I'd love to go on it, but my Greek tour conflicts with it.

I got in touch with Jacob Shoshan, an Israeli guide who is highly recommended. He may guide our November tour of Israel. We exchanged several faxes. I'll meet him when he comes to Englewood at the end of March.

But the main reason I haven't written is I need a total reassessment of my attitude towards tours.

Writing in the Third Person

Jack Gerbaud wanted to organize tours to Hungary, visit folk festivals, immerse himself in the culture and customs of the country. He wanted to learn the Hungarian language. Early in the morning, he awoke after six hours' sleep and began his language study. Verb after verb, noun after noun, adjective and adverb, one after another. Strange sounds poured into his head; slowly the linguistic barriers fell before him.

He focused on the Hungarian magazines, especially descriptions of folk traditions.

Writing in the third person felt heavy and strange in his hands. Was this the proper method, approach, the proper device? He got the idea after reading *Beneath the Wheel,* by Herman Hesse, one of his favorite writers. Swept up in the story, he wondered, Wouldn't it be interesting to focus on theme, plot, and the third person? It would distance himself from his writing and might make it easier to edit.

He had been writing a journal for years, pouring out his thoughts and feelings. He loved the mental cleansing of this discipline and form of meditation.

But the closeness of writing in first person—I, I, I—made it so difficult to edit. Third-person writing would be a transparent device. Yet it could be good and worthy.

In a few hours he would be meeting his guide, Andrew, and his tour group. They would be driving their minibus to the medieval town of Szentendre, an hour's drive from Budapest. On the way, they'd stop at the ruins of Acquinum, an ancient Roman town. Perhaps he could do some shopping in Szentendre, buy some Hungarian blouses and vests for his boutique in the United States.

The next morning, Jack read a wonderful line in *Narcissus and Goldmund* by

Herman Hesse: ". . . we all have a slight tendency. . . to confuse our wishes with predestination."

It so easily applied to him. Had he bitten off too much? Could he run five tours to Hungary the following year? Organizing tours was easy. He had done it for years and knew the technique. The difficulty—and magic—lay in selling them. Could he get enough people to fill five tours? This season he had hardly filled one. Now he was running five. "Filling" might mean only four people. But if this happened, he would still be making money if he didn't lead it himself. In order to expand, he could not possibly lead every tour.

This was the reason he planned to work with Adam. This former editor of Shaman magazine whose doctorate was in Turkish studies, would be the agent, tour organizer, and leader in Hungary. He might be the guide, too. Jack could stay in America and run his Jack Gerbaud International, Inc.

Jack had taken a Marxian qualitative leap. He was about to enter a new world, the world of delegating responsibility, management, even sales.

Was he destined to run a larger tour business? Could he? Did he even want to? What was the difference between *his* personal desires and predestination? Would it be better to put his efforts into selling his books and promoting himself as a writer, rather than organizing and selling tours? Was he wasting the limited amount of time he had in this lifetime? What did God want from him? He felt an irresistible pull to expand his tour business; yet pulling in the opposite direction was a desire to retreat into his private world, live the life of an artist, and spend minimal time selling.

Could he do both? All of his adult life he had mixed art and business. Was he squandering his energy and time with such a mix? What about focus and concentration? Wouldn't he go further if he did only one thing?

Perhaps God had put him on earth for another purpose——to work out the conflict between personal desire and predestination. He knew the conflicting wishes of his ego; as for predestination, he could only listen to the voices of intuition for hints, then watch as his life unfolded.

That morning he had some transient problems, too. Adam had visited him in the form of a nightmare monster threatening to beat him up. No doubt this was for giving the Szentendre tour to Andrew, a mistake which could easily be misinterpreted as a double-cross. Jack had put the needs of his tourists first. Customers would be satisfied even if Adam was not. On the other hand, Adam might understand the fluidity of tour business situations.

What about voices? Was a third person being born? Should he add the "fourth voice" of an interlocutor?

"Adam, let's go to the Gerbaud for an espresso. We can discuss next year's tour program."

"Good idea, Jack," Adam agreed. "What did you do today?"

"We went to Szentende."

"What? I thought you were going to the Jewish Museum."

"We were supposed to, but our tourists wanted to visit Szentendre. They wanted to save money and go by train, and they wanted me to lead them. I didn't want to, so when our former guide, Andrew, showed up, I asked him to lead them and told him I would pay for it. I made the decision on the spot. Sorry you were forgotten. On the diplomatic side, I suppose it was a mistake. I can only say that, as for pleasing my customers, it was the right decision. By the way, I ended up going, too. Sorry about the trouble you went to, and about my half-promise to do the Szentendre tour with you. It just didn't work out. Next year I'm sure it will be different."

Jack didn't know if Adam would accept this explanation. But it was the best he could do. Then he put aside his concerns and moved on.

Jack sat in the Kempinski Hotel restaurant drinking an early morning espresso and reading the story of Madame Butterfly in Hungarian. The hotel desk clerk had already given him a "new" American name for Madame Butterfly: *Mrs. Butterfly,* he called it. Jack liked that name. From now on, Puccini's opera, *Pillangókisasszony* in Hungarian, would be called "Mrs. Butterfly" in English.

He churned out those Hungarian words. Reading the electronic libretto translation in Hungarian while the performers sang in Italian pushed along his *magyar nyelv* linguistic skills at a rapid pace.

One day left in Budapest: Tomorrow his group would return to New York. He continued reading Hesse's *Narcissus and Goldmund* with wonder and jealousy. Why couldn't he write like that? Perhaps he could, with more commitment and work. But he was so divided between so many works, worlds, directions, and lives.

Imagine, Margit Kovacs was Jewish! Who would believe it? What a tribe those Jews are! What a *torzs;* what a *shevet.* And why not write in three languages?

Why not write in more than three? Throw in sprinklings of Hungarian, Hebrew, Turkish, Greek, and Bulgarian. Sew the whole thing together with English. It could be an incomprehensible creation. What would critics say?

Not a problem, since critics didn't *read* his writing. Who did? No one. He was not ready to make it public. He felt deep in his reptilian subterranean gut that an unknown force was holding him back. It was no longer fear of criticism. Rather it seemed like a secret disdain, as if publishing itself was demeaning. Publishing would detract from the eternal process of creativity, the foreverness he experienced during bursts of artistic illumination. Writing put him in touch with the Hidden Hand of Creation originating with the higher forces above, below, and within. The writing process was a good-in-itself. Publishing felt like an afterthought. Why bother when without it such an epiphanic experience could be reached?

Writing was also a means of perfecting the relationship between God and man. The first five of the Ten Commandments spoke of this relationship; the second half of the one between man and man. The latter could not exist without the former. Man-and-man relationships came "almost" as an afterthought.

The key word here was *almost*. Could it be that Jack was being carried away by the powerful and revelatory character of the writing process? Writing in mad passion, he had forgotten the second half of the ten commandments. His revelations *felt right*.

But feelings, although the motor of man, were are not his rudder. Feelings could fool you into believing you were experiencing an eternal truth, whereas, upon reflection, you might only be creating an illusion, fooling yourself, seeing only part of the picture. Secretly, Jack wanted others to read and appreciate his writing, to join in his revelations. Even deeper, he wanted them to join *him* in his revelations. All people are connected to the eternal truth. The process of writing simply reveals it.

Thus, on a deeper level, no difference existed between writing in his room and communicating with his audience. He could forget about the publishing problem. There existed a Higher Mind continually reading whatever he wrote, communicating it telepathically to all other minds. Most of these minds did not realize it consciously, but they "knew it" unconsciously. It was communicated to them through the vast underground stream, a kind of eternal subterranean internet connecting people to each other. At this profound level separations were only superficial distinctions. In reality, no one was alone. All were connected by the publishing network of Eternity, Inc.

Thus, even as he sat in his room, Jack wrote for a public; he published every word, every edited correction. Every sentence and paragraph he created was public property, part of the universal Publishing House of Creation.

That afternoon he met Adam. They sat in a restaurant on Vaci Street, straightening out details for the 1997 tour itineraries. Two hours later he left with a feeling of accomplishment. Complete itineraries had been planned. Happy and relieved, he was now eager to leave Budapest. America was waiting. So were the eager arms of his sweet wife, Jezebel.

I'm reading *Live Life First Class* by Kenneth Thurston Hurst. He is Paul Brunton's son and a fine positive writer in his own right.

I've returned from Budapest—and to writing in the first person. I wrote in the third person under the influence of Herman Hesse. It also had something to do with setting up those five 1997 Hungarian tour programs with Adam Molnar. Here I was leading my most unsuccessful tour in years—only four people, a quantitative failure—and instead of contracting, withdrawing, and leaving the tour business through the back door, I expanded into five future Hungarian tours.

Perhaps I used third person because I couldn't face failure and misery. How could I not feel these painful emotions leading a tour to Hungary with only four souls, trying to make an impression on Adam, Andrew, Paul Laifer, or anyone else in the tour business?

This even though program and services were excellent and our four clients had a good time.

As Adam said, "You need clients."

Don't I know it.

Do I dare expand when my market is contracting? Dare I waste Adam's time when my hopes of getting new clients are so low? I see dried-up markets, desiccated half-clients, up ahead; I see a road strewn with barren tours, a year of mucho work with few results. Yet these negatives are not stopping me. Somehow and for some unknown reason, I am still developing new Hungarian tours and aiming to accompany one or two of them if I get enough registrants.

I start most new projects with some optimism. This seems to be the first I'm starting with skepticism. Yet I am starting.

Why? Partly it is the challenge of making a nearly impossible project succeed. It is also a new way of organizing tours. Finally, I want my tours to give me "retirement" income and security while I sit at home reading, writing, playing guitar, studying, running, and doing yoga. Of course such an idea is unrealistic. Running more tours will mean more work for me, not less. But simply because the idea is unrealistic does not stop me from trying it.

I am more of a dreamer than a practical person. Give me a dream, a cloud; raise me from the earth. I thrive on the unrealistic, on nebulous dreams falling from the sky. It is part of my nature. That is why I am planning these tours with such low expectations. I doubt I'll pour lots of new money into advertising. I'll continue my ads in folk dance magazines and *International Travel News* and mail out my new brochures; I'll slowly collect new names and expand my mailing list. If I should be doing something different, I can't figure out what it is. Perhaps I'm walking on the ground floor of a new idea and cannot see its implications yet.

Writing

A minor miracle occurred in writing class yesterday. When I told Barry I was sinking into a quantitative journal writing swamp, turning out page after page with no direction or end in sight, he said that my writing form *is* journal writing. Suddenly, I saw some form of journal publishing down the line.

My journal represents the physical, mental, spiritual aspects of my development. It shows growth of a soul through the adventures of a wandering mind.

My new writing goal may be publishing parts of my journal. Just as this idea occurred, Terry Rodgers called to tell me about his friend in the publishing business who prints small runs of books. Is this a mystical direction call from above, a sign from the Hidden Hand of Mr. Destiny and Mrs. Fate?

My exercises also need a new goal. I reached 150 push-ups, sit-ups, and squats. I need something new, but I don't know what.

Yesterday I ran a seder at Miki's. I put the kids, Jeremy, Alison, Jenny, and Akira, near me. Miki, Bernice, Paula, and Christie said I ran it very well.

The goal of rewriting our Passover Hagaddah is slowly forming. I'd like to put it in my own words, make it comfortable for myself and our family. Such a project will take a few years to complete. It will mean mastering, not only Hebrew and the bible, but studying other hagaddas as well. There is an exhibition of hagaddot at the Ridgewood Library this week. I should visit it.

Writing a hagaddah would be a good project. It would put my struggle for artistic expression, financial and emotional freedom, and my battle against physical, mental, and spiritual slavery, into a historic context.

I cannot edit my journal. It is too close to me. What final form it will take, I still do not know. Perhaps I must write many years of journal before I can have the perspective to look back. Ten, twenty, thirty years of journal writing. I may be dead before I finish. _

I can forget about order, style, meaning, communication, or publication. I simply write. I can pour out thousands of pages, exploring philosophies, personal developments and retrogressions.

But the time *will* come. Have faith. I cannot force growth or predict when my tree will bear fruit.

Patience, vigilance, and constant work are the only answer. I'll keep exploring the ups and downs, walking the soul's slow upward path towards unification.

This morning, when I read the stock pages, I saw patience working. Xoma was the most active OTC stock. It had risen the highest percentage. I used to own it but sold it at a loss. Had I waited two years, I would have broken even. Had I waited three to five years, I'd have made money. But I got impatient and sold it too soon.

The rise of Xoma after so many months in the dumps is proof of the power of patience, vigilance, and constant work. Believe in the process; have faith in the glorious helplessness of it.

Patience in journal writing. . . let it roll on at its own pace even for years. Patience in tourism. . . write off 1996 as a miserable year. Realize, if I stick with quality tours, eventually my stock will rise.

Taking My Daily Dose of Writing Medication

I decided to stop writing—to trade my daily writing habit for editing my journal. Both efforts failed. Evidently, I never want to give up journal writing. It is simply too good.

Writing frees me from my demons. There is something magical about the process. Ever since I started my journal, depression has diminished to near zero. The only time it returns is when I stop writing. Writing is a medicine I must take daily.

I don't know why I am built this way, but I am, and I'm lucky to have discovered it. The magical medicine is already affecting me. Energy is creeping back into my soul.

How low I sank by giving up writing! I even decided not to bring my computer on tour to Greece. That would have meant ten days without medicine. Why hammer a nail into my foot? I'll *bring* my medicine to Greece!

The night before the Russian Weekend I stood on the Solway House grounds, looking at a star-filled sky. All alone at that dark, deserted hotel, I got the same chills of primal fear that almost made me walk off the porch in Oaxaca twenty-five years ago. Scary cabalistic heebie-jeebies.

Then I decided to focus on a concrete task, like running my Russian weekend. Fears disappeared. The idea of serving others saved me from the heebie-jeebies. I thanked my concrete thought. Two days later, as I stood on the ground of Opus 40, thinking about my power in putting together a wonderful weekend, a stabbing pain hit my temple. By the end of the weekend that pain had turned into a splitting headache. Fears of grandiosity and hubris had dammed up my flow of elation.

I had been bounced between terror and hubris.

Only a concrete foundation can save me from these extremes. The best one I can build for myself is daily journal writing, coupled with focus on customers.

Seeing Myself as a Writer

Reading my writing is like reading my own bible. It has messages from God as well as man. Is it hubris to say this? I think not. It is realistic. I have been studying, thinking, pondering the ideas of my heroes for most of my life. They are me; I am them. I have absorbed their teachings while adding the unique twists of my personality. The boiled-down distillate is a compilation of everything I know.

A new self-image is forming. Amazing how long an old one can last: ten, twenty, thirty years, even a lifetime. But it's breakthrough time. Spring thaw is here.

Is it possible I refused to read my writing because, when I did, I heard an old critical voice shouting, "Amateur! Student! Unworthy! You are not really a writer. You don't even know grammar; you got lousy marks in school; you are not an intellectual. You might qualify as an artist, but as a user of words to convey *ideas*? Never! Go back to being a nice guy, smiling and playing in the park. Only great French intellectuals can write. They're in a class way above you, so don't even bother."

Hard to believe such an inferiority complex lasted so many years. Lack of confidence is the reason I never considered myself a writer—and this after writing four books! But the old self-image is setting in the West; a new sun is rising. I have to thank my writing class, along with thousands of word-seeds I planted in my writing garden.

Maybe I'm afraid if I read my work I'll admire the gifts God gave me—humor, outlandish fantasy and delight in the absurd, love and appreciation of beauty.

Yesterday I took my first baby steps towards a new life.

I played guitar but thought in terms of recording. I envisioned making tapes of all my classical guitar pieces, my songs, even some readings.

Then I packed for Greece, went to the bank, picked up my car from Quirk, took an afternoon nap, cleared my den, and got ready for the big event: placing two thousand-page piles of New Leaf Journal on the dining room table! Next to it I piled edited versions with Barry's comments written on the back, then added a pile of songs I'd written. I finished by placing a box of my former concerts tapes on top of the song pile.

I'll use a two-pronged approach: First, edit my journal. I see five to six books. Second, prepare tapes of my classical guitar pieces and songs. Then comes a book of songs. Along with this is a taping my "World of Guitar" record.

I sat down on my couch at read the first pages of my *New Leaf!* I tried not to think about editing or changing anything, just reading it as a "disinterested" observer. I was amazed how good it was! Easy reading, a fluid style, full of ideas I want to remember. Then I thought, Why not? I just read "Songs and Stories for Open Ears," which I'd written twenty-five years ago. I loved it! If I could write so well then, why not now? Notes and messages from above, the best parts of me in print. What a joy to read someone with whom I really agree!

A wave of unbelievable sadness rapidly swept over me. Imagine, I have talent, the ability to capture beauty on paper, a sense of the lovely, a passion for the sublime. I've had it all my life! Why have I been hiding it so long? Why can't I accept it? I read the words to my song "Who Am I?" written when I was my twenties and living in Greenwich Village. I remember performing it in a cafe. How the audience loved it! So did my girlfriends.

Philosophical and meaningful: it was too profound for me to face. I wrote it, recorded it, but retreated from further expressing such powerful emotions. Instead I backed into my known world of humor.

I have been aware of these transforming visionary thoughts ever since I heard Beethoven's *Eroica* symphony at age thirteen. But I hid them in the well-protected confines of my heart. Others might ridicule me; I was afraid to make them public. These spiritual parts were too raw, tender, and important to take a chance. They might be destroyed. I hid them for years. Occasionally, they leaked out in a guitar piece, song, gesture, or stray word.

Then about three years ago I started my *New Leaf*. The leak grew to a trickle, then stream, river, flood. Soon a Niagara Falls of spirit-cleansing waters burst across my pages.

I broke down the door and stepped into a new world. Yesterday afternoon I sat crying on my living room floor, releasing demons from years of imprisonment. Suddenly, the fear of looking back fled. Why had I been so afraid? What had been the big deal? I saw a glorious past blending into a glorious future. My cleansing cry has made it all so simple. Why did it take years to discover my better self?

The Editing Life

I had supper with Don Kmetz last night. We sat in an Italian restaurant in New York on Eighth Avenue drinking wine, eating crispy green salads and angel hair pasta dishes. We talked about writing. "Writing the first draft is easy, because you're carried along by your inspiration," Don said. "Editing is hard; it's constant decisions. Editing creates beauty."

I am ready for the editing life.

I vow that every page I write will be edited, not once or twice, but several times. I'll edit on the computer and on hard copy.

Complaints, How I Love Them!

I have been off the mark ever since I returned from Greece a month ago. Love my tours, ha! Book of love, ha! What is this love charade? This delusion has put me on a slope sliding into depression valley. Thinking about love is fine, but try *doing* it! Sure, I know it is lying somewhere at the base of my spine and periodically emerges to say hello. But it is always a brief hello.

I'm exchanging the Book of Love for the Book of Complaints. Instead

It cannot compensate for lack of faith.

Look past the window of ego. Can you see the starlit night and brilliant, windblown day? Can a clam float on air?

Can turbulence blow a plane off course? Can an elephant crush a spider with its thoughts? These worthy questions must be considered. Dollars and high finance cannot answer them.

The "Elmore Leonard Writing Method"

I saw Elmore Leonard on TV last night. He has written thirty-three books and is working on his thirty-fourth. He writes about one a year. He writes them *by hand.* Imagine, no computer, only by hand! Then he revises, rewrites, edits, expands, contracts, etc. He writes four or five *good* pages a day. He writes all day: from about nine in the morning to six at night.

Why is Elmore Leonard's method important to me? First, he writes *by hand;* second, he spends his day rewriting and polishing the raw written pages. At the end of the day he has the *satisfaction* of having created four or five "perfect" pages. Like God, he can look over his creations and rest on his "seventh day" evening Sabbath.

Should I write like that? September is seed planting time; new habits are being fertilized in the soil. Could writing a few perfect paragraphs or pages a day become my new habit? It would signal *a new approach to writing:* I would truly be *turning over a new leaf.* I could even write in my hand-written journal, then spend other time during the day copying, recopying, rewriting, editing, and polishing what I've written. I would have a *finished product* at the end of the day.

I can start today with my Bulgarian hand-written journal. I wrote it this summer in Bulgaria.

Writing

This morning, for the first time in weeks—or is it months?—I fell into that old-time depression with its painful feelings of loss, worthlessness, loneliness, directionlessness, and nothing-I-do-is-worthwhile. This morning's depression is old and familiar: the *non-writing depression.* It is a call from above. God says, You'd better write or else all meaning and purpose will be drained from your life. Simple as that.

I like organizing and leading my tours, weekends, folk dance classes, the of filling my journal with love stories about my tours and the happy energies I expend running them, I'm much better off complaining about low registration. Sure, I always have the same complaints. But life is a circle. Just as the sun rises and sets each day, so I rise and set each day with a new series of old complaints.

Where the fuck are my clients? Why don't they sign up?

How many times have I screamed these miserable cries of help? Answer: since I started the tour business. I'd like to be original and offer brilliant new insights, but all I have is my mantra of old complaints to repeat.

Ah, but it feels so good!

What have business frustrations cost me? First, my retina detached from my vitreous. I see flashing lights in my left eye when I look to the left in a darkened room.

Does this have to do with looking left politically? Am I being punished for veering to the right? Or am I simply mad at people for not registering? Are the flashing lights actually lighting bolts hurled down from the sky, striking each potential customer and broiling them into sizzling well-done under my hot gaze of anger and frustration?

How about the floaters in my eye? Are they floating tourists passing by without deposits? Does their floating symbolize lack of commitment?

Last night, after turning our mattress, I got a neck cramp that paralyzed my shoulders and arms for a few moments. Did that come from seeing imaginary customers hiding under the bed?

I am beginning to wonder whether these ailments that have popped up during the past few weeks are physical. Perhaps they are psychosomatic phantoms, ghosts of former tour potentials.

I am somewhat embarrassed to keep complaining about the same themes. What is the matter with me? Can't I find other subject matter? Must I be so boring and repetitive? The answer is *yes*. Otherwise I write nothing. Instead I create physical and psychosomatic pains for my body.

Writing Calms the Mind

Writing calms the mind. Its smooths flows of word play, lists of smiles and easy pearls, uprooting, moving, swirling in ponds of turgid putridity. All serve the giggling goddess of laugher.

Money slips and slides around me. I'd like to hold it, but. . . do I really care that much?

warmth and security of my wife, family, and friends, the physical exhilaration of yoga and running, the delicious taste of language study on my lips, the sensuality of guitar playing. But these have nothing to do with writing. Writing is another mode: it is the process of serendipity and freedom, the meaning-giving center of my life.

What about wife, family, and friends? Is writing as important as they are? Comparisons are odious. I need to eat and drink in order to live. Family, friends, and work are my food; writing is my water. Or vice-versa. I need both.

What kind of writing do I need? I edit to put myself in the process of completion. But to handle non-writing depression, my transcendental wake-up call, I need the free radical base of open, serendipitous writing, the adventure of sitting down at the computer and pouring out whatever comes to mind.

I'm writing now. The more I write, the better I feel.

The Peace of Flow

Yesterday Bob told me his article had been published in the *Record*. "Mazel tov," I said. "See what happens when you stop coming to writing class?"

"Are you still writing every day?" he asked.

"Yes," I answered. "I've been trying to put my journal into categories, but I can't do it. I should, yet I can't."

"Your life is like your journal," Bob said. "You jump from studying languages to running tours to leading folk dance classes, to running, to yoga, to reading, to whatever. That's the way your life works——also your mind. Why not leave the order of your journal just the way it is? Make it a "Day in the Life," or "Year in the Life" kind of journal. It doesn't need an "artificial" order imposed on it. It might already have an inner order you haven't considered yet."

Bob hit pay dirt.

What kind of order do I want? The idea of putting my writing into categories seems logical and reasonable enough, yet I can't do it. Perhaps, even though it is reasonable and right, for me it is unreasonable and wrong.

My journal may indeed reflect life as it really is. Look how it skips from one subject to another or mixes subjects; it mirrors the wildness and unpredictability of life. The order of the known I try imposing on life rarely works.

Evidently, life has other plans for me. My *New Leaf Journal* is no exception.

Like monkey mind, my journal jumps from one branch to another; it is never still. There may be a unity behind it but I don't know what it is yet. I'll go along with the jumping mishmash of "daily events" I have written. It keeps the flow going even though I don't understand it.

My journal is about inner and outer travel. How about a title like: *The New Leaf Journal of Inner and Outer Travel: Volume One*. The unity I am searching for may be in this title. I can add volume two, three, four, etc. Giving *this* kind of "organization" to my Journal means accepting what I am already doing. It inspires me to write, which keeps me sane, healthy, and fulfilled. If that is true, could it be so bad? *The New Leaf Journal of Inner and Out Travel* title combines the inner world of imagination with my outer world of push, challenge, and business. It fuses my need for a hermit-monastic-cell existence with my social-cenobitic one. I need to work on at least two levels: inner and outer, contemplative and business, study and action. When I combine them, I end up a whole person. I must be executive, salesman, and entrepreneur, then withdraw for a periodic revitalizing drink at the inner spring.

Behind the dualism of the title lies the unity I have been searching for. It is the *peace of flow*, the satisfaction of riding a river between the mountains.

LANGUAGES

Pre-bedtime Greek Vocabulary Practice: Habits Make the Man

This morning after coffee and a glance at the local Ocala newspaper, I sat reading *Teach Yourself New Testament Greek*. I found it in a bookstore in Sarasota. It is the only book I've ever found on biblical Greek. I bought one for myself and one for Peggy Kirshenbaum. She's a former classics scholar and teacher of Latin and ancient Greek. Yesterday morning I studied Hebrew. I read the Book of Joshua, wrote down each Hebrew word I didn't know, and tried memorizing them. *New Testament Greek* suggested a new way of learning: read the list of new Greek words before bedtime. Don't try to memorize their meanings. You'll be amazed at the power of this pre-bedtime practice. I'll try it.

Very satisfying studying Hebrew for an hour. If I did it every day I would quickly improve. I could also do it with New Testament Greek.

Clean-up

Yesterday I spent all day cleaning house. First I went through the dining room brochures and put them on the dining room table in four piles: Czech, Slovak, Romanian, and Hungarian. I couldn't find my *Teach Yourself Romanian* book. I checked the language section in my den, dining room, and basement. Nowhere in sight. I *never* throw out books. Where could it have gone? I decided to buy another one at Barnes and Noble. Then I cleaned out the basement. I threw out seven cartons of old brochures, fliers, books, and folk dance tapes. I've never thrown out folk dance tapes before. It was a new cleansing experience. I arranged the basement shelves in Bulgarian, Greek, Hebrew, Hungarian, Czech, Polish and foreign dictionary sections.

I took five hours to finish my basement clean-up. Then I went upstairs to work on the dining room. I threw out a half-carton's worth of unneeded brochures. By seven o'clock I had five neat piles of books on the table. First was: *Teach Yourself Modern Greek, The Oxford Dictionary of Modern Greek,* and *I Kaini Diathiki,* the New Testament; the second: *Ha Yesod, The Shilo Pocket Dictionary* of Hebrew, and Torah; third: *A Course In Modern Bulgarian,* a Bulgarian dictionary, and *Pod Igoto,* Under the Yoke by Ivan Vazov; fourth: *Learn Hungarian,* a Hungarian dictionary, and *Egri Csillag,* Stars of Eger, by Geza Gardony; and fifth: *Teach Yourself Romanian* and a Romanian dictionary.

Cleaning up the house was the first step in my five-language study program; laying out my inspirational books was my second.

How did I find my "lost" Romanian book? It appeared "miracu lously" at the end of the day when I had finished cleaning and laid out all my language books on the dining room table. I looked again in the old language section of the basement, and there it was, right in front of me! It had been there all along, but I hadn't noticed it. Finding it must have been my reward for the clean-up. Was it a message from God, too?

My next step will be to find five language teachers.

Words

I collect sounds in the form of words. Then I draw from my collection. Foreign names are fine; so are local colorings, deep-dyed Old English words, Teutonic roots, Slavic, Hebrew, or even Albanian. I like place names, geographic locations, mountains, or valleys. What difference does a Galilean tone make or the rolling hill sound of Hellenic names in provinces like Gaulanitis, Auranitis, Batanaea, Trachonitis or even Scythopolis, Greek names in the Roman Decapolis. These place names, managed by either a one-fourth ruling Tetrarch or Roman procurator, feed the hind quarters of my brain and water my frontal lobes as well.

How pleasant to mention the fortress at Jotapata or the rebel, John of Gischala, the general Vespasian or his son, Titus. These names leap from the past.

Their sound and usage are one of the strongest connections I have to history. The tone and nuance of their names enter a fluid-filled corner, a hidden cistern of my mind, feeding a subterranean need, watering and illuminating thirsty cells.

I have found an emotional connection to names, events, and places of history through tone.

The framework of history is involved, too. But I have never been able to make that passion connection. Alas or not alas, I am *not* an intellectual. I am a romantic, a mystic, an aural person, a lover of intuition. Spiritual enterprises ring in my brain, burst in my ears, bathe my eyes.

Then why not use them?

Let my tongue wrestle with the languages of English, French, Hebrew and Latin, Babylonian, Aramaic, Hindu, and headstrong Sanskrit embedded in sandstone

I *love names*! A new world opens. How I love new worlds!

LIFE

The Future Is an Illusion

In his wonderful book *Healing into Immortality*, Gerald Epstein tells his readers to write a new book called: *The Future Is An Illusion*. The subplot is called: "The Past Is an Illusion." Ninety percent of my conversations with others are about the past and future. Thus, ninety percent of what I talk about with others——and also with myself, my ongoing inner dialogue——is an illusion.

How can I change such a powerful thought habit? Epstein says, Become a watcher of your thoughts, a witness, an observer. Become a *thought manager*.

The first step is to become aware of your constant use of past and future tenses.

That's a good beginning. Epstein says it takes three weeks, twenty-one days, or multiples thereof, to develop a new habit. It would be good for me to develop this new thought-management habit. It would affect all my work.

Yet even as I write, I can see how the illusion of futurity creeps into my thoughts through the future conditional grammatical construction of "would be." Better to change it to the ever-truthful present tense: _It *is* good for me to develop this new thought management habit. It *is* a bottom line habit. It *affects* all my work.

The Windshield Wiper of My Mind

My mind needs a thorough cleansing, a purging of the snows. I need a writing bath, a flood of words, a mind-wash with soapy verbiage. My brain is stiff, taut, and bulky. Where is the lithe, svelte form of yesterweek?

My only cure is to write, write, write. It doesn't matter what, where, or to whom I write. The writing purification process can free my mind from the heaviness of snow-bound depression.

I am sick of "depression." That word has never described my state. It is so clinical, lacking in feeling, and void of nuance. It smells of drugs, pills, institutional sympathy, and a pharmaceutical and psychological industry waiting for my inner collapse so they can pounce on my prostrate body to "cure" me. They are hungry for business. If I don't get depressed, *they* will.

I hate feeding the depression industry.

The word has outlived its usefulness. I might use parts of it to describe my state like "de," "down-pressing," or "press-shunning."

Inner Glow

I need metaphors to stimulate my brain. Too much snow shoveling has dulled my wit and left my mind in shambles. Time to recover, recuperate, shovel my *own* sidewalk, dig a trench through the rubbish and debris to my *own* temple where mental winds blow strong.

Writing is like washing your face in the morning, taking a bath, cleaning up, or organizing a messy house. In the process, good ideas and new directions emerge; sometimes I hit on helpful hints for others. This cleansing brings hope and light to a tired morning. Every day, through the savage attacks of imaginary time and space, my soul gets covered, polluted, and soiled with materialistic demands from the waking world. It needs purifying time alone so light, glow, sparks, and the blessings of eternity can shine upon it. Without light, why bother living? Some question whether life has purpose. But it definitely has a glow. Purpose and meaning are lower forms of glow. So are goals—those necessary illusions created by the mind to light up the tired day.

Why struggle? To rekindle, see, and feel once more the vibrancy of that inner glow.

But glow, although eternal, is fragile in its radiance. It is easily forgotten. Experience and memory of enlightenment, of en-*light*- enment, lasts only a few moments. One business meeting, social distraction, or bad night's sleep, and you've forgotten it. No wonder some religions pray five times a day. It helps remind you of the glow you are constantly forgetting; it helps you remember the wisdom and reason for staying alive on this earth.

Light struggles against darkness. The struggle is forever.

Although morning sun cuts the darkness you must have more than sunlight for a thorough house cleaning. You need to brush your teeth with music, sweep with a writing broom, and let a good calligraphy soap pen clean your paper.

Some people can clean their house without art—a walk in nature, a business deal, a run, a swim in the lake. We are experiments of one. There are as many paths to cleanliness as there are human souls. But though the roads may vary, all lead to the same glow.

I'd like to remember this truth. But I'm sure I won't. Like my fellow humans, I will follow the path of forgetfulness. It will begin shortly after I have written this piece. Even though the Bal Shem-Tov said, "Forgetting is exile; remembrance is redemption," and I say, "Forgetting is hell, remembrance is bliss," nevertheless, I will still forget. It's one of the drawbacks of being human.

One needs constant reminders. Writing reminds me. So does running, guitar playing, reading, meditation, and singing. Even snow shoveling can be one, especially when I get into its rhythm.

Life is full of metaphors; basic reminders of glow are everywhere. But we forget so often.

But I Forget

The speed of forgetfulness amazes me. How important can worries, concerns, joys, hopes, and sorrows really be if I forget about them so quickly?

It is only when I wake up in the morning, lost and wondering, and ask myself, What shall I do today, why, and for what purpose, that I am forced to face the big question. Then thoughts of transcendence and higher destiny return.

How important is anything I do if I forget the world and its troubles so quickly? The answer is "not very." The preacher in Ecclesiastes was right: "Vanity of vanities, all is vanity." Belief in God was his answer to life's questions. I am reaching the same conclusion.

I like it. I hope I don't forget.

Lack of Faith

The biggest problem in my life is lack of faith. What is worry but that?

Do I have free will? Or are my decisions illusions of freedom created by God to teach me responsibility?

God created the lower world for people like me. Here we make apparent decisions affecting all kinds of apparent events.

But who really makes these decisions?

Parents let children make independent decisions to teach them about responsibility. Does the Higher Power allow the same for us?

Perhaps He knows the results beforehand but allows us to believe we make independent decisions so we may learn about responsibility and higher thoughts.

Worry about the future is play acting. It is a disguised form of idolatry. Worship of a graven imaged called The Future breaks the second commandment by trying to step into God's place and usurp His power. I do it every day, worshiping worries created by my ego, because I don't have enough faith.

Last night at Ruth Ross's party I talked to Carol and Larry Kaplan. I used to know her as Carol Pasternak, an old friend from Camp Wochika and Wyandot.

I spoke with confidence and authority about everything I was doing. I was using my "selling on the phone" personality. It frightened me. Who am I to be so knowledgeable and confident? Who am I to answer so quickly, to respond and dominate the party conversation? Where did that shy, timid, retiring, reserved party person disappear to? I dominated the conversation, not only with my talking, but with my presence. I went into Ruth's party thinking, *I am working; I'd better psyche myself up for the job ahead.* Yet I wasn't "working." I was a guest at a party, and I was supposed to "relax." But what is "relaxing," and how do you do it? Plus, I like working; I like to be *on.*

When I am in public I have two choices: either retreat and sit quietly in a corner, or engage the people in conversation. At parties of the past, I'd speak to people about pleasant but unimportant things while the best part of my mind remained apart, free to think about ideas that really interested me. In other words, I hid from others. I opted to protect my true nature, the meditative, studious, introspective self with its happy, childlike fascination for the world. I chose never to reveal my identity, to shield its precious mystery, goodness, and desires to attain loftier goals by talking about trivia, babble, or making jokes.

But my reservations disappeared last night. In their place I offered beliefs, real concerns, my true interests in tours, folk dancing, running, philosophy, and mysticism. Result: I came off as dynamic and forthright.

Although this change of public personality frightened me, I know the fear will disappear. There is no other way to go. The old route of hiding in a cave and reserving my best thoughts for myself is slowly coming to an end. Now I'm more relaxed and charismatic at parties. I even enjoy them.

It seems inner life, as expressed in my journal, is going public. Since my New Year's guitar concert, the door to my mind has burst open. I let anyone enter. I don't mind telling them about myself.

Business and self have merged in a "phone sales personality." Now I always sell. It helps create a public purpose in life. I no longer want to keep my real passions a secret. Inner blocks have been busted. I am ready to talk at parties and anywhere else.

By dropping the idea that sales are bad, evil, and only for capitalist pigs or low-life entrepreneurs, I am traveling on a new road of comfort with the outside world. I am sick and tired of beating myself with the same negative communist philosophy every time I sell something.

Truth is, sales are good for me. Better yet, sales are great for me!

They're a dominating positive force. Paradoxically, sales as a long-time nemesis, are an expression of my love and need for others. Communist shame prevented me recognizing it. Sometimes it takes years, decades, a lifetime, even many lifetimes, to break down walls. But thank God, mine are starting to crack.

The Birth of James Saint-Salesman

Am I better off as saint or salesman?

If I have to choose, I'd better choose salesman. I feel the energy of fear and excitement in my sales gut. Sainthood is abstract and other-worldly. Can I trust my desire for sainthood? Am I fooling myself by thinking I'm traveling on a higher path?

What is right? I don't seem to know anymore. If, as Ramakrishna says, the renunciation of women and gold is the path to enlightenment, I am on the wrong path. I have renounced neither. Which of these paths is better? Can they be combined? Perhaps through the *spirit* behind my sales personality.

What about the name "Saint Salesman?" Why not? Look at Camille Saint-Saens. He wrote *and* sold his music. Why not adopt the surname James Saint-Salesman, just as Camille adopted the surname Camille Saint-Saens? James Saint-Salesman could head the sales department for Jim Gold International, Inc.

Little Letters

Arrived in Sarasota yesterday. We're staying with Lou and Ann Paige. Beautiful house. I taught some folk dances last night to Ann Kessler's group. Fine group, lovely night.

I woke this morning up with a roaring headache. Was it the pillow? My bed? Traveling without time to reflect or study?

As I write my neck muscles loosen. A slow, calm, relaxing mental fluid moves slowly into my shoulders. Writing magic is working. It is my alone time for meditation, reflection, and focus on the inner vision creating my universe.

Focusing on all the folk dancers, greeting them, moving through the Sarasota world, if done in extreme, distracts me from my inner source. At all costs, I must remember the HaShem home located deep in caverns behind my mind.

Shoulder, neck, and head relax further as I meditate in my writing cave. Ha Shem, the capital letters you receive put me off this Sarasota morning. I need the elegant feel of a small letters on my lips. Give me a half-dribble lodging behind my tongue, cleaning my teeth, loosening the inner uvula hanging upside-down in right-side-up mouth vision.

Oh Little Letter, you ring out subtle vibrations on the vertebral xylophone of my neck. Without my ode to you, I am odious. Free me, Little One, from these heavy chains. I know you will if only I remember you.

Five years ago I decided to focus on study, mysticism, and business, and take family and friends for granted.

Even when visits with friends faded to once a year and intervals between family get-togethers moved from weeks to months, I nevertheless pursued pathways to inner and outer self.

Yesterday when I finished writing my European guides and cleared my desk, I realized I was "finished" with two months' work. I felt empty. What now? I asked. Should I expand my tours? How can I grow?

I knew I needed something new, but couldn't figure out what. At first I ruminated on business and self-study. I thought about running tours to many countries without me—an old idea I still haven't figured out how to get enough customers to do it. Then I thought about starting smaller folk dance classes, run by other teachers whom I would train—an Arthur Murray approach to increase the folk dance base and also find more clients for tours. But none of these ideas clicked. Had I reached my limit? Was it time to find *something completely different?*

How about family and friends? To spend some time, even a few moments a day, thinking about them would be a mental change, an accomplishment in itself.

I took them for granted. But they are like the air I breath: I don't think much about the air, yet without it I would die.

It Is You

It is so satisfying to know your deepest desires.

Is the search for such desires selfish?

No. The selfish aspect is only apparent. In reality, following the egoistic desires of the "I," takes you on the descending elevator. Down, down, down, lower, lower, lower. Soon you reach the ocean flowing beneath the illusory forms of reasoned reality. You arrive at the beach. Take off your clothes; step out of your body; jump into the ocean.

You swim by material forms unaffected by their superficial attraction.

You swim forever, floating in the blissful embryo of oneness.

You have shed the longings, contradictions, and pressures of ego, bypassed the temporal engines of emotional and mental destruction.

Your inward road leads you to your new liquid home, your permanent post office box address floating on the cosmic sea. The world pulls you no more in its ancient, hypnotic way.

You are one; you are at peace.

Follow your desires to the end of their road. Know your true identity. See the higher light. It is you.

Mr. Holland's Opus

We saw *Mr. Holland's Opus* last night. It began so slowly I went outside and bought a candy bar to eat. Gradually, the movie picked up. By the end, I was totally engrossed.

I have said not one word yet about the theme or plot of the movie. What concerns me more is my reaction to movies in general. The medium is simply too powerful. I get swept away, forget my identity, and merge with the actors. Then the movie ends. I leave the theater completely lost. What happened to all those people on screen I identified with? I become melancholy realizing the transience of material reality. The movie brought back memories of the High School of Music and Art, the terrible mood swings and uncertainties of youth, and the feeling that, in the end, everything one does boils down to nothing. Oh sure, Mr. Holland had an effect on his students, even though he felt himself a failure, unloved, and unfulfilled. All his students "proved" that he was worthy and had transformed their lives. The teenage girl in his class who plays clarinet so poorly ends up governor of the state. She gives a beautiful speech at his closing surprise party. Her appearance touched me most of all. Imagine, this twerpy little girl who could only squeak on the clarinet, so brittle, frail, shy—but determined to do something well in her life—ends up governor of the state! It reminded me how simple, ugly people can fulfill a great potential. It also reminded me how important my actions are and how, in unseen ways, they affect others. Good deeds go a long way; so do evil ones. Deeds remain the best form of teaching.

Spring Planting: New Goals

Time for new goals. I've felt the need since returning from Budapest. Spring planting is here. Bring on the fertilizer! Uproot dead trees and flowers. Plough the April ground.

The first signals came from lower back pain. Then came over whelming fatigue and loss of enthusiasm. My only breath of fresh air came from languages. Yesterday I took Flaubert's *Madame Bovary* off the shelf to read in French, then I went to the basement, picked out *Isten Rabjai,* by Geza Gardonyi, from my Hungarian book collection and read it in Hungarian. The Torah sat in the living room; I read it in Hebrew. I took out Bulgarian and Czech grammar books; I went to the Greek section of the basement and selected the New Testament to explore in Greek. These are mucho languages. Soon I'll add Czech and Bulgarian.

I'm reading languages like symphony scores. Without looking up words or translating them into English. I am trying to "think in the language." In a sense, all these languages are merging into an endless river of words and foreign sounds. I will commit several hours a day to this new linguistic goal, which will feed my interest in tours as well.

As enthusiasm for foreign language study increased, I realized I was in transition. The search for new goals began with Adam Molnar and our five Hungarian tours. A qualitative tour leap. When transitions come, everything seems to change at once. New vision shine on the transforming self. New goals put new life into my miracle schedule.

Visceral Winds

I'm waiting for a visceral wind to blow me in a new direction.

Oh a one has already blown through my linguistic mind.

Yesterday it blew through my guitar mind: I'm playing slowly and listening, squeezing the juice out of each note and phrase. Focusing this way makes it impossible to miss a note.

A visceral wind has not yet blown through my tour mind. The "Adam experience" is still intellectual. Although I'm contemplating an expansion, it's not gut-level yet. Perhaps running tours without going on them is not my style. I can get enthusiastic about our March 1997 tour—five days in Budapest and three days in Western Hungary, with a day trip to Vienna—and our summer tour—with three days in Budapest, three in Central Hungary, and two at the Jaszbereny Festival. I can also get enthusiastic about our ten-day trip to Romania, which will precede our summer Hungarian tour. I'm enthusiastic because I plan to go on these tours. I'll experience them. I am not accompanying the July and October Southern Hungary and Red Pepper Festival. If I did, I might get enthusiastic.

What does this say about me? Do I really have to go to be enthusiastic? What about sending others without me? Doesn't that feel more like pencil pushing, paper work? True, I'd make money, but without the hands-on thrill, can I really get excited?

Something to think about in terms of direction, visceral winds, personal motivation, and happiness.

I have not done yoga or run for a week. I haven't had such a period of physical inactivity for a long time. Waiting for a visceral wind to blow and point me in a new direction. So far none has come.

New Directions on the Path of Exercise

I just invented a running warm-up routine—"fast yoga." It consisted of an extended salute to the sun routine done quickly and at least twice. It works up a sweat and heartbeat before running.

After the run I do slow yoga—same salute to the sun, only slower. A running yoga cool down. I end by practicing new postures. My three primary exercises are moving from quantity to quality.

When I started doing them in September—bi-monthly 2½-hour runs, "150s" routine of 150 squats, 150 push-ups, and 150 sit-ups, it took an hour. Now it takes about forty-five minutes.

These primary exercises are established in their parameters. Now I want to direct these exercises downwards into the depths or upwards into the heights. Do them faster, add yoga warm-ups and warm-downs, and develop new postures.

The Exercise Road to Unity

Yesterday I started out with a half hour of yoga warm-ups; then I ran 2½ hours; I followed my run with another half hour of yoga cool-downs. I was tired the rest of the day—tired but proud! I had taken a step upward on the road to unity.

Progress is measured by movement from diversity to unity. Running and yoga used to be separate exercises. Now I am combining them, making them one. What was once a series of exercises is becoming one routine, a type of yoga dance. I am thinking "one." That's progress.

The Law of Attraction

Does one attract what one thinks? Is the law of expectations really the Law of Attraction in disguise?

In business, I expect few people to register for my offerings. In social situations, I expect few to listen. I expect little interest in what I have to say. Others must convince me of their interest before I bother revealing my important and deepest thoughts. Otherwise I oil my body by laughing, making jokes, seeming cool, so the burdens of others will slip off my mind, leaving me free to create in peace.

Since I got back from Hungary I've been thinking of the Law of Attraction and its disguised form, the law of expectation. It showed why I have so few people have registered for tours, weekends, and dance classes, even why business never really takes off. This is what I expected; this is what I'll get.

But there is another way of looking at it. Although I profess to want more customers, perhaps I really don't. Expecting little from others and from business may not be a bad thing. Although it keeps business small, it frees me from time constraints and demands that service to others would impose. Low expectations and their self-fulfilling prophecies give me free time to explore the realms of my artistic mind. On the other hand, business success would give me an overwhelming stream of clients. I'd have less free time for creative endeavors.

My low expectations may be a secret way of protecting my inner artistic life from the demands of the outside world. That life gives me a bottom-line reason for existence. By expecting less from others, I protect my most valuable treasure.

That is why a heaviness overcomes me whenever I think about expanding my tours, my customer base, and most other things I do in the day-to-day material world. I have reached my full business capacity, enough to fill those needs on earth. Wanting more may be crossing the line from need into gluttony.

I was put on earth to create. Supporting myself is necesary——but secondary. The roots of my tree lie in art. It can lose a few leaves or branches but without roots it will die.

All along, my instincts have protected me. My business fits. It *should be* small. I shouldn't try to enlarge it beyond its proper place.

Rediscovering the Witness Exercise

My mind popped out yesterday as I performed forty-five sit-ups. It sat outside my body and ego, calmly observing, watching my emotions, wishes, dreams, hopes, fears. I observed myself from above doing sit-up after sit-up.

Strange, weird, scary, wonderful. This "witness exercise" is not a feeling. It is beyond feelings, an experience of freedom and release combined with a breath of the infinite.

Can I incorporate the witness state into my life, remember it, re- experience it daily? I've thought about it for years. I remember returning from an hour and a half run at the farm, huffing and puffing up a steep, long hill. Suddenly, as I approached the top, my mind drifted out of my body and hovered like a cloud about two feet above my head. Perhaps it hovered like the cloud of HaShem above the tabernacle as the Israelites traveled in the desert. This cloud observed and witnessed me, without judgement.

That witness experience was more annoying than inspiring. It made me nauseous, then gave me a headache.

What does it mean to slip out of my body? What does it say about the importance of hopes, dreams, and a commitment to succeeding in daily life? How important can goals be if one can sit outside the body and observe them dispassionately? If this witness exercise represents a manifestation of a higher power, doesn't it, in its long perspective, trivialize the importance of earthly desires?

Not ready to face the wisdom in my witness experience, I got nauseous instead. But in my gut I knew that observing myself from the witness seat was home, a place of meditation, a happy attitude. I wanted to be there.

It also reminded me of attachments. I want, want, want! I cling to every desire, fear, and hope. So many wishes and goals. The witness exercise shows their relative unimportance.

Ultimately, what I really want is to reach a space of inner beauty where the sun shines. Bathing in wondrous light is the home of true success. But as I cried, "Not yet, not yet! I'm too young to relinquish desires, excitements, and frustrations in exchange for heavenly calm. Give me problems, hopes, worries, fears, and daily frustrations. Pain keeps me alive; worries fill me with glee; frustrations are my bread and butter. I feel alive when I suffer. Who wants happiness, anyway? Better to *hope* for happiness. Let it exist as a goal in the distant future."

No wonder the witness exercise made me sick.

Yesterday the witness returned during sit-ups. I'll take another look at it. Maybe I can incorporate it into daily life.

I slept nine hours last night.

I'm tired because I'm pushing yoga and running. Yesterday morning I did an hour of yoga, ran half an hour, and followed it with half an hour of yoga warm-downs. In the afternoon, I visited Isaac Mozeson's house and picked up ten copies of his book *The Word,* which claims Hebrew as the root language for all the world languages, truly one of the most fascinating books on language I've ever read. I want to sell this book or give it away to friends. After talking to Isaac, Bernice and I took Gus and Marilyn Wander out for lunch. I told Gus about *The Word.* He bought it immediately. Smart guy. When we came home I couldn't focus on anything. I needed exercise to center myself. I did another hour of yoga. All told, yesterday I did two and a half hours of yoga plus a half hour of running. Exercise hours are adding up. The cumulative effect is why I needed nine hours of sleep last night.

As I intensified my yoga and running training, I saw the light of improvement flashing. Over a period of weeks and months, I can feel my body changing, my skills improving. It is easier to do squats, sit-ups, push-ups, the lotus position, legs over my head, stand on my head, balance on my forearms, sit on one squatted leg, and do the duck walk. I created these goals two years ago. I see slow progress.

I'm putting so much time and effort into exercising, it's frightening. Am I *too* passionate and intense? Am I mad? Beauty and terror reside in these passions.

On the other hand, intense long-term effort and commitment bring results and improvement. It is so satisfying to see progress.

Create long-term focused goals with exercises. Do it with other interests, too.

The hardest part is focus. Focusing means excluding, discriminating, putting on blinders, as well as creating unity. My mind jumps so easily from one thing to another. How to focus it is always a question.

I could start today by turning over a new leaf. I'll focus on languages—

even one language at a time. Also guitar, exercises, and putting my journal into some kind of order for publishing. I must put on the blinders to see the light. Where does business fit in? It doesn't. I must make money in order to support my miracle schedule habits. It is a realistic necessity. But just because it is a necessity doesn't mean I have to make it a priority. It could just as easily be a secondary. My main efforts and energies can remain focused on writings, languages, exercises, and guitar. In some mysterious way they also feed my business.

This path helps me think clearly and keep my values straight.

Fading Interest in the Sport of Get Jim

Last night we ate out with Arlene at a Turkish restaurant in Moonachie. Excellent food, homey atmosphere. We had a good time. Towards the end of the evening the subject of last May's Greek tour came up. Arlene told me all the things I could do to help my customers get better service, especially handling baggage in the chaotic port of Piraeus.

Soon the conversation degenerated into "Get Jim," with Bernice joining in. They said I would lose customers if I didn't improve baggage handling and other services; they kept pointing out all the complaints of my unhappy tourists.

Such suggestions for service improvements are old news. So is the "Get Jim" sport, which begins the instant I try to defend myself. But last night I thought: why? It will lead nowhere. Sure, if I return to the Piraeus and take a cruise, I'll know baggage will be a problem. Previous experience *might* enable me to handle things differently, or it might not. Some service improvements, although desirable, may be impossible to make. Tourists suffering baggage-handling chaos often cannot be avoided. It is part of the travail of travel, the nature of the business.

I count on my intuition, instincts, reason, and whatever other powers I can summon up to handle the immediacy of tour situations. Naturally, some people will complain; others will not care one way or the other. Some will register for future tours, some not. I've come to accept that. I no longer feel so threatened when these "Get Jim," "Improve Jim," or "Criticize Jim for His Own Good" attacks take place.

Criticism, complaints, and glory are part of leadership. People count on you when you lead. Some expect near-impossible things from you. I work to satisfy myself and my customers. I do the best I can. If I help others in the process and can make some tourists happier, all the better. But I can't *expect* to make my tourists happy. Even when they tell me they are, often it turns out they're not. Conversely, sometimes when they sit quietly in the corner, it turns out they've been satisfied by some insignificant thing I've either done or not done.

I can't promise happiness on my tour. Happiness is a personal choice. I can only promise to work the best I can.

On one level it makes me sad I can't please everyone. Some people have remained angry with me for years. Evelyn has a personal vendetta against me and bad-mouths me at every turn. I'd rather be loved than attacked. But the only way I can avoid attacks is to hide in my room, never make a public appearance, and never put my work and name on the line. Since I don't live in a cave, public attacks are part of business, part of the game of life.

To my satisfaction, my fascination with the "Get Jim" sport is fading. That's progress.

Loving My Work

How I *love* my work! I am a man of many parts.

I am a man of many parts. One part wants to join a monastery; it is a romantic way of life dedicated to silent retreat and the pursuit of art and excellence, where I can remove myself from the vicissitudes and distractions of the material and business world, the world of action, of *assiyah*.

Another part lives in the world of action. I am forced to struggle there in order to survive. Loving my work means I also want to live in the world of *assiyah*, the world of folk dance teaching, weekends, and tours.

If I do, I must stretch for a place beyond the mystical. What realm is this? Paul Brunton calls it the realm of *philosophy*. I like that word. He says there are three levels of ascending spiritual development: religious, mystical, and philosophical. Philosophy synthesizes the religious and mystical. This needs further thought.

Return to Studies

It has been a whipsaw week. I have been tossed right and left, up and down, across the room and back. Total focus has been on organizing, reorganizing, dropping, then reconstituting tours. In the process, I gave up disciplines that kept me sane, balanced, hopeful, and inspired.

I'm putting myself back on track, wiser for my suffering; I'm returning to studies with a passion bordering on vengeance.

Perfection or Passion?

We heard Pinchas Zuckerman play at the John Harms Theater last night. I swooned as his gorgeous Beethoven violin sonatas soared above the piano accompaniment. Such sweet tone produced with impassive face. You'd never know he was performing except for the beautiful sound cascading through the hall and the movements of his fingers. He looked asleep. Yet riding on his notes, we traveled to heaven.

When I picked up my guitar this morning, I thought about him. I tried producing the same slow and beautiful tones. I succeeded. *Perfect!* Then I thought: I'm ready to move beyond perfection. What about passion? Sometimes passion disappears into the calm water of perfection.

It takes daring and an adventurous spirit to play with passion. The hope for perfection, on the other hand, is governed by the fear of making a mistake; it has a quiet, middle-of-the-road beauty; it seems to be based more on status quo than explorations down the tortured, twisted, beauty-strewn, bursting path towards the Infinite.

I'm stepping off perfection road for awhile; I'm slipping into the witch's cauldron for a passion hot bath.

Perfection as a feeling of inner peace that has nothing to do with accomplishment or creation in the material world. You can perform beautifully and feel awful, or perform terribly and feel wonderful. Balance is perfection; peace is perfection. It is a state of mind rather than a materialized actuality. Only you can judge whether you have achieved it. Thus it is possible to "be perfect" even as you create one imperfection after another.

Perfection and imperfection exist together simultaneously and harmoniously in the human psyche. So do passion and peace.

But they exist on different levels.

Giving it All Up

Fear lies beneath my guilt: Fear of separation, ostracism, loss of possessions, loved ones, and death. Guilt, with its handmaiden anger, often serves to cover up my fear.

How then can I handle my present situation? How can I recover the aesthetic vision of Beauty that makes life worthwhile?   Accept loss. Imagine I've lost my wife, family, friends, possessions, everyone and everything that is important to me. I am alone and forgotten, floating in the upper world of nonattachment. Acceptance of loss is the only way I can escape from my prison and reopen the doors of Beauty.

I'm talking about an attitude, about mental detachment. *Mentally*, I have to give up. A herculean painful task. But I don't want to live in prison. Who needs guilt whippings, oceanic waves of anger or gut-wrenching, bilious-gripping, bottom-dropping fear? I want to breath fresh air again.

Paradoxically, happiness means mentally releasing everything I own and want; all possessions and desires out the window.

Difficult, but who said life was easy?

How to Handle Jealousy

Jealousy is a call for self-improvement.

Mihai David gave us a Romanian dance workshop last night. Great Romanian dancing! Watching him dance his standards plus his new *Trei Pazeste* thrilled me. How can a man leap and dance that way! So energetic, beautiful, inspiring.

Why can't I do that?

Mihai's dancing made me jealous. That sick, sinking feeling returned: Why can't I dance like Mihai?

Then, as I played guitar this morning, the cure to jealousy came to mind: *use it as motivation to improve!* This beats wallowing in envy. I may never dance as well as Mihai, but at least I can put myself on the path of Romanian dance improvement. I can start today.

What a wonderful way to handle jealousy!

Jealousy is your heart screaming out your deepest yearnings. It points out a path of passion and love on which, for some reason, you hesitate to travel.

Look at my past.

I was jealous of Bob Dylan's song-writing talents. It tore me up that a folk singer with such an awful voice could write such powerful songs. Why couldn't I do that? Jealousy highlighted my passionate need to express myself through the written word. Writing is a path I am still following.

I was jealous of the flamencan guitarist Juan Serrano and classical guitarists Julian Bream and Andres Segovia. I'm still following that guitar improvement path.

I was jealous of performing artists reviewed on the entertainment pages. Why couldn't *I* be reviewed? Why couldn't *I* be recognized and famous? I still have the need for recognition; I have been following that path ever since.

What about wealth? Although I don't have the same admiration for the rich, I do wish I had more money. But strangely, I am not jealous of wealth people. Deep down, I know money is a means to an end. It buys me the mental freedom to dance.

Mama and Papa, Where Are You?

Today I just want to complain and whine until I drop. I know it isn't manly. I see black clouds floating above me. I'm writing to blow the clouds away and clean up the sewer running through my brain. This morning I'm crawling in the pits and heading lower.

Why have they forgotten me? Where are the calls and registrations? Even my stocks went down.

Last night I had a nightmare. Cezare from Balkan Tours told me our group had the best seats—better than first class, on the most beautiful plane that ever flew to Bulgaria. "Don't cancel on me," he said. I woke up humiliated. I knew I had lied to him about the true number of registrants. I said ten when I actually have only seven plus two cancellations, with one uncertain which makes four definite so far.

On one level, four isn't bad. But that's the lowest level.

My wife says I complain too much. "Go to a shrink," she says. "I can't stand hearing you complain anymore." I can't blame her. Every cycle I experience the same loss of perspective, hopelessness, and sense of doom. These cycles have plagued me most of my adult life. They started after I graduated from college. Before that I had a good thing going: Mama and Papa were taking care of me!

Mama and Papa, how I miss you! Please take care of me. Promise I won't have to worry about money, tour, weekend, or folk dance registrations. Take care of my money worries. Fend off humiliations. Protect me from the promises I make to tour agents and hotel owners. How can I stay in business if I don't lie? Who will hold my seats on the plane if I tell the truth?

Mama and Papa, take care of this mess. Let me play at the fountain or practice violin in peace, high in my ivory-towered room, dreaming of glorious flight among musical stars, soaring above the moaning earth, singing hallelujahs for angels inhabiting the seventeenth-century woods of my Amsterdam violin.

But Mama and Papa, you are gone. I am in charge. It's cold at the front lines. Still, I've got a faded picture of you in my wallet stored in the basement of my mind.

Animal Tours

Tired, hungry, battered, I want warm breasts, compassionate smiles, and loving eyes caressing the infant me lying in the arthritis-free security of Mama's arms.

Am I really in such sad shape? Must I return to the womb to find happiness again?

Unfortunately, this morning's answer is yes. All because Karl Finger has fifty-five people registered for his Bulgarian tour and I have only five.

Returning to the womb is not an accepted way for a mature man to think. Nor is it the way of the hero I'd like to be. But, if my journal is to be the repository of inner truths and visions, transitory or permanent, glorious or disgusting, perverted or heroic, dynamic or pathetic, then I must write down everything. By returning to the womb or early infancy, I can visit my ancient, long-forgotten homeland and get some fresh juice to drink. I can crouch on the ground with my ancestors to talk about tree climbing and coconut gathering.

As we grunt, scratch, gurgle, and swing gently from branch to branch gathering coconuts for the evening meal, we can argue over the relative merits of bus travel versus brachial locomotion. Then, I could pile my hairy ancestors and their gorilla cousins into a tour bus, drive to Bulgaria's Balkan Mountains, climb the trees of the Shipka Pass, and as we sit in the branches, throw coconuts at Karl Finger's fifty-five tourists, who should be punished for not registering with me. A drive-by coconut drop.

No one has thought of a coconut tourist attack before. I'll dress my animals as tourists, get through customs, then drive across Bulgaria in hot pursuit to capture Karl's tourists. Then they can "choose" to join my tour.

It's one way of expanding my tourist base. Instead of stuffing the mails with fliers and brochures or flooding the phone lines with sales calls, I might do better promoting my tours in the zoo. Those cages hold hundreds of potential customers. An untapped market. I could easily convince them to fill my bus. True, a traveling clientele of lions, tigers, monkeys, giraffes, turtles, South American exotic birds, arctic bears, sea lions, antelopes, gazelles, gorillas, snakes, frogs, and fish might not be able to pay the full tour fee. However, there may be government funding. Perhaps a grant for the zoo-abused.

Animal Tours may be an idea whose time has come. Instead of ecotours with humans visiting animal habitats, why not have animals visiting human ones?

I could dominate this new market.

Jersey Pains Versus Minnesota Fears

Focus on the sun. You can't let storms or clouds control your life.

But control my life is exactly what they have been doing. I have been riding on a downwards stream for a year. Yesterday it broke its banks. A flood of understanding washed over my being. It appeared as old understanding reborn.

Old understanding is new understanding on a deeper level.

Now my mistakes are deeper, more profound. I make them on the vertical plane rather than the horizontal.

Making progress is so often a question of pain versus fear. When the pain of holding becomes greater than the fear of letting go, a cataclysm "click" occurs. You drop the old and take a step forward.

Under grey skies opponents take the field. Battle lines are drawn: It's the Jersey Pains versus the Minnesota Fears. Both teams are dressed in their respective showdown uniforms, the Pains in casual spiked pullovers and razor blade pants, the Fears adorned with cement hats, iron vests, and loose trembling pantaloons buffeted by the Midwestern winds.

Today's game will be held in Yourbrain Field. The contest will pit Pain-holding-on against Fear-letting-go. Fans sit in Cerebrum box seats and Cerebellum bleachers. They cheer and eat popcorn as Medulla throws out the first ball. Pain and Fear are off and running, whacking brains at every chance they get.

Fear fans hold up their sign: "Beat the Pains! Hold on! Tighten up!"

Pain fans hold up their sign: "Beat the Fears! Release! Let go!"

This game may go extra innings. Suddenly, New Attitude, wearing fresh diapers and a halo, crawls across the field.

Jersey Pains and Minnesota Fears return stop their play. Fans sigh. The sun is shining.

Grace Breaks the Cycle

How do you break the cycle of fear and pain? How do you let love shine through?

Souls wrapped in personhood travel their road to enlightenment. The path is strewn with nails, broken glass, gaping holes, oil slips, toe-stubbing rocks, and boulders. Stalked by bloody drive-by dragons, trapped in claustrophobic traffic jams of debt and financial worry, bearing their own cross, they tread towards Golgotha, where crucifixion awaits them. Suddenly, for no apparent reason, their burden lifts. Fear and pain melt away. Grace, unknown and incomprehensible, lifts the clouds above. Souls stand revealed and content under the Mediterranean sun.

Love

Focus on what you love. Leave the rest to God.

This means a reorientation of the way I think. Focus on each Czech word. It means my *rush* to mastery is over. Make slow, small, steady love gains. "Gains" implies progress. "Being" is better. It focuses on the moment, where the power of love resides.

To run a business with love is a challenge.

Focus on what you love. Leave the rest up to God.

How to Unleash Passion

Repetition releases passion. Repeat to the point of pain.

Follow repeats with rest periods.

Guitar: practice pieces and passages over and over again.

Exercise: repeat push-ups, squats, sit-up, scorpion position, other positions, whatever, over and over again—three, six, nine times, whatever.

Language: Repetition of words and phrases.

Editing: Rewrite over and over.

History and Philosophy: Reread a sentence (or fact) over and over again.

Index Finger Points to Power

Where does power come from?

What is the relationship between power and love?

Here are guitar conclusions: The right index finger symbolizes personal power. Focus on it. Show its power to the audience. The index is ego power, the power of my smaller self.

True power comes not from ego but from the Divine. Body and mind are instruments for divine use.

Ego can only succeed when backed by the full funding power of God.

The Power of Pain: Heel Spur and Tour Fear

Disease, pain, and sickness are teachers. I create them in order to learn.

I can hardly walk this morning, much less dance. My left heel spur hurts more than ever. It got worse before last year's Bulgarian tour; it got worse before this year's Czech Republic and Slovakia and Poland tour. Is there a relationship between heel spur pain and tour fears? If there is, that means my thoughts can cure it. My tour fears are "expressed" through my *left* heel. This coordinates with the detach ment of the vitreous from my retina, and the floaters in my *left* eye. Such psychosomatic episodes with my left side have occurred before. The first took place years ago in Aix-en-Provence, when my *left* side got "paralyzed" after my first love affair ended. I thought I was going blind. Yes, I was blind—with rage and fear. But I didn't know it. It wasn't until after two months of self-torture, doubts, and worry about my health that I went to a neurologist who told me my nerves had created my disease. I was all right, but my nerves were blinding me.

Could it be the same now? Are my nerves injuring my left eye along with my left heel? Thinking this would give me hope for a cure. Otherwise, I sink into the hopelessness of physical determinism, believing physical pains are caused by mysterious outside forces over which I have no control.

Let's concentrate on my heel spur. Is it caused by some "outside" force invading me, destroying my cells, enlarging my heel spur, and increasing my pain? Or is my mind creating pain so that I will learn, grow, expand and ultimately benefit?

Practicing Philosophy

I'm going to "practice my philosophy" by focusing on heel spur as an expression of upcoming tour fear. I'll see if the pain diminishes.

Heel spur stabs my heel just as tour fear stabs my brain.

The heel spur is hobbling, crippling my walk, just as the tour fear is hobbling, crippling my thought processes. (I can't focus on anything.)

Every time my heel spur hurts, think "tour fear." Tour fear is located in my heel. Every time I step on it, its poison fangs bite me. Suppose I change my thinking: every time I step on my tour fear, I crush it.

Pains will test the power of my mind.

How powerful is my mind? Can it really create such pains, pleasures, problems and solutions? Does it really run my world? How much effect do superior powers have on it? They watch over my mind. I should be talking to them.

I may not have complete control. But I have much more than I think.

Death and Endings

Suppose jumping from one ritual to the next, flitting from one business to another, one worry to another, is simply an attempt to escape death? Suppose self-improvement, hopes for a stock market and personal financial rise are all a disguised attempt to escape from the inevitability of ending?

Is this a depressing thought or an elevating one? I rush to perfect myself but for what purpose? Are all my vanities merely a shield to escape from the fear of ultimate decease?

Facing the inevitability of death, how can I worry about tourist registrations, paying my bills, or whether my books will be read? Why should I care about playing a perfect Alhambra so audiences will love and respect me? How long does fame last? After centuries and millennia, rocks disintegrate. What chance is there for the creations of my humble ego?

Viewed long range, the quest for wealth and fame is a ridiculous short-sighted waste of time. Only the pounding ego and skipping mind beguile me to promote these illusory goals. Fluff swirling in the passing wind.

But what if death and birth are an illusion? Suppose they are merely doorways of learning? Suppose life never ends?

Tours Revisited

Sad and listlessness. I am mourning the end of my Czech tour.

I am suffering withdrawal pains. Tours are the crowning achievement of my folk dance business. They bring incomparable adventures.

Countless travel and business frustrations often obscure my love for tours. They hide the adventure, fun, and privilege of running them. I enjoy recounting the negatives of my tour business. What about the positives? I rarely talk about them.

How about the thrill of landing in Israel and kissing the ground, working with fine guides, meeting Igor Moiseyev in Moscow, opening doors of a darkened Soviet factory in the town of Pskov to find a folk orchestra, full-costumed folk dance troupe, and tables laden with food standing ready to perform only for our tour group? Indescribable human experiences. They are the real reason I run tours. What beauty!

I lost my purpose when my Czech tour ended.

Should I create a new purpose by planning tours to thirteen European and Middle Eastern countries? It may be an impossible dream, but so what? Dreams create motivation. That is what is important, not the result.

Success and failure are up to God. I can only make the effort.

A noble effort it is. Filled with adventure, experiments, frustrations, minor catastrophes, headaches, and balancing acts beyond my wildest dreams. I love the languages, the music, dance, and songs, the architecture, art work, customs, costumes, people, map reading, transport, dealing with a hundred foreign faces, and even handling the complaints of difficult tourists. Although I may scream in the privacy of my frustration, I still love the challenge and adventure.

Why not expand my tour business? Let heavens burst and earth explode! Let rivers, streams, and oceans bathe and boil me in their white-hot waters. I can't do everything. But why not try?

This means throwing myself into the tour business one hundred per cent! Put folk dance classes second, weekends a distant third; guitar playing, writing, study, running and yoga, will feed my soul. They are my invisible foundation. In the quiet retreat of their meditation they shape the essence of my tours, weekends, and folk dance classes. Without them my desire and reasons for doing business would crumble. Tours are a fundamental organizing principle of my life.

They're also a good reason to leave the house.

Auschwitz

Our couples group met last night. We had a pizza supper followed by our meeting. Marilyn asked me to tell us about Auschwitz. George said Ilsa had lost both parents there. I got very quiet; then started talking.

Visiting Auschwitz was the black cloud hovering over my tour. I'd feared the visit for a year. Yet how could I visit Crakow and avoid it? Auschwitz

(*Oswiecim* in Polish) was a pilgrimage I had to make, had to know about. So I made it part of our itinerary.

Auschwitz is simply too overwhelmingly horrible to describe or understand. Words seem only to diminish its magnitude. Yet words are all I have, so I'll try.

After talking to the group about my Auschwitz experience, I felt overwhelming fatigue for the next few days. I can't get it out of my mind, can't forget. It gnaws at my brain, haunts my person, and saps my energy. How could such a horror exist in the world? How low can human beings sink? I am a human being. Could I? How about other "normal" people, ones who go to work every day, my friends, members of my family? Could they, given the right background and upbringing? Evil exist in every person. How strong can it be? Auschwitz shows the enormity, the magnitude, of evil possible in this world.

The trip from Crakow to Auschwitz took about an hour. We drove on a good road. The sky was blue, the sun shining. But my heart beat in my mouth. When we arrived I saw tour buses parked in front of the entrance parking lot. Restaurants and book stores stood in the background; crowds of people milled about. The atmosphere seemed more like that of a shopping mall than a memorial.

We bought tickets and entered with an American student group from Ohio. Our Auschwitz guide, dressed in a suit and tie, said, "This is a Memorial Museum. There will be no gum chewing, shouting, or loud talking, out of respect for the millions murdered here. People like to know about their guides. You probably want to know something about me. My name is [he gave a Polish name I forget]. I am sixty-five years old. I come from a family of teachers. Both my parents were killed by the Nazis. Auschwitz was originally a Polish army barracks. In the beginning, the Nazis used it solely to imprison and exterminate the Polish intelligentsia and political prisoners. In 1942 the Nazis decided to use it as their main extermination camp for Jews. By that time, most Polish intellectuals and political prisoners had been killed. Poland lost twenty percent of its population during the war."

We started walking. The sun shone on this eerie quiet site. On one level, it seemed so normal. Tourists milling about snapping pictures, groups led by their guides forming here and there, quiet red-brick buildings, corridors, paths, walkways. We walked through the "Arbeit Macht Frei" arch and entered the camp.

The Joy of a Disciplined Life

I'm getting back to normal—or abnormal, whatever my natural state is.

How did I do it? I began my morning by writing. Then I did a half hour of yoga warm-ups, followed by an hour and a half run. During breakfast I read a story in the *New York Times* sports section about an Olympic runner who came in seventy-third in a race a year ago. His friend told him he didn't have the right attitude to make the Olympics. He agreed. At New Year's he made a resolution to change his attitude. Along with this he changed his training schedule. He began getting up at seven a.m. every morning, ran an hour, then went to work teaching in a school. In the late afternoon, after school, he trained with a local track team. At night before bed, he did one hundred sit-ups and two hundred push-ups. He gave up all social life during this period.

After three months he felt great! His running times improved. He passed the Olympic trials and made the Olympic team.

An inspiring story. It reminded me once again how satisfying and beautiful is the disciplined, high-goal life. I could follow it, create my own Olympic trials. I don't even need an Olympics to do it.

But I *do need a discipline*. I feel better today because yesterday I followed my athletic discipline.

This *Times* story inspired me to do even better. I can begin a new program based on the *three times a day athletic rule*. The rule is: *exercises of one sort or another, early morning before breakfast, late afternoon, and before bed.*

My three exercises are: running, yoga, and the triple-threat three: one hundred fifty push-ups, sit-ups, and squats. To the triple-threat I have added one-legged squat practice and "hand-stand" push-ups. These fit in with both the Olympic folk dance training program I developed in Greece and my desire to learn a hand stand reborn at Dolna Krupa castle in Slovakia under the direction and tutelage of Romeo Pascone.

The three times a day rule could also be applied to guitar playing, writing, and language study. Can it apply to business?

Glories of Work and Discipline: I

I needed elevation. Read something noble, I thought. How about the bible, Paul Brunton's notebooks, Eastern philosophy, or books on Kabbalah?

But these books teach me what I already know——and if I do, why not focus on remembering it? Instead of looking outside for inspiration. Look within. Edit my mind.

Editing is becoming a lifetime calling. I am throwing page after page of early New Leaf journals into the garbage can. I am amazed how much I throw away. It is both humbling and freeing. I used to think whatever I wrote represented a creative act worthy or recognition and remembrance. Through editing I see almost everything can be tightened, improved, cut. It no longer pains me to. I am more detached. This must be good.

Glories of Work and Discipline: II

A new calm has descended on me since we visited Dolna Krupa Castle in Slovakia. I'll call it my Dolna Krupa calm. It has been created by a number of factors. First, I no longer feel responsible for the happiness of my tour participants. I try the best I can to create a good program along with good services. But it is *not* in my power to bring them happiness. Only they can do that. Somehow that lesson sank in at Dolna Krupa Castle.

Another factor in my calm is journal editing. I don't know why this is, but it is.

My new three-times-a-day exercise discipline rule is part of it. I am pushing slightly above my head, structuring my day with a no-matter-what, no-matter-where mentality, forcing myself to follow structure and discipline with no excuses.

This discipline holds me together, gives me confidence, brings elation, and puts me on the path to self-improvement.

But the goal is not self-improvement, which comes as a by product anyway, but rather, *staying on the path*. By working hard, aiming slightly above my head, staying in the process, following the discipline—practice, practice—I have found a most important ingredient for happiness.

Go for the Passion!

I like cloudy weather because I can stay home and work. I will not hear the ancient remnants of mother's and father's voices saying, "It's such a beautiful day. Stop practicing. Go outside and play. It's a shame to waste a beautiful day staying inside."

These voices come up during good weather. But truth is, the weather is better inside my mind than outside. Sparks are flying all over the room I work in. The harder I work, the hotter the sparks, clearer the sky, brighter the sunlight. I used to feel guilty about it. How can I separate myself from my wife, friends, and family by retreating into my wonderful world of work, work, work, by strapping myself on the glorious, self-fulfilling cross of labor, seeing my soul ascend to heaven even while my feet are planted firmly on earth. Isn't it selfish? Shouldn't I feel guilty?

No, no, no! Go for the passion! Ring up the ecstasy! Three cheers for death on the work cross with its divine payments of resurrection and transfiguration! Why piddle around with half-way "hobbies"? Better to step into the puddle and, through glorious work and effort, transform it into an ocean.

I Am an Olympian

Yesterday morning I ran forty-five minutes; in the afternoon I did fifty minutes of yoga; in the evening, at nine-thirty, I did a few sun salutation warm-ups followed by one hundred fifty push-ups, sit-ups, and squats. I took the one-hundred-fifties slowly, stopping to rest every so often. But I finished them.

It was a huge exercise day.

I went to bed worried.

I woke up tired this morning. Was I really tired or just scared about all the exercise I had done? In other word, did I frighten myself with *my potential?*

As soon as I said it, I knew I was. Had I really done all those exercises yesterday? Wasn't it too much? Would doing such extensive routines cause me to have a heart attack, pull a muscle, or break a bone? Was it healthy or unhealthy to push so hard, to reach so high?

No one can answer these questions except me. I am an experiment of one. Exploring my potential is exploring the unknown. No one knows what mysteries and possibilities, I will find within myself. True, by pushing and adventuring in these unknown regions, I am opening myself up to injury. But how else can I discover my potential?

I may hurt myself. But I may also discover a new world.

I've decided to walk the edge, go for the potential adventure, push, explore, grow, take a chance on the injury downside.

I have made a discovery: I am *not* tired——merely hesitant, worried, afraid. This means yesterday's exercises didn't hurt me. They didn't even make me that tired. They simply opened up another door to my potential.

It is amazing how far people can go when they try. Olympic training is within my grasp. It is hard to imagine myself as an Olympian, with muscles, athletic prowess, and skills. It is so far from my self-image. And yet, these exercises, in releasing potential, are telling me I can rise to unknown heights. If I train like an Olympian, think like an Olympian, step into the flow and process of becoming an Olympian, I can actually *be* an Olympian.

Since I am doing all these things now in my own Olympic training program, I *am* an Olympian.

Now there's a radical thought!

Death and Useless Things

Yesterday we went to Dr. Daniel Smith of Columbia Presbyterian for a second opinion. No luck. She needs a hysterectomy.

As she was being examined, I took a walk down the hall. I cried. True, the operation may go smoothly and she won't die. But maybe she will. Even though we've got a great doctor working for us, there is the possibility of things going wrong.

Even if everything goes right, there is always the ever-present question of death. No one escapes. If not today, tomorrow; if not tomorrow, in the future. This operation puts the finality of death squarely in front of me. I have a short reprieve before I die; so does she. So do we all.

Does it really matter much if things are postponed? Does it matter if we get a few more years or not? You bet it does! I want a reprieve. I don't want to be alone. I don't want to die.

"Big deal," says God. "Who cares what you want. I designed this life. I'm choosing how many years you'll have on this earth. I'm choosing for her, too. So shut up. Go back to your corner and sit down."

Who else do I have to talk to except God? Who else can soothe me, answer my questions, and tell me the final truth? Yes, I'm worried about being left alone for the rest of my life; I'm worried about death and transformation, about the pain, loneliness, and loss of my uxorial mental and spiritual limb. How will I handle life alone? Will I even want to?

These are the terrible but realistic fears I am facing. No one has an answer. Sure I can study medicine and learn to "be more comfortable" in hospitals, waiting rooms, and among doctors and nurses. We're not talking comfort here, though, but about death, the final calling. It is coming, if not today, then "soon" in the future. What's the difference whether "soon" means today, tomorrow, next week, or in twenty years. If time is an illusion, then so is "soon." Why deny death or run away? I might as well accept it and get it over with.

Consider death every moment. It is good to remember. Everything I touch, do, and think is transitory, even the most precious and beloved things I possess.

Do I really possess my wife, children, home, family, friends, and on down the line? Do I possess anything? Isn't it all a transient, a fleshy loan from God, placed in my hands to feel and hold before I pass it along? What an illusion to think I can possess anything. How silly, petty, and temporary are my worries. Even money, my biggest nemesis, it is puny next to losing her. Besides, one of the reasons I want money is to make her happy. But if she is not around, how can I make her happy? What kind of security does money actually give me if we are all soon to die?

Everything I think and own is a figment of my imagination, a flesh-dressed illusion walking down the street. Ghostlike worries and phantom fears feel so important and real when they visit me but in the light of the transitory nature of life. Why bother with them?

I'd love a reprieve. But whether I ask for it or not, God has already decided. Destiny is written all over her face and mine as well. Complaints are useless; so is worry. But I do it just the same. I like useless things.

Staying in Touch: the Importance of Family Gatherings

Yesterday our family met in our back yard. Miki came with my nephew Danny who lives in Connemara, Ireland, his kids, Jasha, and Tanya, and Ben and Paula.

Towards the end of the visit, while we were eating dessert, six-year-old Jasha cuddled up to me and asked, "Can I sit next to you?"

"Of course," I answered. I picked him up, sat him next to me, and gave him a hug. Four-year-old Tanya was already sitting on my other side. I felt so surrounded by loved ones. I hadn't lost my touch with kids; I was part of the family—all of us huddling together for warmth.

When the kids left, I felt sad. I'm anxious before family gatherings. Yet, when they end, I feel relieved but nostalgic.

Family contact and gatherings are important to me. Yet I have put them in second place—behind business, arts, athletics, and personal development.

I have lots of rituals, repetitions, and disciplines related to business, arts, athletics, and personal development. I follow these disciplines every day. Yet I spend almost no time thinking about family relationships. I take them for granted. Yet they are the pillars of my work. When I think about making money, succeeding in life, I think not only about personal satisfaction, but about how it will please others. Who are these "others"? My wife, children, brother, sister, nephews, nieces, cousins, aunts, uncles, on and on even to my extended family, my friends. This is a long chain of connection; I daily take if for granted.

The discipline of following a repeating ritual is the foundation of success in all business, artistic, athletic, and spiritual pursuits. It is also the foundation of family commitment. I'd like to start putting part of my consciousness and energy into the ritual of seeing my family. It's an effort. But without such effort I feel distanced and alienated.

The sadness I felt when Danny, Jasha, and Tanya left was my wake-up call: Put effort into organizing family gatherings and staying in touch.

Back Pain Medicine

When my back hurts, it is usually not my back but my brain.

My brain is killing me this morning. I'm going to Bulgaria in a few days.

I'm suffering from pre-trip anxiety. I hate leaving the secure, comfortable routines of home. Morning coffee, computer in my den, guitar in living room corner, philosophy and language books on the shelf, running shoes ready and waiting in upstairs bedroom, basement rug waiting for yoga, friends, phone, mail, stocks, relatives—everything I love is at my fingertips. Why leave this ease and comfort to run a trip to Bulgaria?

Facing my anxiety diminishes it. Deny it, and I develop physical symptoms. Pain in my lower back is my biggest signal. So are pains in my knees, neck, shoulders, heel, throat, and stomach. The lumbar aches I've been feeling the past few days reflect mounting anxiety about the trip. It is hard to believe that simply facing my fears will make my lower back pain go away. Hard . . . but true.

Even as I write this I can feel the pain diminishing, leaking out of my coccyx. The miracle of verbal medicine soothes my nerves.

I got a fax from Cathy Springer a few days ago. She said Ilyana Bozhanova will gladly meet our group in Plovdiv and give us a dance workshop. She also said that the economic situation it Bulgaria has gotten much worse, and crime is up. Should I bring my computer? Will it be robbed from my hotel room?

In the past I have always accepted the possibility I could have my computer stolen. I'd mentally written off the thousand-dollar purchase price as a business loss. But this year, since I'm behind financially, I thought losing a thousand-dollar computer is a big deal. Maybe I shouldn't take a chance this year.

Second, I've needed a break from writing. The Bulgarian tour would give me a good excuse to take one.

Third, Barry wisely said, "A writer cannot take a break. He feels too guilty. Editing is a part of writing: Use this opportunity for editing."

I felt relieved. Barry touched on the essential: a writer must write. Spending two weeks in Bulgaria without writing would torture me. Editing would solve my problem. I wouldn't have to bring my computer.

"What about depression?" I asked.

"Write by hand."

Good idea.

I told Bernice. She said, for you writing and editing serve two completely different purposes. Editing is exacting and confining; writing is freeing, relaxing, and helps your spirit soar. You need both.

Another good idea.

I'll do both. I'll edit my journal in Bulgaria *and* bring a paper notebook to write in. I'll not have to lug or worry about my computer. A hand-written journal combines painting and writing, drawing and language. Perhaps I'll edge my way into art. When I return to Teaneck, I'll copy my hand-written journal into my computer. This will be a pain in the ass. However, as I copy, I'll be editing at the same time, which may be a positive.

We'll see where this experiment leads. I can also practice writing Bulgarian in my hand-written journal. The Cyrillic alphabet is so beautiful.

My back feels much better already. I have nothing else to say. I am drained…but cured.

Depression as Vacation

I need a vacation. What is a *vacation?* I have never dealt with this problem before. I try to live my life as if I'm on a vacation all the time, by doing things I like. I've succeeded.

But I still need a vacation from doing the things I like.

Funny thing is, even though my conscious mind doesn't want to take one, my unconscious forces me to; but instead of a "vacation," it appears in the form of depression.

Depression is when I no longer have the interest or energy to work at what I want but somehow feel I must work at it anyway. I experience this on a daily basis, usually after lunch. That's when I "take my depression vacation." I eat, nap, lie on the couch, and generally feel aimless and miserable.

I also experience these downs on a cyclical, six-week basis.

I have been taking these mini-vacations for years. Since I like progress and self-improvement, perhaps depression vacations are a form of self-improvement through gestation.

Path of Progress Lesson: Accepting the down Days

Tomorrow I'm leaving for Bulgaria without my computer. I haven't been without it for years. Well, big deal. Instead I'll edit, read, and write in Bulgarian. My skill grows. Now I find *A Course In Modern Bulgarian* easier to read.

How fulfilling to walk the upward path of progress, hurl myself upon its discipline, and see the slow dawning of the Bulgarian understanding linguistic sun rising in my back yard.

I can make progress in anything. I just have to invest the effort, spend the time. This means staying on the path despite slow, fast, down, or up days.

Part of the price of progress is accepting, not only the down days, but down weeks, months, even years. When you walk the path of progress, most of the time nothing seems to be happening. Only habit, routine, and ritual keep you moving. "Why bother?" you often ask as one day turns into another with no apparent improvement in sight. But you continue the daily plodding, looking up one Bulgarian word after another, forgetting it, and looking it up again. Over and over the same thing, day after day, week after week, month after month, year after year. The path is slow, torturous, relentless, and often seems meaningless. You try reminding yourself of its importance. Periodic sunbursts appear, lighting your face, illuminating your mind. Then you cry: "It's worth it!" Now you know the beauty of discipline, understand the rewards of practice and importance of following a daily routine. These sunbursts are transient reminders, shinings along the trail. They act as your guides.

As I depart, remember the path of progress. Focus on it during my tour.

"Ever a Room Unfinished"

I got back from Bulgaria three days ago. I spent the first day sleeping, the second getting up at 1:00 a.m.; then I half slept and half worked. Today, the third day, I'm getting up at 2:30 a.m. with my first desire to return to a "normal" life. I'm trying to rediscover it by writing.

I'm putting together my tour schedules for the 1997 season. I've got the hand-written Bulgarian 1997 tour journal to read, edit, and analysis. On top of this—or under it—I've got all my New Leaf journals to edit. That's my biggest project. It is overwhelming, especially since I don't know where it's heading. I keep adding new pages every day.

Ever a "room unfinished."

Let a Miniature Push-up Be Your Guide

When panic or depression start, and mountains run their rivers into the sea, and bibles bend their purpose to cover land masses, what twisted road can bring you home?

It is the road of Doing. Its opening is behind the back door at the end of the mind's alley. The miniature push-up, small, seemingly meaningless, purposeless, inane, insignificant, infant movements, the quarter-way sit-up, one-inch squat, one word, one note, one step danced in right or wrong direction: any micro-particle of activity giving you *control* over your destiny will place you on the road to purpose and meaning. With each step forward, panic and depression recede. Clouds break up, then evaporate as you progress on the sunlit path of Doing.

Let a miniature push-up be your guide. The road to happiness, although passing through clouds of panic and depression, is the road of miniature deeds. Miniature deeds done on a grand scale. Do them constantly and everywhere.

Take your first step by pointing your toe towards heaven.

I Need Outer Travel, Too

I've always known how much I need my life of inner travel.

I thought *outer* travel was an annoyance, a necessary expedition into the world to earn a living. My deepest desire was to become a hermit, a monk, a recluse. Then I could study, write, or play guitar all day long.

I was wrong.

I need inner *and* outer travel for balance. Too much of one or the other gives me a headache, and makes me miserable. This morning I want the outside world to visit my doorstep. Give me calls, checks in the mail, registrations, signs of life from beyond the walls, signs my audience is alive and still wants me. They can express their love best when they call me to work.

But I can't count on them. Therefore, I'll take the initiative. I must call *them*. Take control. By doing so feelings of power and accomplish ment will return, whether I succeed or fail.

On Reading Jephte's Daughter

Yesterday I finished reading Jephte's Daughter, by Naomi Ragen. When I immerse myself in novels or classical music, I am often so transported I "lose touch" with the world at hand. I rise into the stratosphere, encountering celestial beings who inhabit higher planes. I remember such experiences to this day. In my St. Marks fifth-floor walk-up apartment in Greenwich Village, sitting in my stuffed armchair for almost two days straight reading The Last Temptation of Christ by Nikos Kazantsakis; or missing my subway stop as I sat on the subway reading Look Homeward, Angel by Thomas Wolfe; or forgetting classes at the University of Chicago as I read Martin Eden by Jack London.

I gave up listening to classical symphonies, sonatas, and concertos after high school. I "traded them in" for earthbound folk music—short, simpler music over which I had more control. Hearing classical music had become too painful. I couldn't combine soaring on wings of Mozart and Beethoven with my need to function on the daily lower planetary levels.

Part of me wants to drift into space, fly away, leave the planet, exchange earthly life for celestial travel, soar with birds, with angels. Earthly existence feels so banal once you have experienced celestial flight.

Yet I have strong legs. Yearning to attach themselves to earth. They relish material existence; solid and stable, they fight for survival against the fantasies of my mercurial mind. My legs struggle against classical music and novels that raise me above the earth, feed my errant mind, and toss me helter-skelter through an ethereal universe.

I live in a divided land, torn between earthly cares and heavenly desires. Is there a compromise? Can one read novels, listen to classical music, and still function in this world? Do I have enough mind control? Or will this division last as long as I live in my body.

Reading Jephte's Daughter added richness, color, and forgetfulness to my life. I rode on the currents of its plot and lost myself in its characters. With more self-control I could add novel reading and even classical music to my life.

The Joe Elias Weight Reduction Method

1. When eating out, walk to the restaurant. The more miles away, the better. Best is to live in Port Jervis and eat out in New York City.
2. Put heavy weights on forks that carry cholesterol-bearing foods.
3. Use rubber chopsticks.
4. Eat soup with a toothpick.

Wise men and yogis without hair on their head are not bald. Rather, their hair grows inward.

Ordering Myself into Witness Mode

How do I calm angry waters?

Is it my job to "cure" and make things better? I want others to stop being mad at me. Yet I know this is impossible. If they decide to get mad at me, there is nothing I can do to stop them. They makes their own decision. Sometimes, I happen to say or do something that calms her down. But these are accidental acts, places where God steps in to feed me a morsel. I can count on God in the long run, but in the short run I've got to count on myself. The only thing that works is lifting myself above the situation by putting myself in witness mode.

Sometimes I feel guilty stepping out. Is it a residue from a former life? This guilt habit tells me I am responsible for the feelings of others. If they are angry, happy, sad, anxious, worried, tense, it is because I have caused it. I am also responsible for making their life better.

This attitude of responsibility for others is not only disgusting but also the height of chutzpa. How can I be so blind, dumb, and power hungry to elevate my puny ego to such magnitude? What hubris! Yet believing myself responsible for their feelings gives me a sense of power and connection. Without it I have to face the truth that each ego is alone in the world; each autonomous self makes up its own mind, creates and follows its own feelings. This puts me in a lonely position. I hate being left out. I want to be part of the show. Therefore, when someone blames me for something, anything, I gladly accept it even though I have nothing to do with it. They are feeding my desire for power, telling me I am strong, dynamic, forceful, muscular, heroic, and godlike, and that I, simply by existing, have a powerful influence on them. Even though they call me moron, stupid, idiot, and curse me, I accept it. In my inverted way of thinking, they are offering me a form of love.

That's why I accept their criticism. There's something in it for me. My ego screams from the mountain top: Thank you for cursing, blaming, and making me feel important.

I want to get off this illusory power ride, to rise to the vision of witness world. How do I do it? Just *do* it. Take the plunge. Start out by saying "No! Never again!" Make it an imperative, a captain's order, a law, a general's command. Then follow orders. Everything else will fall in place.

The Dips

I have been suffering from "the dips." Why, I'm not sure.

Look at a few surface vicissitudes: cutting my Darien group back to one night a month, Paula's high blood pressure, Ron's upcoming quadruple bypass. Although reason for a blip on my vibrational scale, these are not enough to cause a significant slide.

On the positive side, business is not bad. I've even had some success in the stock market.

Then why the dips?

It's because my six-week energy cycle ended.

It makes sense. I returned from Bulgaria at the end of August; my first folk dance class was September 18. Thus I began my fall 1996 work cycle around the middle of September. It is now November 6. About six weeks have passed. Isn't it time for my period?

Indeed it is.

What can I do about the dips?

Take a mini-vacation. Do something else. Eventually the dips will end with the birth of a new energy cycle.

What is the best way to handle dips? Ride and observe them.

TV Self-Protection Program

My ego struggles to break free of its dark crust. Every morning it heads out the door questing for light, hoping to find a star caught in slime. Why am I in slime today? Why do I feel so stuck?

Last night I sat for hours in front of the TV. I could have been reading, writing, doing push-ups, playing guitar, anything but watching TV. Instead, waste, waste, waste!

Know what to cling to and what to avoid. Cling to my rituals. I've discovered riches in them. "Who is rich?" asks the *Pirkei Avot*, Ethics Of Our Fathers. "The man who is satisfied with his portion."

Why is it better to fall asleep in the basement than watch five minutes of TV in bed? Because the hypnotic power of TV turns five minutes into fifteen, thirty, sixty, two hours, and more. I am rarely strong enough to resist. Watching TV is like cake in the house. I pig out and feel disgusted.

"Take a peek" at the TV or sit down for "just a few minutes." Before you know it the screen's hypnotic tentacles wrap themselves around you, weaken your resolve, poison your brain, and paralyze your decisiveness. Soon you're vegetating helplessly, your energy sucked out, your time wasted. You wake the next morning feeling used up. TV watchers experience a slow degeneration of their brain cells.

I must start my TV Self-Protection Program: Insist on *not* watching it. This will soon develop into a habit that will protect me, not only from TV, but from videos as well. It will "force" me to do something useful with my time, like reading, push-ups, guitar playing, calling a friend, learning a folk dance, taking a walk, studying a language, memorizing a word, or reading the bible.

Playing Guitar in the Garden of Eden

I see monks walking among the dandelions near the rosette of my guitar. They stroll between the strings, over the ebony fingerboard, gaily playing *satori* games, leaping into the sound hole.

Now they have turned my Ramirez into a swimming pool, splashing and twisting their purified bodies in a Buddhist mitzvah stew, preparing their elegant limbs for a morning *mikvah* dip.

Rolling crescendos and frying peccadilloes frolic in the marshes of yesterday's turmoil. The sun stretches its palm wings, flooding the lily fields with fountains of light.

Gates of practice open. Museums stand at attention; daffodils play with rakes. It is a scene worthy of my suburban town. Long ago the elders named it "Garden of Eden." Only one in New Jersey.

Rents aren't too bad. There's diversity, too: ants, fish, rice heaps, antelopes from Costa Rica, Bolivian birds living in sandwiches, three clusters of nettle, and most recently, an ethnic settlement of weeds.

What Is a Calling?

What is my calling? Can you have several? When does it appear? At the beginning of life? Teenage years? In your twenties? At mid-life? Beyond?

Is music my calling? Or writing? What about folk dancing, sports, yoga, running, and studies? Or my social director personality. Is that a calling, too? Can personality be a *calling*? Or does an inner voice speak?

Meditations for My New Life

I woke up at five-thirty this morning, had coffee, read the *New York Times*, studied Hebrew words, then played scales on my guitar. Suddenly, the Romanian tunnel dream returned, and I started to cry. I couldn't play anymore, so I went back to bed.

An hour later I awoke wanting to begin a new life. I knew it would have the same form as my old life. But I wanted the content and substance to be different. What could be different? Perhaps "meditation on others."

How does running, yoga, or writing become a meditation on others? How about aches and pains?

It is in the thoughts themselves. For example, while holding a yoga posture that stretches the quadriceps, I might think about the quadriceps of others. If it affects the stomach, heart, or spinal cord, I might think about the stomachs, hearts, and spinal cords of others. The guitar notes I play would be send to all people in the world. The "luxuriate in people" and "meditation on others" approach would be a qualitative change, a new stage of life.

Such meditations uplift me. Will they chase away fears of financial disasters, poverty, sickness, loss, endings and death?

Love, Truth, and Beauty as Motivators for a New Life

Yesterday all sense of purpose and mission vanished. Why bother living? Even suicide crossed my mind. I knew I was in bad shape. But why? I have everything I want. I love what I do. I look at my life and must admit I've got it all. What a paradox! While I stand before the mighty "I've got it all," I am contemplating ending it all. Unusual, indeed. I hope my wife doesn't read this. She may take it literally and have me committed.

As an older, experienced person, I realize I have been through these emotions before. With slight variation, I am going around in familiar circles, rising and falling in the same cycles. What does this new one mean? Obviously, I am approaching an ending. What is suicide, death, and its gloomy earthly counterpart depression, but a symbolic form of ending? Energy and matter can neither be created nor destroyed but only transformed. Therefore, I am approaching a transformation of some sort.

It has to do with a return to the world of business and sales. Specifically, the season of tour selling is approaching. My brochure just came out. It is a masterpiece of color, craftsmanship, font, and design. My envelopes are ready; so are the newspaper articles on my tours; my mailing is sealed, weighed, and ready to go. Everything is set for the 1997 business push. I've just spend three months in semi-isolation and retreat, working on my guitar, Hebrew, bible, yoga, editing, and reading novels. Basically, I wanted this time to set new directions and rejuvenate myself. Now the three months are over. I am ready to move ahead. Resistance to moving ahead is mirrored in flashing visions of suicide and depression. They signal the death of my three-month retreat and semi-isolation.

After death comes rebirth. I'm preparing to slide out of my old skin into a new one.

There is one important attitude I changed during this three- month retreat: I lost many obsessive concerns about money. This has been the most freeing aspect of my retreat, and perhaps also why it was successful. I retreated without financial worry. I have less money than before so why I did not worry I do not know. Let me simply accept the birth of this new attitude as a blessing and move on.

But with disappearance of financial worry, my motivation to make money by promoting my business also disappeared. If earning money was no longer my prime motivator, what would motivate me? An old question.

Truth is, I had better return to work and reignite my business or else! If I don't, the answer is quite clear: suicide, death, and depression, in whatever order comes first. This proves I have a visceral need to promote my events even if money is no longer my prime motivator. Maybe it was never was. I fooled myself, creating a financial fear to scare me into action; I hadn't faced the importance of my calling; I didn't want to see that my work is not merely a matter of credits and debits, money, finance, and security, but rather a matter of life and death, and that without the meaning and connection it gives my life, I will surely die.

So I have found a motivator even more important than money: Beauty. *Beauty*? Who ever heard of such a ridiculous motivator? Okay. Instead of beauty, what about love? *Love*? Are you *kidding*? Who ever heard of love as a business motivator? Money, yes, but love? Okay. Instead of love, what about truth? *Truth*? You *must* be kidding. Who ever heard of truth as a business or sales motivator? Money, power, fame maybe, but truth? Never.

But now that the phantom of financial worry has been chased away I am left with beauty, love, and truth as my bottom line. What is love? What is truth? I have never understood them. I don't know if I have ever experienced either. But I know beauty and have felt it deeply. Poets say that love, beauty, and truth are the same. If that is the case, then I can say this trinity is my motivator. That's quite a revelation for three months of retreat.

Focus on the Main Event

I'm at the Paramount Hotel in my favorite room, 45. It's peaceful.

Playing guitar beautifully. My fingers are flying. I'm dropping the details to focus on the main event.

The main event of the guitar tremolo is the base notes. Trebles are details. The four-finger tremolo has three trebles to one base; the five-finger tremolo has four trebles to one base.

I've moved beyond "proofs" to focus on the base. It is bringing wonderful results.

I'm playing fast fast but not thinking fast fast. I'm playing fast fast and but thinking slow slow.

The Inferno of Translation

I'm reading Dante's *Inferno*. The translation by Mark Musa is excellent, yet I'm getting bored and impatient because it is a translation.

I'll never read a book in translation again. The sound of the language is too important. In the future, only read the original, even if I don't understand it. Better to learn a new language than to read a translation. What is a translation anyway but a shadow of a shadow? A word of Dante's *Inferno* in the original may be enough to inspire me not only to study Italian but to run a tour to Italy.

MONEY AND ITS BRETHREN

Morning Monsters

The weather report said it's going to snow again next Monday. It will kill my Monday night folk dance class. It may snow Tuesday, too, and kill my Tuesday night class. It's going down to ten degrees tonight as well. That will put a damper on my Friday night Darien folk dance class.

Winter weather is killing my business. As I look into the future, I see black clouds, fog, rain, snow, hail, and darkness. Yet the whole picture may be a lie. Things could get worse, better, or remain the same. Why do I write about it and put such future illusions to pen? To expunge, purge, and vomit up these miserable images of frustration, failure, doom, insecurity, and collapsing fortune. I see them all in front of me, great walls blocking my path, boulders strewn around me, giant billboards rising before my eyes screaming headlines: *No tourists! No registration! No money! Jim Gold has been forgotten. Only gloom, doom, and rejection will be his future lot!*

These fearful monsters, luminaries of the lower world raised in projection to stellar worth, are my morning porridge. They are phantoms gone wild, running unimpeded around my mental gym, the playpen of my creative head. I call them "phantoms" because I cannot know the future. The misery I am creating this morning can be easily turned into happiness with only one positive business phone call. Imagine, any moment, someone may call up booking twenty people for my Budapest and Prague tour. In one minute it could move from disaster to heart-thumping success! All it takes is one phone call. True, the chances of this happening are small, even microscopic. Yet my fertile head and dynamic imagination can easily create a beautifully scenario with mucho money coming into my coffers, and mucho happiness to myself and Paul Laifer, my booking agent. Too bad it is not true. How happy will Paul be when I tell him my tour only has one person? How embarrassed *I* will be. Frustration and disappointment: I am doing more advertising this year than last, but instead of twenty-five people, I have only one.

This proves only the present is real, true, and valuable. The past, although sometimes a lovely illusion, is still a can of phony and useless memories. The future is also an illusion, painted by hopes. If I want a quick return to the Garden of Eden, I'd better look to the present. I'm spinning illusion after illusion in an effort to break free from illusion and return to the awe-filled, ever-loving present.

Nevertheless, creating illusions is part of my business and life style.

Why Worry?

I canceled folk dance classes this week because of the blizzard. I canceled the first week of January, too. I've resigned myself to no work this week. I'll spend my "snow vacation" playing guitar, writing, stretching, and reading the Torah in Hebrew. Bible stories are beautiful.

No business or no money coming in. Otherwise I'm having a good week.

Suppose my problem is not losing business from the snow, but rather guilt over enjoying this mini-vacation. If I don't worry about losing business I might feel *too* good. Instead, a voice reminds me I should be working, making money. It's a *small* voice, because doing business this week is close to impossible. But it is a voice nonetheless.

If I had no financial fears, I'd have no guilt, either. Then I would dive into Torah studies, writing, guitar, yoga——and into happiness.

Could I live with such happiness? While everyone else is a earning a living, I'm home doing "nothing." I don't care what others say about this, but I do care about *my* miserable little voice of conscience. "Jim Gold," it says, "you'd better work, or your world will fall apart. If you're not going to work, at least worry about it. Otherwise you'll end up penniless, homeless, a bum, starving, sick, living on the street, or lying in some gutter in frozen New York City or sweltering Bombay. Who will take care of you if you don't work? At least worry. Worry is a substitute for work!"

I could answer: God and destiny are taking care of me. So why worry?

The Importance of Pursuing the Impossible Dream

I am still "suffering" from lack of fear. Even though my business has been terrible since November, I am unafraid. Is this stupidity, bravery, or something else?

As my phone sits quietly on its desk, my mail box remains free of registrations, and my bank account dwindles, I remain remarkably calm. The vicissitudes of life are beyond me. Like a witness, I sit in my inner viewing chamber and watch.

How long will such detachment last? Is it good? Realistic? Have I evolved to a higher yogic state of nonattachment? Has the gut-wrenching worry, and ever-present fear of financial ruin, homelessness, and attachment to my business, really disappeared?

After putting out the most beautiful brochure of my life and taking out more ads than ever before, my Budapest tour is on the verge of collapse—but I'm not worried. I watch in wonder.

Could it symbolize the end of an era, a new calm, meditative, philosophical stage in my life?

I am seeing a repetition of the business cycle. I've been through similar ones before: folk dance weekends with hundreds of people diminishing over the years to weekends of tens and twenties; large tours diminishing to small tours, followed by rebirths like the successful 1995 tour season.

How can I get excited or worried again? I know business is cyclical. I can fight for tour registrants, and nothing happens; or I can do nothing, and my phone rings off the hook, my mail box fill with registration checks.

Perhaps I "know too much." That usually means knowing nothing at all. Am I fooling myself by believing the trough is the same as the crest or rising wave? Am I a step closer to non-attachment? Is it a creative hiatus, a break between cycles?

I am not unhappy with this calm state, but I am not happy either. It is an extended limbo. I pass my time developing non-business interests like running, yoga, guitar playing, and bible studies. Or waiting for a new idea to propel me.

Once an idea is fulfilled it is dead. That's why a great success often signifies not a beginning but an end. Last year was my most successful tour year. Did it signify an ending?

My original idea, born fourteen years ago, was to develop a tour business with many tours. I had planned to go on three or four a year and run the others with different guides and tour managers. I tried expanding my tour business simultaneously but my market diminished. Soon I gave up hopes of tour expansion. After a year's depression, I decided my personal participation on each tour was its best selling point and that I would go on all my tours. With that decision, I gave up my original tour dream. Is it time to return?

What was my original dream?

I saw my job as exploring and developing tours in Western and Eastern Europe countries, and the Middle East. I would know the hotels, guides and services in these countries as well as tour managers back home, like Ginny, who could lead my tours. I would collect tour monies and spend most of my time making deposits in the bank. This idea didn't work. Instead of becoming a millionaire I went into debt; instead of increased registration, my participant list got smaller. In order to be competitive, I had to lead my own tours. With this realization I adopted realism as a business philosophy.

Nothing kills a dream more quickly than realism.

It is time to return to my original dream. It may never be realized, but at least the hopes, goals, and growth it creates will act as long-term inspiration. I will set up an impossible dream good for my entire life time. It will be an unattainable goal, like reaching God.

I'm the kind of romantic who likes pursuing unrealizable goals and impossible dreams. Realizable goals because of their nature, are subject to the cycle of birth, death, and rebirth. But unrealizable goals and impossible dreams can never be fulfilled. Thus they, like God, last forever.

Pursuing an unrealistic goal may be the ultimate in realism.

Pursuing the impossible dream may be the best uplifting medicine for my psyche and emotional well being.

Suddenly, Wealth

Suddenly, I feel free. By abandoning hopes of wealth through tourism, I have stepped out of tour prison. I am giving up my quest for it. If it ever comes, it will come by "accident."

It may not be my destiny to attain great material wealth. Perhaps I am already "wealthy" but do not recognize it. My riches are a good wife, good family, good health, good work, and good friends. These are riches well beyond the money belt. I'm returning to focus on survival. Why not continue that pattern instead of beating myself over the head pursuing wealth, which somehow never comes? Besides, the reason I want it is to free my mind from worry so I can pursue scholarly and artistic interests. I'm doing that already without wealth. I was brought up to scorn wealth. Perhaps I've overreacted to my upbringing.

Downsizing

I've written almost nothing during the past week. Such "vacations" often come during transitions.

I am going through a business transition. I am downsizing all my operations. Fewer people are joining my weekends and tours. I'll have to think smaller in order to survive. Perhaps thinking smaller will bring on a surge of creativity.

It already has.

I've decided to run small tours of five to six people. That means I'll be making about a thousand dollars a tour. Not good for two weeks work, but not bad either. Plus I get a "free" trip, and a chance to practice language and history.

I'm downsizing weekends, too. I'm eliminating guest teachers next season. I'll aim for five to ten people; I'll run small, personalized weekends. This will give me a profit of about $300 to $600 dollars a weekend. Not good, but not bad either. I'll run about four weekends a year. If I get even lower numbers I can cancel it without much loss; and, of course, if the market turns, I'll make even more.

What does this mean in terms of my expenses? Probably not much. I still want to make beautiful brochures which I can proudly send out to potential customers. So I doubt if brochure expenses will go down.

How about my mailing expenses? They probably won't be going down either unless I create two mailing lists, one for local folk dancers and weekenders, and another for tours nationwide. If I do that, I'll save on mailing and printing costs, but not much. It may not be worth the bother.

Downsizing has an immediate advantage: my focus *is off* making lots of money and *on* doing what I like. It makes me creative. I'm thinking about a small tour to Sicily next year, also Romania. Taking chances will be easier since not as much will be at stake.

It's good for me to stop focusing on money so much. At heart I am still an artist.

How does the artistic approach differ from the business approach? A businessman looks for a public need, then tries to fill it. An artist looks to an inner need, fulfills it, then looks for customers to buy his creations.

Marketing precedes creation for the businessman.

Creation precedes marketing for the artist.

During the past fifteen years I've worked to become a businessman, an entrepreneur. To a certain extent I have succeeded. Nevertheless, I slip easily and naturally into the artistic mode.

I see why Arlene said I didn't seem enthusiastic about my work. I wasn't. My focus was on money, and running tours to known destinations in order to make even more money. I went for what I knew rather than the new. An ending. It was similar to my concert career: once I put together a good program I was afraid to change it, especially when people paid me such good money to perform. How could I take a chance experimenting, trying out new material? But performing the known slowly dried up my creative juices. Soon my concert career ended.

The same thing is happening in my tour career. But this time I have past experience to guide me. I am aware. I don't want my tours to die like my concerts. In fact, as I'm thinking about this, perhaps I should bring back my concerts again—in downsized form.

Worry and focus on making money has distanced me from the creative source. Thinking small may be the best thing I can do for myself. It will feed my roots. Downsizing may put me back on the right trail again.

Discipline, Ego, and Transcendence

How can I keep my spirits up when business stinks, money trickles, and, I am humiliated by numbers? This morning I got a fax from Adam Molnar in Budapest: "I am a bit surprised that you have such a small group," he wrote. Stab, stab. Once again, humiliated. As our future Hungarian tour guide, I want to make an impression on Adam. Bringing such a small group to Budapest——four people——is hardly a way to make an impression. I've already accepted the financial misery of this trip. Accepting the humiliation is even harder.

But I'm not canceling. I'm facing my humiliation. I've faced it so many times before. I'm learning to "live in the embarrassment." I feel bad for Adam. He won't make much money working with me. I know I have a negative, miserable attitude. How can I keep from sinking into black holes? Discipline. Self-control. Unwavering adherence to my miracle schedule.

Disciplines cure me. Writing lifts me out of black holes. So do my other disciplines of music, business, exercise, and study. They are my cures, my salvation. By forcing myself to get out of bed and step on their stone-strewn path, take my first baby steps towards the light; I am crawling out of the cave of discouragement, ignorance, and death, and stepping into the radiance.

Discipline is the answer to problems of worry and humiliation.

I have to admire politicians who run for office. Daily they face humiliation and rejection from voters, but they keep coming back to fight again.

What is being humiliated? My ego. Transcend it and there is nothing left to humiliate. Easier said than done. But that doesn't make it any less true.

PERFORMANCE

New Business Beginnings: Rebirth of Business Energy

Something snapped over the New Year's Weekend. Two concerts gave me the keys. After the first, I concluded that a classical-guitar-only concert was not my way.

During the second concert I led a community sing. Wonderful, easy, flowing, natural——no problems at all. Group songs are my element. But how can I impress an audience if I open with "Irene, Goodnight," which has only three chords? How can I prove what a fine guitarist I am? How can I make an impression? I finally concluded an easy opening to an evening program is best for me. It takes the courage of the humble plus a vow of guitar poverty. What better symbol of guitar poverty than three chords? Use "Irene, Goodnight" as a group song opener. Take the pressure off. Do the simple and easy thing; open myself to simplicity.

Leading group songs and talking with the audience comes easily to me. It's a talent, so effortless I don't even recognize it as one. Playing classical guitar in public is difficult. I've always felt giving a concert *should* be easy. That concept went up in flames during the New Year's Weekend. Over its ashes, a hurricane Phoenix of new energy is rising. Short-range, it means promoting tours, weekends, and dance classes. Long term, it means promoting concerts and writing. I have no idea how to promote concerts and writing. The time is not yet ripe. Yet I feel someday it will be.

Business energy has been released.

Means to Mitzvah

Think of the audience. Serve others on the road to mitzvah. Use them on the road to mitzvah. It's the Jewish way.

To tremble and quake before audience judgement is one way. But a different one is to think of them as belonging to you, as part of yourself. Thus you serve a unified higher self.

I need a new way of thinking. I refuse to perform, edit, or publish until I find *a new reason for doing it.* That is why I have withdrawn from concerts, editing, and publishing. It takes years for old attitudes to exhaust themselves and die. I'm waiting for a new attitude light to shine on me.

Thinking of the audience as means to mitzvah may be that new radiance. It is a radically different way for me to think, totally opposite from my usual way. Since opposites attract, I'm on the right track.

Continuing as a Soloist

Since the Russian Weekend I have stopped writing, guitar practice, and language study. First, fatigue was my excuse. But I've been fatigued before and it hasn't stopped me. Why now? This morning it hit me. Two weeks ago I decided to edit my journal and publish it. For some reason, whenever I think about editing and publishing, I stop writing. These thoughts stop my flow. I must consider never publishing again. How sad. The only thing sadder is not writing. When I stop writing, I lose energy and sink into depression. Writing is my key to self-discovery and morning happiness. I find such fulfillment in no other activity. Paul Brunton wrote his journal for thirty years and died without any desire for publication. If not for his son and a small group of devoted friends, none of his incredible work would have been published posthumously.

What will happen to my journal? Could I go on for the next thirty years, piling up page after page, leaf after leaf, without publishing a word? Paul Brunton is one of my heroes. Would I be able to emulate his attitude?

As my writing and guitar practice become more and more private, they keep improving. No one hears the former except Barry and my writing class. As for my guitar playing, who will ever know about my improvements? By offering my writing and playing to others I am giving my best. Yet I don't want to go public. The best parts of my iceberg may remain submerged. When it finally melts, there may be no trace of me. I will be forgotten. I can find solace in practice, however; it implies a never-ending search for perfection, a daily walk on the path to higher power. The purpose of my writing and guitar practice has changed. They have become private forms of meditation, paths to self and Self-discovery.

Guitar Performing Challenge

Yesterday I did nothing; I lived far from my routines and rituals. I rested. Yet the day was not wasted. The guitar-performing challenge dropped me into a vat of rumination for the entire day.

First I thought about improvising. Five minutes later I canceled that idea. Then I decided the challenge was to play before an audience. Years of practicing had finally borne fruit. I had solved the problem of inadequate technique. It boiled down to *the ability to accept mistakes!* For decades I lived under the restricting wall of perfection's call. Mistakes were anathema. I played slowly and cautiously. As soon as I tried playing with feeling, looseness, expression, and abandon, I missed notes. Back and forth I went for years trying to iron out these errors, striving for perfection but never attaining it. A month ago, I gave up.

"Perfection is hopeless," I said. "Play with abandon. Damn the mistakes!" I settled for imperfection and vulnerability.

As soon as did, I made that decision, my playing improved dramatically. Most mistakes disappeared. Fear dropped out of sight. In its place came loose, expressive playing, everything I had always wanted.

A New Look at Performing

Last night at Rama's we heard a performance by Ray Gombac h, a sacred story teller. After a beautiful introduction filled with wisdom, he did a dramatic reading of Jewish stories called "Moments of Illumination." An excellent presentation.

Ray Gombach's performance made me long for my performing career. It even made me jealous. Why shouldn't I perform before such a fine, intimate audience? First I thought I ought to study storytelling. Then I realized it was not storytelling I needed but the thrill of performing. I missed my old performing life. Yet I had no desire to pursue a performing career or even chase after a performing job. My conflict over performancing still had not been resolved.

When we came back to Teaneck I told Bernice about my feelings. She said, "Why not make performing your hobby?" She's been saying that for years. But last night I listened again. Could I return to performing as a *hobby?* My career is established in folk dancing, weekends, and tours. Guitar—and writing—are established as "hobbies." I haven't made money in them for years. I like it that way—at least for now.

Perhaps I can return to performing and do it for nothing. If I didn't care about money, career, or fame—all former performing goals, then I wouldn't care whether my audience walked out on me or not. I could play classic guitar with mistakes, misinterpretations, pauses, memory lapses, and stumblings, and it wouldn't matter. I wouldn't get nervous.   But is it possible—or even desirable—to perform *without* getting nervous? Nervousness is an old habit I have held onto for years. I don't know if I could perform without it. But I could try.

If I have no ambitions, goals, desires, or hopes, but play with the love of music and audience energy, maybe I could start out on a new performing path.

I Am a Jumper

Jumping from guitar to writing to yoga to running to Hebrew to Romanian to dancing to organizing to touring to business to reading—and back to guitar. I do many things, perform many actions. On the surface I am pulled in many directions. But, in actuality, I only perform one activity—jumping.

I am a jumper. What is *jumping* but an expression of vital flow; a bursting forth of energy within. Who is at the center of this energy? Oneness. My jumping masks unity, the many faces of God.

Pot of Gold

Performing is my personal burning bush. It illuminates awe and wonder.

I have been on a twenty-year quest to escape the terror of performance. Yet, even thought my playing has "gotten better," the terror is still within.

Improvement cannot conquer it. The pot of gold at the end of the rainbow is filled with trembling. It is the creative pot, the cauldron of awe, the vessel of the Creator.

The Audience Is My Burning Bush

The audience is my burning bush, a constant reminder of something higher than myself. Audience is angels in disguise, sitting in front and all around, drawing out the best, forcing me to stretch beyond my self-imposed limits. Alone, I prefer to focus on my ego with its contradictory desires, fears, hopes, and illusions. The audience is my sign post, pointing out the straight and narrow, forcing me into the cavernous maw of raw, latent cosmic energy, the burning mouth of God.

The audience places me before the light. There I tremble before the power of my creative force, the messenger connecting me to the center of the universe.

Fresh Start

My temporal lobe has been making sandwiches for two weeks. Great washes of sound have pulverized the thirty-foot protective wall of my musical Constantinople; it crumbled before the Nevele Hotel onslaught. Hordes of hotel guests tramped down to breakfast, fine-tuning their urchin rumbling stomachs for the upcoming Supper Gastronomicus topped with athletic buffet of gastrocnemius steaks and Achilles tendons. What a dinner! Tables laden with wine and pork guarded by tall muscular Brazilian waiters with quivering noses and darting eager eyes, they stood ready to pounce on any dancing cutlet from Bulgarian *pravo* to Italian *tarantella*, panting before any serpentine Hellenic *syrtos* or macho belching Arabic *debkha*. The backslash weekend of folk dance and yoga blasted any hopes of a relaxed vacation behind the golden wall of ancient habits. Instead, rays of a future imperfect cosmic tense shone upon a rising guitar career. Soon, guitar in hand, I clocked my way toward the stage guillotine and placed my head squarely in the Tale of Two Cities.

But the second hand on the cosmic clock withered. So did the first. I am back! Yes! Question mark has been replaced by an exclamation point. Ploughing on the plains of Esdraelon, planting in the *buba* fields east of the Egyptian Deltas, scaling my fingers in the musical slave pits of Pithes and Ramses, I finally cooked my pharaonic brain in the hieroglyphic cauldron. Holding Osiris in the left hand and a shining pyramid in the right, a new "me" was born.

I played *Renaissance Dances* on my Ramirez as the Red Sea parted: I sang *Drill Ye Tarriers, Drill* and entered the barren freedom of the Sinai Desert. Torrid with enterprise, I knew that future delights awaited me.

The question rose from the neighboring Nile. "Why now? I was ready. For what, I don't know, but for something". An ibis stood by the door singing in dulcet tones. I am ready to perform, never perform, or make performing besides the point.

I am ready to take pleasure in the guitar—and singing, too.

Uncle Nat was right. "You've exhausted all other routes, " he said, standing in front of his tent. "Take pleasure. There is no choice."

Death and Resurrection in Darien

The swirl of errant folk dancers never showed up. They stayed home Friday after Friday. Registration descended to four. Call *that* interest? Years of driving to Connecticut twice a month. So much effort. Even when attendance was low, I went anyway. I refused to give up. I twisted my mind in any direction to keep hope alive.

This season, instead of meeting every two weeks, we tried running classes every Friday night. Result: mediocre to miserable attendance. Marjolein taught last week, and only five people showed up. I thought more people would come on the following Friday, when *I* led. Wrong. Same five-person attendance.

My mind collapsed, along with my hopes. I told my dancers they were witnessing the death and resurrection of our Darien folk dance group: We were changing our format to meeting the first Friday of every month: *First Friday Folk Dance Party*.

Financially, First Fridays can't be much worse than the last two years. Some evenings I taught for forty or fifty dollars a night, sometimes even less. I failed to realize my goals in Darien. I wanted a minimum of fifteen dancers to register and to create a beginner class. We achieved neither.

When I arrived in Darien last Friday and only one person showed up for the beginner class, I decided to end it. By 8:30 when three more people trickled in, I knew my decision was right.

I celebrated alone by eating in Boston Chicken.

But I hadn't counted on the mourning process. Death needs a funeral. I had to mourn before I could move on. What a fool I had been to only be elated! I don't give things up that easily. Usually I stick and stick and stick. I went through the stages of dying: first came shock and depression; then anger at the folk dancers who didn't register or show enough interest to support our folk dance venture; then came disappointment that I had failed in my purpose, and sadness with the lose of my group. This morning I finally accepted the demise at Darien.

Soon I'll be ready to move on.

Fast Fast Fast: Passion and Exhilaration in Speed

Frozen fingers can be released by playing fast fast.

I mean *really* fast! So fast I even miss most of the notes.

For years I have secretly wanted to play fast, faster, and fast fast fast. I rationalized away my wishes thus:

1. *Practice slowly; eventually I'll be able to play the notes faster.* I've tried this approach for over twenty years, and it hasn't worked.

2. I'm not good enough to play really fast.

That's about it. Only two rationalizations. But if I remember when I started classical guitar lessons with Rolando Valdes-Blaine, I didn't have problems with tremolo or speed. I never thought much about missing notes. Maybe I did, but I don't remember.

But I *do* remember guitar playing problems starting when I left Rolando and took lessons with Alexander Bellow. He changed my right hand position. I started practicing slow slow slowly. Soon I could hardly play at all. In retrospect, lessons with Bellow sent me down the wrong path. But perhaps I was destined to go down the wrong path anyway; I was too stubborn to listen and give credit to my inner voices; I *wanted* to hold myself back for some psychological reason. I cannot blame those years of slow playing and lack of excitement and passion in guitar playing on Alexander Bellow, even though I'd like to. I chose him for a teacher, chose to follow his directions and use his Segovia-based method of guitar practicing. Only it never bore fruit.

Now I'm returning to my intuitive base, listening to the inner voice of intuition. I'm playing fast fast, and fast fast fast, and loving every exhilarating minute of it! It's too good to be true—playing with passion, excitement, abandon, fervor, speed, verve, and freedom!

Perhaps this is what happens after you play guitar for about thirty-five years. There are breakthroughs all along the road of life, but you never know when they'll come. This morning as I played *Leyenda*, missing half the notes, traveling with incredible speed, I broke down crying. I knew I was taking my first steps down the right path. My muscles have to learn how to accept and live with speed. So does my mind.

Talents

Last night Sasha (Alexander Antchoutine) performed three incredible Russian dances. While he changed costumes, I sang Russian folk songs.

"What can you say after a dance like that?" I said, after he performed a Moiseyev number. "Such a performance can only be followed by the letter L." I sang "Moscow Nights" with L's in five different languages.

After Sasha's second dance, I said, "What can possibly follow such a magnificent dance? I can only think of reading my brochure for you." These lines were funny. But they *felt* like genius! I've been given a talent for verbal creations.

The classic guitar is a talent, too. . .but a lesser one, something like my calligraphy. Best is to accept it this way. One of my talents is to stand before people and improvise with my mouth. In performance, I do it around a folk song base.

BUSINESS

Refuse to Give Up: Project Hungary!

I told Paul I have three people registered for my Hungarian tour. I lied: I only have one.

Today I must face the possibility that my Hungarian tour will be cancelled. I am looking failure straight in the face. I don't like it. I've tried all the usual approaches—mailing, advertising, even phone calls. I called my long list of good possibilities, but not one of them has come through.

What should I do? Give up? Move onto something else? I'd like that. This tour's potential failure hangs over my head like a black cloud; it makes me mad and sad. Part of me wants to forget it; another part refuses to give up.

Which part should I listen to?

Refuse to give up! My tour of Hungary haunts me for a reason. I am simply too stupid, dumb, bull-headed, determined, stubborn, and proud to give up. When pushed to the wall, I hear my screams. "No, no, no! Never, never, never! I won't give up. Kill me first." Deep down I know that, if I give up, I'm finished. I would destroy an essential quality. Is it dignity? Refusal to be humiliated? A combination of both?

I can't say I'm proud of my inability to give up. But I'm not ashamed of it either. It's a quality I admire in others. I admire it in myself, too. It is the reason I am still in my own business, surviving on a shoestring or whatever other string comes along.

I don't consider myself a fighter but a nice guy, smiling a lot, trying to please others and make them happy. I'm not a rebel or idealist fighting for a higher cause. But that may be a public mask I wear to protect my inner core.

What am I afraid will be destroyed? That small voice telling me about transcendence, Beethoven, Mozart, playing the violin, a mystical vision of sparks, a dream with a million virtues beyond words.

I wade through social waters. At parties, holding my cocktail, smiling, and chattering, my essence hides out deep in the recesses of my being, untouched and unaffected by small talk and the social whirl. I want to keep that core unblemished; it reminds me that life is worthwhile and worthy, and that eternity is here, now, and forever.

I cannot give up. It is a question of life or death. Fighting is life; giving up is death. That is why I fight for my Hungarian tour. I don't have to win. The future is not mine to predict. I fight for the here-and-now. Going down in that struggle is the noblest way for my Hungarian tour to die.

I'll make phone calls, mail off letters, and walk around the block thinking about Hungarian tour promotion. During the next three weeks all my efforts will go into selling Hungary. If my efforts fail, at least I'll have given the tour my best shot. Then I'll give up with pure heart and peace of mind.

The winds are howling outside my window in a vicious morning storm. It's almost sixty degrees outside. Snow is melting.

After picking up my corporate kit with its seal and letter of incorporation from Bob Baumol two days ago, I met with Mike Bellini, my accountant; he has gone into his own accounting business. He said incorporating would cost me more money, and that it didn't necessarily protect me. I told him how Bob had said it would. I had to "convince" Mike that incorporating, with its liability protection, was good for me. I called it catastrophe insurance. While discussing incorporation, I hit on the idea of raising capital by selling shares in Jim Gold International! This idea inspired me. It felt like the first new business idea I've had in months, perhaps years.

I didn't even think how to sell shares or why anyone would want to buy them. Instead I thought: What would I do with the money? The answer: advertise!

Why is this significant? It means I have more confidence in my tours. The technical aspects are in place; my apprenticeship is over. I know what I am doing. The fact that my first thought was to advertise my tours means I am ready to proclaim the gospel. I believe in myself and its extension—my tours—without reservation.

I have also created a fictitious extension of myself, Jim Gold International, Inc. It has taken over a decade to make this decision. The years from 1984 to 1994 were preparation and training.

The 1994 season was good, the 1995 season sensational. 1996 is here. It looks like the worst year ever. I have hardly any customers. But "worst year" could be an illusion. It could be a planting year. New ideas and concepts are germinating.

From November to December of 1995, while business was dull, a guitar breakthrough was taking place giving me a freedom well worth the drop in business. A long, quiet time of reaping and planting, of mental and spiritual unfolding. building a raised platform on which to launch my future life.

A breakthrough is also occurring in business. By incorporating Jim Gold International, Inc., I have created a new entity, a symbol and metaphor for a new business, new life, and new level of existence. My corporate entity feels like a new "self." I am now two "people": The individual Jim Gold who works as an employee, and Jim Gold International, Inc., the company employing Jim Gold. I am both employee and employer. I own my identity; I also work for my identity. There is something intriguing about this schizophrenic existence. Freeing, too. Incorporating is a long first step down a new road. I don't know where it will lead, but it feels good. Certainly it feels different.

My New Smorgasbord Brochure

Here's an idea for my next brochure. Since I am selling myself, my talents, skills, and ideas, why not list all my talents and sell them in one brochure? A "catalogue" brochure. It would contain not only tours, weekends, and folk dance classes, but boutique items like such Hungarian vests, "229 Folk Dances," T-shirts such as "Folk Dancers Can't Be De-Feeted," the books I have written, other books such as Greek folk dancing by Alkis Raftis, and my school-show and club-date fliers. This would offer potential customers every service I can perform.

From a distance, blades of grass in a field all look the same. But up close each one is unique. I am a blade of grass. I grow in the human field. No one can take my place or grow the way I do. If they could, why would God have bothered creating me?

Catalogue Brochure

It's easy to get an idea. But one has to wait and see if it will actually be executed. A truly good idea means one it will be acted on, actualized. How do I check out a good idea? Simple: As soon as I get one I try forgetting it. If it is a good idea, it will return to haunt me. If it doesn't go away after a few days or weeks, then I know it is a good idea; I've struck pay dirt. Fulfillment comes almost effortlessly. The idea itself propels me to act. I simply follow its orders.

Is my catalogue brochure idea a good one? Will I act on it, fulfill its dictates? I'll forget about it and see what happens. In it, I will be writing my own copy, ads, and publicity——a major step. I have always resisted such writing. My hostility towards writing my own advertising usually turns into humor. In the past, such humor has been rejected by my publicity gurus. So I "hired it out" to Arlene, my publicity person.

But Arlene is moving to Florida. I can still work with her "long distance" but it will be difficult. Her move means it is time to try something different, like writing my own brochures and ads. Even if I follow this route, I can still keep working with her; she can send out press releases and even become my Florida tour representative.

I just spoke to Jackie Leidenfrost from Larsen Publications in Burdett, New York, on Lake Seneca, just forty miles from Ithaca and Cornell University. They publish Paul Brunton and put out a beautiful book catalogue with top authors. Yet they're hardly selling anything and struggling. I could put out a book catalogue, hardly sell, and struggle, too. Why not? Let my catalogue brochure be my first catalogue.

As if to confirm my insight, the phone has just rung with two new registrants for my tour to the Czech Republic, Slovakia, and Poland in July!

Leaving for Hungary Today

I started reading *Beneath the Wheel* by Herman Hesse last night. What a pleasure to read a novel again.

Why not put novel reading in my daily routines? Something for my unconscious to mull over and for my conscious to think about as I board the plane.

* * *

First day in Budapest. Staying at the very expensive Kempinski Hotel. We ate at the Matyas Pince Restaurant last night. Excellent food and atmosphere.

Our small group of four ladies, is lovely. Each one is high-spirited in her own way, and generous, too. No problems with money. They easily tip the waiters and gypsy musicians. Very unlike some of the cheap people I sometimes get on tours who count every penny even though they are often rich.

I'm meeting Adam Molnar this morning for the first time. We'll try map out a tour plan for this week and the future. My other tour guide, Andrew Solyom, also called. I'm meeting him tomorrow morning. Now I have two tour guides. I have almost as many guides as I have tourists. I feel split, even disloyal, to Andrew for wanting to work with Adam. Perhaps I *should* think of having two guides to work with instead of one. Adam is a folklore specialist; Andrew is a specialist on Hungarian Jewish history. I could use them both for different reasons. Of course, it's all immaterial if I don't get any customers.

I had a wonderful sleep last night—almost nine hours! I feel peaceful this morning. Perhaps that's why I don't have much need to write.

Folktours with a Classic Touch

Last night I went to bed 3:00 a.m., tossed and turned, woke at 6:30, and went right to breakfast. A miserable night, and terrible way to begin the morning. But perhaps I needed such a night to establish myself in Hungary and celebrate my new beginning.

I love the name "Folktours with a Classic Touch."

"Classic touch" means classical concerts and tours of historic music spots; it means Liszt, Bartok, and Kodaly in Budapest, Dvorak and Smetena in Prague. It also means fine art, folk arts, crafts, music, and villages museums.

I am setting up five 10-day tours with Adam Molnar for the 1997 season. Each one will include a different folk festival. I plan on going on one or two. The March and late October itineraries will cover Western Hungary and include a day trip to Vienna.

I envision adding a one-week "extension" tour to the Czech Republic. I'll arrange it with Jasan Bonus. This would include four nights in Prague and two or three in the country, visiting villages and meeting with local dance groups. I'll run it in conjunction with the Hungary tours.

I could run this kind of five-time-a-year program in Bulgaria, Greece, even in Turkey and Israel. Certainly I could run it in Bulgaria. Plenty of folk dancing and villages there. But I don't have a Bulgarian specialist like Adam or Jasan. I'd have to work directly with Balkan Holidays. Maybe it's possible. The same problems exist in Greece, Turkey, and Israel. I should start by "practicing on" Hungary, the Czech Republic, and Bulgaria for one 1977 season. Developing, and especially selling, such a program is a major project, the expansion I've been looking for. I came to Budapest with only four tourists because I sensed an expanded vision. Now, slowly, it is coming to fruition.

This may be the beginning of a Folktour type travel agency. There has always been an invisible force pushing me towards such an expansion even as part of me resists, saying I should stay in my monk's closet, write, and be an artist. Two opposing visions live side by side in my mind. I have to feed them both. Somewhere up ahead there may be unity... but it may come after death.

Great and Greater Expectations

My five 1997 tours to Hungary *symbolize* a new direction. More important, they symbolize the rebirth of a *new attitude*. Could it be that low business expectations drew low client response? That is, by *expecting* small tour registrations, I drew small registrations?

True, I have no control over who and how many register. But *I do have control over my thoughts,* which are generally negative regarding registration numbers for my events. I am usually "surprised" when anyone registers; I see such registrations as acts of grace, gifts from God aided by some effort on my part.

If I change my expectations, will the registrations change?

Whether they do or not, certainly such positive thoughts will help make daily life more pleasant.

On that basis alone, positive thinking is worthwhile. But I wonder if, in a mystical way, positive thinking will actually *draw* people to my events.

I'll try an experiment. I will expect more registrations and see if expectations turn into actualizations.

As of today I'm expecting a registration of twenty people for my Czech Republic–Slovakia–Poland in July tour, and twenty people for my Bulgaria tour in August.

Smaller May Be Better

Last night's dance class was so wonderful it made me sad. I've built up a fine group. Two years ago they could hardly walk. Now they are dancing! The class has a friendly warm spirit.

Why does it make me sad?

Ninety percent of my tour customers come from my dance classes, so the way to find more tour registrants is to build up dance classes. I can supplement my customer search with ads in the folk dance magazines. Trying to reach beyond the folk dance community is only worth a little effort. This means my tour business will always remain small. This is not so bad——except for last year's Bulgarian and Budapest tours, I've never made much money in tourism. The potential has always been there, but it has never materialized. Every seven years I get a bonus of large tour registrations. Beyond that, tours have always been small. Last night's dance class made me sad because it pointed out these limitations. I am a prisoner in the folk dance compound. Not a bad place to be. Like the prison of my body, it gives me pleasure and pain. Nevertheless, it is a prison. Recognize it as such.

Prisoners must also recognize that smaller can be beautiful.

I have more *fun* leading folk dancers on tour. We have a common interest. I am not even sure I want a giant tour business. I only want the money it will bring. But who says that bigger will make more money? Could be that bigger only means bigger problems, bigger worries, and a bigger future bankruptcy.

True, small could lead to smaller problems, smaller worries, and smaller future bankruptcy. Nevertheless, small may be better for me.

I am coming to terms with the reality of my business existence. Increasing customers is no longer the route for me to pursue.

I should concentrate on the fine jewel customers I already have, focus on giving them better service, talking to them of the phone, trying to satisfy some of their desires and wishes.

Small is personal: I know everyone's name.

Giving up the Guilt Power Trip

Helena just called. She is canceling the cruise portion of our Greek tour.

I realized the power of guilt. I disappointed her. By feeling guilty, I assume that, by doing enough advertising, making enough sales calls, I could have gotten enough registrants to run my tour. Yet this year I put more money and time into phone calls, ads, mailings, and brochures than ever before. The result has been the smallest registration in years.

Evidently I can put together the most beautiful Greek tour and still get zero registration. I may have control over my product but not over markets. Such vicissitudes are the stunning facts of all business ventures.

But by feeling guilty over small registration, I am saying it is within my power to *control* markets. By choosing guilt over realism, I am choosing hubris over reality. When the winds of fortune blow down my tour, I can take credit by saying I didn't try hard enough. *Thank God, it's my fault! I still have the power!*

Worse than guilt is realizing I do *not* have the power. Although I can do my best, business vicissitudes, fate, and predestination are stronger than I. Tour boats sail on seas of changing markets. I can choose to sail my boat, but I cannot choose to fill her.

Guilt as Protection against Helplessness

Last night I had a sickening thought: I may not go on my Greek tour. Cally, from Cloud Tours, called yesterday. She said our tour would cost over $2,000 per person. I said fine. I thought it included one free—namely, me. Later I realized there was no free; I would have to pay for myself.

I don't like making little money; I don't like breaking even. But losing money? Certainly not.

If I have to cancel, maybe I can convince my three people to go with Bob. If they do, fine. If not, I can refund their money or ask them to join me on another tour. I'll apologize to my customers and Bob Salem as well. But paying $2,000 to go on my own tour is not a wise business decision.

Disappointing everybody hurts me—especially Helena. It's her first tour ever. She's dreamed about going to Greece all her life. Will she go without me? I hope so. But whether she goes or not, what I tell her will certainly hurt her. It'll hurt the others, too. Margaret is tougher, a more seasoned traveler, and Natalie has never been sure about going anyway. Maybe I can convince her to join the Czech Republic or Bulgarian tour.

I feel guilty disappointing these people. I "promised" them a wonderful travel experience, and now, as we approach departure, I have to cancel my personal leadership. I've tried my best, made many sales calls, put ads in journals, talked it up at folk dance classes, gave it the best sales shot I could.

Cancellation due to lack of registration is not my fault. Yet part of me still believes it is. And this even though I can't think of anything I did "wrong."

Why do I feel so guilty when I can't find anything I did wrong? Of course I can look for "mistakes." Was I "selfish" to include Thessaloniki and Kastoria on our itinerary simply because *I* wanted to visit them? But even those cities could be seen as a service to customers wanting to visit off-beat places. I also had "promises" from twelve members of the Lee family. But as their promises turned to shit, my tour registration slowly went down the toilet.

Low registration was not my fault. Would I rather feel guilty than powerless? Would I rather feel there is some unknown power I could have exerted rather than acknowledge that fate, destiny, markets, and God are in charge? After exerting every effort to organize, sell, and run this tour, at a certain point one crosses the line into helplessness; greater powers than oneself take over. The fisherman can bait his line and throw it in the water. Whether fish will bite today, tomorrow, next week, or never, he cannot know. He can only wait for a bite. I am that fisherman. My survival instinct tells me I cannot go on this tour. Everything points to my faultless cancellation.

Yet guilt remains. How can I get rid of it? Does powerlessness equal guilt for me? Is such guilt based on hubris? Is it felt when man forgets his place in the universe?

Have I forgotten mine, stepped beyond my limits by daring to hope, nay, *expect*, a result from my actions? Was that the beginning of my slide into arrogance? Hubris and guilt are defenses against the awesome helplessness one feels before the supreme powers of fate, destiny, and the divine.

I face market rejection every day. That means I face my helpless ness and powerlessness every day. They are my worst fears. Paradoxically, they may also lead to my greatest strength. Facing them can open the doorway to the divine.

Learning about Nonattachment and Providence

I am suffering from terminal tour drainage. Putting my Greek tour together has been like traveling down a narrow twisting Greek mountain road.

I am a prisoner of tourism. I need a new career, but I refuse to give up my present one. I am stuck and disgusted because my efforts seem to lead nowhere. What can I learn from these frustrations? Nonattachment. Acceptance of providence.

Life is loss, gain, and change. If I can learn nonattachment from my tour frustrations, they've been wonderful after all. Perhaps ups and downs, gains and losses, hopes, fears, jubilations, and emotional crashes are blessed teachers visiting me in small packages of emotions.

What about guilt at not being able to satisfy my customers? A wise teacher once said: "Do all you can for your children—or customers. But remember, they have their own providence. They have chosen this life, and there is only so much you can do for them."

Good ideas to meditate upon: nonattachment, customer providence. . .and my own as well.

I m on the Right Road: Accept the Bumps

Susan says that work is what pays you money. I said everything is work whether it pays or not. Thus running, yoga, guitar practicing, bible study, language practice, all my "sidelines," even eating and going to the bathroom, belong to the world of work. *Everything* is work: This is because I see work as play. "Side" activities are part of my research and development department.

She thought I was nuts and had never "really" worked a day in my life. She missed the point of what I was saying; maybe she is unable to understand it. Nevertheless, for me the important thing *was* saying it—and believing it. I didn't have to convince her, only myself, and I was. I had unified the opposites of paying and nonpaying work.

Business is awful. Is that a reason to be down? Should I worry because money has temporarily stopped coming in?

It'll pick up again.

Right?

In that question lies the answer to my problem.

It is a question of belief over experience.

My experience tells me that somehow I'll get along, I'll man age—something comes along to "rescue" me, business picks up again, I remain alive.

So speaks the voice of experience.

But my belief says that, in spite of past experiences, business won't pick up, I won't make it. Success and positive experience make no dent in these ancient worries. Experience may influence my belief, but does not necessarily change it. It is a problem of attitude.

I don't need more experiences. I need faith. If I have it, I continue in a calm matter-of-fact way. With faith my way of life will not change, but my vision of it will be totally different.

Dionysus Ballas taught easy Greek dances at last night's folk dance workshop. We had the largest crowd ever. It was a beautiful event. He and his Greek folk dance performing troupe created a great mood. I felt proud of all the phone calls I had made to help bring out such a crowd.

A few days ago Julie said David Lee was mad at me. I assume it's about something that happened on our Bulgarian tour. Today she's meeting his wife, Lenora, for lunch to find out about it. It bothers me. I consider the Lees to be friends and supporters. If they're angry, why can't they speak to *me* about it?

Another threat: they may cancel their Greek tour. I had hoped they would bring, not only themselves, but members of their family as well—about twelve people. Lenore's family came from Kastoria. I put it on the itinerary to entice them. If they don't go, I'll lose a dozen people, almost the whole tour.

What do I do about it?

Assume the Lees and their family *are not* going to Greece. That will remove both the expectation and threat.

My next project is to call all the Greek, Czech, and Bulgarian GPs. I'm giving up on the Budapest and Prague tour. At this point, only a miracle can save it. I'll decide whether or not to cancel it when I return from Florida.

Why Can't Business Be Holy?

Why can't business be holy? Why not admit I believe in soul, God, and reincarnation? Why not admit that marketing my services is a *mitzvah?* Why not admit I am a spiritual person who longs to spread the gospel and reach higher states? Why not verbalize this to others?

I can still hear my mother's voice: "Religions are stupid. Believers are idiots."

My mother worshiped music and the arts. Suppose I related "spiritual" and "religious" to musical epiphanies? She'd understand that.

Perhaps I have created my mother in my own image. I have no idea what she really felt or thought, what was really going on in the deepest recesses of her haunted soul.

If the vision of my mother is my own invention, why not reinvent her? Create a new mother, one who accepts my feelings, thoughts, and longings.

This is a worthy task, one my mother—whoever she is—would be proud of.

I chose my parents to teach me certain lessons in this life. They may have been smarter than I thought. Perhaps they taught me the secular communistic life because they knew as I got older, I would, in true dialectical Marxist fashion, oppose them by searching for synthesis through spirituality.

These thoughts are creations of my brain. But so are my parents.

This morning I feel that special blend of nausea, anger, and disgust that tour leaders experience once their tour business collapses. I stand in awe. How can such a thing happen? It seems too unbelievable to be true. Yet it is taking place right before my eyes.

Is it me? I doubt it. I am the same as last year.

Is it my tour programs, my prices? I doubt it. Both Budapest and Prague prices and programs are the same as last year; Greece prices and programs are almost the same, too.

I have forgotten how quickly a stock can collapse after a tremendous run-up. I had a tremendous tour run-up last year; my stock zoomed to its highest ever. This year my stock is zooming to its lowest.

I have forgotten those miserable years when I tried to expand. Six years ago I ran many tours. Most got few or no people. I decided to give up the tour business. I did, got depressed, and realized I shouldn't give up too quickly.

Discouragement is a form of mental masturbation, something to do in my spare time.

What should I do about my Budapest and Prague client? I use the singular because I have only one. What a disgusting situation! I put thousands of dollars into making a great brochure, advertising in most folk dance journals, plus ITN and the lawyer's journal, and the result is one client! Have I done anything wrong? I've advertised, mailed, made countless telephone calls to potential customers, enthusiastically talked up Budapest, Prague, and all my tours during folk dance classes and weekends. The result is one customer! Maddening and absurd. Is God trying to teach me humility? I can't figure it out.

The more I think about the Budapest and Prague tour failure, the madder I get. Registration for this tour has never been worse. Israel was once this small, and I had to cancel. But Budapest and Prague? *Never.* What the fuck is the problem? Could the lesson and challenge here be how to set up a tour for one customer?

I have no idea why the registration is so laughable. But I'm not laughing. Just frustrated. I'll curse the skies, shake my fist, scream, kick, and blame the heavens. Vent, vent, vent. Greece is also a disappointment. Again a long list of GPs has dwindled into a long series of no's. What a fucking year! One downhill after another. Last year registrations flowed in. This year my stock has been dumped for a new lover. It seems the harder I work, the worse it gets.

Maybe that's the problem. Last year's tour orgasm is over. I've been trying to have my next tour orgasm too early. My market is too tired. I may have to give my tour business a rest.

Once a wave of success reaches its peak, it is followed by descent and regrouping to gather strength for the next wave.

The stock market is my teacher. Look at Micron Technology. Down almost seventy-five percent, from a hundred to thirty. If this can happen to such a great company, why couldn't it happen to Jim Gold International, Inc?

Have I gone down seventy-five percent this year? Let's take a look. Last year I had twenty-two people for Budapest and Prague; this year I have one. Last year I had twelve people for Greece; this year I have five. It's too early to talk about my summer tours to Czech Republic, Slovakia, and Poland, and Bulgaria.

My Greek numbers are in half. Bad, but not as bad as Micron. My Budapest and Prague numbers cannot be compared to Micron Technology. They can only be compared to a terrorist bombing where the entire plane has been destroyed and one live person crawls out of the wreckage.

Bulgaria might get ten people—that would be down seventy-five percent. Czech Republic–Slovakia–Poland is a "new product." I can see it getting five or six people.

This year's tour business compares to Micron Technology—down seventy-five percent coupled with the "natural" disaster of Budapest and Prague.

Looking at the upcoming year overall, it's bad but not as bad as I thought. Only Budapest and Prague demonstrate the absolutely worst. It can't get worse than losing everything.

Sales Restore the World

The light is hiding.

Not a drop of business is coming in. Each attempt I make feels like it's failing. I am secretly hoping for a small messiah who, using forklifts of bookings, registrations, telephone calls, and checks in the mail, will lift me out of the failure pit. When all your efforts bring zero results, what else can you do?

On one level, my prayers are addressed to customers; on a higher level, they are addressed to the Light Itself. Years ago, in Greenwich Village, separate and alone, I hoped to merge with the outside world through success and fame. I wanted my audience to love me, cushion and caress me, protect me from the vicissitudes of life.

Now I rarely use the word "audience." It has turned into "market," or "customers." But words screen higher reality. Behind "audience," "market," and "customer" I see the word Love. I want my ego to disintegrate, wash away, and lose itself in the ocean of love?

Marketing pins my love on others. Without customers I cannot merge with Higher Forces or enter the universal essence. If they don't join my tours, weekends, or folk dance classes, I remain alone.

Is this a sales concept of redemption?

I cannot be saved alone. I must work to repair the world, restore it to oneness by gathering sparks for *tikkun olam*. That is why I hear a constant inner wailing.

"Audience," "market," and "customer" represent the other half of myself. I must merge with them before I feel at peace.

Happiness occurs briefly, during rare moments when sparks appear. Most time on earth is spent living in a dark room, hoping for a gift of grace, a ray of upstairs light.

One cannot enter heaven alone. The world must enter with you. This is the very essence of *tikkun olam*.

The doctrine of artistic and personal independence has dominated my life.

But independence is a myth. In essence I am connected to everything and everybody else. My desire for artistic separation is an illusion. I cannot save myself alone. We enter heaven through the eye of the needle, together or not at all. That's why I have to convince people to join my tours, weekends, and folk dance classes. Only by joining other sparks, uniting with adjacent souls will I create fulfilling events.

Therefore, I must sell. On a higher level, audience, market, and customers are me. Even an audience of one is enough for redemption.

Save one life, you save the world.

Through sales, I can save my world. It will save others, too. The mud of sales connects to the heaven of *tikkun olam*. "Man is not alone" says Joshua Heschel.

I say, "Man is alone—until he makes a sale."

Selling the Gospel

The gospel is a sales program promoting Higher Reality. It sells a Higher Education program.

I am selling a gospel, too—but in a different form. Tours, weekends, folk dance classes, all are archetypal representations of the divine light. They educate indirectly, using subtle forms of vibration and light.

When I sell my gospel to a customer, I feel light. Thus I achieve en-light-enment.

Birth of a "New" Tourist Vision

What am I learning? Have a will of steel. Steer my ship through the storms towards original goals and itineraries.

I can never know who will register. Therefore, satisfy myself. I have no control over markets and registrants, but *I do* have control of what and where I want to go. If I give up my desire to make lots of money, I can run my tour with three people, ten, forty, or even if no one registers. I can thus guarantee none of my tours will ever be cancelled.

Run tours for myself! No more catering to so-called "demands" of the market. Nobody knows what these demands are anyway. All I can know is my own dreams and desires.

Deep in my heart, I know what I want. But contrary desires, confusion of goals, and listening to others instead of myself, have thrown me off the path of my original touristic vision.

I want to please others. . . but I rarely can. Even when they tell me what they want, I can't be sure. How many times have people told me they were signing up for a tour only to change their mind later on. Sure, they may be sincere the moment they tell me. But "other events" prevent them from keeping their promises. My best bet is to go with my own vision.

It's not even a matter of money. It's having my brains squeezed by the endless vicissitudes, the countless ebbs and flows of market forces. I can't run tours like a cork on the ocean. I need moorings, a stationary boundary, a bedrock granite peninsula I call home. I won't find it in customers and markets. It is located in the islands of isolating decisions in my mind. They are the best and only safe havens.

Am I Ready?

Valerie may have turned the key.

The first step took place when she and her friend, Edy, bought $75 worth of my books. It was the biggest boutique sale of the Russian Weekend. Wonderful for my ego! I haven't sold any of my books for a long time. Suddenly, *bingo,* a big sale!

The second step took place when Valerie asked for copies of *Handfuls of Air;* she also wanted to buy a tape of my "World of Guitar" record. Aside from the wonderful flattery of someone wanting to buy, her request opened up new directions.

Should I tape my old records and sell them? Should I make new tapes of classical guitar, folk songs, and sell them? Should I focus on selling my books? Should I put my journal into book form?

I reread *Handfuls of Air.* How I love to read my own writing, but how painful it is! Most painful is recognizing my writing is good, original, and worthy of publication. It can stand with pride before the world. I have been avoiding such confidence all my life. I shy away from my own goodness. I am more comfortable with a negative self-image that pushes me to improve. Nevertheless, Valerie's requests may have planted the proper seeds in my present mind.

But before seeds can grow, my garden has to be ploughed and hoed. Part of this year's ploughing has been tourism. Over the past years ten years I have devoted ninety percent of my energies to developing that business. This year I have given up the idea of making it large; I have been whittling down my dreams to personally leading three or four tours a year.

Will the creation of new tapes and books fill that semivacuum? Suppose I made tapes and books my top priority? Better yet, suppose I looked at both activities as potential *money-making activities!*

I'll have to put my energies and efforts into promoting them. Will I? If my tourist business will no longer occupy ninety percent of my mind, what else is there for me to do?

It's possible to make money selling my books and tapes. I can start with my mailing list, then branch out. Most important, however, will be making a commitment to promoting them.

The aches, pains, and incredible fatigue I've experienced during the past few days are a signal that my mind and body are preparing for a change. New thoughts need new tendons, sinews, and muscles to support them; new directions need a new body. Fatigue symbolizes the death of my former pathways. This death also plant seeds for my future resurrection.

Am I ready?

Athens Prelude

It's noisy in my Greek Herodium Hotel. Outside kids are playing in a schoolyard. I'm exhausted from jet lag.

Last night we ate at Sophocles Prison Restaurant, then walked to the Plaka to check out tavernas for dancing. Today I slept all afternoon, then walked to the Plaka, stopped at an outdoor restaurant for coffee, cake, and orange juice, studied my *Teach Yourself Greek* book, then started writing in my notebook. After an hour I was almost back to normal again.

I wrote "Kirios kai kiries," (Ladies and gentlemen) in Greek in my notebook. Then I wrote:

But I love my tours—the dancing, language, and adventure.

A sudden spark of hope and energy. How important writing is to my psyche! I'd better write my journal soon—or else!

I practiced more Greek letters, paid my restaurant bill, and headed back to the computer in my hotel room. A step upwards.

1996–97 Olympic Folk Dance Goals

Last night we saw the Olympia Folk Dance group. Their lead dancer, Costas, couldn't be there because he had a job in Athens. This shows the importance of charismatic leadership. The group performed without enthusiasm; it felt leaderless. Nevertheless, I have to thank Costas's brother, who did some twists, turns, and leaps in the Tsamiko. His performance gave me my 1997 *Olympic Folk Dance Goals*:

1. Learn to do a *one-legged squat*
2. Learn to *turn on one squatted leg*

3. Learn to do a *back bend from a squatting position*
One-year project. My goal is to master them by the time I come back to Olympia next year.

A beautiful Delphi morning. I had 7:00 a.m. coffee in the Kastalia Restaurant, overlooking a magnificent mountain and gorge. So far this morning my mind is mostly blank. Perhaps I'll leave it that way and do some editing.

We're in Kalambaka, getting ready to visit the great Meteora. No espresso this morning. The bastard downstairs said the kitchen was closed. A good service would have made it for me anyway.

Last night I taught folk dancing to our group in the hotel dining room. Kalambaka is a good place for me to teach: there's nothing else to do at night. After the dancing I went upstairs and copied my bus-edited journal into my computer.

It is the last day of our tour. I can't wait for it to end.

The Gift and Talent Hosannah Highway

Why did I wake up with a terrible headache in Kalambaka yester day?

I learned a lesson I must never forget.

It all started after our arrival in Kalambaka's Edelweiss Hotel. After we settled into our rooms, walked the town, and had an eight o'clock supper, I noticed we had the whole dining room to ourselves. A perfect time and place to lead folk dancing, I thought. After dinner, I took our my tapes, tape recorder, and speaker, and lead an hour of dancing. It created beautiful climax to an excellent bus tour of Greece.

When the evening ended everyone was feeling great, including me. That was the problem: everyone was feeling great including me. *Feeling great* was the origin of my headache! This completely inappropri ate reaction to good fortune would amaze me except that it has happened so often before. After the dancing I went up to my room, mentally surveyed the past days of touring, and realized our tour had been fantastic. Excellent program, good hotels, fine folk dance performances and dancing in the Athens Tavernas of the Plaka, the Touris Club in Olympia, and the dining room at Kalambaka. _

Thus, success equals a headache.

Something is wrong here.

After a day of quasi-nausea and misery I finally figured it out as I *enjoyed* editing my journal. I also enjoyed our tour, dancing, people on tour, and the entire travel experience. Now it was ending, completed, successful, and finished. I *felt joyful.*

Joy had given me the headache! My reluctance to appreciate gifts and talents, my creativity, and creations had made me sick.

Is reluctance to appreciate God-given talents a sin, a reverse kind of hubris? What about hallelujahs, hosannas, and praising God?

It's time to sing hallelujahs. If I don't, I get a headache.

No doubt, I am at the talent-and-gift-appreciation stage of life. If I don't appreciate myself, I'll get a headache.

What better way to pray than through hosannas and hallelujahs about the talents He gave me. Singing my praises is singing His praises. It should be a daily practice. In doing so, I will probably get rid of my headaches, and ninety per cent of my guilt, too.

Why have I been reluctant to appreciate my talents? I fear the loss of control. I would rather not appreciate them than face the shining glory of the Higher Power. The tiny ego often speaks without recognition of itself as an instrument. It says: "I did that? I created that tour? No, I couldn't have done that. It must have been someone else. It was you, Mr. Customer, you, Mrs. Audience, you, Mr. and Mrs. Tour Participant. I couldn't have done it without you. You are more important than humble me. I just work here. Thank you for appreciating my efforts and talents, but it really isn't necessary. I am nothing. The shine and halo you see around me are merely projections of your own wishes.

No question it is hard to take credit for yourself. But I'm going to try. I'll begin by fighting hubris, false pride, false lack of pride, and false modesty. I am building the Gift and Talent Appreciation Highway.

"Basically". . . The Joy Factor

Today is the last day of my tour. Our group, now led by Bob Salem, is taking the island cruise. I'm flying home. This trip was a great success. I love Greece. I love the tour business, all the places it brings me, and all the goodies it drops in my lap. What sheer fun to listen to Greek folk music and dance in the Plaka's Stamatapoul os and Sisyphus tavernas, to meet many friendly Greeks, and to do it with the good people in our tour group.

I am full of joy this morning; I don't know quite what to do with it. I *do* know I'd better recognize my gifts express them—or else! Big responsibility and obligation. It will improve the health of my body and mind. If I don't, I'm up joyless headache shit's creek.

Tour Business as a Psychological Need

Overwhelming fatigue since I got back from Greece. There is a churning, a shifting back and forth in my mind. Everything weighs heavy.

I'm also down about "giving up" the tour business. It has been such a rich source of challenge.

I could continue my guitar and writing routes *and not* give it up. Do all three. I can run tours with four (to six) people. Small tours aren't ideal, but at least I'll be able to run a tour business. I'll price it so the first three people pay for my trip. After that comes profit. I might make $600 to $700 on four people for ten days to two weeks of work. That averages down, after about $300 in taxis and other expenses, to $300 to $400 profit for two weeks of work, about $200 per week. This is the worst case scenario.

This is what I make on a bad week of folk dance teaching. But classes will continue while I'm away, so I'll be making about $300 per week.

Now I know why I'm so fatigued: It's depression from the idea of giving up. Thus, my tour business is as much a *psychological need* as a financial hope.

I struck pay dirt. My tours are here to stay.

Giving them up would be like cutting off my leg.

The tour business is one of my organizing centers; it motivates and inspires me. Perhaps I shouldn't use the words "tour business." Too objective and impersonal. My tour business is very personal and subjective. The paths I have discovered are part of me.

Their directions are both horizontal and vertical. The former have slowed. Now I move mostly vertically. Explorations and changes will deepen my knowledge of these paths. I've gone through a year of tour hell. But I have moved a step deeper by seeing their personal, psychological, mental, physical, and spiritual importance. They form an important vivifying challenge. No matter how frustrating, disappointing, and difficult, never give them up.

Guitar, writing, folk dance teaching, weekends, running, yoga, languages, history, and philosophy study are also constellations shining on my life; they are the fountains from which the feeding waters flow.

Today I am back to square one. But it is a wider square lodged deeper in the earth.

Stick with My Original Visions!

When Cally suggested I join Bob Salem's group, I jumped at the chance. *That was my mistake!* By doing so I thought I could offer my tourists a cruise, a private bus, and improve our small registration situation. On one level I was right. The tourists all had a good time. But on a personal and business level, I was wrong. By changing my tour itinerary, I got two cancellations. This, along with Bob's low tour price, forced me to break even instead of make a profit. I also gave up an opportunity to explore new areas of Greece—namely, Thessaloniki and Kastoria— which was the original purpose when I designed the tour. *Thus in one poor decision I gave up both profit and adventure.*

What can I learn from my mistake?

Get back to artistic truth. Go with my gut feeling, the original idea. It is most often the right one.

Sadly, the pressures and vicissitudes of the marketplace affect me. Few-to-no people register. Brilliant intuitions, beautiful ideas, and beatific visions have little or nothing to do with the market place. I may be in charge of my vision, but God is in charge of markets. Whether He wants to hand me some customers or not is up to Him.

I can learn from my Greek tour mistake: *I must stick with my original vision!* If I don't, if I let market pressures throw me off course, *it will make me sick!* Better to suffer sales humiliations and depressions following my original vision than whipsaw myself trying to second-guess the market. It is practically impossible to know "what people want." The only way I can "know" is when they send deposits for a tour.

I screwed myself by putting so-called customer's needs above my own. After all, it is *my* tour. Customers, no matter how important, must come second! The customer is not always right. I am! If only I can remember this important truth.

This philosophy is completely opposite from what most business men will tell you. It may be why my business stays small. Nevertheless, this "artistic approach" is the only one I can operate under. Artistic vision is my organizing and motivating principle. If I throw it away trying to "please customers"—something I never truly know how to do anyway—I will end up with a depression and headache.

That's why, since I returned from the Greek tour, I have been sick with anger. *I had given up on myself!* I'd given away my most precious possession: my vision and my dream, traded it in for a nonpaying, uninspiring classical tour of Greece, the exact itinerary I did last year. Only the hotels and their locations were new.

Can I stand up against the pressures and vicissitudes of the market place? Can I sustain my vision?

If I give it up I'll have *no reason to go on my tour.*

Thus, I *have to follow my vision.* If I don't, I'll die a slow torturous death, stretched on a wheel of headaches and depressions. Self-disgust at my cowardice will poison me; worms of self-hatred and loathing will eat me up. The result will be I'll never run a tour again.

Artists look inward. They hope their vision will please the public. Inner satisfaction comes before outer recognition.

Businessmen look outward. They find a public need, then develop a plan to fulfill it. Outward recognition must come before inner satisfaction.

Perhaps the courage to follow my tour vision is the courage to run small tours. At least that way my tours will stay alive.

Returning to Tours "With a Vengeance!"

I cannot say whether my tours need me or others need my tours. But there is no question *I need them.*

They are an organizing psychological principle, focusing my life outwards, arranging my year; they put language, history, and religion studies together. I am surprised by this, since I am an artist who likes to live with the Muses high on Mount Parnassus, somewhat oblivious to the world below.

But I also have a practical side that revels in Dionysian joy of a banquet on earth. I want money, earthly power, and to make things happen; I love to sink my teeth into the juicy richness of a project and see it grow before my eyes.

The tour business expresses my Dionysian aspect.

Therefore, when I start thinking about giving up the tour business—I am talking about giving up my other half. That's a lot to give up.

It is painful to run a tour business. But it would be infinitely more painful if I gave it up.

Giving up is the worst thing I can do. It is infinitely better to go down fighting. Leonidas with his Spartans defending the pass at Thermopylae against Xerxes and his Persians did the right thing. Consider struggle as a fight to the death. The other alternative is the torturous death of inertia and let worms of defeat devour your body.

Return to the tour business *with a vengeance!* It is the only cure. Even if nobody registers I must still return. I have underestimated how vital it is to me. It is my dream in concrete. It may never be realized, but nevertheless, it is one of the motivating dreams of my life. I have not only taken it for granted, but also demeaned it by considering it solely as a financial venture.

Coffee in the Morning

Yesterday we arrived in Prague and settled into our Fortuna Quality Inn. I like it a lot. I did forty minutes of yoga, fell asleep on the floor, took a shower, then fell asleep again in bed.

At three o'clock in the afternoon, Rosa arrived with our bus. We drove off to a local folk dance festival.

I went to bed at ten o'clock, woke up at four a.m., and tried out my new coffee maker. What a winner! Smartest thing I've done in awhile. Thank you, Bernice. Now I can have fresh coffee in my room whenever I want! A major victory. I can begin my mornings the Teaneck way, drinking coffee, studying a bit, writing, then exercising. After performing these morning rituals, I feel I have done something useful with my life. Now I can bring my rituals on tour with me!

Raising Tour Prices: Rebirth of my Tour Business

Last night I spoke to Ruth and Sam Diamond about my tours. By the end of the conversation I had decided to "take the plunge," by raising my tour prices. If I take fifteen people, that is enough justification for doing so. I often get less than fifteen. But if I raise prices 20 percent that would give me a reasonable profit margin. If get six people, the tour will be worth running. Even four would be passable. That is the worst-case scenario. It is certainly better than last year's Budapest tour, when I got four customers and made $400.

Four to six would be my cut-off point. Less would not be worthwhile. I might get more. That would be nice.

The risk is that, by raising prices, I might get almost nobody. But this is happening with low prices. I'm traveling with few people and making so little money it's not worth running my tours. I'm reaching the point where I either raise prices or close the business. So raising prices is worth the risk. If I do, I *may* get customers, and *may* have a tour business. If I don't, it won't matter anyway. I'm at that "I've got no choice" point.

If I aim for four to six people—hopefully more, and limit tours to fifteen, then I can not only run tours with my own leadership, but also with other leaders, namely, Ginny, etc. If she leads and I get four people, I still make money. And *I don't go!* Now that is a good deal! I can *expand my tour business,* keep it special, and run folk tours to several countries at once! I'll revitalize my old original dream of running tours to thirteen European and middle eastern countries. It doesn't even have to be thirteen; it could three. But the main idea is one of expansion by running tours *with and without* my personal leadership.

Raising my prices may be one of the wisest decisions I've made in years.

It's only day three. The first storm has come. A Minnie Horell headache hit when I woke up this morning.

Should I take her off my mailing list? Should I make sure she never comes on another one of my tours again? Hobbling along on fifteen feet, only poetry might save her. Her incessant, meaningless, empty banter and slow hobble slows down our group and give me a headache. She reminds me of the worst aspects of my mother and the prison she created. Ma, up there in heaven, although you are my guardian angel and protect me here on earth, your powerful wings often hid the sun and shroud me in darkness. True, I want protection—but not too much. Our new guide, Gabriela Gogova, represents the lively aspect of my mother. She's anxious, but kind and funny, too. I like her even though she is hyper and somewhat overprotective. The combination of opposites, Minnie and Gabriela, has created my morning headache.

Writing about it makes me feel better. Thank you, Mr. Computer, for coming on tour. Your wisdom, kindness, imagination, and creativity are my islands of refuge in this sea of noisy people.

Writing about Minnie, her ilk and symbolic meaning, frees me. I dwell once again in the land of the Righters, the Writers. I think of Britta, one of our tour jewels: a calm sea in the whirlpool of turbulence, an island of palm trees, sand, and sun standing quietly in the middle of a tropical storm. I like her. Will the illusion explode as our tour continues, or will it grow to palm tree height?

Here is the tour ritual cure for me: rise at four or five a.m., wash, drink my coffee, write, then do yoga. This is a curative, wonderful, healthful, happy tour routine. Early to bed and early to rise.

God has sent me Minnie for a reason. She is a character in the divine path of study He devised for me, a lesson plan in half-crippled form. What will I learn? Tolerance? Survival? How to prune misery from my mailing list?

Finding Time by Giving up Tour Breakfast

I've discovered the way to find time in the morning: give up breakfast! That will give me an extra hour to write, exercise, etc. Instead of sitting in the dining room eating, I can pack the breakfast food in my shoulder bag and nibble at it during our morning tours.

Beethoven Pays Me a Visit

We're staying in Dolna Krupa castle in Slovakia. It is a nineteenth-century mansion where Beethoven stayed.

Last night Beethoven visited me in a dream. He said, if I want to perform with confidence on the guitar, there has to be a change in my personality It has to be a qualitative change so strong I would forget my old guitar performing personality.

Qualitative change of personality: This is a long process. I have been going through it for years. Does it mean, when I get back to America, I am ready to relinquish my old performing personality and enter a new relationship with myself, one of fearless, focused, concentrated guitar playing? Beethoven stands in one place, I in another. There will never be another Beethoven or Jim Gold. In this lifetime, each individual is given a unique personality along with unique opportunities, paths, and missions to fulfill. No one can take anyone else's place. Only he or she can fulfill it.

My performing transformation will only be complete when I have forgotten my old self. Then I can step into my new clothes and stride down the street.

Return of the Witness Exercise

The ghost of Beethoven haunts Dolna Krupa Castle. It visited me the first night and brought good thoughts for my future development. Last night it came again, but in negative form. After swatting a mosquito, I hid under the covers. Then, as chills of fear swept through me, I chased it away by "watching." I used the witness exercise. It worked!

Ghostly visits are probably the most frightening aspects of kabbala. The fear they create puts you at the borders of insanity. Fear of ghosts, haunted houses, ethereal visits from the netherworld, fears Ma will visit me in spectral form or Pa will come out of the walls—this bone chilling terror must be what insane people experience when they retreat into themselves to live among *their* ghosts.

Last night I had visits from the darkest recesses of my mind. They also visited on a Thursday night in April, when I stood alone on the empty Solway House grounds. Standing outside the hotel in deserted darkness, I watched forms of trees and houses silhouetted in the moonlight around me and felt the fear of the underworld returning. At that time I had my first victory by chasing these evil spirits away with thoughts of customer service on the upcoming weekend. It worked! I was saved. I found a technique for dealing with fear: concentration on concrete thoughts and tasks like work, people, yoga, running, or playing guitar. Anything to control my mind and keep it from drifting along the haunting negative path with its images of hell and the devil.

Last night I found another method of saving myself: the witness exercise. As I lay in bed, visits from Beethoven wraiths passed over me. I knew they were figments of my own imagination. I "watched" them passing, "witnessed" my body contort and tremble. I "witnessed" these supernatural creatures invade the lower parts of my mind, haunt my body, and cover my flesh with goose pimples. And as the witness aspect of my mind—my higher mind—watched them, they slowly lost their force and disappeared! A major victory!

I should apply the witness exercise to my tour. True, there are no bone-chilling fears here, just normal ones. Nevertheless, it is good practice. To live more of my life under the aegis of the witness exercise would be a great advance for me.

Used my fan against the mosquitoes and closed the windows as well. Also used the witness exercise. Very good. I slept beautifully.

We're leaving Dolna Krupa this morning and heading for the Vychodna Folk Festival.

Pride

We arrived for the Vychodna folk festival yesterday.

This morning I came to breakfast early at our Club Hotel in Kezmarkok, sat alone at a table, and wrote in my hand notebook about my terrible neck, shoulder, and arm pains.

It's frightening. A heart attack? I doubt it. My collapsed cervical vertebrae acting up? Probably.

Part of my pain has a physical cause: so much sitting on the bus, at restaurants, and concerts. But much of it is mental, too. On a deeper level, physical and mental are one.

Let's talk mental. I'm carrying the weight this tour on my shoulders. That's why they hurt so much. Part of this tour is also a pain in the neck. That's why my neck hurts so much. Oxen have yokes. I have the tour. I also have neck pain from strangulation. Aspects of this tour are strangling me.

Is rage finding a new location in my neck? Shouldn't I have some? Strangely, I don't feel anger. I don't feel sadness or happiness either. Yet I have not been anesthetized. Beneath neck, shoulder, and arm pain, a new feeling is revealing itself. *Pride!* The pride of the hero. Forty-nine percent of me is in tour prison. But fifty-one percent is strutting in the pride of tour heaven.

In spite of the arrows of criticism shot at my tour leadership, in spite of the whining, bitching, and petty, miserable complains from a few customers, I am proud, not only of the job I'm doing, but better yet, of the inner peace I feel. I'm proud of the way I am running this tour, proud of how I'm handling the barbs and criticisms. Proud I'm not folding within. Proud I feel no guilt or rage. I am proud of my "witness exercise" and how I've been using it to handle, not only Beethoven's eerie nocturnal visit at Dolna Krupa Castle, but my tour participants during the day as well.

Nothing is fazing my inner peace.

This is too good to be true. But why not? I've been running tours a long time. I'm experienced and older.

What about my neck pain, tour burden, and the restrictions of tour prison? Anger, rage, pain, and hurt may well be located in those regions of my upper body. But it is only forty-nine percent. That leaves me with a fifty-one-percent pride factor.

The neck factor represents an old, fading self. It is based on memories, the pains, angers, and fears of former tours.

The *pride factor is the new element in my tours.* It contains both "witness exercise" and inner peace. It is *an island of light existing apart, that cannot be touched by outside forces or events.* Sunlight on this island is shining down through my shoulders!

Neck and shoulders are *gates*. A kabbalistic light radiates through my neck and shoulders.

The weakness I feel in those regions is my *resistance to its powerful new rays!* Weakness in my shoulders, arms, and neck represents *the dying of my old self!*

Thank you, Gabriela. It happened under your watch. The turning point took place after our walk and talk at Dolna Krupa Castle. We spoke about Minnie Horell's complaints.

Paradoxically I have to thank Minnie Gorell for these revelations. Her complaints about the Trnava tour, coupled with her miserable personality, have provided the fodder for my revelation. She is the sand grain that helped create my pearl of new wisdom.

We visited Spiss Castle today. I found a sign for a Sri Chimnoy Peace Run. It was a sign for me. It means I must *rededicate myself to running.*

Advertisement: Are you tired of depth? PAUSE AND PEEP TOURS: The superficial approach to tourism.

Pop and my Polish Roots

I'm writing in my room at the Hotel Continental in Cracow. This is my first day in Poland. We drove over the Tatras Mountains from Slovakia last night.

Our first Polish stop was in the mountain resort village of Zakopone. We had just come from a two-hour rafting trip down the Dunajec River in Slovakia. I had a splitting headache. Our bus parked five blocks from the center of town. We got out and walked to the main shopping area. I left the group to wander about alone. I stopped for an espresso in a restaurant, said, "Djankoje," or something like that for "thank you," and drank my espresso as Polish workmen fixed a broken pipe under the bar counter. Their speech was more animated than the Slovak I had heard in Slovakia, and certainly more lively than Czech.

This milieu felt very comfortable and familiar. In spite of my fear of Polish anti-Semitism and prejudices against Polish people, I liked these working Poles, their language, intonation, and body movements. I recognized that all I knew about Poland were my prejudices. I felt at home.

After my espresso—which made a small dent in my headache—I wandered down the crowded streets. Groups of musicians on the sidewalk played Polish folk songs and classical music. I even heard a band from Peru.

I kept asking myself: Why does this country feel so familiar and comfortable? Suddenly, I thought of my father. I broke down in tears. Although he was born in America, my unknown grandfather came from Poland. I was walking on ancestral ground.

Imagine finding my father's roots—and mine—on the streets of Zakopane! After ten minutes in Poland I was crying.

We got back to the bus and headed for Cracow. I slept during the two-hour trip, trying to rid myself of my terrible headache. When we arrived at the Hotel Continental I went to my room, groaned for twenty minutes, and decided to take a long walk by myself. I took the elevator down to the lobby and stopped into the dining room to tell my group I wouldn't be eating supper. I sat down with Arlene, Hilda, and Minnie. I sipped a little soup, drank some strange Polish juice, nibbled a salad, then advanced to the main veal dish. My spirits lifted. I ended up staying for the whole supper. Miraculously, soon my headache disappeared.

Recognize Death

Recognize death. Then all boundaries fall away. Borders, separations, fragments, creations of outside "objects" to help us control our destiny, all are illusionary means we use to escape from our fear of death.

We're leaving Cracow this morning and heading back to Moravia. On the way, we will stop at Auschwitz concentration camp. I have dreaded the visit since I organized this tour. Somehow, our guided tour of the Jewish quarter in Cracow with Lidia softened my fears. I don't quite understand why.

We arrived in Koprivnice, Moravia, last night. The entrance to this city looks like a disaster zone. Our hotel, the Hotel Beam, is a real shithole. What a comedown from the beautiful Continental Hotel in Crakow. We are in an area rarely traveled by American tourists. Our supper was delicious, the staff friendly and warm, and our folk dancing in the salon an excellent way to raise our group spirits. This morning at breakfast I discovered we're sharing the hotel with European ping-pong champions who are having a match today in the nearby town of Frydek-Mistek.

Last night we also drove through the Moravian town of Pribor, where Sigmund Freud was born. At breakfast this morning I edited my New Leaf Journal. To my happy surprise, I am getting many "new," inspiring ideas from it. Editing it is becoming a lovely place of refuge from my tour and tourists.

Mornings, when my mind feels empty is the best time to edit my journal.

Yesterday, in the Moravian town of Kromeriz, Arlene complained about all the tension among our tour participants. "I can't stand hearing another hysterical woman!" she said. She leaned on my shoulder and almost cried.

Later I asked her about a farewell dinner tomorrow night. "The group feeling here is just too bad," she answered. "Let it pass."

Her comments made me feel low. But as I walked the medieval streets of Kromeriz, I realized those views and feelings were *hers*. Not mine. If people in the group are fighting and arguing among themselves, there's little I can do about it. It is *not* my problem. Sure, I'd like them to be happy and harmonious. It makes a better tour. But if their personalities occasionally clash, so be it. I'm traveling on my solo path, marching on the streets of Kromeriz, to my own drummer. Happily, I can step out of my tourists' petty squabbles and not feel responsible for them. I can admit I'm enjoying myself on this tour. Although our hotel is miserable and this area of Moravia somewhat ugly, it is nevertheless a travel experience I've never had before. Who knows where it will lead? I liked Kromeriz and the medieval capital of Moravia, Olomouc, too. My feeling of inner peace, contentment, even pride, are still with me.

Yesterday afternoon, I sat outdoors in a coffee shop in Olomouc, watched the traffic pass before me on the trolley-railed, cobblestoned streets, and edited my New Leaf Journal. I am happy to find so much wisdom, inspiration, and direction in it. The ideas I wrote are helping me, reminding me of my best attitudes. I can use them on my tour. I feel I am reading and editing someone *else's* guide book to life.

Wen we got back to our Tatra-Beam Hotel in Koprivnice yesterday afternoon. Somehow, it looked better. Attitudes certainly color one's vision. If it can happen in Koprivnice, it can happen anywhere.

On Tipping

This tipping stuff is bothering me. What is right? Whom do you tip? How much?

If service is bad, you shouldn't; if service is good, you should. I know you should tip the bus driver, guide, porters, and leave a little extra after you pay for a drink. But how about the museum guides and restaurant musicians? I know you tip gypsy musicians, but what about other musicians?

What is the custom in this country? What is expected? Is tipping an insult? Or is it an insult *not* to tip? New Zealanders and Australians consider it an insult. Demeaning. But our Slovak guide Gabriela thinks it's not a question of humiliation but of money. Partly, she is right. I want our group to do the right thing tipping-wise. I'm just not sure what it is. Whenever I ask other guides or service people, their answer is: "It's up to you."

If I can't find a more concrete answer, I'll have to make up some rules for myself. Then I can pass them on to my group.

Positive Benefits of My Czech Republic/Slovakia and Poland Tour

The tour is over. We're leaving Prague today. I'm calm, even. Definitely a new state of mind for touring.

I looked at the stock pages in the *International Tribune* yesterday. Technology stocks have been blasted. Micron Technology is down almost five points. My other stocks are either down or haven't budged. It may be two years or more before the technologies recover. Not much to look forward to in the market. I'd best forget about stocks for awhile.

It's hard to find any redeeming features in Minnie. Her removal from my mailing list will be one redeeming feature.

I take satisfaction when I realize that, except for the Tatra P. Beam Hotel in Koprivnice, this has been a physically difficult but very professionally run tour.

I take most satisfaction from my state of mind. The personal squabbles and personality clashes on this tour, first among Minnie, Ruth, Arlene, and everyone else, have not affected me. Personality clashes are the creations of the personalities involved. I create and offer tours, not personalities. Thank God, I've moved beyond feeling guilty and responsible for them.

I'm going home with new ideas. Raising my prices twenty percent plus promising small tours—fifteen to twenty people maximum—is an excellent idea. It may destroy my business or resurrect it. In making this decision, I don't have to offer fancier hotels, better service, a stronger program, or even anything new. These things exist already. But promising small numbers is a service I can succeed in providing. Small groups offer a higher quality of service for my tourists. Large groups are only good for two reasons, both having little to do with the good of tourists and everything to do with the good of the tour company. Large numbers bring in large dollars and pump up the egos of tour directors and their companies. There is something macho about saying I've got forty, fifty, sixty people on my tour. It is one kind of success measurement: The more people on your tour, the more worthy you are.

Obviously this has nothing to do with good service or tour quality.

Am I threatening my business by raising tour prices twenty percent? Hard to say. However, raising prices and lowering tour participant numbers gives me a new direction, along with a concept I believe in. I can get enthusiastic about ten, fifteen, or twenty people. Once I got beyond thirty, I start hiding the numbers from potential customers. Deep in my heart, I realize larger numbers are not a selling point. Tour quality starts to suffer, and I know it.

By raising prices and lowering tour participant numbers I am improving the quality of my tour service. That in itself is a worthy goal.

My calm and even state of mind is my most positive personal accomplishment on this Bohemia/Moravia/Slovakia/Poland tour. My change of direction, symbolized by a 20-percent price rise along with a promise of a lower number of tour participants, is its major benefit. Also, always bring a coffee maker and coffee!

I returned to Teaneck two days ago to find a descending stock market, no checks in the mails, and lots of bills. I got angry about the "reality" I didn't face on tour. But a newly discovered part of me remained calm—the same calm I discovered at Dolna Krupa Castle in Slovakia, where Beethoven wrote the "Moonlight Sonata."

I've also made strides on the guitar. After two weeks' absence, the Villa-Lobos "Prelude No. 5," "Leyenda," "Alard," and "Alhambra" are "easy." They flow fast and smoothly.

Rafting on the Dunajec

"I am the second best rafter in Slovakia."
"Who is first?"
"All the others."

Return to Categories

I'm working on next year's tour and itineraries.

I've been getting up at 3:00 and 4:00 a.m. I love it! Can I keep such a schedule after I recover from jet lag and start working again?

I've also starting a new exercise routine. I do an hour of yoga—"warm-ups" as it were, then go for a half hour to forty-five-minute run. It all lasts a little over two hours. I love this, too. Can I continue once I start working again?

What about writing? This year's "direction" is towards tightening and focus. I want to edit my writing.

My first habit, developed two years ago, was daily writing in my journal. These first drafts created the early pages of my journal.

Last summer I began my second habit: editing my first drafts. Now I am ready for my third habit: categorizing every journal entry. In this process, order and date do not matter. Today's writing can be mixed with yesterday's, last year's, or whatever. This will be a year of categories, boxes, and focus. My philosophical quest will be to find the relationship between limitations, focus, security, and beauty.

Finding the Monastery Within

I've got four beautiful tours going to Hungary thanks to Adam Molnar, and one beauty going to the Czech Republic and Slovakia thanks to Jasan Bonus. I will have a beauty going to Bulgaria thanks to Balkan Tourist and Dannie Kotseva. My only question marks are Greece—a historic beauty but not a folklore one—and Romania with Roxanna Kraus of Quo Vadis tours.

My experiment will be in my Hungarian and Bulgarian tours. I will run them without my personal leadership. First I must write out all the Hungarian itineraries Adam has sent me. Then, I'll create my two-week Bulgarian June Rose Festival tour, guided by Dannie.

I feel limitation, focus, security, and beauty in my tours this year. The pain from last year's low tour registration is bearing fruit. By raising my prices and offering smaller tours I have both increased my options and reduced my failure rate. I might even make money.

Last year's debacle has nevertheless destroyed my hopes of making *mucho* money on tours. But if I could survive last year's miserable registration, I can get through anything. In spite of registration falling from peak to pits, my tours survived! That is a good sign. Thank you, Pain and Misery, for your teachings.

I have lost interest in reading about philosophy, religion, and mysticism. These readings have been incorporated into my being. I no longer need books to remind me about *Fsitchko e edno*—all is one. It reminds me of the incident at the Batchkovo monastery in Bulgaria this summer. As Dannie lead us past murals by Zaharie Zograph, I left the group and wandered about the monastery alone. I visited a few guest rooms upstairs, where I met one of the monks. We talked about the simple cells with their iron cots; then I named the monastery the Batchkovo Hilton. We both laughed.

Suddenly, I realized I no longer had my anchorite urge. For years a voice within had called me to join a monastery. Deep within my soul lived a monk. It was the call for inner peace, a higher calling from God, a reminder that I am more than my body, mind, business, and social and public definition.

What did its disappearance mean? I had internalized my monk's call, built within my body, mind, and soul my own personal monastery. The walls, cells, rooms, refectory, courtyard, mosaics, icons, candles, and saints were ethereal but firm. From that quiet inner spot I could view the world. I had become my own monk. Divisions in my soul had been healed. Withdrawal from life and working in the world had been fused. I could lead tours yet simultaneously dwell within my private inner monastic sanctuary. I was at peace.

Amazing and beautiful. Another path of inner growth.

Bulgaria or History

I am reading the travel book *Bulgaria,* by Phillip Ward. I'm focusing in on the *imagination approach* by first reading a line, then imagining its contents, imagining the face and shape of Boris, ninth-century Tsar of Bulgaria, imagining what Shumen might have looked like under Turkish occupation, when builders removed stones from the ancient Bulgarian capital of Preslav and used them to build a new mosque in Shumen.

"Out, Out, and Never Come Back Again!"

My Wednesday and Friday night folk dance classes opened with very small attendance and registration. So far no one has registered for my October Yoga and Folk Dance Weekend. Business is dead. Bills and debts are mounting. Is it an omen for the future, or am I simply using worries as fodder to make me write? Without worries, would I write at all?

These are old questions. I have never been able to answer them in the past. I will not succeed now. I can say nothing about the "reality" of dead business and its future earnings. These are in the hands of God. But I do know that A feeling of financial panic is gnawing at my stomach.

What should I do? My answer used to be work towards financial rewards. But I am thinking differently. I've had financial panic many times before, and it has rarely if ever propelled me to work harder. Rather than motivate me, panic paralyzes me.

I *do* have a business plan. I finished writing my fliers for the 1997 season. I'll soon make a 1997 brochure, put ads in magazines, call customers, and mail them individualized letters and fliers. Calling and mailing to individuals will be the heart of my business sales plan for the 1996–1997 season.

The only thing I don't know is results. I never can. I can only decide to follow my path, walk my walk, work my work, do my deeds.

What about panic? It is a passing cloud. I know how to deal with it: do something you have power and control over. No questions or debates. Just start! As Brother Achalananda said about his own misery and depression, "I mentally screamed, 'Get out! Get out and never come back!' The depression was instantly gone and never returned.

"A pattern can change in an instant if the will and desire to change it are strong enough. Such is the power of mind when connected to the power of God."

Change my patterns, then. Out, out! Never come back again! Tough love chases away the rodents of worry gnawing on my mind. No *questions*. Just *start!*

Collapse of Business Expectations Brings Peace Of Mind

When Terry walked into the Darien folk dance group last night, I gave her a big hello. In the back of my mind was the expectation she and her husband would go on my Greek tour. Last March she had pleaded, "We can't go now. Please, run a tour to Greece next year. We'll be on it."

So I decided to run the tour one more time. (I also wanted to visit Salonika.) Terry's enthusiasm and "promise" were a major factor in my decision.

When I handed her the Greek flier last night, she said, "Oh, we can't go this year. I decided to buy furniture instead."

My heart sank. Another kick in the face.

I deserved it. When will I learn people's desires and "commit ments" to go on my tours, weekends, or anything else mean practically nothing? Only when I have their deposits in hand can I attach some meaning to their decisions. Even those aren't foolproof. Witness Dorothy. Last year she gave me a deposit for the Czech/Slovak/Poland trip but cancelled two months before going. "We can't go now," she had said. "But next year I definitely want to go on your Romanian tour." When Dorothy walked in last night, I handed her my 1997 Romanian tour flier. She read it, looked at the price in dismay, and said the date wasn't good. She didn't say no, but I'm not waiting for her yes either.

These two reversals show me once again how I can count on almost *no* one in this business. I have learned the lesson over and over again. What is so frustrating is, no matter how many times I learn, I forget it. Somehow I refuse to let it sink in. Perhaps I have the mistaken belief that, if I remember my lesson, it will kill my hope, desire, and even ability to organize a future tour.

But I know that is not true.

By lowering my registration expectation to zero, I plant the seeds for personal happiness, which frees me to realize that all events I run have the potential for failure even though the event itself is excellent.

I can put together a fascinating tour or weekend, write a marvelous book, plan an exciting concert, and still there is the possibility no one besides myself will show up.

This has happened to countless others in history. Why shouldn't it happen to me?

Is it possible to run a business and expect *no* customers? Can such an "artistic" approach ever work? Sometimes. But when, I'll never know.

There *is* an answer to my dilemma: I have to start business from the beginning, not only every year, but every *day*. Find a new customer base, new folk dancers, new tour and weekend participants. In unpredictable business situations, the only thing I can count on is an attitude of low-to-no expectations. Start fresh. Look for a new base.

This may be the end of my business. But also the beginning of peace of mind.

Return

It began when Barbara Tapa finished my 1997 brochure and Jim Fessel printed 2,500 along with 2,500 envelopes. Now I have the equipment. I am ready to return to business, to start selling my 1997 tours.

I've spent the last four months in retreat, four months of study in the cave of choice: my Teaneck living room armchair. That period is coming to an end.

I accomplished a great deal during that period: I moved to another level of guitar playing, I solved my right index problem, studied Hebrew, Judaism, and the bible, edited mucho *New Leaf Journal*, progressed in my yoga postures, read novels and fiction, and, very important, even though I earned less than ever and sank further in debt, I stopped worrying about money.

My retreat has served its purpose. It is time to use my new skills and mind mood in the outside world. First, I am putting my external house in order. I'm pruning my mailing list of twelve hundred people down to about five hundred. I've got mailing labels ready. I'm mailing to these dead woods one last time. If they don't register for one of my events, I'll dump them.

I also met with my accountant yesterday. I'm going to reorganize my finances, keeping business and personal accounts separate. I'm also going to keep an exact record of my expenses so I have a better idea of where my money is going. It'll be good for taxes, too. This tighter financial reorganization goes along with my tighter mailing list.

Smaller, quality, more focus and personal control is what I want.

I also want to bring the sparks I have discovered during my four-month retreat into my daily business life in the outside world. Jesus had forty days of meditation in the desert. I've had four months. Jesus found his direction. It's time to find mine.

GOD

Miracle in Reverse

I am totally pissed-off, frustrated, and in rebellion against God. What's the matter with Him? Why isn't He sending me customers? Why isn't He filling up my beautiful Budapest Festival tour or raining down registrants for my Greek tour?

Today I stand in total disgust, shaking my fist at heaven. I am sick and tired of begging, pleading, falling to my knees, and praying for customers. Isn't there a better way? I've supplemented my supplications with abundant ads in journals, a beautiful brochure, and many phone calls.

The result is: one customer for my Budapest trip. It is the worst showing I've ever had. What irony. An excellent tour with the most publicity and sales calls, and the result is less customers than ever. No wonder I'm pissed at the pittance of clients He has sent.

I could take the pressure off Mr. Lord by blaming myself. That sounds humble enough. But I don't believe it. If I'm doing something wrong, I can't figure out what it is. In fact, I feel like I'm doing something right. The tour is great, advertising better than ever, phone call follow-ups have been done once and twice. But the result of this labor and expenditure of time and money has been zero. It's a business miracle... but in reverse.

Perhaps that's what "explains" it.

If God can create miracles to inspire people, why can't He create miracles in reverse to out-spire or per-spire people?

Perhaps this is God's version of a sense of humor.

Getting customers this year is like pulling teeth. I'm wading through molasses, reaching for tourists. Every major effort brings a minor bite. I'll have to adjust my expectations downwards. But though business is painfully slow, I'm still optimistic.

Phone calls lie at the base of my business. Last night I spent two hours calling all my Greek GPs. The ones I'd hoped would come decided not to. One registered for the Russian Weekend, one will come to a folk dance class, one will do nothing this year. My optimism is based, not on my customers' reactions, but on *the fact that I am calling them. Last night I even saw my phone calling as relaxing, socializing, and pleasant.* A major attitude breakthrough. So far there have been no business rewards, only the satisfaction of a selling job well done.

Enjoying my phone calls! It's too good to be true. Not many people have phone call epiphanies. It might lead to new lands; new doors may open. Dualisms of outside and inside, work and play, socializing and solitude, are breaking down. I can see hermits entering the world, monks retreating from their cloisters, artists descending from their mountains, all on the road to *fsitchko e edno.*

Faith

How can I have more faith in myself?

I am all alone on this quest. No one can help me. My search is beyond language and words. Every morning I start out on a new path, searching for another facet of the infinite diamond shining within. I wake up lost, start to write, and soon, through my writing meditation, I rediscover my strengths. The Higher Force talks to Me through me.

It is all very strange. Who am I to dare speak about such things? Who am I to say that a Higher Force is speaking through me, teaching me to transcend my ego? Others may think I suffer from delusions of grandeur. I may think the same thing. But, as Dr. MacIsaacs said, "You're not enough of your own hero. You believe too much that others have solutions." It's true. I read the great works, study the lofty books, all in a search to find what is already in me. Answers would come more easily if I had more faith in myself. Better to be my own hero than find my heros in others.

But I am going beyond this by saying Higher Forces exist within me, speak to and through me. I am comparing myself to prophets of old.

What will happen to me if I do? Am I fooling myself, slipping into hubris? It might help to realize that, throughout history, countless others have discovered the same thing: the Higher Power is within. No one can discover it for you. Others may show the road, but you have to walk alone. No one is talking about ego here. Rather it is about bypassing the ego, forgetting and throttling it, reaching for the Mighty Force that resides within.

I fear such powers. Will they alienate me from others? Will they destroy me?

But my search for them is also the source of my salvation.

Acceptance of God and His Works

I'm having early morning espressos at the New Olympic Hotel in Olympia and writing in my hand-written journal.

Could my new direction be *focus on the concrete?*

It symbolizes an acceptance of God and His works; it can be expressed through:

1. Language
2. Performance—guitar, folk dancing, other
3. Writing and editing

4. Business

My search for God, religion, and unity has crystallized with an acceptance of the Hasidic sparks inherent in concrete tasks.

Scraping the Bottom

Oh Lord, blow a breath of life into my nostrils. That would be good this morning. I am scraping the bottom, searching for applicable foodstuffs. Where is my handle? I want to travel in disguise, hit emotions sideways. A thin cover of boredom hides my inner landscape. Does it hide a creative thrust?

I am tired of old tattered visions. I am thrashing, splashing, bashing, and dashing to find a new road map.

Something has changed. The author of Dante's *Inferno* might know what it is. Can I meet him for lunch to discuss it? If he won't travel to the Forum Diner, perhaps we could sit in my living room and prepare for a traveling psychic hour. Dante will have lots to say about my infernal state. Or is it Purgatory? If he doesn't want to speak, I know he'll be a good listener.

All anchors have fled. My boat has been cast adrift. Biblical behemoths crawl at my ankles, licking calloused calves, and biting knotted thighs.

INVENTIONS

Rumjana in Shiroka Luka

Staring beneath the banister, walking where canes never met, Rumjana sits in a Greek mode, counting ants and twisting her pinky in Turkish coffee grinds.

All is quiet, soft, and dank in the still morning air. Far away, a nightingale sings. Arrows pierce her heart, broken at the root. Will Turkish win the day, or is another lecture on Romanian in sight?

As the morning sun shines on turnips and berries, only the brave wait for the Bulgarian seamstress to make her descent from the hills of Shiroka Luka. Treading the soft path, she wends her Thracian way towards the music school across the *gaida*-shrill Shiroka River. Warm castle turrets puncture the pure Rhodopian sky. Orpheus once stood here, and so did Euridice. Is it Rumjana's turn today?

Panic thunders in the distance. Black clouds drift overhead; a torrential mountain rain threatens the town. Microbes from nearby Pamporovo drift towards Shiroka Luka. Only a welter of fish can save Rumjana now. Can she tread this one, too? Will one-two be enough?

A walkway is in sight. She smiles. The wisdom of writing for a naked pancreas cannot be easily silenced.

King Diamond

Adam Hausner sold diamonds on 48th street. His narrow store was squeezed between a diamond emporium and a Greek restaurant. Merchants, hundreds of potential customers, cyclists, pedestrians, police, motorists, tourists, prostitutes, shoppers, and assorted kings and queens from all walks of life paraded up and down the street.

Adam was something of a philosopher. Often he drove to work early—before the rush of the city descended upon his narrow preserve—and sat in the back of his store behind his small desk. From this position, away from the display cases of diamonds, necklaces, rings, and green carpeting, and with the tranquillity that only a good night's sleep can bring, he liked to take a step backwards into Philosophy Street in the city of his mind. There he wandered aimlessly, wondering about the nature of the world. Was life really a waking dream? Who created customers? Who created diamonds? Who had created Adam?

He never came up with answers. Often, just as he was getting close to understanding the relationship between body, mind, and spirit, he would be interrupted. One day it was by a heavy-set man with dark glasses, wearing a black overcoat, who walked through the door, pointed at the display case, and asked. "What're ya gettin' for dis stone?"

Adam looked at the diamond set in a gold ring. "Eighteen hundred dollars."

The customer glared at Adam, grunted, turned, and, without a word, walked out.

Adam returned to his thoughts. What was the real nature of a diamond? he asked himself. Then it struck him! *The diamonds he sold had no intrinsic value.* They were, rather, reflections of the inner worth, symbols of the "real diamonds" people searched for in themselves.

He was selling *reflections*.

Thus, in a sense, his business was superfluous. Was he a fraud? Maybe he should have listened to his father and become a teacher. Then he could have given people something useful, guided them, helped them find their lost parts. His father knew value; he could tell the difference between a lasting truth and a bauble with an ephemeral shine.

Another thought came to him: People owned "real diamonds," but they weren't aware of them. And the few who were didn't know how to find them. By selling his precious stones, Adam was performing a social service for his customers. He was supplying them with reminders.

His brain was really cooking that morning. He thought up new copy for his next ad: *When you're feeling down...and out, remember your diamond within.*

He unlocked the display case, picked out his most valuable DeBeers gem, and slipped it into his vest pocket just above his heart.

He drove home in a good mood that evening. When he hit a traffic jam on the Long Island Expressway, he turned on the radio and listened to Bach while exhaust fumes and waiting cars piled up around him.

After a fifteen-minute wait, the traffic began to move again. He cruised through Queens. At the Great Neck sign, he patted his vest pocket. *There was nothing there.* He began to tremble. Where was it? Hadn't he put it in his vest pocket? Or had he? He couldn't remember.

With sweating hands he searched his pockets but found nothing. His mind flew back to the store. Mentally, he combed the display cases, desk drawers, safe, the rows of catalogues lying open on his desk. It was all a blank.

He pulled over to the side of the road and stopped to search the front seat, the glove compartment, the floor. Still nothing. He panicked. Where could it be? How could he have misplaced—or worse, lost—such a valuable jewel?

He finished the drive a physical wreck and slumped in his living room armchair, unable to touch the martini his wife brought him.

He gazed into space. Try to remember...try to remember. His finger inadvertently slid over his breast pocket. Try.... *There* it is! He touched it. His diamond had been with him all along, safe and secure. How could he have forgotten where it was?

He held his hand over his heart. He pressed gently against the precious stone and resolved never to forget it again. Then he fell fast asleep.

"*Dinner's ready!*" Laura had prepared a huge spaghetti repast. All three kids charged down the stairs, plopped onto their chairs, and began grabbing food. "Wait a minute!" Laura snapped. "Don't be pigs! Wait until everyone is seated."

Adam yawned, stretched, and took slow, leisurely strides towards the dinner table. The kids eyed him eagerly. As soon as he sat down, they dove for the food. "Where are your manners?" Laura shouted. The kids started yelling at each other. Adam's peace of mind vanished. "Shut up around here!" he said, slamming his fist on the table. "I want quiet when I eat!"

"Listen to your father," Laura echoed.

The dinner continued in silence until Liam, the eldest son, dumped his plate of spaghetti on the floor and ran upstairs.

Adam's appetite disappeared along with the spaghetti, which he forced Liam to clean up and flush down the toilet.

He took a walk around the block to help digest what little food he had eaten. As he passed the candy store, the old panic returned. Where was his diamond? He wanted to touch it, see it, feel it. He wanted to remember how valuable he was. But he kept forgetting. And when he did, a terrible panic ensued, a heavy cloud darkened his world. He felt like a fool, weak, even stupid. Why must a grown man need to touch a diamond for hope, security, sustenance, self-knowledge, and wisdom? Did everyone need a diamond as he did?

He bought four halvah bars in the candy store and raced down the dark side street, tearing off wrappers and shoving the bars into his mouth one after another. He hardly chewed them.

The sudden rush of sugar softened his fear and gave him hope. But the energy surge soon ended on a low plane of lethargy and despair. He had lost it again.

He sat on a park bench. The night air was cool and clear. A breeze blew, then stopped. No cars passed. The leaves above his head were still. Adam listened. His heart stopped pounding. He sighed and slouched forwards as his shoulders relaxed. Then he felt the stone moving against his heart. His eyes lit up. Found. Why had he ever been afraid? Why the panic? It had always been there.

Why was it so hard to remember? No matter how many times he tried, he kept forgetting. His treasure lay, always and forever, deep within him. But he needed diamonds to remind him.

He headed home along the darkened streets thinking about reminders.

Brain Arthritis

Jack's brain was getting stiff, his body too—slowly becoming more mechanical and rigid. When he spoke to people, words often stiffened in his mouth and fell out like sticks.

He decided to see a doctor, who immediately did a brain scan. "You are suffering from brain arthritis," he concluded. "It is curable, but the treatment is very painful."

"So is the pain, Doctor. I'll do anything to get rid of it."

Good." The doctor nodded. "A positive attitude is very important in this treatment. Traditionally, we have given patients only aspirin. However, a laboratory in New Jersey has just developed a special drug for treatment of brain arthritis. It is now available in pill form. At your stage, the disease is very advanced, so only concentrated doses can help you."

The doctor reached into his drawer and pulled out a small bottle. "Take these. They'll make change easier and lessen the pain. Take them every day for one year. After that, you won't need them anymore. You'll be able to change by yourself."

"Thank you so much, Doctor," said Jack. "I feel better already."

"That's one of the miracles of these pills," the doctor exclaimed. "You feel better even before you take them."

Jack went home, ate lunch, and took his first pill, a round one with a sweet fragrance. Then he went for his usual afternoon stroll. Every day for twenty-three years he had been walking the same street and turning right on Baker Avenue. That day, however, for the first time, he turned left.

The pills were working.

He passed the dull red-brick house. Suddenly, he noticed sparkling window panes, polished handrails, and the black-shingled hooded roof. When he passed the old maple tree, it seemed to stand proud and straight, its sturdy branches to vibrate like powerful hands reaching towards the sky.

He glanced at the sidewalk, then at the street. How its asphalt shone!

Everything looked so new that day. Even the fire hydrant head surveyed the neighborhood like a conqueror.

Then Jack felt uneasy. Enough adventure for one day.

When he returned home he sat down in the old living room armchair and opened *A History of the Black Sea Trade; its Cumulative Effects on the Eleventh Century Expansion of the Byzantine Empire,* by Heinrich von Schled. The book's 543 pages had been translated from German into English; many sentences went on for two pages and more. Jack, feeling always he had to finish whatever he started, read on, even though the von Schled tome was a marvel of dullness. In time, he had read every word, comma, period, page number, and footnote up to page 34. By page 35, he was almost asleep. Suddenly, a new daring rushed through his stomach and shot adrenalin straight into his right arm. He slammed the book shut and threw it across the room. It smacked against the wall and fell into the garbage can, where it belonged. Jack smiled triumphantly, picked out *Martin Eden* by Jack London, and, licking his lips, sat down to read.

Jack soon began changing attitudes in many ways. He learned to think a thought and, if it didn't work, change his mind to a more fruitful one. As he became more flexible, he took fewer pills. In time he didn't even need them anymore. Although, like all sufferers, he had a tendency to relapse, he struggled to begin each day afresh, ready to shift his plans if need be. Brain arthritis had loosened its grip on him. He had a better grip on life.

What Are Friends For?

Tom was suffering from writer's block. I think a visit to Jack's house will relax me, he thought. Jack lived on the other side of town, and since Tom needed exercise, he walked.

On the way he passed trees, houses, children playing, a tunnel, and a truck. Finally, he saw Jack's place up ahead.

And a magnificent house it was: Beautiful shutters hung from each rectangular window; a bright red brick facade shone in the afternoon sunlight; a slate roof crowned the wide second floor, and white smoke poured from the tall, majestic chimney.

Then Tom noticed that smoke was also coming out of the *windows.* He saw even more smoke creeping from the sides and bottom of the front door. *Jack's house was on fire!*

Tom pushed open the front door and rushed into the living room. He ran down the hallway until he found Jack, in the bedroom, suffocating from smoke and coughing out his guts. Dragging him by the hand and collar, he managed to get him out just as the roof collapsed behind them.

"That was a close call," gasped Jack, sitting on the front lawn. "Thanks for saving my life." He brushed sweat from his forehead. "But am I worth saving? I've been so down ever since my novel was rejected for the sixteenth time. I appreciate your effort, but it would have been better to save the sofa."

"Cut it out, Jack!" cried Tom as the last wall slumped into rubble behind them. "Any life is worth saving, especially a friend's. . . . How did it happen, anyway?"

"When you hear the reason you'll know I'm a true friend," Jack replied as fire engines came screaming down the street. "*I lit it.* I love the sound, the smell, the warmth of a fire. And the reason I lit this one is—" Jack gasped for air again— "is to give you a subject to write about for your next story. I did it for *you,* Tom, I did it for you!" As he uttered this last, he inhaled more smoke and crumpled to the ground.

"What a friend," said Tom with admiration.

At that moment the fire captain told his men not to bother throwing water on the house.

Tom turned away from the fire engines and started up the block. Glancing back, he said, "The embers from Jack's house will glow in my mind forever. I'll dedicate my next story to him."

The Personality-changing, Mental Meat-Grinding Machine

Thomas suffered from IPD—Intractable Personality Disfunction, a disease inherited from his mother. How could he become more selfless, caring, sensitive, and open? How could he break out of Ego Prison, with its delicious meals and thoughtful staff?

A Personality-Changing, Mental Meat-Grinding Machine on sale in Pathmark for $29.95 gave him hope. He jumped into his Mitsubishi and drove down to buy it.

He put the machine on his living room table, dialed "Warm, Sensitive, and Caring," opened the steel door, put his head inside, and threw the switch. Warm currents heated his brain. When he heard "ping!" he was done. The door opened; out came a new Thomas—kind, caring, and sensitive. There was only one drawback: His head had burnt to a crisp.

Still, over the next week he grew more and more enthusiastic about his new personality. He told his friends. Many jumped into their cars and headed for Pathmark.

A-Muse-ing

I was waiting for my muse to show up. I like her. She always runs around naked when she comes. But that's not so great, since I can never catch her. She's light-footed, lighthearted, and full of fun. Even so, there's something devilish about her. Maybe it's her enigmatic smile.

At last she appeared. "Muse, you *beauty*," I said. "I hope you stay here forever."

"I'll do as I please," she warned.

A thought occurred to me. *Chains!* That's *it!* I'll chain her to the computer. She'll never escape.

I took the chain out of my desk drawer. When she wasn't looking, I grabbed her, threw her against my keyboard, and chained her up. Now she was mine!

I gazed at her bound to the letters A and L, waiting for her to give me an idea. But nothing happened.

She laughed. "Chains can't hold me, you dope. You're wasting your time. Let me go. If you keep doing this, you'll never catch me!"

She was right. A chained muse meant nothing to me.

Sadly, I released her. "Is there anything I can do to keep you?" I asked.

"One thing."

"Yes?"

"Forget me."

"How can I do that? I need you."

That enigmatic smile again. "Forget me," she repeated, and strolled out the door.

For a whole week I felt sad. I shopped, read, jogged, watching TV, and took walks.

A month passed.

Then, one morning, I awoke feeling fresh. I went straight to my desk and. . . *voilá!* There she was, standing next to my chair, naked and beautiful as ever. "I never expected to see you again!" I said. She was so alluring. How could I have forgotten her?

She pointed to the blank screen on my monitor. "Sit down," she commanded. "Get to work."

"Yes, ma'am!"

I sat down and wrote this piece.

Paying off a Loan

I charged into the bank Monday morning, frantically looking for money to pay off the loan shark swimming behind me. The teller said, "Go downstairs to the vault." I took the steps three and four steps at a time with the shark snapping at my heels. Luckily the vault was open. I raced in, tripped over a bag of coins, and fell headlong into a pile of cash. With a feeling of relief I gathered the piles together and stuffed them in the loan shark's mouth. His huge jaws snapped greedily at the greenbacks. When he'd had enough, he swam clumsily out of the vault and up the stairs. His fin got stuck in the revolving door, but he escaped down Ocean Avenue.

I sat in the remaining pile of cash, sweating. That was a close call, I thought.

Just then a beautiful woman came towards me. She had long blonde hair down to her waist and a slender lithesome figure. Her skirt was very tight and had cash receipts printed all over it. Her legs were so close together, I could easily tell she was the bank mermaid.

"What are you doing here?" she gasped. "Help! Help! A *robber!*"

"Please! *Please* don't shout," I said. "My ears are very sensitive to pressure. I'm not a bank robber. I only came in for a quick loan. I had to pay off a debt in a hurry, and now that I have, I feel much more relaxed. Perhaps you'll sit down and we can talk?"

She looked me over hesitantly, then calmed down as she realized I was harmless. "We've had a lot of robberies lately," she said, perching on a stack of hundred-dollar bills. "I guess I'm a bit jittery."

We sat for a half hour discussing the banking business, foreign currency, and the falling value of the dollar. "Imagine," I laughed, "soon those hundreds you're sitting on will be just about worthless."

"Yes," she answered. "It's a real problem. Sitting on dollars won't keep inflation down."

Her name was Esther. I wrote down her phone number as we left the bank together. We saw each other during the next few days. I was so happy to be free from debt. Now I could love again. And what a beautiful woman I had to love! It made me realize that banks can offer more than just money.

On Friday afternoon, when I went to the bank to meet her, suddenly I saw the loan shark coming after me again. "What do you want?" I growled. "I just paid you off!"

"Like hell you did!" said the shark angrily. "Those dollars you gave me ain't worth shit anymore. I wanna be paid off in gold. Ain't you heard about inflation?"

Now I was scared. The old panic returned. I started to run. The shark began chasing me. How could I repay him? I ran ahead of his ferocious snaps, heading towards the bank. It was my only hope. I charged through the revolving door and dashed down the stairway, leaping three and four stairs at a time. Luckily the vault was still open. I raced in, tripped over a bag of gold coins and fell headlong into a pile of cash. "Take the coins," I yelled. "Take the coins!"

I picked up handfuls of coins and shoved them into his greedy mouth. I could hear his sharp teeth grinding them into dust. As he swallowed, I knew that, soon, his digestive enzymes would compact it into gold bars. Finally, the shark had had enough. He swam clumsily out of the bank and down Ocean Avenue. I sat in my pile of cash, waiting for Esther.

When she arrived, she looked concerned.

"What happened?" she asked. "I was worried about you."

"The shark was after his money again," I said. "But don't worry. I gave him the gold in the vault. He's satisfied now." I wiped my sweating brow with my handkerchief. "Why don't we go out to supper together?"

"Good idea." She took my hand. "You've had a rough day."

I agreed. We headed for a nearby seafood restaurant, entered the back room, and sat down in a quiet corner.

"Relax," said Esther in a soothing voice. The waiter was soon bringing out orders out. "It's all over now. Put your mind at ease and eat your fish." She looked closely at my plate. "Hmm," she hmmmed thoughtfully. "Looks like shark."

I studied my plate for a long moment. "You're right," I said, gleefully jabbing my fork into it. That night I ate with a vengeful smile of satisfaction.

Patience Is a Virtue

One cold winter day, Larry went to the store to buy some milk for his mother.

He trudged ankle deep in snow along Garrison Avenue. Several cars driving past splattered gray slush and water in his face. Larry picked up a rock and wrapped clean white snow around it. When the next car splashed slush in his face, he threw the snowball at the driver. It smashed against the window, cracking the plate glass in a flower-like design. The driver screeched to a halt as Larry ran off.

"Gimme some milk quick!" he panted.

"Patience," drawled the grocer. "Patience is a virtue."

Larry threw a dollar on the counter. "Gimme some milk *quick! Pleeease!*" The grocer held up his index finger. "Calm yourself, young man. Patience is one of the few virtues left in our society." Just then Larry saw the car driver rushing through the door. His face was cut and bleeding from the splintered glass, and he had an insane look in his eye.

"See how it pays to be patient?" said the grocer. He handed Larry the milk container just as the driver's fist smashed into his arm.

Larry ducked the next punch, grabbed the milk and ran out the door. As he fled down the street, he heard the grocer calling after him. "What's the rush, young man? Patience is a virtue."

Blood Flow

"Blood flow is controlled through metaphors," said Dr. Breathdare to Jason Peabody, who lay under the thirty-third Street sign. Blood oozed out of the wound beneath his sixteenth vertebrae, forming a puddle on the sidewalk. Yet Jason remained calm. He watched his blood flow south towards thirty-second Sreet and meditated upon the Danube and how smoothly it flowed by Slovakia, Hungary, Bulgaria, Romania, and through the Dobruzhian Delta into the Black Sea. A dark stream now trickled past bankrupt Macy's, the IRT subway station, and Madison Square Garden.

Dr. Breathdare kneeled next to Jason and said with quiet assurance, "You've made your point, Jason," he said. "People are beginning to stare at you. It's time to stop this attention-getting device and get back to your office. Stop this blood flow: *Now!*"

Jason concentrated on the command. He placed the clamp of his mind on his arteries and slowed his heart beat. His wound clotted. "Thank you, Jason," said kindly Dr. Breathdare. "You have performed an outstanding public service. It's better to speak up than bleed in public. People *will listen* to you."

Jason rose. "Thank you, Doctor," he said, picking up his briefcase and heading towards his travel office in Penn Plaza. "Now I can finish writing that Eastern European guide book."

Paul's Piano Lesson

"Can't we hurry this Beethoven sonata?" Mrs. Pathby asked at her son's lesson. He was quite goal oriented.

"Absolutely not. Play it *more* slowly," his teacher, Mrs. Moreon, repeated.

"What?" shouted Paul. "You must be mad. Music must have goals. When I play the Beethoven *Pathetique*, my goal is to finish! That's why my fingers fly so fast. It's a contest. First pianist to finish wins. I play to win!"

Mrs. Moreon blew her nose, then spat on the floor. "Pretty bad," she sneered. "Luckily your mother pays me a pretty penny to tolerate your cyclopean, boorish, buffoonish, materialistic perfectionist attitude. Otherwise, I'd take your piano and stuff it down your ungrateful throat!"

Mrs. Pathby piped up from her seat by the window, "Steady now, Mrs. Moreon. There's no reason to berate my son. His goal-oriented way has brought me benefits. Last week he took up dancing. Then he waltzed to the store to buy my groceries."

"Goal-oriented attitudes belong in the sewer!" Mrs. Moreon sizzled. "Crass, crass. I've never heard such a materialistic, communistic, jingoist, jargonistic, hedonistic, bullshitistic attitude. Luckily you're feeding my coffers with mucho cash. Otherwise, my high standards could not be compromised."

"That's easy for you to say, Mr. Moreon," said Paul, looking up from the watermelon he had squeezed between the piano keys. "Not everyone can attend the Laptop Computer School of Music as you did, or graduate summa cum cumquat from its fruit department."

Paul's piano lessons continued until the termites ate his house.

A Guitarist s Manual

What is the best position for playing guitar with the feet? First the guitarist leans against a chair, puts his head on the floor and both legs in the air. Then, by placing his left hand on the foot stool while right hand supports the guitar, he frees both feet to play.

The hammer stroke is the most effective way to strike a string. A metal hammer is best. When struck by finger or toe a beautiful tone is produced though a hammer will also destroy the guitar.

Another method of striking the string is called the free stroke. It is often executed while the guitarist is in midair. If air is not available, the free stroke is performed in a vacuum and the guitarist is executed.

Thus, a skilled guitarist can execute a hammer stroke or a hammer stroke can execute the guitarist.

Of the guitarists using an upright position, the most famous was Gilfry Goosepimple. Once during a concert he tapped his foot so hard it broke through the floor, causing the ceiling below to collapse into a basement pool hall and, enraging the pool players, who ran upstairs, broke down the concert hall door, wrecked the chairs, fractured the bones of everyone in the audience, and finally, not only broke Jack Goosepimple's guitar, but his head as well. Since that day, foot tapping has lost its popularity in the concert guitar world although it has been adopted in the construction business.

Few manuals have dealt at length with guitar drainage problems. Water often seeps through the body of the instrument during wet weather, causing small pools to accumulate within. If this water is not properly drained, it can soon be inhabited by frogs and fish. An audience is often discomforted when, in the middle of playing a guitar masterwork, a frog croaks—thought some guitarists have used this to advantage. Mortimer Flapjack, in his "Water, Frog, and Human" trio, emphasizes not only croaking but gargling as well.

Some players have expanded upon the water concept and turned their guitars into row boats, though this is still more common among cellists.

The best guitar draining method is to attach a sewer pipe to the mouth, form a hole in the back of the guitar, then blow through it. The breath forces the water out the sewer pipe. Although the hole utterly ruins the guitar, the instrument can still be used as an antique.

Rage

Snorting, she grabbed the armchair and ripped off the cover with her bare hands. She squeezed the stuffing out of the pillow and stamped on the armchair frame, quickly turning it into a heap of smashed wood and splinters.

Without bothering to open the window, she hurled the sofa through it. Shattered glass flew in all directions.

"I *hate* this house!" she yelled, driving her foot through the plaster wall.

"I can't stand looking at you, either!" she screamed at her husband, who was hiding in the corner. Grabbing him by the scruff of the neck, she crushed his starch collar. It sent his shirt buttons flying in all directions.

"Martha, you're overreacting," were the last words he spoke before she heaved him across the lawn into the rose bushes.

"I can't stand the smell of those roses either," she shouted as she ripped out the bushes and ploughed them under with her heel.

Finally, her rage subsided. She found a pear in refrigerator and sat in the corner munching it while all the paintings on the wall hung trembling from their hooks.

The Underachiever

We are an achievement-oriented society.

Often, in our unending drive to find success, we leave friendship and family behind.

Let us therefore take a stand here and now for underachievement. Let us proclaim the wisdom of doing less!

Underachievers are everywhere.

Why, even *achievers* often feel they are underachievers. Just to prove they aren't, they fight to achieve even more.

Support your local underachiever and you will be supporting your friends, family, neighbor, mayor, councilmen, merchants—even your local police.

Underachievers have time: time for friends, for their families, for fun and love. Everyone knows that time is all around us. Yet only the underachiever seems to have enough time to enjoy it.

Underachievers, unite! You have nothing to lose but your facades. The slaves of achievement may work all day and burn bright fires, which many can see, but only the underachiever can enjoy the natural light of the sun.

Mama Clock

Mama Clock led her son Ben down the road. She had his wrists tied to a watch and his brain strapped to a schedule. Although Ben lived in a lovely village surrounded by trees, fresh air, and flowers, he couldn't see its beauty. Too tied down, he dwelt in Time Prison, handcuffed and ruled by Mama Clock.

She controlled him. There was no deviation from her schedule. Every day was exactly the same; changes came only once a month, on Sundays. If Ben avoided his schedule, Mama Clock would shake her rusty and, twist her tin face into a scowl, and shout: "Moron, get back on schedule! I'm not ticking away here to *amuse* you. You can only pull yourself out of your stupidity swamp by following my *schedule*. It will tell you exactly what to do, and your wristwatch will tell you exactly when to do it. Follow my advice. Until you can run your own life, *I will run it for you!"*

Mama Clock called Ben stupid so often that by now he believed it. He became a docile and willing prisoner. Even the thought of freedom frightened him.

One day he met a thin, lively girl with dancing blue eyes. Her name was Frieda. She had a spirited way of talking, laughed easily, seemed unafraid, and had a good time wherever she went. Her smile and easy abandon made Ben sad.

"Why can't I have fun, too?" he asked Mama Clock.

"You're too dumb for fun."

But Frieda thought Ben was just as smart as anybody else.

"Mama Clock wants to keep you prisoner by convincing you you're stupid, "Frieda told him. "If she keeps you handcuffed to your wristwatch, you won't find out how smart you are."

Ben had many talks with Frieda. After lunch, they'd walk in the park, or sit by the ocean watching the waves roll in. He began to understand he wasn't stupid after all. Slowly belief in himself grew. As it did, so did his fights with Mama Clock. Fearing he might break out of Time Prison, she hurled one accusation after another at him.

"Stupid, blithering, blundering idiot! Your brain is softer than an egg yolk. How can a moronic, loathsome creature like you expect to succeed in the world?"

Ben defended himself, fought off each accusation with his newfound belief. The more he fought, the more he emerged from Time Prison. He unlocked his wrists, dropped his wristwatch in the gutter, then tore up his schedule. Soon he was able to say goodbye to Mama Clock.

He held Frieda's hand as they danced down the road together.

Mama Clock screamed when she lost her son. When that didn't work, she shook her fists. When that didn't work, she calmed down. She took a few easy breaths, muttered "Finally," to herself. She smiled.

Then she waved to her son. "Good luck, Ben," she said. "And have a good Time!"

Waiting for the Mail

"I sure hope I get some mail tomorrow," Lance said as he fed his pigs. He shoveled slop into their trough and continued to glance at page 63 of Ovid's *Metamorphosis*. Holding the book open with the heel of his work boot and letting the sun illuminate the text, he began reading the luxuriant hexameters. How he loved Latin! Every morning before feeding his pigs, he sat at his desk under the cozy light of his table lamp. Coffee in hand, he would spend a meditative hour, poring over each word, looking up meanings in his Latin dictionary, then checking with Webster's for any Indo-European roots or connections between ancient and modern tongues. Lancelot believed a thorough understanding of etymology not only enriched his life but provided the innovative ideas needed to run a successful pig farm.

Not that his farm was successful. Far from it. Pigs often died, especially when he wanted them to produce beef. His feeding methods, although innovative, were questionable, for when he ran out of corn meal and slop, he tore pages from Dante's *Inferno*, or even *Lives of the Saints*, and threw them in the trough,

One morning, he was crossing his farmyard, pondering important problems while stroking his chin. On the right stood his favorite pen. He kept questioning himself as he entered it. Was he wasting his life as a pig farmer? Should he become a Latin scholar?

He squatted beside a sleeping hog. "Tell me," he demanded, "what is more worthy? To place pork chops and ham on the dinner tables of distant city folks, or to study Virgil and read Cicero in the original?"

The pig snorted, grunted, wiggled its ear, and turned over. Its snout widened. In a low, rumbling voice, it replied, "Lance, I'd think it over a bit more. Mid-life changes take time." It snorted again before closing its eyes and burying its snout in the mud.

"You think so?" Lance replied. "But what do you know? You're only a hog. Besides, I work by consensus. I'll ask the others." He trudged across the pen. "I feel foolish asking pigs for answers," he grumbled. "They're not as smart as they look. What do they know beyond the pen? Better for me to leave this farm, see the world, expand my horizons, and become a credit to the human race. Besides, I want to read Virgil in the original."

So he made plans. The very quest that had convinced him to buy his pig farm was now pulling him away from the security of his pens and propelling him into the world of men, women, dogs, and commerce. Would he be able to study Latin or read Virgil and Ovid in such a world?

On Tuesday morning, Lancelot Hogsfeld packed his suitcase, put the farm in the care of his aged parents, locked his front door, and marched down the country road.

Soon he passed a farmhouse. An old man was sitting in a rocker on the front porch. Lance had seen old men, but this man was older by far.

Lance came closer to look him over: Torn shirt, baggy overalls, gnarled fingers, white beard. "Who are you?" he asked.

"I am the god of tooth-fillings," the old man explained.

"My teeth are fine," Lance said," but my *life* is full of holes. How did you sleep last night?"

"I never sleep. I watch the stars. My cousin was a star. So was my uncle. But now I'm a professional Old Man. I make house calls, visit hospitals, pick up the mail."

"I don't get mail," Lance complained. "People only write my pigs."

"Hire me," the Old Man advised. "You'll see mail pile up to your ceiling." He hitched up his suspenders. "Tell me, son, why do you want to get mail?"

"I'm looking for a goal," Lance answered. "Maybe I can find it in the mail."

"You need a commitment, son." The Old Man raised his arm, swatted Lance across the face, and sent the pig farmer flying off the porch.

"What the hell'd you do that for?" Lance yelled when he got up.

"I want you to pay attention to your pigs, son."

Lance rubbed his chin. "I feel like punching you in the mouth."

"I wouldn't do that, son."

Lance clenched his fist. "Okay. What do you have to teach me?"

"I already did, " the Old Man replied. "But there's more. Go back to your pigs. Wait for the next mail. It's coming tomorrow."

Florence

Florence turned her head toward Fred. Her blue eyes burned into his sockets. "Fred," she said, "You know my struggle. After I read *Paradise Lost*, I decided to battle God for control of the earth. Today I am still fighting. It's a tough fight. God is everywhere, and I am nowhere. This fight may take my whole life."

Fred shrugged. "Who am I to question God?" he asked. "Why don't you go back to Jamie's Meat Market? Being a butcher made you happy. It gave you a feeling of fulfillment. What happened? Did it become just another job?"

"I still like butchering. But I want to go *beyond* cows, sheep, pigs, and chickens. I want to expand big time. That's why I took such a low-paying job with Satan, Inc. They swear they'll put God out of business in five years. They've got fourteen branches in the city already and expect to open in the suburbs next year."

"Fine job for a young woman," Fred mused.

Florence agreed. "I want to be president some day."

Fred looked concerned. "I hope you'll be happy. Such high expectations can lead to lots of frustration."

"I don't expect to fail," Florence assured him.

Frogs

I used to be a tadpole sitting placidly on the highway, waiting for that Great Fourwheeler of the Sky to crush me into churning insignificance. Yes, I was a run-over child lost on the super highway of Frogdom. While all my friends graduated into frogs, I sat forever on a pole of lard, sinking and swaying beneath the Mother Elm tree hovering over our backwater Pond of Illusion.

But I was a happy tadpole. What did I know of suffering? Nothing but undulation. Yes, undulations of pond moss were my only pain—and an occasional smack on the ear drum from a falling pine cone, dumped on our pond by a hapless chickapea bird whose only mission was to teach suffering to the likes of me.

But I soon grew beyond that.

One day as I sat on my bench under the pond, dining on grass blades, I spied the unctuous piles of His Royal Sauciness. Who was this giant urchin lard keeper? And why had he visited my pond?

"Oh, holy tadpole, son of frog," said His Royal Sauciness. "It is your duty to suffer. Suffering is good for you. It fills your belly as it shreds your soul. It helps you climb your inner mountain, raising your ashes to the stars and bringing heaven hurtling downward into your webbed feet. Your feet, and the very soles you jump on, filter the stardust of heavens untold and unappreciated spires. Sure, it hurts to spring on them. Why shouldn't it? Jumping from leaf to lily pad with such spikes in your feet is no joke. Neither is sitting on them. Yet how else will you attain heavenly vision? Only the spikes in your toes and nails in your heels will fill you with the necessary elevation to shoot you heavenward so you may mingle with the stars. And mingling with the stars is its own reward."

The Nowhere Revolution

Join the Nowhere revolution. When your friends ask you where you've been on vacation, be the first on your block to answer proudly: "I've *been nowhere!*"

Going nowhere takes the pressure off. Going nowhere is relaxing. It's the greatest undiscovered destination in all twenty-first-century travel. Virgin tour guides know this. That's why they are virgins.

Nowhere is where all the saints have been. It's the final destination. It's not depressing, but freeing.

We'll take you there! Write us at Nowhere, Inc., Central Pillar Plaza, Empty Place, WI 64703, for our free Nowhere brochure. We'll put you on our mailing list. Be the first in your family to travel nowhere.

Voice

That lousy rotten Voice! Who does he think he is? Left me. Just like that! You call that gratitude? And after all I've done for him. I gave him the best place in my body—and he leaves.

I'm not the kind of girl to let just anybody in. I've got my standards. I'm very particular. But this Voice was real nice. You know the type—smooth and soft-sell yet strong and macho, super-masculine yet somewhat laid back. And oh, so attractive! All the other girls in the office wanted him. At first I didn't mind sharing. But after awhile I wanted him all to myself. I've got so little time. After working all day typing papers, serving coffee, bringing buns into executive meetings where all those dark-suit creeps clean their hands on my public and private parts—oh, they are disgusting! I hate them! But I had to do it. I had to.

After all, what could I say? I had no Voice.

But then I found my Voice. Ah, sweet Voice. He's protecting me, speaking up for me.

Why should I have to share him with the other girls?

Let them find their own voice.

Morgan the Gorgon

Morgon the Gorgon had difficulty making friends. Snakes grew out of his head; they hissed whenever anyone came near him. Morgon was very upset. The number of snakes were increasing each year.

Finally, in desperation, he went to a snake doctor, who understood his problem immediately. "There is a snake coming out of your head for every evil deed you have committed," he said. "The only way to get rid of them is to reverse the effects of the evil deeds. This is a very difficult task."

"I'll do anything to get rid of the snakes," said Morgan.

"Then follow me to the Room of Mistakes." The doctor led Morgan downstairs to a large underground chamber. As soon as they crossed the threshold, the snakes started hissing furiously. "Shut up!" shouted Morgan. But the snakes kept hissing. He had no control over them.

"If you look through this window," said the doctor," you will see the Field of Evil Deeds."

"What evil deeds have I done?" asked Morgan.

The doctor laughed. "There are so many, I don't have time to tell you all of them. However, judging from your most prominent snakes, you have robbed mailboxes, cheated your friends, lied to your parents, stolen from your classmates, and bullied little children. I see countless others, too." The doctor put his hand on Morgan's shoulder. "You must go to the Field of Evil Deeds," he said. "Uproot every plant you find."

"Will it get rid of the snakes?"

"Absolutely."

As Morgan explored the Field of Evil Deeds, he found it extended much further than the doctor's basement. It spread over many city blocks. Morgan couldn't see the end of it. Some plants were taller than he was. One looked like a small tree, with iron blades growing out of its trunk and razor blades coming from its leaves. There were cactuses, rose bushes, and nettles. It might take weeks to uproot one plant alone.

He got down on his hands and knees and started weeding. The first plant he pulled up cut his thumb. He worked for hours on a huge cactus; his fingers blistered and bled. After nine hours of weeding, he had uprooted only four plants.

He fell on the ground, exhausted. It seemed hopeless. But when he awoke, he saw that two of his snakes had fallen out. They lay dead on the ground beside him. Encouraged, he spent the next three days weeding furiously.

He worked in the field, ate in the field, slept in the field. When his hands got bloody, he bandaged them and continued weeding. He weeded for months. Every few days another dead snake fell off. After a year had passed, the field was completely cleared.

Morgan felt much better. He visited the doctor again."Look at yourself in the mirror," the doctor said. Morgan did. The snakes were all gone. He looked wonderful without them. *"Fantastic!"* he exclaimed. He was ready to face the world again, no longer as Morgon the Gorgon, but as Morgon the Fair.

Hystation: He Wasn't There

Is hystation a preventable disease? Or is it simply a part of the life cycle?

These questions were proposed by Dr. Kinnewhat at the opening meeting of the Society of Invertebrates in Salt Marsh Estuary, Massachusetts. Several frogs in the audience croaked when he proposed his theory of Cyclic Indifference, but the cheering tadpoles drowned them out.

A generational split over the issue was taking place.

As the commotion subsided the doctor pulled up his shirt, manifesting a large gurp on his chest. "That's what happens when you're at the bottom of your cycle," he said, fondling the gurp. "The energy just drains out of you. You feel like a shell of your former self."

As the doctor spoke, you could see his body beginning to unravel. His energy was draining fast. His inverted brain began pouring its contents down his spinal chord and collecting in fetid pools of hystation. It looked like someone was pulling the threads of his skin apart. His legs shortened, torso shriveled, arms fell off, and face collapsed.

As the symposium watched the hystation taking place, one of the frogs tried saving the doctor's brain. He hopped to the lectern, reached for it with his tongue, but was too late. Only the thought of the doctor remained.

"Where's the *doctor?*" shrieked the frog's wife. An after-image flashed behind the lectern and a frog shouted,"There he is!" The audience turned to look. . . but he wasn't there.

How Tommy Typed His Way to Cold Turkey

The winner of the typing contest would get a free trip to Turkey.

Tommy entered. He'd always wanted to see the poppy fields.

When the gun went off, forty contestants began typing: "Thumbs" Goldberg flew at incredible speed; "Thirty Fingers" Halligan pulled into the lead at three hundred words a minute. Content was superfluous; only speed counted. Tommy won by kicking out Halligan's electric typewriter plug, turning over Goldberg's table and pouring glue on the keys of comma virtuoso Luke Looseness.

"Congratulations, Tommy," said Mr. Keys, who'd organized the contest. Using the pantomime techniques perfected at the University of Serif, he handed Tommy two imaginary stubs. "Here they are Tommy: two tickets to Turkey via Typing Carriage. Just put your clothes in the roller and you'll be off."

"What?" said Tommy, pushing aside the proffered hand."I want the real thing! Give me a real trip, or I'll turn you in for pushing dope."

Mr. Keys drew back. "Call in the Lettermen!" he cried. Four Letters entered the room. "Take this young man and put him on the first plane to Turkey. He wants the real thing."

"North Turkey?" asked the short Letterman, dressed like "0."

"Exactly," answered Mr. Keys.

What a surprise it was for Tommy when his plane landed in the Pontic Mountains of Northern Turkey. It was freezing; snow was falling, and a chilling north wind was shaking the needles on the pine trees. "I'd better slow down," he said through chattering teeth.

Tommy stayed there one month. During that time, he kicked his fast typing habit cold turkey.

Mother at the Museum

Despite my therapist's orders I took my mother to the Metropolitan Museum. I haven't been there for about a year. I arrived half an hour early and had a chance to wander the halls.

I love museums, and have a special, personal way of visiting them. I don't look at the exhibits; I listen to them. I proceed slowly and pensively, breathing in the serenity of the place, looking at the people, listening to the sounds. Museums are places of meditation. I'm surrounded by history and silence, momentarily separated from the busy world. What a pleasure—a moment's respite from letters, phone calls, bills, and responsibilities. A free moment to simply let my mind expand, float over timeless statuary, ancient monuments, incorporeal emanations from Egyptian mummies, slow-vibrating vases from ancient Greece, paintings by long-gone painters, high ceilings, wide floors, spacious halls, and a general feeling of protection from the fleeting forms of buses, parking tickets, vendors, and traffic just outside the door on Fifth

Avenue.

Well, that got busted when my mother arrived. Leaning on her cane, her eighty-year-old weight bore even more heavily upon me when she took my arm and used it as a second cane. It's not the physical weight of her body that pushes me down; it's the mental weight of her comments.

The Van Gogh exhibit was sold out, so instead we passed through the Impressionist section until we came to the 20th century room. Before me stood *Autumn Rhythms,* by Jackson Pollack. I remarked to my mother what a piece of shit I though it was. She reprimanded me severely, saying that the word "shit" was disrespectful to the artist. I said I meant it to be, and that if Jackson Pollack had any respect for me he wouldn't have painted such garbage—or at least wouldn't have showed it to me. We argued about the subtle and gross implications of the word "garbage" until I realized I had been through that scene before, namely all of my *life*. Growing up in the Gold household, that's the way it was. You always fought to express your feelings, especially negative ones. And if they were about politics or art, the only two religious subjects in our family, watch out!

After about forty-five minutes in the museum my mother got tired. But as usual, instead of *saying* she was tired, she told me I was tired and we should leave. Whenever she has a feeling she doesn't like she tells me it's mine. I grew up this way. Her feelings immediately became my feelings; mine were pushed aside, disregarded, forgotten. Today at the museum was just a repeat of countless past episodes. I'm beginning to understand the psychological dynamic. Still it's sad to think that the highlight of my morning was when I put her on the bus and said good-bye. (It wasn't really *that* sad.) Afterwards, I returned to the museum and wandered through the halls for half an hour, regaining my serenity.

Carlos the Cloud

Carlos floated across a Spanish sky.

Every morning, Father Sun rose, dressed him in a moisture suit and sent him out the east door to travel across the heaven.

Carlos played with the other clouds, and at the close of each day, he settled above a tree. There he gathered moisture and slept as the stars passed over him.

Every morning Carlos ate a large moisture breakfast.

He grew larger and stronger; his nebulous muscles bulged until, one day, he burst, feeding hundreds of the plants, trees, and rivers below him.

Carlos looked up at Father Sun. "Raining is fun, Father," he said. "Can I do it again?"

But after awhile, Carlos began to see the drawbacks in his condition, too. He said to his father, "I was so big and strong. Now I'm small and weak. Why grow, if this is what happens to me?"

"You have just watered the earth and made hundreds of plants, trees, and rivers happy," answered the Sun. "You have helped them grow. When they grow, you grow, too. Don't worry. Next time you have your moisture breakfast, think about plants, trees, and rivers. Then, when you grow, you'll grow in wisdom, too."

"Who cares about wisdom?" said Carlos. "Who cares about plants, trees, and rivers? I want *muscles*. I want to be big and *strong* again."

Father got angry. "Listen, lad, stop pestering me. Filling and emptying is a cloud's job. That's the nature of a cloud."

Father Sun pointed a ray at a group of men below him, standing in front of a hardware store. "See those people? Filling and emptying is their job, too. They pass across the earth, gathering their talents and giving to others. After many years, I call them home. I give them a short rest before sending them back to work."

Next day Carlos again drifted across the early morning sky. Darkness still blanketed the earth. The smell of trees wafted up to him, and the cool, fresh morning air brushed against his nebulous body.

Father Sun appeared in the East and saluted the earth. Morning rays lifted the night, and Carlos felt his vision expand.

"Where were you last night, Father Sun?" he asked. "Did you die?"

"Of course," his father answered. "I die every night and come back the next day. Dying is part of my expanding nature. It's an important part of my travels."

"That's easy for you to say, Father. You're an old man."

"You can die at any age, Carlos. And, at any age, it's an expansion."

"I want to expand, too," said Carlos. "I want to accumulate. I want to become a *cumulus*. I want to become Carlos the Cumulus, the biggest and strongest cloud in the sky!"

"Naturally, Carlos. Every cloud wants to get bigger and stronger, to grow and expand and float across the sky. But it is also a cloud's nature to burst into rain and disappear. All clouds are temporary, transient, limited. Carlos, you will certainly grow bigger and stronger, and perhaps even attain your wish and become the biggest and strongest cloud in the sky. But don't think about your size too much. Think rather about *giving*. That is the nature of both sun and cloud—even when we make what the humans call "mistakes," by destroying cities with hurricanes, swelling rivers with downpours, scorching crops and creating droughts of endless summer heat. The sun shines and the clouds rain both through destruction and creation. Mistakes and glorious days are part of the light and part of the rain.

"Carlos, you are learning what it is to be a cloud. Learning too, is a form of giving. Now, travel with your cloud friends. Play with them. Grow. Expand.

"And float over the Spanish sky."

Trip to Nepal

Lance saw the flying soul heading towards the Tibetan gate, red hot, with olives trailing.

I suffer from computer shoulder. I can't stand the pain." He turned to his girlfriend, Veronica O'Toole, whose green glass eyes blazed like Malaysian fireballs. "Please, massage the nape of my neck."

"I cannot," Veronica replied. "I'm off to Nepal where the good napes dwell."

Lance gripped his pancreas. "I can feel my flow tightening. My stomach is bursting with burpo gas."

"Drop your napes!" Veronica commanded. "Stop complaining. This tasty Tibetan porridge will welk your loins."

"Thank you, dear Veronica. May you successfully climb Mount Ever Rest."

Jones Corners the Water Market

It was a new day in the life of If-The-Shoe-Fits-Wear-It Jones. He was, after all, president of First Caterpillar Firm whose motto, "Down the Pillar!" turned Greek columns into delicatessens.

First Caterpillar banked on the Danube. Water flowed into its coffers. Indeed, its currency was neither the Franc, Forint, Deutschmark, nor dollar, but water. As First Caterpillar's vaults filled with hydrogen and oxygen, Jones watched his water empire grow. He hoped to corner the water market. Water banks rose everywhere.

That's when the staff realized Jones was a madman. Everyone knew except his water-worshiping wife, Penelope. Jones had his eye not only on the river sources of Europe but cast an acquisitive glance on the Atlantic and Pacific as well. "If I can corner those markets, I'll be water king of the world!" He roared. "No one will ever dump on me again!"

His eyes filled with tears as this vision of perfection gathered in his loins.

That morning, he visited his therapist, Dr. Eyehav Urine.

"Doctor, what is my prognosis?" he asked in a watery tone. "Will I be able to conquer the water markets of the world? Or will I be forced to sit in my closet all day drinking bottled water?"

The good doctor got up. "I have to go the John," he said.

Jack and Jill and the Big Bad Wolf

Once upon a time there was a boy named Jack. He was a normal eleven-year old except he was thirteen feet tall. One other thing: his left foot was a size thirteen, and his right foot was six miles long.

When Jack walked across country, his right foot demolished cities and towns. He went west from New York heading for California. He started on his left foot. Clump! His right foot landed on Cleveland. That was the end of Cleveland. Then, St. Louis. Clump! Albuquerque: Clump! Finally, he arrived in the battered, flattened, and former city of San Francisco and took a walk on the beach.

There he met a eleven-year-old girl with braids named Jill. Her left hand was average but her right hand was six miles long. Also, she never walked, only skidded.

Jack liked her right away. "Let's be friends," he said.

She held our her right hand. "Sure," she said. "Shake hands."

"Hold on," said Jack. "Friendship takes time."

They swam in the ocean and frolicked on the beach for two years. Then they got a phone call from the mayor of Santa Fe. The Big Bad Wolf had retired from the book he was living in and taken up residence in the Sandia Mountains. Every Wednesday, at midnight, he would come into Santa Fe for a snack and eat up a townsperson or two. The population was going down. At first, the townspeople had merely been frightened, but now, with real estate values falling and the threat of becoming a midnight supper, they were terrified.

"Come right over, Jack!" the mayor pleaded. "Bring Jill, too. We need all the help we can get."

Having read in the *San Francisco Kabbalah Beach Book* that every mitzvah creates an angel, Jack and Jill agreed to go immediately. Holding hands, they clumped and skidded towards Santa Fe.

Wednesday night found them waiting for the Big Bad Wolf in the town plaza. Sure enough, at midnight he arrived. Big, hairy, his gray coat streaked with black, his mouth salivated as he imagined his midnight snack.

Jill walked right over to him. The Big Bad Wolf bared his teeth. He growled ferociously.

Jill shook her head. "Bad manners," she said. "That is not the way a civilized person greets you. A civilized person shakes hands."

The wolf, puzzled by a sudden identity problem, said, "I don't have a hand."

"A foot will do," said Jill. "Or a paw."

The wolf put out his paw. Jill shook it with her six-mile hand. That was the end of the Big Bad Wolf.

Jack and Jill became local Santa Fe heros.

And that's why the towns people in Santa Fe love these sandwiches so much.

Zane's Brain

What's in Zane's brain?

Yesterday I had a chance to examine it with my magnificence microscope. Here's what I saw:

There is a giant fire burning on the right side of Zane's Brain. It must be over a hundred feet high; maybe it's a thousand, or a million miles high shooting flames into the sky and burning up much of the planets, the Milky Way, and several galaxies beyond. It's hard to say exactly how big the fire is. Let's just say it's awfully large.

On the left side of Zane's Brain is a great lake. It must be hundreds, thousands, even perhaps a million miles wide. It is very peaceful and beautiful, and it just sits there quietly absorbing the sun. Like all other lakes, this lake is full of water.

Well, one day, the Fire on the right side of Zane's brain had an idea. "I'm dynamic, creative, innovative, adventurous, curious, expansive, and smart," it said. "I like to experiment and try out new things. I think today I'll try something different. I'm going to make some money." Fire scratched its hot head thoughtfully. "Should I steal it or borrow it?" it asked. "Well, borrowing is just plain boring. I'm going to *steal* it! That's exciting and fun (especially if I don't get caught.) I'll start off by stealing a dollar. I'll get a slice of pizza with it. Then I'll steal $10, then $20, $100…$1 million! I'll soon be the richest fire in the world! I'll steal more and more until I steal the whole world. And what will I do with the world once I steal it? I'll burn it, of course. "Ha, ha, ha! That's what fires do!"

Fire laughed diabolically for fourteen days. Then it stopped and thought: "Wait a minute. I'm part of the world. If I destroy the world by burning it up, I'll destroy myself! That's not a good idea. I like to have fun, but I don't want to die! Maybe this isn't such a good idea after all."

And Fire sat down on a hot stump to think it over.

Meanwhile Lake heard about how Fire wanted to try stealing, and how his uncontrolled desire would eventually destroy the world. "That hothead!" said Lake. "I'm part of the world, too. I don't want to be destroyed. I don't want to die. I know Fire gets carried away with himself sometimes. He often doesn't know what to do with all that extra energy he carries around.

I'd better stop him before it's too late."

So, beneath his calm surface, Lake started making waves. "I'm going to take my water and dump it on his stupid fire-filled head! I'm going to dampen him real good! I won't let him destroy me!"

So Lake dumped 50 million buckets of water on Fire. It made a sound like *sssss*. Soon Fire's desire to steal a million dollars fizzed down to $1,000, $100, $20, $10, $1, and finally to none. Fire's flames relaxed.

"Thanks, Lake," he said. "I'm feeling much better. I don't know what came over me. I just got too hot, I suppose."

Then Fire took Lake by the hand, and the two of them went out for pizza.

Wow, Look At That!

Once upon a time there was a little girl who always said, "Wow, look at that!" (She was full of awe and wonder.) When she went outside and saw the sidewalk she'd point down and shout: "Wow, look at that!" When she saw a car pass by or an airplane over head, she'd point to it and say: "Wow, look at that!" When she saw a bird, mouse, dog, or cat, a flower, tree, or pony, a man, woman, child, she'd shout: "Wow, look at that!"

One day a bad fairy came to her house and said: "You're a stupid moron!

What's the matter with you, anyway? Don't you know that it is not only impolite to shout: 'Wow, look at that!?' Worse, it is wrong. The things you are pointing at are not only ugly and bad, but you are completely silly to think they aren't. You should be suspicious of what you see. Things are not the way they seem. Dogs rot, cats die, chickens get roasted, flowers fade, children age, old men and women die and leave you, cars break down, planes get rusty, mice get run over by cars and rot on the street. The world is full of misery. Remember it next time you want to say 'wow, look at that!'

The girl now felt terrible. How could she have been so wrong? She began looking at the world differently. She soon said nothing when she left the house. The smile quickly faded from her face. Her eyes grew dead. Her face soon looked like a pancake after it has been run over by a bus.

She got sadder and sadder. But she couldn't even cry because now she thought that smart, sophisticated little girls didn't do that sort of thing. One day she finally hit bottom. She lay down on her living room floor and fell asleep. A distant dream reminded her that once upon a time the world had been filled with awe and wonder. What had happened?

Suddenly, a good fairy appeared. "Hello," it said. "I'm the good fairy. The bad fairy and I work together, teaching little girls about life. We're really the same fairy, but we wear disguises and try to fool you by looking different. The bad fairy teaches you so feel sad, and finally to hit the bottom. Why? So that when you finally wakes up you know for sure that the best and frankly, the true, real, and only way to go out the door of your house is with the words: 'Wow, look at that!'

Snoring

Jack Jock snored. Every morning before the alarm sounded, a nightmare originating in his lungs rose, wreaked havoc in his trachea and produced an emission of Series A snoring gas.

Now completely awake, he saw the wraith Irving Incubus, arm in arm with his wraith, Sarah Succubus. This couple had been together since the 8th century and were spending their declining years frightening dreamers with bone-chilling nightmares.

Jack drew the bed sheets over his head in terror.

"Jack Jock, thou art a churlish curl," Irving growled. "Snoring, what? Why, but for the kindly protection of thy blessed mother, this secret snoring would be stiffly punished. I condemn thee to fill out government forms for thirty days!"

Sweat jiggled on Jack's forehead. "Oh," he groaned, "anything but that!"

"I'll not joke with thee, Jack Jock." Irving cackled as his jowls jingled. "Beware! In the future, no mercy for the likes of thee will I show."

Succubus nodded in agreement. Irving took her hand and both departed.

Jack Jock panicked. What would he do? Filling out government forms was a punishment worse than an accounting course. He paced the floor. His heels ground into the wood, turning it to pulp, and then into the *New York Times,* whose headlines read:

"Interest Increases in Incubus-Succubus Income Teams: Income Incubating Schemes Now A Thriving Business."

The headlines shocked Jack Jock. Could it be that Incubus and Succubus were a hoax? Were they headquartered in Washington? Or had they been hired by his mother?

Suddenly, he heard footsteps outside his bedroom door.

"Mom?" he called.

A high voice from behind the door sighed, "Yes, dear?"

"What are you doing out there?" he cried.

"Just putting a couple of my medieval puppets back in the attic, dear," she answered sweetly.

"At 5:00 a.m.?"

"Yes, dear."

The answer soothed Jack. Mom often did strange things. He relaxed, turned over, and went back to sleep.

An hour later he was snoring "Til Eulenspiegel" in utter satisfaction.

A Brief Groan in the Timeless Warp

When the pecker trees in the dingwhat doorways bloomed, the first ring mascot rose to bread his stallions. Aye, they were a fetid lot of great balls hanging from trees of iron. Behind the stables, rotting peeperpods dingled beneath the dew droppings. Indeed, Genghis Khan never rode like this, nor did he ever have it so good.

But what of the yesteryear? Could a cantaloupe dewdrop so lightly? What about Pecktopod Slantworth Poopinghatch, the hydrangea of all goosebumps?

Before her sex change, Slantworth asked these questions. As a him, hers no longer belonged to He anymore.

"Can't I laugh a Darth?" she groaned. "If only a bottom could be bound to a top. I've forgotten how to pepper a new leaf. Nor can I sanction it." Slantworth bent her ant in place.

Sycamores dewed lightly as she strode before her horse.

Sense is being slaughtered this morning," she lathered. "And we can no longer Parcheesi in good fashion. Too bad. A slip won't beckon to the timorous anymore. And what about Sebastian? Is he ready to be cooked? Or are only leopards to be leaped?"

Thus concluded a brief groan in the timeless warp.

Too Many Hours at the Computer

When the new year began Paul Crewball knew the time had come to give up dopehanging, sky gliding, and cliff changing. Newlyweds no longer inhabited his year. Old tiles, decrepit busters, and cream-puffed windows that so long cleared his apartments of red brick establishments had flown deftly and silently out of his mind.

Was he going mad again? Or was this simply a change in atmo sphere, an old hangout in new wolf's clothing? Hard to say when skies walked backwards and moons hung their rumps on backyard clotheslines to cry.

Well, the sky was falling. But who cared? Long ago, when the land of wet mouths left the atmosphere, flying skyward on a three ring circus, plants had changed hands. It was time for a break and everyone knew it. Too many hours at the computer had dulled Paul's fingers and turned his tongue into red iron.

Swamp Disorder

John and Martha were lovers of premier order. Their roars, cries, laughter, tears, and general bedroom antics were the talk of the neighborhood. People heard their joyous screams miles away and often called the police or fire department when the sounds of love were just too overwhelming.

"A noisy bunch" complained Lesley Parsnips their itinerant neighbor.

"Shut them up! We can't sleep a wink" complained Parsip McCullough, their other neighbor.

"I wish they would watch TV," cursed Peepod Poley, their across the street neighbor.

So generally, John and Martha were burning up the neighborhood with their loves cries, causing friction, jealously, and hatred among neighbors, and destroying the very fabric of society with all their fun.

One day, John read an add in the *New York Crimes:* "Are you looking for happiness satisfaction, and inner peace? Does your stomach cringe and twist every time you go to work? Do you feel your innards turning to outwards every time you walk out your door? Do you hate your neighbors, love your enemies, and generally walk backwards in forward times? If you suffer from any of all of these debilitating diseases, come to Henry's Place.

"We'll give you a cool drink of beer, some tasty pretzels, and a taste of the after life. Some say we're heaven on earth but we say we're earth in heaven. But whatever anyone else says, or whatever we say, you must experience our joy connection for yourselves. Come visit us. You won't regret it.

"We're located on Fisher's Island just across the causeway. To reach us, simply drive straight down Route 16, pass the Great Swamp on your right, and you'll see our sign nestled in the Andes Mountains."

John put down his morning coffee and looked up at Martha. "Read this add," he said. "It sounds good. Let's visit Henry's Place this afternoon."

Martha put down her soup bowl, put her reading glasses on backwards, and read the add. "Okay, she answered. "I love you, John. I'll do anything for you, anything to make you happy. But frankly, this Henry's Place sounds like a loud of shit. What is this happiness crap, bliss, contentment, higher powers stuff? Who believes in that? Sounds like whitewash from the sixties. But, as I say, I'll do anything to make you happy. If you want to go, I'll go with you."

"Thank you, dear. You're always trying to please me, You're so selfless, so unconcerned with your infant ego. In fact, I don't even think you have an ego, but if you do, it's only the size of a shoe."

"Thank you, dear. That's because I shop at Pathmark. You can reduce your ego size if you shop there, too."

"Not for me. I like a big ego. In fact, for me, the bigger the better. I go for Tarzan egos, larger and powerful egos, elephant egos, lions roaring and dogs pissing egos. I hate small fry egos that go nowhere, and that remind me of mice scurrying into their holes to hide from rabbits. Nevertheless, I love your ego. That's because yours is not a small ego. Yours is invisible. It is completely hidden under a cloud of shopping."

"Thank you, John. Your support of my habits encourages me to expand my skills, to move from mere food shopping to clothing and even expand to shopping for grains." Martha smiled. "I can't visit Henry's Place this afternoon. I've got an appointment with my mouse sitter. But how about Saturday? Crossing the causeway to have beer and pretzels sounds like such a fun way to celebrate the Sabbath."

"It is clear the neolithic bulaboos cannot clear the deck for morning fornicators. Such suds and deer-bottoms never miscalculate. Nor do they ventrilicate in subtle wanders. No, the only path is straight to hell. That's the best one, no denying it. An upwards mobile style, whether it be through cell phone or protoplasmic devolving, cannot tie the tides to the moon whether it be in individual or community."

John rested his case.

"I cannot abide such loose and incomprehensible talk," chided Martha. "Your babblings is are incomprehensible, ununderstandable, and irrational. They rise, no doubt, from the deep cesspool of your unconscious. Nevertheless, although they are a part of you, I'll have no part of them. They're out of my league. I am not one who loves baseball. In order for us to communicate as rational, loving, interested. full human beings we need a complete openness to our failings and short comings. There is no better way to do this than with a good fuck."

John peppered his wart, drew back, then covered his wounds with saliva. He slobbered and hissed, then fell back into "normal" mode. "All right, dear," he said, holding the calm of Jupiter high above his head. "I know you hate moving sidewards or backwards, upwards or downwards. Therefore, let us move in the only other direction available to us: the rational forward. You stated a desire to visit Henry's Place with me. Well, I suggest we move forward, jump in our car, and drive forward across the causeway."

"In plain language, you mean we should go there now?"

"Yes."

Martha squared her bottoms, tucked in her shirt, juggled her breasts, farted, then passed an unconscious hand over her vulva. "I'm ready," she said. "Let's get going."

They climbed into their Mercedes Benz, raised their right arms, said a quick "Heil Hitler!," and turned on the ignition. The car sputtered into Teutonic mode; its exhaust pipe spilling out German phrases from Goethe's Faust and Sorrows of Young Werther. Driving the Mercedes, its windows automatically went down, and phrases of *Gotterdammerung* could be heard coming through the back door speakers. One could also even hear Wagner spouting about the harmonic affects of anti-Semitic phrases on Nordic operas. This car was certainly Judenrein and Tom and Martha were happy about that. Even though, of course, there was not a shred of anti-Semitism in their loving, sweat-filling, psychoanalyzed bodies. All anti's and uncles had been flushed out by years of broom clearing, brush pounding psychotherapy which left their vats dry and their innards looking like the outers of freshly plucked chickens.

Following the driving directions to Henry's Place, they headed down Route 16, passing houses with freshly painted lawns, farms, and a brick graveyard. A forest of maple trees, lined with single warts, and hydrangea beds freshly covered with linen and wool blankets, donned and dawned their path. Indeed, it was a scenic drive as the sun shone down upon their Teutonic car roof with full Brandenburg force; the wind pushed the scattered clouds across the sky with jack-booted speed.

When they drove past Murphy's Drug and Food Mart they came to an open field. Two miles of nothingness stood before them. A wide open road. Then suddenly, on their left, the Great Swamp appeared. Strangely, it appeared on their right as well.

"Look, there's the Great Swamp on our right," said Jack.

"It's on our left," Martha corrected.

"Can't we agree on anything this morning?" asked Jack. "That's our right."

"Sorry, dear, you're wrong about this one. It's on our left."

"It is not. I'll call Dr. Abramowitz. He'll know."

"You don't have to consult your therapist for everything. It's on our left. No doubt about it. Count on me this time. I'm right."

John scratched his head. "All right. You win. What's the differ ence whether it's right or left, anyway? I'm an up and down person."

"Suit yourself, dear. In any case, stop the car. I want to check out this swamp."

"Martha. don't you want to spend the full day at Henry's Place? We don't have time to look at this swamp. It's just a swamp, anyway. You can look at it from the car."

"You must be kidding, Jack. Do you think I would ever pass up the opportunity to look at a swamp? You know me better than that. I *have to* look at this swamp! It is beyond a need; it is my compulsion."

"My name is John."

He pulled the car to the side of the road. The haunted couple got out, and walked towards the Great Swamp. John gazed at the sun and watched the clouds passing. But Martha stood in front of the swamp totally transfixed. "This *is* a swamp!" she said in amazement. "I've rarely seen one like this. In fact, I would say I've never seen one like this but that might be an exaggeration. In any case, I can't stand it. This swamp cannot last. It must be eradicated, cleaned up. I *hate* swamps! All swamps. I cannot abide their existence."

"Oh, let this one go, Martha. We'll never get to Henry's if you start."

"There is no stopping me, John. I *must* start. It is my calling. The calling of the Hebrew prophets was nothing compared to my swamp clean-up calling. Mine comes directly from God—although I am an atheist, or rather a secularist, or both. I'm not sure which. But I am sure of my calling. I know we cannot move forward one more inch until this entire swamp mess is cleaned up!"

"But it will ruin our day. We'll never make it to Henry's Place."

"Fuck Henry's Place. It can wait. I don't care about Henry's Place anyway. I'm more concerned with improving the environment and world peace. We must clean up this swamp!"

Jack paused, looked over the swamp, and reflected a moment. "Well, all right. It doesn't look that big. We'll give it a try."

"Good, Thank you dear for being so understanding. The lovers of world peace and pure environment also thank you. The world will be a better place if, when, and after we clean up this swamp. After all, cleaning up messes is my business. I wouldn't have started Messes, Inc. if it weren't so."

They opened the trunk of the car, took out two shovels, a pair of scissors, and three band aids; then they started clearing out the Great Swamp.

"This shouldn't take us more than a day or two," said Martha cheerily.

"I hope you're right. But I think it'll take at least a week. We'll see. But whatever it takes, do you still want to go to Henry's Place when we're finished?"

"Of course, dear. Isn't that where we were going in the first place? I never break a commitment although, in truth, there are sometimes delays before I can fulfill my obligations."

"Certainly swamp cleaning can create delays."

"Indeed."

Four weeks later:

Gus "Weed" Dreamtree, president of Swamp Therapies, Inc. said: There is one important word in life. Contrary to popular philosophical opinion it is not God, truth, or even justice. It is *communicate!*"

John wrenched his finger. He looked Gus straight in the eye. ""Fuck communication!" he answered belligerently. "All this emphasis on communication only serves to obfuscate what's beautiful, creative, and vital. I will not hang my artistic soul on a cross of communication!"

"What then are you afraid of?" asked Gus. "Are you afraid some of your originality and imagination might leak out? You don't have to worry about that here. We at Swamp Therapies are dedicated to what's right, not what's wrong. We promote what is healthy not unhealthy. Speak to some of my partners."

Gus introduced the staff. There was Madeleine Aldull and her sister, Genevieve Totaldull. the Dimwitter brothers, Clyde and Romaine, Clyde Dumwater and his sister, Clara Dumwaiter, and the three legged pair of twins, Jake and Jake Dumwitter and Dimwitter, the Dumbeller twins, Dimwat and Dumwich, and finally the president himself, Gus "Weed" Dreamtree.

Gus looked at John in amazement. "You expect to lead a normal life *and* be an artist, and have an artistic temperament? You must be crazy."

John stood up to the weed man. Yes, that's me. I am an artist. I have an artistic temperament. It is one of the reasons I am exciting, dynamic, charismatic, and loved by the women. It's another reason why I'm so driven—but I love that, too! Yes, Gus, contrary to your swampy notions, my imagination is alive and flourishing. Imagination: that's what an artist is and does. It flourishes because of and in spite of my artistic temperament. Artistic temperament goes with the territory.

"You can take it or leave it. But whether you do or not, I am. I'm taking it. I *am* it. So be it.'

"Besides, the artists are the elite of the world! I always knew it. That's why I say fuck the proletariat! Fuck the bureaucrats, the board of education rote teachers, the list making accountants, mechanical financial executives, social workers of the "helping" profession, and their psychotherapeutic psychoanalytic hand-maidens. Fuck 'em all! Sure they exist—but on a lower level. Philosophers and religious people sometimes may come close—but not close enough. Only the mystics have it. They too are part of the elite. But what are artists, after all, but mystics with skills."

John broke down in tears of ecstasy. "I've done it, I've done it, I've done it! he cried. "I've broken through!"

Leyenda, Alard, they're easy. I can play them! Yes! Oh Lord, thank you. I've been on the cross for so many years.

But now, at last, I've fallen. And by falling, I have been raised, reborn, resurrected! I'm free! I've broken through! I've done it, I've done it!"

Four months later:

The damwhats bickered incessantly. Henry's Place seemed far away. Turds of fostered excellence still floated down the river into the Great Swamp. Martha turned to John, a huge frankfurter roll of disgust on her face.

"Who is polluting this swamp?" she hissed. "I can't stand polluters! Root them out! Destroy them, fuck them, kill them!" She gripped the handle of her pocket grenade, pulled the pin, then tossed it in a litter basket just north of the swamp. An explosion of methane gas ensued. Police from Land's End, the Dynamic Brothers, hurled themselves to the rescue. Surrounded by revolution and followed by a squadron of backlashes, these surly tulip-tipped coppers backgammoned their way towards Martha and John. The smell of fresh turnips beaded with broccoli emanated from their loins. These were sexy policemen, true vegetables of the higher Broccolian Order, vested with authority by the lamplight himself, Poop Pie Us the Third, head floor sweeeeper on the Vati Can. Now, pebbled with putrescence, these stalwart masters of the legal realm approached Martha and John. "Polluters?" they asked. "Only show us their dastardly faces and we will quickly pullulate and pomulate their pupicks."

www.ingramcontent.com/pod-product-compliance
Lightning Source LLC
Chambersburg PA
CBHW051034160426
43193CB00010B/941